Forging the American Character

Forging the American Character

Readings in United States History Since 1865

Volume II

Second Edition

John R. M. Wilson, Editor
Southern California College

Prentice Hall, Upper Saddle River, New Jersey 07458

Library of Congress Cataloging-in-Publication Data

Forging the American character / John R. M. Wilson, editor. — 2nd ed.
    p. cm.
      Contents: v. 2. Readings in United States history Since 1865 —
v.2. Readings in United States history since 1865.
      ISBN 0-13-576661-3
      1. United States—Civilization. I. Wilson, John R. M.
    E169.1.F745 1997
    973—dc20   96-23386
                                              CIP
                                              Rev

Acquisitions editor: *Sally Constable*
Production editor: *Jean Lapidus*
Copy editor: *Maria Caruso*
Manufacturing buyer: *Lynn Pearlman*
Cover design: *Bruce Kenselaar*

This book was set in 10.5/12.5 Palatino by The Composing Room of Michigan, Inc.
and was printed and bound by Courier Companies, Inc.
The cover was printed by Phoenix Color Corp.

 © 1997, 1991, by Prentice-Hall, Inc.
Simon & Schuster/A Viacom Company
Upper Saddle River, New Jersey 07458

Printed in the United States of America
10 9 8 7 6 5 4 3 2 1

ISBN 0-13-576661-3

Prentice-Hall International (UK) Limited, *London*
Prentice-Hall of Australia Pty. Limited, *Sydney*
Prentice-Hall Canada Inc., *Toronto*
Prentice-Hall Hispanoamericana, S.A., *Mexico*
Prentice-Hall of India Private Limited, *New Delhi*
Prentice-Hall of Japan, Inc., *Tokyo*
Simon & Schuster Asia Pte. Ltd., *Singapore*
Editora Prentice-Hall do Brasil, Ltda., *Rio de Janeiro*

Contents

Preface

A long United States history textbook may run to 1000 pages. Although that length may seem intimidating to students, it does not allow extended treatment of a wide variety of fascinating topics. A book of readings does. The theme of this reader is the American character. I trust that the concept will illuminate American history without being overly restrictive.

A reader like this enables students to explore subjects ranging from the moral aspects of the American "invasion" of 1492 to the debate over multiculturalism in the 1990s, from the horrors of life and death in the Civil War to the national obsession with the Kennedy assassination. The nature of the selections varies. Some offer new interpretations of the past; others introduce readers to new findings; while still others synthesize the writings in a historical subfield. The readings do not pretend to cover every possible topic; rather, they explore various areas that shed light on the American character yet suffer comparative neglect in many textbooks.

Trying to define the American character can be very frustrating. No one has been able to develop a widely accepted definition of the concept. Authors often use different meanings in the same piece of writing—for instance, referring interchangeably to the character of the individual American and to the character of the mass of Americans. National character, especially in a country as big and heterogeneous as the United States, can be useful only as a large-scale generalization to cover the most prominent characteristics of the national culture. Some scholars have criticized efforts to capture the national character, suggesting that in many cases they may be merely intellectually sophisticated forms of racial stereotyping. Yet the practice persists, perhaps because it is so convenient to group people and thus make them more manageable. Perhaps the most useful definition would be that national character means generalizations about a nation or nationality developed to elucidate the ways in which it is distinctive.

A national character suggests tendencies on the part of a people, not fixed positions held by everyone. It means that, all things being equal, the people of a given nation are more likely to believe or behave a certain way than those of another nation. There is an inherent comparison implied in suggesting a national character, although studies of the American character generally tend not to explicitly explore other nationalities.

The genre began very early in the history of the United States with the publication in 1782 of J. Hector St. John de Crévecoeur's *Letters from an American Farmer;* the immigrant asked the famous question, "What then is this American, this new man?" Crévecoeur's pioneering inquiry into the American character ran up against geographical and cultural heterogeneity, which has become a vastly greater obstacle in the succeeding two centuries. The most famous inquiry came in the 1830s when Alexis de Tocqueville wrote *Democracy in America* and provided penetrating French insight into the nature of the conforming, religious, liberty-loving joiners he observed. Over the years, historians and other social observers have sought to explain American distinctiveness through such characteristics as abundance, exposure to the frontier, pragmatism, belief in progress, and mobility. They have debated the relative influence of mother England and the wilderness, and in so doing have illuminated American self-understanding—without providing any final answers. The quest continues, as the popularity of *Habits of the Heart* (1985) attests.

This collection suggests that Americans have defined themselves not only by what they are, but by what they are not, and the latter negative definition is an important component of Americanism. By and large, Native Americans have not been allowed to share their heritage with Europeans. For other nationalities, conformity to the English cultural model was long required for acceptance in the United States, although a more pluralistic, open society seems to be emerging in the late twentieth century. Yet over the past half century, the increasingly diverse American population has frequently defined itself less by what it is than by what it is not—as antifascist and, especially, anticommunist.

This book should help to clarify some of the various forces, ideologies, people, and experiences that have helped forge today's distinctive

American character. If, as Socrates said, the unexamined life is not worth living, then this excursion into the life of a people should help make it more worth living.

In closing, I'd like to thank the reviewers of my book, John Powell, Pennsylvania State University at Erie, and Anthony N. Stranges, Texas A&M University.

John R. M. Wilson
Costa Mesa, California

1

The New View
of Reconstruction*

Eric Foner

Eric Foner (1943–), both educated and educator at Columbia
University, is one of the fine scholars engaged in exploring the gaps
between perception and reality in the Civil War and Reconstruction era. He takes particular interest in blacks and radicalism. Two
of his books indicate his area of expertise: *Politics and Ideology in
the Age of the Civil War* (1981) and *Nothing but Freedom: Emancipation and Its Legacy* (1983). In 1988 he published a full-length
and well-received treatment of the subject of this article: *Reconstruction: America's Unfinished Revolution, 1863–1877.*

  In this 1983 selection from *American Heritage,* Foner offers a
clear picture of the view of Reconstruction that prevailed from the
1870s through the 1950s and explains why it is no longer convincing. Reconstruction provides a good case study of historiography,
the history of history. As long as white racism was the social and historical norm, radical northern attempts to force black equality on
the South during Reconstruction appeared misguided, if not
downright malevolent. The civil rights movement in the 1950s and
1960s forced historians to reevaluate both their attitudes toward
current racial issues and their interpretations of the past. This new
look led to a shift in the roles of heroes and villains in Reconstruction. Now the Radical Republicans became the good guys and

*Reprinted by permission of *American Heritage* Magazine, a division of Forbes, Inc.
© Forbes, Inc., 1983.

President Andrew Johnson and southern obstructionists the obstacles to racial progress.

Foner suggests that a new, more radical, view has emerged: Reconstruction was simply not radical enough. The failure of the Radical Republicans to provide "forty acres and a mule" or any economic stake in the new postwar society left the freedmen at the mercy of their former masters—with the resultant economic gap lasting down to the present. Nevertheless, the door of hope was opened and blacks have been struggling through it ever since what W. E. B. DuBois termed the "splendid failure" of Reconstruction.

The American character is not static. Frederick Jackson Turner argued that the frontier was the most important factor forging it. Foner's article depicts human, political attempts to reshape it. The debate over Reconstruction is in part a debate over whether the Radical Republicans, promoting greater racial equality, or the Southern Redeemers, seeking continued racial supremacy, were truer to what the American character has been—or could be.

In the past twenty years, no period of American history has been the subject of a more thoroughgoing reevaluation than Reconstruction—the violent, dramatic, and still controversial era following the Civil War. Race relations, politics, social life, and economic change during Reconstruction have all been reinterpreted in the light of changed attitudes toward the place of blacks within American society. If historians have not yet forged a fully satisfying portrait of Reconstruction as a whole, the traditional interpretation that dominated historical writing for much of this century has irrevocably been laid to rest.

Anyone who attended high school before 1960 learned that Reconstruction was an era of unrelieved sordidness in American political and social life. The martyred Lincoln, according to this view, had planned a quick and painless readmission of the Southern states as equal members of the national family. President Andrew Johnson, his successor, attempted to carry out Lincoln's policies but was foiled by the Radical Republicans (also known as Vindictives or Jacobins). Motivated by an irrational hatred of Rebels or by ties with Northern capitalists out to plunder the South, the Radicals swept aside Johnson's lenient program and fastened black supremacy upon the defeated Confederacy. An orgy of corruption followed, presided over by unscrupulous carpetbaggers (Northerners who ventured south to reap the spoils of office), traitorous scalawags (Southern whites who cooperated with the new governments for personal gain), and the ignorant and childlike freedmen, who were incapable of properly exercising the political power that had been thrust upon them. After much needless suffering, the white community of the South banded together to overthrow these "black" governments and restore home rule (their euphemism for white supremacy). All told, Reconstruction was just about the darkest page in the American saga.

Originating in anti-Reconstruction propaganda of Southern Democrats during the 1870s, this traditional interpretation achieved scholarly legitimacy around the turn of the century through the work of William Dunning and his students at Columbia University. It reached the larger public through films like *Birth of a Nation* and *Gone With the Wind* and that best-selling work of myth-making masquerading as history, *The Tragic Era*, by Claude G. Bowers. In language as exaggerated as it was colorful, Bowers told how Andrew Johnson "fought the bravest battle for constitutional liberty and for the preservation of our institutions ever waged by an Executive" but was overwhelmed by the "poisonous propaganda" of the Radicals. Southern whites, as a result, "literally were put to the torture" by "emissaries of hate" who manipulated the "simple-minded" freedmen, "inflaming the negroes' egotism" and even inspiring "lustful assaults" by blacks upon white womanhood.

In a discipline that sometimes seems to pride itself on the rapid rise and fall of historical interpretations, this traditional portrait of Reconstruction enjoyed remarkable staying power. The long reign of the old interpretation is not difficult to explain. It presented a set of easily identifiable heroes and villains. It enjoyed the imprimatur of the nation's leading scholars. And it accorded with the political and social realities of the first half of this century. This image of Reconstruction helped freeze the mind of the white South in unalterable opposition to any movement for breaching the ascendancy of the Democratic party, eliminating segregation, or readmitting disfranchised blacks to the vote.

Nevertheless, the demise of the traditional interpretation was inevitable, for it ignored the testimony of the central participant in the drama of Reconstruction—the black freedman. Furthermore, it was grounded in the conviction that blacks were unfit to share in political power. As Dunning's Columbia colleague John W. Burgess put it, "A black skin means membership in a race of men which has never of itself succeeded in subjecting passion to reason, has never, therefore, created any civilization of any kind." Once objective scholarship and modern experience rendered that assumption untenable, the entire edifice was bound to fall.

The work of "revising" the history of Reconstruction began with the writings of a handful of survivors of the era, such as John R. Lynch, who had served as a black congressman from Mississippi after the Civil War. In the 1930s white scholars like Francis Simkins and Robert Woody carried the task forward. Then, in 1935, the black historian and activist W. E. B. DuBois produced *Black Reconstruction in America*, a monumental reevaluation that closed with an irrefutable indictment of a historical profession that had sacrificed scholarly objectivity on the altar of racial bias. "One fact and one alone," he wrote, "explains the attitude of most recent writers toward Reconstruction; they cannot conceive of Negroes as men." DuBois's work, however, was ignored by most historians.

It was not until the 1960s that the full force of the revisionist wave broke over the field. Then, in rapid succession, virtually every assumption of the traditional viewpoint was systematically dismantled. A drastically different portrait emerged to take its place. President Lincoln did not have a coherent "plan" for Reconstruction, but at the time of his assassination he had been cautiously contemplating black suffrage. Andrew Johnson was a stubborn, racist politician who lacked the ability to compromise. By isolating himself from the broad currents of public opinion that had nourished Lincoln's career, Johnson created an impasse with Congress that Lincoln would certainly have avoided, thus throwing away his political power and destroying his own plans for reconstructing the South.

The Radicals in Congress were acquitted of both vindictive motive and the charge of serving as the stalking-horses of Northern capitalism. They emerged instead as idealists in the best nineteenth-century reform tradition. Radical leaders like Charles Sumner and Thaddeus Stevens had worked for the rights of blacks long before any conceivable political advantage flowed from such a commitment. Stevens refused to sign the Pennsylvania Constitution of 1838 because it disfranchised the state's black citizens; Sumner led a fight in the 1850s to integrate Boston's public schools. Their Reconstruction policies were based on principle, not petty political advantage, for the central issue dividing Johnson and these Radical Republicans was the civil rights of freedmen. Studies of congressional policy-making, such as Eric L. McKitrick's *Andrew Johnson and Reconstruction,* also revealed that Reconstruction legislation, ranging from the Civil Rights Act of 1866 to the Fourteenth and Fifteenth Amendments, enjoyed broad support from moderate and conservative Republicans. It was not simply the work of a narrow radical faction.

Even more startling was the revised portrait of Reconstruction in the South itself. Imbued with the spirit of the civil rights movement and rejecting entirely the racial assumptions that had underpinned the traditional interpretation, these historians evaluated Reconstruction from the black point of view. Works like Joel Williamson's *After Slavery* portrayed the period as a time of extraordinary political, social, and economic progress for blacks. The establishment of public school systems, the granting of equal citizenship to blacks, the effort to restore the devastated Southern economy, the attempts to construct an interracial political democracy from the ashes of slavery, all these were commendable achievements, not the elements of Bowers's "tragic era."

Unlike earlier writers, the revisionists stressed the active role of the freedmen in shaping Reconstruction. Black initiative established as many schools as did Northern religious societies and the Freedmen's Bureau. The right to vote was not simply thrust upon them by meddling outsiders, since blacks began agitating for the suffrage as soon as they were freed. In 1865 black conventions throughout the South issued eloquent, though unheeded, appeals for equal civil and political rights.

With the advent of Radical Reconstruction in 1867, the freedmen did enjoy a real measure of political power. But black supremacy never existed. In most states blacks held only a small fraction of political offices, and even in South Carolina, where they comprised a majority of the state legislature's lower house, effective power remained in white hands. As for corruption, moral standards in both government and private enterprise were at low ebb throughout the nation in the postwar years—the era of Boss Tweed, the Credit Mobilier scandal, and the Whiskey Ring. Southern corruption could hardly be blamed on former slaves.

Other actors in the Reconstruction drama also came in for reevaluation. Most carpetbaggers were former Union soldiers seeking economic opportunity in the postwar South, not unscrupulous adventurers. Their motives, a typically American amalgam of humanitarianism and the pursuit of profit, were no more insidious than those of Western pioneers. Scalawags, previously seen as traitors to the white race, now emerged as "Old Line" Whig Unionists who had opposed secession in the first place or as poor whites who had long resented planters' domination of Southern life and who saw in Reconstruction a chance to recast Southern society along more democratic lines. Strongholds of Southern white Republicanism like east Tennessee and western North Carolina had been the scene of resistance to Confederate rule throughout the Civil War; now, as one scalawag newspaper put it, the choice was "between salvation at the hand of the Negro or destruction at the hand of the rebels."

At the same time, the Ku Klux Klan and kindred groups, whose campaign of violence against black and white Republicans had been minimized or excused in older writings, were portrayed as they really were. Earlier scholars had conveyed the impression that the Klan intimated blacks mainly by dressing as ghosts and playing on the freedmen's superstitions. In fact, black fears were all too real: the Klan was a terrorist organization that beat and killed its political opponents to deprive blacks of their newly won rights. The complicity of the Democratic party and the silence of prominent whites in the face of such outrages stood as an indictment of the moral code the South had inherited from the days of slavery.

By the end of the 1960s, then, the old interpretation had been completely reversed. Southern freedmen were the heroes, the "Redeemers: who overthrew Reconstruction were the villains, and if the era was "tragic," it was because change did not go far enough. Reconstruction had been a time of real progress and its failure a lost opportunity for the South and the nation. But the legacy of Reconstruction—the Fourteenth and Fifteenth Amendments— endured to inspire future efforts for civil rights. As Kenneth Stampp wrote in *The Era of Reconstruction,* a superb summary of revisionist findings published in 1965, "If it was worth four years of civil war to save the Union, it was worth a few years of radical reconstruction to give the American Negro the ultimate promise of equal civil and political rights."

As Stampp's statement suggests, the reevaluation of the first Reconstruction was inspired in large measure by the impact of the second—the modern civil rights movement. And with the waning of that movement in recent years, writing on Reconstruction has undergone still another transformation. Instead of seeing the Civil War and its aftermath as a second American Revolution (as Charles Beard had), a regression into barbarism (as Bowers argued), or a golden opportunity squandered (as the revisionists saw it), recent writers argue that Radical Reconstruction was not really very radical. Since land was not distributed to the former slaves, they remained economically dependent upon their former owners. The planter class survived both the war and Reconstruction with its property (apart from slaves) and prestige more or less intact.

Not only changing times but also the changing concerns of historians have contributed to this latest reassessment of Reconstruction. The hallmark of the past decade's historical writing has been an emphasis upon "social history"—the evocation of the past lives of ordinary Americans—and the downplaying of strictly political events. When applied to Reconstruction, this concern with the "social" suggested that black suffrage and officeholding, once seen as the most radical departures of the Reconstruction era, were relatively insignificant.

Recent historians have focused their investigations not upon the politics of Reconstruction but upon the social and economic aspects of the transition from slavery to freedom. Herbert Gutman's influential study of the black family during and after slavery found little change in family structure or relations between men and women resulting from emancipation. Under slavery most blacks had lived in nuclear family units, although they faced the constant threat of separation from loved ones by sale. Reconstruction provided the opportunity for blacks to solidify their preexisting family ties. Conflicts over whether black women should work in the cotton fields (planters said yes, many black families said no) and over white attempts to "apprentice" black children revealed that the autonomy of family life was a major preoccupation of the freedmen. Indeed, whether manifested in their withdrawal from churches controlled by whites, in the blossoming of black fraternal, benevolent, and self-improvement organizations, or in the demise of the slave quarters and their replacement by small tenant farms occupied by individual families, the quest for independence from white authority and control over their own day-to-day lives shaped the black response to emancipation.

In the post–Civil War South the surest guarantee of economic autonomy, blacks believed, was land. To the freedmen the justice of a claim to land based on their years of unrequited labor appeared self-evident. As an Alabama black convention put it, "The property which they [the planters] hold was nearly all earned by the sweat of *our* brows." As Leon Litwack showed in *Been in the Storm So Long,* a Pulitzer Prize–winning account of the black response to emancipation, many freedmen in 1865 and 1866 refused to sign labor contracts, expecting the federal government to give them land. In some localities, as one Alabama overseer reported, they "set up claims to the plantation and all on it."

In the end, of course, the vast majority of Southern blacks remained propertyless and poor. But exactly why the South, and especially its black population, suffered from dire poverty and economic retardation in the decades following the Civil War is a matter of much dispute. In *One Kind of Freedom,* economists Roger Ransom and Richard Sutch indicted country merchants for monopolizing credit and charging usurious interest rates, forcing black tenants into debt and locking the South into a dependence on cotton production that impoverished the entire region. But Jonathan Wiener, in his study of postwar Alabama, argued that planters used their political power to compel blacks to remain on the plantations. Planters succeeded in stabilizing the plantation system, but only by blocking the growth of alternative enterprises, like factories, that might draw off black laborers, thus locking the region into a pattern of economic backwardness.

If the thrust of recent writing has emphasized the social and economic aspects of Reconstruction, politics has not been entirely neglected. But political studies have also reflected the postrevisionist mood summarized by C. Vann Woodward when he observed "how essentially nonrevolutionary and conservative Reconstruction really was." Recent writers, unlike their revisionist predecessors, have found little to praise in federal policy toward the emancipated blacks.

A new sensitivity to the strength of prejudice and laissez-faire ideas in the nineteenth-century North has led many historians to doubt whether the Republican party ever made a genuine commitment to racial justice in the South. The granting of black suffrage was an alternative to a long-term federal responsibility for protecting the rights of the former slaves. Once enfranchised, blacks could be left to fend for themselves. With the exception of a few Radicals like Thaddeus Stevens, nearly all Northern policy-makers and educators are criticized today for assuming that, so long as the unfettered operations of the marketplace afforded blacks the opportunity to advance through diligent labor, federal efforts to assist them in acquiring land were unnecessary.

Probably the most innovative recent writing on Reconstruction politics has centered on a broad reassessment of black Republicanism, largely undertaken by a new generation of black historians. Scholars like Thomas Holt and Nell Painter insist that Reconstruction was not simply a matter of black and white. Conflicts within the black community, no less than divisions among whites, shaped Reconstruction politics. Where revisionist scholars, both black and white, had celebrated the accomplishments of black political leaders, Holt, Painter, and other charge that they failed to address the economic plight of the black masses. Painter criticized "representative colored men," as national black leaders were called, for failing to provide ordinary freedmen with effective political leadership. Holt found that black officeholders in South Carolina mostly emerged from the old free mulatto class of Charleston, which shared many assumptions with prominent whites. "Basically bourgeois in their origins and orientation," he write, they "failed to act in the interest of black peasants."

In emphasizing the persistence from slavery of divisions between free blacks and slaves, these writers reflect the increasing concern with continuity and conservatism in Reconstruction. Their work reflects a startling extension of revisionist premises. If, as has been argued for the past twenty years, blacks were active agents rather than mere victims of manipulation, then they could not be absolved of blame for the ultimate failure of Reconstruction.

Despite the excellence of recent writing and the continual expansion of our knowledge of the period, historians of Reconstruction today face a unique dilemma. An old interpretation has been overthrown, but a coherent new synthesis has yet to take its place. The revisionists of the 1960s effectively established a series of negative points: the Reconstruction governments were not as bad as had been portrayed, black supremacy was a myth, the Radicals were not cynical manipulators of the freedmen. Yet no convincing overall portrait of the quality of political and social life emerged from their writings. More recent historians have rightly pointed to elements of continuity that spanned the nineteenth-century Southern experience, especially the survival, in modified form, of the plantation system. Nevertheless, by denying the real changes that did occur, they have failed to provide a convincing portrait of an era characterized above all by drama, turmoil, and social change.

Building upon the findings of the past twenty years of scholarship, a new portrait of Reconstruction ought to begin by viewing it not as a specific time period, bounded by the years 1865 and 1877, but as an episode in a prolonged historical process—American society's adjustment to the consequences of the Civil War and emancipation. The Civil War, of course, raised the decisive questions of America's national existence: the relations between local and national authority, the definition of citizenship, the balance between force and consent in generating obedience to authority. The war and Reconstruction, as Allan Nevins observed over fifty years ago, marked the "emergence of modern America." This was the era of the completion of the national railroad network, the creation of the modern steel industry, the conquest of the West and final subduing of the Indians, and the expansion of the mining frontier. Lincoln's America—the world of the small farm and artisan shop—gave way to a rapidly industrializing economy. The issues that galvanized postwar Northern politics—from the question of the greenback currency to the mode of paying holders of the national debt—arose from the economic changes unleashed by the Civil War.

Above all, the war irrevocably abolished slavery. Since 1619, when "twenty negars" disembarked from a Dutch ship in Virginia, racial injustice had haunted American life, mocking its professed ideals even as tobacco and cotton, the products of slave labor, helped finance the nation's economic development. Now the implications of the black presence could no longer be ignored. The Civil War resolved the problem of slavery but, as the Philadelphia diarist Sydney George Fisher observed in June 1865, it opened an even more intractable problem: "What shall we do with the Negro?" Indeed, he went on, this was a problem *"incapable* of any solution that will satisfy both North and South."

As Fisher realized, the focal point of Reconstruction was the social revolution known as emancipation. Plantation slavery was simultaneously a system of labor, a form of racial domination, and the foundation upon which arose a distinctive ruling class within the South. Its demise threw open the most fundamental questions of economy, society, and politics. A new system of labor, social, racial, and political relations had to be created to replace slavery.

The United States was not the only nation to experience emancipation in the nineteenth century. Neither plantation slavery nor abolition were unique to the United States. But Reconstruction was. In a comparative perspective Radical Reconstruction stands as a remarkable experiment, the only effort of a society experiencing abolition to bring the former slaves within the umbrella of equal citizenship. Because the Radicals did not achieve everything they wanted, historians have lately tended to play down the stunning departure represented by black suffrage and officeholding. Former slaves, most fewer than two years removed from bondage, debated the fundamental questions of the polity: What is a republican form of government? Should the state provide equal education for all? How could political equality be reconciled with a society in which property was so unequally distributed? There was something inspiring in the way such men met the challenge of Reconstruction. "I knew nothing more than to obey my master," James K. Greene, an Alabama black politician later recalled. "But the tocsin of freedom sounded and knocked at the door and we walked out like free men and we met the exigencies as they grew up, and shouldered the responsibilities."

"You never saw a people more excited on the subject of politics than are the negroes of the south," one planter observed in 1867. And there were more than a few Southern whites as well who in these years shook off the prejudices of the past to embrace the vision of a new South dedicated to the principles of equal citizenship and social justice. One ordinary South Carolinian expressed the new sense of possibility in 1868 to the Republican governor of the state: "I am sorry that I cannot write an elegant stiled letter to your excellency. But I rejoice to think that God almighty has given to the poor of S. C. a Gov. to hear to feel to protect the humble poor without distinction to race or color. . . . I am a native borned S.C. a poor man never owned a Negro in my life nor my father before me. . . . Remember the true and loyal are the poor of the whites and blacks, outside of these you can find none loyal."

Few modern scholars believe the Reconstruction governments established in the South in 1867 and 1868 fulfilled the aspirations of their humble constituents. While their achievements in such realms as education, civil rights, and the economic rebuilding of the South are now widely appreciated, historians today believe they failed to affect either the economic plight of the emancipated slave or the ongoing transformation of independent white farmers into cotton tenants. Yet their opponents did perceive the Reconstruction governments in precisely this way—as representatives of a revolution that had put the bottom rail, both racial and economic, on top. This perception helps explain the ferocity of the attacks leveled against them and the pervasiveness of violence in the postemancipation South.

The spectacle of black men voting and holding office was anathema to large numbers of Southern whites. Even more disturbing, at least in the view of those who still controlled the plantation regions of the South, was the emergence of local officials, black and white, who sympathized with the plight of the black laborer. Alabama's vagrancy law was a "dead letter" in 1870, "because those who are charged with its enforcement are indebted to the vagrant vote for their offices and emoluments." Political debates over the level and incidence of taxation, the control of crops, and the resolution of contract disputes revealed that a primary issue of Reconstruction was the role of government in a plantation society. During presidential Reconstruction, and after "Redemption," with planters and their allies in control of politics, the law emerged as a means of stabilizing and promoting the plantation system. If Radical Reconstruction failed to redistribute the land of the South, the ouster of the planter class from control of politics at least ensured that the sanctions of the criminal law would not be employed to discipline the black labor force.

An understanding of this fundamental conflict over the relation between government and society helps explain the pervasive complaints concerning corruption and "extravagance" during Radical Reconstruction. Corruption there was aplenty; tax rates did rise sharply. More significant than the rate of taxation, however, was the change in its incidence. For the first time, planters and white farmers had to pay a significant portion of their income to the government, while propertyless blacks often escaped scot-free. Several states, moreover, enacted heavy taxes on uncultivated land to discourage land speculation and force land onto the market, benefiting, it was hoped, the freedmen.

As time passed, complaints about the "extravagance" and corruption of Southern governments found a sympathetic audience among influential Northerners. The Democratic charge that universal suffrage in the South was responsible for high taxes and governmental extravagance coincided with a rising conviction among the urban middle classes of the North that city government had to be taken out of the hands of the immigrant poor and returned to the "best men"—the educated, professional, financially independent citizens unable to exert much political influence at a time of mass parties and machine politics. Increasingly the "respectable" middle classes began to retreat from the very notion of universal suffrage. The poor were no longer perceived as honest producers, the backbone of the social order; now they became the "dangerous classes," the "mob." As the historian Francis Parkman put it, too much power rested with "masses of imported ignorance and hereditary ineptitude." To Parkman the Irish of the Northern cities and the blacks of the South were equally incapable of utilizing the ballot: "Witness the municipal corruptions of New York, and the monstrosities of negro rule in South Carolina." Such attitudes helped to justify Northern inaction as, one by one, the Reconstruction regimes of the South were overthrown by political violence.

In the end, then, neither the abolition of slavery nor Reconstruction succeeded in resolving the debate over the meaning of freedom in American life. Twenty years before the American Civil War, writing about the prospect of abolition in France's colonies, Alexis de Tocqueville had written, "If the Negroes have the right to become free, the [planters] have the incontestable right not to be ruined by the Negroes' freedom." And in the United States, as in nearly every plantation society that experienced the end of slavery, a rigid social and political dichotomy between former master and former slave, an ideology of racism, and a dependent labor force with limited economic opportunities all survived abolition. Unless one means by freedom the simple fact of not being a slave, emancipation thrust blacks into a kind of no-man's land, a partial freedom that made a mockery of the American ideal of equal citizenship.

Yet by the same token the ultimate outcome underscores the uniqueness of Reconstruction itself. Alone among the societies that abolished slavery in the nineteenth century, the United States, for a moment, offered the freedmen a measure of political control over their own destinies. However brief its sway, Reconstruction allowed scope for a remarkable political and social mobilization of the black community. It opened doors of opportunity that could never be completely closed. Reconstruction transformed the lives of Southern blacks in ways unmeasurable by statistics and unreachable by law. It raised their expectations and aspirations, redefined their status in relation to the larger society, and allowed space for the creation of institutions that enabled them to survive the repression that followed. And it established constitutional principles of civil and political equality that, while flagrantly violated after Redemption, planted the seeds of future struggle.

Certainly, in terms of the sense of possibility with which it opened, Reconstruction failed. But as DuBois observed, it was a "splendid failure." For its animating vision—a society in which social advancement would be open to all on the basis of individual merit, not inherited caste distinctions—is as old as America itself and remains relevant to a nation still grappling with the unresolved legacy of emancipation.

QUESTIONS TO CONSIDER

1. Prior to 1960, who did historians describe as the "good guys" and "bad guys" of Reconstruction? Why?
2. What caused that long-lived interpretation to crumble?

3. What was the focal point of Reconstruction, according to Foner and Sydney George Fisher?
4. In the long run, how did Reconstruction most fail the freedmen? Why did it happen and why was it critical?
5. Does Foner conclude that Reconstruction was a success or a failure? What do *you* conclude?

2

The Inner Revolution*

Thomas Cochran

One of the most distinguished historians of the twentieth century, Thomas Cochran (1902–) served as president of both the American Historical Association and the Organization of American Historians, the two most prestigious professional bodies of the discipline. Originally an economic historian, he broadened his area of inquiry in later life, as book titles such as *Social Change in America* (1972) and *The Uses of History* (1974) attest. In 1985 he published some of his reflections in *Challenges to American Values: Society, Business, and Religion.* "The Inner Revolution," the title article of a 1964 book, demonstrates an insightful grasp of intellectual history.

In this selection, Cochran argues that a series of intellectual breakthroughs in the late nineteenth and early twentieth centuries caused a revolution in the perceptions and values of Americans. Undermining accepted truths, such as a morality based on abstinence, frugality, and saving, the new theories in psychology led to the acceptance of promiscuity, high consumption, and living on credit. Psychology and physics combined to undermine belief in the objectivity of reason—and left nothing to replace it. While intellectuals were beginning to adopt the new ways of thinking before World War I, the ideas reached the American masses through shifts in religious thought, child-rearing practices, and John Dewey's progressive education following the war.

The nature of the American character as it existed in the nineteenth century and before was shattered by these intellectual changes. In his influential book *The Lonely Crowd* (1950), sociologist David Riesman lamented that Americans had shifted from inner direction to other direction—that they had lost their independence and become conformists. In "The Inner Revolution," Cochran explains why: Americans had been left with their internal compasses destroyed as they attempted to cope with twentieth-century ideas. While it is less obvious to the casual observer than the staggering material change since 1900, the inner revolution reaches right to the core of the individual and has probably had an even greater impact.

Advanced thinkers of the seventeenth century warned that science had taken God away from nature and from man. Early in the century John Donne lamented that the world was maimed and cursed:

> *And new philosophy calls all in doubt,*
> *The element of fire is quite put out;*
> *The sun is lost, and the earth*
> *And freely men confess that this world is spent,*

But in spite of the implications read into the new Galilian cosmology religion survived and flourished, and nowhere more than in the northern colonies of America. The Puritans, Quakers, and other dissenting sects built religious precepts and language into the growing society, and the middle class character of American life fostered continuing religious strength.

Consequently, the weakening of religious certainties and religious behavior that had come gradually over generations to Europeans occurred rapidly in America from the 1890s on. And weakening religious beliefs had more effect on the rest of the value structure of American middle class society than seems to have been the case elsewhere.

It was in this atmosphere that Americans turned to the study of social science, and a few saw history in a new role. A society sure of its values had needed history only to celebrate the glories of the past, but a society of changing values and consequent confusion also needed history as a utilitarian guide. Hence, the social science approach to history . . . arose largely from the inner destruction of values, from the loss of the historic certainties of nineteenth-century Americans. The seminal importance of this inner revolution in values calls for more analysis of some of its details.

The basic weapon of destruction in America, as in Europe, was the skeptical, experimental attitude of science. A series of discoveries around the turn-of-the-century in fields as diverse as physics and psychology were more emotionally upsetting than any scientific findings since those of Galileo. In the first quarter of the twentieth century new scientific ideas and attitudes permeated the means, such as child-rearing and schooling, by which the old culture was sustained. While among the middle and upper class groups that could consciously espouse new learning there had been some skepticism in the nineteenth century, in 1900 social behavior based on Christian morality, study of the Bible, and the use of a religious language were still generally the rule. The fact that, historically, a disproportionately large part of the professional elite had been of New England origin had probably helped to spread and preserve religious values in the late nineteenth century. These leaders had made a cold peace with the older science, including evolution, and had continued to preach, and to a degree practice, the virtues associated with a divinely directed society. On the secular front, classic laissez-faire and an equally unscientific Social Darwinism joined with Christian morality in providing clear, if somewhat contradictory, laws and principles for the conduct of a society.

Before World War I only an advance guard of Americans had absorbed the upsetting scientific ideas, but by 1925 the well educated urban leaders of opinion saw their relations with the world and the universe in new scientific contexts. Aided by social and economic forces an inner revolution had occurred. The cultural change was not the result of any one line of reasoning following from a particular scientific statement. The upsurging of learning and research accompanying the growth of science, resulting technological changes and ultimately new conditions of living all operated to alter attitudes within American culture. As John Dewey saw the process in 1899: "Habits of living are altered with startling abruptness and thoroughness; the search for truths is infinitely stimulated and facilitated and their application to life made not only practicable but commercially necessary. Even our moral and religious ideas and interests . . . are profoundly affected."

In America the cumulative force of belief in the need for experimentation, in the inapplicability of traditional values to a changed present, in the concealed pitfalls of rationality and in the relativity of truth must be seen against a background of heavy non-Protestant immigration, the physical inadequacies of unplanned cities, the rapid growth of bureaucracy, and the great promise of new technology. The essence of the resulting change was not the supercession of an old set of values by new ones, as had occurred in the Protestant Reformation, but rather the demolition of a central part of the value structure with no substitutes offered. The nineteenth-century American whether conservative or radical, religious or atheistic recognized the existence of certain fixed values that he had to be for or against. By 1925 the well-educated man was skeptical regarding principles or values whether in bringing up his children or forecasting the business situation.

Physics and psychology, in particular, forced the intellectual world to consider the profound meanings inherent in their methods and findings, but the thrust of the advanced thinking in these two sciences was reinforced by almost equally significant work in other fields such as biology. While, obviously, no survey of the hypotheses of science upsetting to major social values can be attempted, a brief description of the most significant work in psychology and physics is an essential background for understanding the inner revolution.

Late nineteenth century experimental psychology and other scientific approaches such as historical analysis of the Bible and anthropological study of human behavior cast doubt on the authority of many older moral values. William James's *The Principles of Psychology*, published in 1890, was one of the earliest books to spread the new scientific ideas. "The human being who appears in James's psychology," writes Edna Headereder, "bears little resemblance to the rational man of earlier years." Later in the decade John Dewey, as we shall see, began applying the new psychology to child-rearing and education.

During the next generation academic psychologists were effectively undermining the religious ideas of will power and rationally controlled activity, but for the educated urban middle class the theories of Sigmund Freud were more dramatic and exciting. The popularity of his ideas in the United States in the 1920s fitted the social trends arising from urban industrialism as well as from the whole complex of experimental attitudes. History texts emphasize how the initial Freudian emphasis on sexual repression as a primary cause of neurosis fitted well with post-war ideas regarding elimination of the double standard of morality and more freedom for women. Bringing sex "into the open" went with short skirts and equality with men in smoking, drinking, language, and voting. But the more important and lasting effect of Freudianism, one that later revisions scarcely weakened, was to cast doubt on the objectivity of reason. Rational processes according to Freud were guided by unconscious urges. Given the same situation two "reasonable" men would, because of different infantile sexual repressions, select facts that reached different conclusions. While later clinical experience has broadened the scope of what is repressed, and lengthened the period over which the unconscious is conditioned, these later scholars have not restored confidence in reason and conscious "will power" as guides to conduct. Ideas have remained ideologies, and truth relative to its context.

In the United States, particularly, the attack on reason was carried to an extreme. Experiments with the conditioned reflex in animals led the University of Chicago psychologist, John B. Watson, to advance a system called Behaviorism in which all "thought" was merely the verbalizing of conditioned reactions. The existence of consciousness was held to be a delusion akin to religion, myths, and other superstitions. While too extreme to convince the majority of experimental psychologists, a few big university departments were won over to Watson's views. Easier to understand than Freud, and more concerned with normal psychology, many middle-class parents became Behaviorists. Behaviorism also influenced writers on child-rearing and specifically incorporated in *Infant and Child Care*, a booklet widely distributed by the U.S. Department of Labor.

While Watson made all morality a matter of conditioning rather than thought or will, Freud, in effect, turned old-fashioned American morality upside down. Repression of self-indulgence by the use of will power in order to abide by divine precepts was now seen as psychologically dangerous in the case of the young and probably futile in the case of adults. The repressed desire would find some alternate and perhaps more subtly dangerous form of expression. As in the case of Freudian ideas regarding sex, the new morality, or amorality, of indulgence suited other social trends. A relatively mature industrialism in the 1920s was emphasizing greater consumption. Since from 1923 on lower-class purchasing power per capita was scarcely increasing, greater consumption had to come from luxury spending by the upper income groups—those who were most influenced by the new psychological ideas.

So the older American morality of abstinence, frugality, and saving was for many replaced by an acceptance of promiscuity, high consumption, and living on credit. As with Behaviorism, later attitudes have modified some of the revolutionary extremes of the 1920s, but the general acceptance of the view of mental processes generated by Freud's theories remained the rule in medicine and the social sciences. It is also interesting that the continuing needs of the economy, written into respectable economic doctrine by John Maynard Keynes, prevented a return to earlier views on the immorality of high-level mass consumption.

Physics joined psychology in showing the limitations of both verbal logic and sensory perception. The roots of the upsetting knowledge that man could not perceive the nature of the physical world through his senses or describe its processes by verbal logic goes back at least to Clark Maxwell's work on electromagnetism in England in the 1870s. But the philosophical significance of this earlier work was not clear to many intellectuals before Einstein's dramatic solution in 1905 to the paradox of the transit of Mercury. His field equations based on treating space, time, velocity and mass as dependent variables became widely known, if not understood, before World War I. More upsetting in the long run to any mental image of the nature of things was the work done by Lord Rutherford, Max Planck, and Nils Bohr in the second decade of the century on the structure of the atom and the nature of energy. The net result was to show that ultimate substance, if such existed, was so infinitely small in relation to the space it seemed to occupy as to be negligible, and that what we perceived as matter was an extremely complex structure of electrical relationships. As John Langdon-Davies put it: "Science . . . has taken the very ground from under our feet and substituted a nightmare myriad of atomic and solar systems."

All of this knowledge was deduced from the interpretation of indirect tests and expanded into theories by mathematical logic. When existing mathematics would not provide answers which accorded with the data, as in the case of Planck's quantum theory, new systems of mathematics were developed. To some devout physical scientists, like Sir James Jeans, God could be pictured as the master mathematician.

Although this might seem to go back to the Thomist view of the essential rationality of God, the new rationality was expressed in a flexible mathematical logic incomprehensible to the common man. It was difficult to convey the new theories even to nonmathematical intellectuals. But the fact that physics had destroyed the old concepts of the universe and its matter was widely known by the end of World War I. The hope that physics had opened the door to a new age of faith was not substantiated. The more general reaction appears to have been doubt regarding man's ability to understand the nature of his environment, and increased skepticism regarding all doctrine.

The reaction against traditional forms or values and the rise of radical experimentation that were encouraged directly or indirectly by the new science can be seen in all the arts. But even a brief account of the trends in music, painting, sculpture, architecture, design, poetry, and literature would raise controversies unimportant from the standpoint of our two main theses. Here attention will be focused on philosophy, the social sciences, religion, child-rearing and education; on parts of the culture in which the effects of the new science and its attitudes were direct and largely explicit. These also include the chief agencies by which the culture shapes the personality and learning of successive generations.

Philosophy was directly challenged by the new methods and concepts of physics. A generation of philosophers, led in the second decade by Bertrand Russell in England and Ludwig Wittgenstein in Germany, contended that philosophy should forego its quest for metaphysical conclusions and devote itself to a scientific study of the nature of truth or systems of verification. This narrowing of the scope of philosophical inquiry was resisted by many academic philosophers such as Americans Paul E. More and Irving Babbitt who defended a classical humanism, but most of the younger philosophers followed Russell and Wittgenstein. The result of this refocusing of attention on the nature of logic, rather than on philosophical systems was to make philosophy into a second order discipline unlikely to provide new values or goals, one concerned with means rather than ends. Whereas William James, for example, had advocated a pragmatism in which truth was discovered by experiment, reason, and some divine intuition, his successor, John Dewey, evolved more precise statements of truth in relation to given contexts, statements that apparently left no room for intuition, divine guidance or other metaphysics.

The pause for questioning forced on philosophy by mathematical logic was quickly reflected in the social sciences. The scholars in each discipline became more acutely conscious of the problems of verification and objectivity in their own work. Furthermore, in their research sociologists and economists had somewhat the same type of experiences as the natural scientists. What had seemed to be simple systems controlled by a few variables turned out to be infinitely complex aggregates concerning which theorizing had to be highly tentative. In part this was the usual result of more intensive research, but also involved was the relentlessly questioning attitude arising from knowledge of the problems of natural science. The more philosophically minded historians were forced to recognize the extreme difficulty of verifying any important generalization, recognize the elusive character of true objectivity, and to adopt Dewey's concept of contextual relativism.

These trends in learning illustrate the pervasive character of the change in the highly educated man's view of his situation. But for the change to affect Americans as a whole, the new ideas had to penetrate to the central beliefs of middle-class culture: to attitudes toward religion, child-rearing and education.

Because of the strong impact of Spencer's Social Darwinism in the United States, and the rise of critical historiography in the seminaries in the late 1880s, religion felt some of the pressures of the new scientific attitudes more quickly than most phases of American life. Andrew D. White's *A History of the Warfare of Science with Theology in Christendom*, published in 1896, was widely read. The more basic influence of science, however, seems not the attack on certain theological assumptions, which always find new defenses, but the undermining of general religious authority in the more liberal Protestant churches, and as a result forcing appeals for support to rest on social rather than on theological grounds.

European writers such as Ortega y Gasset would urge that man had been "coming out of Christianity" from 1400 on, and historians can argue that this process had been going on in America since 1620. They point out that New England Calvinism quickly departed from European theology in order to hold the support of Americans. But in spite of substituting less rigorous doctrine for irrevocable predestination the churches had preserved their ultimate moral authority. No matter how much some businessmen and politicians disregarded Christian ethics they felt it wise to talk the language of Protestant doctrine, and many, like John D. Rockefeller and J. Pierpont Morgan, were devout believers.

The change from the mid-1890s to the mid-1920s was subtle but basic. As the advanced Protestant churches in the larger cities tried to move in the direction of rendering social service by means of Sunday schools, parish houses, social clubs, and missionary work aimed more at social than religious advance, the ministry became more influenced by the ideas of the parishioners. The successful preacher in a prosperous urban parish sought through experiment to achieve a good adjustment, to be a good businessman and a good social leader.

Thus educated urban Protestants (and one might say the same for Jews) had come to apply the questioning attitudes of science to their religious life. Faith survived, but it was in the background. It was not the active implicit faith of the midnineteenth century. Parishioners valued their church as a social institution; doctrine was approached more pragmatically on the basis of its credibility and utility; church attendance was seen as a social as well as a religious ritual. The offspring of the immigrants who poured in at the turn of the century tended to similar views. "The church to them was only too often just one of the many ethnic institutions that had to be maintained . . . "

Invading the old-time religious preserves of child-rearing and education, the experimental psychologists, psychoanalysts, and educational specialists insured the perpetuation of the new attitudes through altered personality in the ensuing generation. Since material on child-rearing practices is notably absent from biographies and autobiographies change must be chiefly inferred from the written advice offered to parents. Analysis of some of the available literature from 1865 to 1929 shows the same tempo of scientific invasion of this sensitive area that is illustrated in other conceptual systems.

In the nineteenth century parents were primarily urged to teach children to know right from wrong, to be respectful of authority and to be reverent toward God. In order to be fit for the life hereafter children were particularly trained to avoid the many guises of evil. The naughty child should be told: you have grieved your parents, "but you have grieved your Heavenly Father much more, you must ask him to forgive you and to help you to be a better child." There was still the assumed unity of divine and natural law establishing what was right and wrong. "Unity in nature and man is the moral, pedagogical and religious solution of our time," wrote the veteran educator Emma Marwedel in 1887. "The church, the school, and the home all aim at the higher moral culture." The First [sic] Commandment to honor thy parents contains, according to Mary Allen West, "an implied command to parents, and furnishes strong ground for claiming God's authority for the careful training of children." The religious tone in the period before 1890 was no doubt strengthened by the fact that a large part of the advisors on child rearing were women and ministers, while very few were doctors.

By the 1890s new psychological ideas were lessening the emphasis on strict, arbitrary discipline and increasing advocacy of freedom of expression for the child. In the Preface to Felix Adler's *The Moral Instruction of Children,* W. T. Harris, Commissioner of Education, wrote: "the new ideal regards insight into the reasonableness of moral commands as the chief end." In this same year Florence H. Winterburn contended that "Parenthood is already looked upon by the more advanced minds as a profession, the time will come when its studies will be reduced to an exact science, ignorance of which will be inexcusable; as it is even now deplorable." But one suspects that regardless of what the "more advanced minds" were thinking most parents still sided with Kate Douglas Wiggin, who parodied the new freedom with the limerick:

> *There once was a hopeful young horse*
> *Who was brought up on love, without force;*
> *He had his own way, and they sugared his hay;*
> *So he never was naughty, of course.*

By about 1905 the effects of the new scientific attitudes were beginning to be more apparent. There was more emphasis on introspection by parents, and original sin and depravity were generally rejected. The effect of scientific questioning is reflected in Ernest H. Abbott's note that in religious training our ancestors had an advantage: "They knew very definitely what they wished their children to do and to believe. . . . Now, although they wish to give their children a full complement of doctrines, they either do not possess the full complement themselves, or do not believe that their children are mature enough to receive it." On the whole, however, Geoffrey H. Steere has found that the admonitions were still in terms of divine will and recognized principles. Attitudes toward sex differed little from the "Victorianism" of the nineteenth century.

By the 1920s the revolution had occurred. "The predominantly religiously oriented text was an anomaly." The measures advanced were generally in terms of psychology or physiology. Writing in 1920, the Editor of *Mothers Magazine and Home Life* came out squarely for experimentation. The child "cannot learn it by looking at it simply or listening to words that adults use to describe it." He warned the mother that "the more she limits her child, the more she handicaps him in his struggle to learn the world in which he must live." Parents were urged to be friends with their children rather than disciplinarians. In contrast to the clergymen and laymen of the earlier periods, the authors were mainly doctors. While there was an emphasis on permissiveness for the child and self-study for the parent, no principles were stated with the unquestioning confidence of the earlier times. Authoritarian parents of the old religious type could find little support in the textbooks. Freudian attitudes toward sex training were usually present, either explicitly or implicitly. In a word, children were being trained not for the hereafter, but for pragmatic adjustments to a changing present.

The new psychologies that affected the life of the middle class child at home altered the environment of the same child in the next most important institution in shaping personality—the school. The midnineteenth century educational philosophy of Horace Mann has been called a "blend of natural law, faith in progress, capitalistic morality, and liberal Protestantism." Late nineteenth-century education was still built around the inculcation of Christian moral truths. "The function of the schools," said John Dewey, "was to indoctrinate their students with a positive pattern of beliefs, political and moral axioms and principles that would guide their acts as citizens."

As early as the 1880s American scholars educated in Germany began to bring back both ideas regarding experimental psychology and methods of teaching. Johan Herbart, an early nineteenth century German educator, was one of the precursors of the twentieth century transformation. He urged the teacher to study the child as well as the lesson. He also advocated courses such as history and geography that were useful for good citizenship. In the 1890s the Herbartians exercised a strong influence on the National Education Association, and formed a society of their own.

But the great world leader in undermining the old moralistic, authoritarian education was John Dewey. Since he was also an instigator of rebellion in philosophy and the social sciences, Dewey is probably the most ubiquitous American representative of the new experimental attitudes. His whole system of thought in both philosophy and education was based on the methods of experimental science. "A human society," he thought, "would use scientific method and intelligence with its best equipment to bring about human consequences." He called the elementary school which he organized at the University of Chicago in 1896 "The Experimental School." The next year he wrote "it is impossible to tell just what civilization will be twenty years from now. Hence it is impossible to prepare the child for any precise set of conditions." Dewey, "suspicious of all attempts to erect a hierarchy of values," could obviously not supply the basis for a new structure of belief.

While from 1896 on Dewey exerted a strong influence on educational thought, his system spread at first to only a few private schools. Not until 1907 were his ideas incorporated in a major public school system. His great influence on the public schools occurred through the work of disciples after World War I. In 1904 Dewey had come to Columbia where Teacher's College was the major graduate training center for school teachers. A National Society for Progressive Education, formed in 1919, and educational articles and textbooks by his Columbia colleagues, such as William H. Kilpatrick and Harold Rugg spread the doctrine of child-centered education. While few public schools could afford a completely progressive system, the Dewey principles were known, perhaps in exaggerated form, to every well-educated teacher. Child-centrism reached its peak in the 1920s and then declined, but the strong emphasis on community relations that survived it was scarcely nearer to the old inculcation of fixed moral values.

Science also influenced education through quite different channels. The scientific management vogue from about 1910 to the 1920s was reflected in educational administration. In 1911 the National Education Association appointed a Committee on Economy of Time in Education which issued four widely read reports between 1916 and 1919. Their major emphasis was on elimination of nonessential studies. School boards subjected teachers' activities to job analysis, and the uses of school funds were studied on a "scientific" accounting basis. In the resulting rise of school management the teaching function tended to take second place. From the management standpoint the function of the school was to prepare useful, conventional citizens. To a degree, this was the opposite of the aims of progressive education, but both shared in the attack on older educational values. Both attacked the traditional content of education, both replaced indoctrination in Christian morality with an emphasis on community relations. The study of languages declined, political science and history tended to become civics or social studies with a primary emphasis on adjustment to current social rather than permanent natural or divine norms. Education had been revised to turn out citizens with cooperative attitudes and lightly held beliefs.

This brief review of some of the social effects of the rise of a pervasive attitude of scientific questioning and skepticism suggests that these early years of the twentieth century may have been one of the major periods of destruction of traditional values. However this proposition may be judged from the Western World in general, there seems little doubt about the magnitude of the change in the United States. The middle and upper class generations born after 1910 found themselves surrounded by the rubble of once imposing structures of truth. This alteration of the coordinates in which the individual saw the mystery of his relations to the world, whether in family life, education, religion or social values, was a change comparable to that from the late middle ages to the early modern, but very much more rapid.

The earlier change is widely regarded as having produced a new, dominant type of modal personality variously called Faustian, inner-directed, or capitalistic. The change of the twentieth century is currently held to have brought to dominance a modal type of personality lacking in strong inner convictions and more in need of external approval than the earlier type. Various writers have called this type the marketer, the fixer, the organization man, and the other-directed man. As the names imply the causes selected to account for the twentieth century change stem from the social conditions of mass-production industrialism. David Riesman, for example, attributes the rise of other-direction to incipient decline in population, material abundance, leisure, and bureaucracy—a world in which other people are the problem. William A. Whyte, Jr., a nonacademic writer whose views have been highly influential, sees his "organization man" as the result of men "belonging" to large bureaucratic enterprises, business, professional, or governmental.

While these and other theories based on changes in the economic and demographic environment appear to rest on plausible assumptions, their premises seem inadequate fully to account for the magnitude of the changes in values. Abundance, leisure, and bureaucracy, for example, operate externally and on the adult. It seems equally probable that motive power for the inner revolution was contributed to by the less emphasized spread of the new findings and experimental attitudes of science with the attendant changes in child-rearing, religious training and schooling.

But the question of causal explanation is less important than the generally accepted result. Deeply disturbed by an impersonal, rapidly changing world with relativistic values, men asked new questions of history. In spite of wars and revolutions, the last few decades have not been a period for high tragedy or exciting drama, but rather one of continual questioning. History, if it is to hold its high place in the field of learning, must suggest policies for meeting current problems.

QUESTIONS TO CONSIDER

1. What was the basic"weapon" destroying the American (and European) value system?
2. How did the changes differ from those of the Protestant Reformation?
3. What was the impact of Watson's "Behaviorism" and Freud's ideas?
4. What was the impact of science on religion?
5. How did the inner revolution affect child rearing?
6. What is your response to the material in "The Inner Revolution?"

3

Ten-Gallon Hero*

David Brion Davis

David Brion David (1927–   ), a professor of history of Yale, has won renown as a specialist in the history of slavery. His profound and original studies, *The Problem of Slavery in Western Culture* (1966), *The Problem of Slavery in the Age of Revolution* (1975), and *Slavery and Human Progress* (1984) earned him a reputation as one of the nation's foremost scholars. His interest in the broader field of nineteenth-century cultural and intellectual history led him to write this article on the cowboy in 1954.

In "The Mountain Man as Jacksonian Man," William Goetzmann argued that the mountain man was not the uncivilized, antisocial being folklore maintained. Davis here explains how the mythical cowboy was a synthesis of the myths of the Western scout and the antebellum Southern gentleman. The cowboy, Davis maintains, outlasted such earlier nostalgic frontier images because he embodied the last of American frontiers. Owen Wister's classic portrait *The Virginian* (1902) appeared just nine years after Frederick Jackson Turner's famous paper on the significance of the frontier on American history, itself occasioned by the "end" of the frontier disclosed by the 1890 census. Through a combination of commercial exploitation and psychological need, the cowboy became a symbol not only to Americans, but to the world.

Since "Ten-Gallon Hero" appeared, the cowboy has fallen from his preeminent position on television and in the movies. He is most evident today in commercials for beer, cigarettes, and pickup trucks, where he continues to embody the ultimate independent, free man. He has been replaced as a hero for preadolescents by Luke Skywalker and other "space cowboys" pursuing the final frontier, free even from the constraints of earth. Another hero of today's youth is the independent, uncontrollable law enforcer in the mold of Dirty Harry. The new generation has paid a price for changing its heroes. While the cowboy was quite clearly escapist in nature, the contemporary setting and plausibility of the violent cops and robbers shows have made heavy viewers far more fearful about the world in which they live. The American character is being continually forged, not only by great ideas, as Cochran suggested in "The Inner Revolution," but by such commonplace things as one's choice of entertainment.

In 1900 it seemed that the significance of the cowboy era would decline along with other brief but romantic episodes in American history. The Long Drive lingered only in the memories and imaginations of old cowhands. The "hoe-men" occupied former range land while Mennonites and professional dry farmers had sown their Turkey Red winter wheat on the Kansas prairies. To be sure, a cattle industry still flourished, but the cowboy was more like an employee of a corporation than the free-lance cowboy of old. The myth of the cowboy lived on in the Beadle and Adams paper-back novels, with the followers of Ned Buntline and the prolific Colonel Pretiss Ingraham. But this seemed merely a substitution of the more up-to-date cowboy in a tradition which began with Leatherstocking and Daniel Boone. If the mountain man had replaced Boone and the forest scouts, if the cowboy had succeeded the mountain man, and if the legends of Mike Fink and Crockett were slipping into the past, it would seem probable that the cowboy would follow, to become a quaint character of antiquity, overshadowed by newer heroes.

Yet more than a half century after the passing of the actual wild and woolly cowboy, we find a unique phenomenon in American mythology. Gaudy-covered Western or cowboy magazines decorate stands, window, and shelves in "drug" stores, bookstores, grocery stores, and supermarkets from Miami to Seattle. Hundreds of cowboy movies and television shows are watched and lived through by millions of Americans. Nearly every little boy demands a cowboy suit and a Western six-shooter cap pistol. Cowboys gaze out at you with steely eye and cocked revolver from cereal packages and television screens. Jukeboxes in Bennington, Vermont, as well as Globe, Arizona, moan and warble the latest cowboy songs. Middle-age folk who had once thought of William S. Hart, Harry Carey, and Tom Mix as a passing phase, have lived to see several Hopalong Cassidy revivals, the Lone Ranger, Tim McCoy, Gene Autry, and Roy

Rogers. Adolescents and even grown men in Maine and Florida can be seen affecting cowboy, or at least modified cowboy garb, while in the new airplane plants in Kansas, workers don their cowboy boots and wide-brimmed hats, go to work whistling a cowboy song, and are defiantly proud that they live in the land of lassos and sixguns.

When recognized at all, this remarkable cowboy complex is usually defined as the distortion of once-colorful legends by a commercial society. The obvious divergence between the real West and the idealized version, the standardization of plot and characters, and the ridiculous incongruities of cowboys with automobiles and airplanes, all go to substantiate this conclusion.

However, there is more than the cowboy costume and stage setting in even the wildest of these adventures. Despite the incongruities, the cowboy myth exists in fact, and as such is probably a more influential social force than the actual cowboy ever was. It provides the framework for an expression of common ideals of morality and behavior. And while a commercial success, the hero cowboy must satisfy some basic want in American culture, or there could never be such a tremendous market. It is true that the market has been exploited by magazine, song, and scenario writers, but it is important to ask why similar myths have not been equally profitable, such as the lumbermen of the early northwest, the whale fishermen of New Bedford, the early railroad builders, or the fur traders. There have been romances written and movies produced idealizing these phases of American history, but little boys do not dress up like Paul Bunyan and you do not see harpooners on cereal packages. Yet America has had many episodes fully as colorful and of longer duration than the actual cowboy era.

The cowboy hero and his setting are a unique synthesis of two American traditions, and echoes of this past can be discerned in even the wildest of the modern horse operas. On the one hand, the line of descent is a direct evolution from the Western scout of Cooper and the Dime Novel; on the other, there has been a recasting of the golden myth of the antebellum South. The two were fused sometime in the 1880s. Perhaps there was actually some basis for such a union. While the West was economically tied to the North as soon as the early canals and railroads broke the river-centered traffic, social ties endured longer. Many Southerners emigrated West and went into the cattle business, and of course, the Long Drive originated in Texas. The literary synthesis of two traditions only followed the two social movements. It was on the Great Plains that the descendants of Daniel Boone met the drawling Texas cowboy.

Henry Nash Smith has described two paradoxical aspects of the legendary Western scout, typified in Boone himself. This woodsman, this

buckskin-clad wilderness hunter is a pioneer, breaking trails for his countrymen to follow, reducing the savage wilderness for civilization. Nevertheless, he is also represented as escaping civilization, turning his back on
the petty materialism of the world, on the hypocritical and self-conscious
manners of community life, and seeking the unsullied, true values of nature.

These seemingly conflicting points of view have counterparts in the
woodsman's descendant, the cowboy. The ideal cowboy fights for justice,
risks his life to make the dismal little cowtown safe for law-abiding, respectable citizens, but in so doing he destroys the very environment
which made him a heroic figure. This paradox is common with all ideals,
and the cowboy legend is certainly the embodiment of a social ideal. Thus
the minister or social reformer who rises to heroism in his fight against a
sin-infested community would logically become a mere figurehead once
the community is reformed. There can be no true ideal or hero in a utopia.
And the civilization for which the cowboy or trailblazer struggles is
utopian in character.

But there is a further consideration in the case of the cowboy. In our
mythology, the cowboy era is timeless. The ranch may own a modern station wagon, but the distinguishing attributes of cowboy and environment
remain. There is, it is true, a nostalgic sense that this is the last great drama,
a sad knowledge that the cowboy is passing and that civilization is approaching. But it never comes. This strange, wistful sense of the coming
end of an epoch is not something outside our experience. It is a faithful
reflection of the sense of approaching adulthood. The appeal of the cowboy, in this sense, is similar to the appeal of Boone, Leatherstocking, and
the later Mountain Man. We know that adulthood, civilization, is inevitable, but we are living toward the end of childhood, and at that point
"childness" seems eternal; it is a whole lifetime. But suddenly we find it
is not eternal, the forests disappear, the mountains are settled, and we
have new responsibilities. When we shut our eyes and try to remember,
the last image of a carefree life appears. For the nation, this last image is
the cowboy.

The reborn myth of the antebellum South also involves nostalgia; not
so much nostalgia for something that actually existed as for dreams and
ideals. When the Southern myth reappeared on the rolling prairies, it was
purified and regenerated by the casting off of apologies for slavery. It
would focus all energies on its former role of opposing the peculiar social
and economic philosophy of the Northeast. This took the form of something more fundamental than mere agrarianism or primitivism. Asserting
the importance of values beyond the utilitarian and material, this trans-
planted Southern philosophy challenged the doctrine of enlightened self-
interest and the belief that leisure time is sin.

Like the barons and knights of Southern feudalism, the large ranch owners and itinerant cowboys knew how to have a good time. If there was a time for work, there was a time for play, and the early rodeos, horse races, and wild nights at a cowtown were not occasions for reserve. In this respect, the cowboy West was more in the tradition of fun-loving New Orleans than of the Northeast. Furthermore, the ranch was a remarkable duplication of the plantation, minus slaves. It was a hospitable social unit, where travelers were welcome even when the owner was absent. As opposed to the hard-working, thrifty, and sober ideal of the East, the actual cowboy was overly cheerful at times, generous to the point of waste, and inclined to value friendly comradeship above prestige.

The mythical New England Yankee developed a code of action which always triumphed over the more sophisticated city slicker, because the Yankee's down-to-earth shrewdness, common sense, and reserved humor embodied values which Americans considered as pragmatically effective. The ideal cowboy also had a code of action, but it involved neither material nor social success. The cowboy avoided actions which "just weren't done" because he placed a value on doing things "right," on managing difficult problems and situations with ease, skill, and modesty. The cowboy's code was a Western and democratic version of the Southern gentleman's "honor."

In the early years of the twentieth century, a Philadelphia lawyer, who affected a careless, loose-tied bow instead of the traditional black ribbon and who liked to appear in his shirt sleeves, wrote: "The nomadic bachelor west is over, the housed, married west is established." In a book published in 1902 he had, more than any other man, established an idealized version of the former, unifying the Southern and Western hero myths in a formula which was not to be forgotten. Owen Wister had, in fact, liberated the cowboy hero from the Dime Novels and provided a synthetic tradition suitable for a new century. *The Virginian* became a key document in popular American culture, a romance which defined the cowboy character and thus the ideal American character in terms of courage, sex, religion, and humor. The novel served as a model for hundreds of Western books and movies for half a century. In the recent popular movie "High Noon" a Hollywood star, who won his fame dramatizing Wister's novel, reenacted the same basic plot of hero rejecting heroine's pleas and threats, to uphold his honor against the villain Trampas. While this theme is probably at least a thousand years old, it was Owen Wister who gave it a specifically American content and thus explicated and popularized the modern cowboy ideal, with its traditions, informality, and all-important code.

Of course, Wister's West is not the realistic, boisterous, sometimes monotonous West of Charlie Siringo and Andy Adams. The cowboy, after all, drove cattle. He worked. There was much loneliness and monotony on the range, which has faded like mist under a desert sun in the reminiscences of old cow hands and the fiction of idealizers. The Virginian runs some errands now and then, but there are no cattle-driving scenes, no monotony, no hard work. Fictional cowboys are never bored. Real cowboys were often so bored that they memorized the labels on tin cans and then played games to see how well they could recite them. The cowboys in books and movies are far too busy making love and chasing bandits to work at such a dreary task as driving cattle. But then the Southern plantation owner did no work. The befringed hero of the forests did not work. And if any ideal is to be accepted by adolescent America, monotonous work must be subordinated to more exiting pastimes. The fact that the cowboy hero has more important things to do is only in keeping with his tradition and audience. He is only a natural reaction against a civilization which demands increasingly monotonous work, against the approaching adulthood when playtime ends.

And if the cowboy romance banishes work and monotony, their very opposites are found in the immensity of the Western environment. To be sure, the deserts and prairies can be bleak, but they are never dull when used as setting for the cowboy myth. There is always an element of the unexpected, of surprise, of variety. The tremendous distances either seclude or elevate the particular and significant. There are mirages, hidden springs, dust storms, hidden identities, and secret ranches. In one of his early Western novels William MacLeod Raine used both devices of a secret ranch and hidden identity, while Hoffman Birney combined a hidden ranch, a secret trail, and two hidden identities. In such an environment of uncertainty and change men of true genius stand out from the rest. The evil or good in an individual is quickly revealed in cowboy land. A man familiar with the actual cowboy wrote that "brains, moral and physical courage, strength of character, native gentlemanliness, proficiency in riding or shooting—every quality of leadership tended to raise its owner from the common level."

The hazing which cowboys gave the tenderfoot was only preliminary. It was a symbol of the true test which anyone must undergo in the West. After the final winnowing of men, there emerge the heroes, the villains, and the clowns. The latter live in a purgatory and usually attach themselves to the hero group. Often, after the stress of an extreme emergency, they burst out of their caste and are accepted in the elite.

While the Western environment, according to the myth, sorts men into their true places, it does not determine men. It brings out the best in heroes and the worst in villains, but it does not add quality to the man who has none. The cowboy is a superman and is adorable for his own sake. It is here that he is the descendant of supernatural folk heroes. Harry Hawkeye, the creator of an early cowboy hero, Calvin Yancey, described him as:

> straight as an arrow, fair and ruddy as a Viking, with long flowing golden hair, which rippled over his massive shoulders, falling nearly to his waist; a high, broad forehead beneath which sparkled a pair of violet blue eyes, tender and soulful in repose, but firm and determined under excitement. His entire face was a study for a sculptor with its delicate aquiline nose, straight in outline as though chiselled from Parian marble, and its generous manly mouth, with full crimson and arched lips, surmounted by a long, silken blonde mustache, through which a beautiful set of even white teeth gleamed like rows of lustrous pearls.

While the Virginian is not quite the blond, Nordic hero, he is just as beautiful to behold. His black, curly locks, his lean athletic figure, his quiet, unassuming manner, all go to make him the most physically attractive man Owen Wister could describe. Later cowboy heroes have shaved their mustaches, but the great majority have beautiful curly hair, usually blond or red, square jaws, cleft chins, broad shoulders, deep chests, and wasplike waists. Like the Virginian, they are perfect men, absolutely incapable of doing the wrong thing unless deceived.

Many writers familiar with the real cowboy have criticized Wister for his concentration on the Virginian's love interest and, of course, they deplore the present degeneration of the cowboy plot, where love is supreme. There were few women in the West in the Chisholm Trail days and those few in Dodge City, Abilene, and Wichita were of dubious morality. The cowboy's sex life was intermittent, to say the least. He had to carry his thirst long distances, like a camel, and in the oases the orgies were hardly on a spiritual plane. Since earlier heroes, like the woodsman, led celibate lives, it is important to ask why the cowboy depends on love interest.

At first glance, there would seem to be an inconsistency here. The cowboy is happiest with a group of buddies, playing poker, chasing horse thieves, riding in masculine company. He is contemptuous of farmers, has no interest in children, and considers men who have lived among women as effete. Usually he left his own family at a tender age and rebelled against the restrictions of mothers and older sisters. Neither the Virginian nor the actual cowboys were family men, nor did they have much interest in the homes they left behind. Thus, it would seem that courting a young schoolteacher from Vermont would be self-destruction. At no place is the idealized cowboy further from reality than in his love for the tender woman from the East. Like the law and order he fights for, she will destroy his way of life.

But this paradox is solved when one considers the hero cowboy, not the plot, as the center of all attention. Molly Wood in *The Virginian,* like all her successors, is a literary device, a *dea ex machina* with a special purpose. Along with the Western environment, she serves to throw a stronger light on the hero, to make him stand out in relief, to complete the picture of an ideal. In the first place, she brings out qualities in him which we could not see otherwise. Without her, he would be too much the brute for a real folk hero, at least in a modern age. If Molly Wood were not in *The Virginian,* the hero might seem too raucous, too wild. Of course, his affair with a blonde in town is handled genteelly; his boyish pranks such as mixing up the babies at a party are treated as good, clean fun, But still, there is nothing to bring out his qualities of masculine tenderness, there is nothing to show his conscience until Molly Wood arrives. A cowboy's tenderness is usually revealed through his kindness to horses, and in this sense, the Eastern belle's role is that of a glorified horse. A woman in the Western drama is somebody to rescue, somebody to protect. In her presence, the cowboy shows that, in his own way, he is a cultural ideal. The nomadic, bachelor cowboys described by Andy Adams and Charles Siringo are a little too masculine, a little too isolated from civilization to become the ideal for a settled community.

While the Western heroine brings out a new aspect of the cowboy's character, she also serves the external purpose of registering our attitudes toward him. The cowboy ideal is an adorable figure and the heroine is the vehicle of adoration. Female characters enable the author to make observations about cowboys which would be impossible with an all-male cast. This role would lose its value if the heroine surrendered to the cowboy immediately. So the more she struggles with herself, the more she conquers her Eastern reservations and surmounts difficulties before capitulating, the more it enhances the hero.

Again, *The Virginian* is the perfect example. We do not meet Molly Wood in the first part of the book. Instead, the author, the I, who is an Easterner, goes to Wyoming and meets the Virginian. It is love at first sight, not in the sexual sense, of course (this was 1902), but there is no mistaking it for anything other than love. This young man's love for the Virginian is not important in itself; it heightens our worship of the hero. The sex of the worshiper is irrelevant. At first the young man is disconsolate, because he cannot win the Virginian's friendship. He must go through the ordeal of not knowing the Virginian's opinion of him. But as he learns the ways of the West, the Virginian's sublime goodness is unveiled. Though increasing knowledge of the hero's character only serves to widen the impossible gulf between the finite Easterner and the infinite, pure virtue of the cowboy, the latter, out of his own free grace and goodness recognizes the lowly visitor, who adores him all the more for it. But this little episode is only a preface, a symbol of the drama to come. As soon as the Virginian bestows his grace on the male adorer, Molly Wood arrives. The same passion is reenacted, though on a much larger frame. In this role, the sex of Molly *is* important, and the traditional romance plot is only superficial form. Molly's coyness, her reserve, her involved heritage of Vermont tradition, all go to build an insurmountable barrier. Yet she loves the Virginian. And Owen Wister and his audience love the Virginian through Molly Wood's love. With the male adorer, they had gone about as far as they could go. But Molly offers a new height from which to love the Virginian. There are many exciting possibilities. Molly can save his life and nurse him back to health. She can threaten to break off their wedding if he goes out to fight his rival, and then forgive him when he disobeys her plea. The Virginian marries Molly in the end and most of his descendants either marry or are about to marry their lovely ladies. But this does not mean a physical marriage, children, and a home. That would be building up a hero only to destroy him. The love climax at the end of the cowboy drama raises the hero to a supreme height, the audience achieves an emotional union with its ideal. In the next book or movie the cowboy will be the carefree bachelor again.

The classic hero, Hopalong Cassidy, has saved hundreds of heroines, protected them, and has been adored by them. But in 1910 Hopalong, "remembering a former experience of his own, smiled in knowing cynicism when told that he again would fall under the feminine spell." In 1950 he expressed the same resistance to actual marriage:

> "But you can't always move on, Hoppy!" Lenny protested. "Someday you must settle down! Don't you ever think of marriage?" "Un-huh, and whenever I think of it I saddle Topper and ride. I'm not a marrying man, Lenny. Sometimes I get to thinkin' about that poem a feller wrote, about how a woman is only a woman but—" "The open road is my Fate!" she finished. "That's it. But can you imagine any woman raised outside a tepee livin' in the same house with a restless man?"

The cowboy hero is the hero of the preadolescent, either chronologically or mentally. It is the stage of revolt against femininity and feminine standards. It is also the age of hero worships. If the cowboy romance were sexual, if it implied settling down with a real *girl*, there would be little interest. One recent cowboy hero summarized this attitude in terms which should appeal strongly to any ten-year-old: "I'd as soon fight a she-lion barehanded as have any truck with a gal." The usual cowboy movie idol has about as much social presence in front of the leading lady as a very bashful boy. He is most certainly not the lover-type. That makes him lovable to both male and female Americans. There can be no doubt that Owen Wister identified himself, not with the Virginian, but with Molly Wood.

While some glorifiers of the actual cowboy have maintained that his closeness to nature made him a deeply religious being, thus echoing the devoutness of the earlier woodsman hero who found God in nature, this tradition has never carried over to the heroic cowboy. Undoubtedly some of the real cowboys were religious, though the consensus of most of the writers on the subject seems to indicate that indifference was more common. Intellectualized religion obviously had no appeal and though the cowboy was often deeply sentimental, he did not seem prone to the emotional and frenzied religion of backwoods farmers and squatters. Perhaps his freedom from family conflicts, from smoldering hatreds and entangled jealousies and loves, had something to do with this. Despite the hard work, the violent physical conflicts, and the occasional debaucheries, the cowboy's life must have had a certain innocent, Homeric quality. Even when witnessing a lynching or murder, the cowboy must have felt further removed from total depravity or original sin than the farmer in a squalid frontier town, with his nagging wife and thirteen children.

At any rate, the cowboy hero of our mythology is too much of a god himself to feel humility. His very creation is a denial of any kind of sin. The cowboy is an enunciation of the goodness of man and the glory which he can achieve by himself. The Western environment strips off the artifice, the social veneer, and instead of a cringing sinner, we behold a dazzling superman. He is a figure of friendly justice, full of self-reliance, a very tower of strength. What need has he of a god?

Of course, the cowboy is not positively antireligious. He is a respecter of traditions as long as they do not threaten his freedom. The Virginian is polite enough to the orthodox minister who visits his employer's ranch. He listens respectfully to the long sermon, but the ranting and raving about his evil nature are more than he can stand. He knows that his cowboy friends are good men. He loves the beauty of the natural world and feels that the Creator of such a world must be a good and just God. Beyond that, the most ignorant cowboy knows as much as this sinister-voiced preacher. So like a young Greek god leaving Mount Olympus for a practical joke in the interest of justice, the Virginian leaves his role of calm and straightforward dignity, and engages in some humorous guile and deceit. The minister is sleeping in the next room and the Virginian calls him and complains that the devil is clutching him. After numerous sessions of wrestling with his conscience, the sleepy minister acting as referee, morning comes before the divine finds he has been tricked. He leaves the ranch in a rage, much to the delight of all the cowboys. The moral, observes Wister, is that men who are obsessed with evil and morbid ideas of human nature, had better stay away from the cowboy West. As Alfred Henry Lewis put it, describing a Western town the year *The Virginian* was published, "Wolfville's a hard practical outfit, what you might call a heap obdurate, an' it's goin' to take more than them fitful an' o'casional sermons I aloodes to,—to reach the roots of its soul." The cowboy is too good and has too much horse sense to be deluded by such brooding theology. Tex Burns could have been describing the Virginian when he wrote that his characters "had the cow hand's rough sense of humor and a zest for practical jokes no cow hand ever outgrows."

Coming as it did at the end of the nineteenth century, the cowboy ideal registered both a protest against orthodox creeds and a faith that man needs no formal religion, once he finds a pure and natural environment. It is the extreme end of a long evolution of individualism. Even the individualistic forest scout was dependent on his surroundings, and he exhibited a sort of pantheistic piety when he beheld the wilderness. The mighty captain of industry, while not accountable to anyone in this world, gave lip-service to the generous God who had made him a steward of wealth. But the cowboy hero stood out on the lonely prairie, dependent on neither man nor God. He was willing to take whatever risks lay along his road and would gladly make fun of any man who took life too seriously. Speaking of his mother's death, a real cowboy is supposed to have said:

> With almost her last breath, she begged me to make my peace with God, while the making was good. I have been too busy to heed her last advice. Being a just God, I feel that He will overlook my neglect. If not, I will have to take my medicine, with Satan holding the spoon.

While the cowboy hero has a respect for property, he does not seek personal wealth and is generous to the point of carelessness. He gives money to his friends, to people in distress, and blows the rest when he hits town on Saturday night. He owns no land and, in fact, has only contempt for farmers, with their ploughed fields and weather-beaten buildings. He hates the slick professional gambler, the grasping Eastern speculator, and railroad man. How are these traits to be reconciled with his regard for property rights? The answer lies in a single possession—his horse. The cowboy's horse is what separates him from vagabondage and migratory labor. It is his link with the cavalier and plumed knight. More and more, in our increasingly property-conscious society, the cowboy's horse has gained in importance. A horse thief becomes a symbol of concentrated evil, a projection of all crime against property and, concomitantly, against social status. Zane Grey was adhering to this tradition when he wrote, "in those days, a horse meant all the world to a man. A lucky strike of grassy upland and good water . . . made him rich in all that he cared to own." On the other hand, "a horse thief was meaner than a poisoned coyote."

When a cowboy is willing to sell his horse, as one actually does in *The Virginian,* he has sold his dignity and self-identity. It is the tragic mistake which will inevitably bring its nemesis. His love for and close relationship with his horse not only make a cowboy seem more human, they also show his respect for propriety and order. He may drift from ranch to ranch, but his horse ties him down to respectability. Yet the cowboy hero is not an ambitious man. He lacks the concern for hard work and practical results which typifies the Horatio Alger ideal. Despite his fine horse and expensive saddle and boots, he values his code of honor and his friends more than possessions. Because the cowboy era is timeless, the hero has little drive or push toward a new and better life. He fights for law and order and this implies civilization, but the cowboy has no visions of empires, industrial or agrarian.

One of the American traits which foreign visitors most frequently described was the inability to have a good time. Americans constantly appear in European journals as ill-at-ease socially, as feeling they must work every spare moment. Certainly it was part of the American Protestant capitalistic ethic, the Poor Richard, Horatio Alger ideal, that spare time, frivolous play, and relaxation were sins which would bring only poverty, disease, and other misfortunes. If a youth would study the wise sayings of great men, if he worked hard and made valuable friends but no really confidential ones, if he never let his hair down or became too intimate with any person, wife included, if he stolidly kept his emotions to himself and watched for his chance in the world, then he would be sure to succeed. But the cowboy hero is mainly concerned with doing things skillfully and conforming to his moral code for its own sake. When he plays poker, treats the town to a drink, or raises a thousand dollars to buy off the evil mortgage, he is not aiming at personal success. Most cowboy heroes have at least one friend who knows them intimately, and they are seldom reserved, except in the presence of a villain or nosey stranger.

Both the hero and real cowboy appear to be easy-going and informal. In dress, speech, and social manner, the cowboy sets a new ideal. Every cowboy knows how to relax. If the villains are sometimes tense and nervous, the hero sits placidly at a card game, never ruffled, never disturbed, even when his arch rival is behind him at the bar, hot with range and whisky. The ideal cowboy is the kind of man who turns around slowly when a pistol goes off and drawls, "Ah'd put thet up, if Ah were yew." William Macleod Raine's Sheriff Collins chats humorously with some train robbers and maintains a calm, unconcerned air which amuses the passengers, though he is actually pumping the bandits for useful information. Previously, he had displayed typical cowboy individualism by flagging the train down and climbing aboard, despite the protests of the conductor. Instead of the eager, aspiring youth, the cowboy hero is like a young tomcat, calm and relaxed but always ready to spring into action. An early description of one of the most persistent of the cowboy heroes summarizes the ideal characteristics which appeal to a wide audience:

> Hopalong Cassidy had the most striking personality of all the men in his outfit; humorous, courageous to the point of foolishness, eager for fight or frolic, nonchalant when one would expect him to be quite otherwise, curious, loyal to a fault, and best man with a Colt in the Southwest, he was a paradox, and a puzzle even to his most intimate friends. With him life was a humorous recurrence of sensations, a huge pleasant joke instinctively tolerated, but not worth the price cowards pay to keep it. He had come onto the range when a boy and since that time he had laughingly carried his life in his open hand, and . . . still carried it there, and just as recklessly.

Of course, most cowboy books and movies bristle with violence. Wild fist fights, brawls with chairs and bottles, gun play and mass battles with crashing windows, fires, and the final racing skirmish on horseback, are all as much a part of the cowboy drama as the boots and spurs. These bloody escapades are necessary and are simply explained. They provide the stage for the hero to show his heroism, and since the cowboy is the hero to the preadolescent, he must prove himself by their standards. Physical prowess is the most important thing for the ten- or twelve-year-old mind. They are constantly plagued by fear, doubt, and insecurity, in short, by evil, and they lack the power to crush it. The cowboy provides the instrument for their aggressive impulses, while the villain symbolizes all evil. The ethics of the cowboy band are the ethics of the boy's gang, where each member has a role determined by his physical skills and his past performance. As with any group of boys, an individual cowboy who had been "taken down a peg" was forever ridiculed and teased about his loss in status.

The volume of cowboy magazines, radio programs, and motion pictures would indicate a national hero for at least a certain age group, a national hero who could hardly help but reflect specific attitudes. The cowboy myth has been chosen by this audience because it combines a complex of traits, a way of life, which they consider the proper ideal for America.

The actual drama and setting are subordinate to the grand figure of the cowboy hero, and the love affairs, the exciting plots, and the climactic physical struggles present opportunities for the definition of the cowboy code and character. Through the superficial action, the heroism of the cowboy is revealed, and each repetition of the drama, like the repetition of a sacrament, reaffirms the cowboy public's faith in their ideal.

Perhaps the outstanding cowboy trait, above even honor, courage, and generosity, is the relaxed, calm attitude toward life. Though he lives intensely, he has a calm self-assurance, a knowledge that he can handle anything. He is good-humored and jovial. He never takes women too seriously. He can take a joke or laugh at himself. Yet the cowboy is usually anti-intellectual and antischool, another attitude which appeals to a younger audience.

Above all, the cowboy is a "good joe." He personifies a code of personal dignity, personal liberty, and personal honesty. Most writers on the actual cowboy represented him as having these traits. While many of these men obviously glorify him as much as any fiction writers, there must have been some basis for their judgment. As far as his light-hearted, calm attitude is concerned, it is amazing how similar cowboys appear, both in romances and nonfiction. Millions of American youth subscribed to the new ideal and yearned for the clear, Western atmosphere of "unswerving loyalty, the true, deep affection, and good-natured banter that left no sting." For a few thrilling hours they could roughly toss conventions aside and share the fellowship of ranch life and adore the kind of hero who was never bored and never afraid.

Whether these traits of self-confidence, a relaxed attitude toward life and good humor, have actually increased in the United States during the past fifty years is like asking whether men love their wives more now than in 1900. Certainly the effective influence of the cowboy myth can never be determined. It is significant, however, that the cowboy ideal has emerged above all others. And while the standardization of plot and character seems to follow other commercial conventions, the very popularity of this standard cowboy is important and is an overlooked aspect of the American character. It is true that this hero is infantile, that he is silly, overdone, and unreal. But when we think of many past ideals and heroes, myths and ethics; when we compare our placid cowboy with say, the eager, cold, serious hero of Nazi Germany (the highcheek-boned, blond lad who appeared on the Reichsmarks); or if we compare the cowboy with the gangster heroes of the thirties, or with the serious, self-righteous and brutal series of Supermen, Batmen, and Human Torches; when, in an age of violence and questioned public and private morality, if we think of the many possible heroes we might have had—then we can be thankful for our silly cowboy. We could have chosen worse.

QUESTIONS TO CONSIDER

1. How is the cowboy complex usually defined?
2. What does Davis see as the function of the cowboy myth?
3. Why has the cowboy image in particular been so enduring?
4. What was the significance of Owen Wister's *The Virginian?*
5. How accurate is the myth's reflection of the realities of work and monotony in the West?
6. Describe the cowboy's attitude toward religion and the reasons for it.
7. What is the cowboy's attitude toward property?

4

Work Ideals and the Industrial Invasion*

Daniel T. Rodgers

Through their first three centuries of existence, Americans had an obsession with work. The Puritans saw industrious labor at one's calling as fulfilling God's plan for the individual, and prosperity was a sign of God's blessing. Over time the religious underpinnings of work were supplanted by those of secular moralists like Benjamin Franklin, who in his maxims praised work both as a badge of civic virtue and as a means to wealth. In the nineteenth century, European visitors were amazed by the enthusiasm for work displayed by Americans pursuing what Charles Dickens denounced as the "almighty dollar."

Yet after midcentury, the nature of work changed at an accelerating clip as large-scale factories increasingly replaced small enterprises. Increased size of operation, more intrusive work discipline, and the demoralizing displacement of skills marked American labor's shift away from Franklin's middle class ideals toward a working class outlook with no hope of advancing to higher social levels. The concept of meaningful and fulfilling work disappeared for factor workers even as their staggering productivity flooded the marketplace with goods.

Daniel T. Rodgers, a Yale history Ph.D., specializes in intellectual history as a professor at Princeton. This selection is taken from his book *The Work Ethic in Industrial America, 1850–1920,* written in 1974.

*Reprinted by permission of the University of Chicago Press from *The Work Ethic in Industrial America, 1850–1920,* © 1974, 1978. All rights reserved.

"Work, work, work," Henry David Thoreau lectured an audience in the budding factory town of New Bedford in 1854. "It would be glorious to see mankind at leisure for once." Like so many of Thoreau's public activities, his "Getting a Living" was a quixotic gesture, a tilt at one of the most formidable windmills of mid-nineteenth-century opinion. It was the kind of irreverence to be expected of a man who could seriously describe his occupation as inspector of snowstorms and anticipator of sunrises. In a land reared on Franklin's Poor Richard aphorisms and the busy bee of Isaac Watts's poem—a land of railroads and heady ambitious, poised on the edge of a thoroughgoing experiment with industrialization—to doubt the moral preeminence of work was the act of a conscious heretic. But in the longer sweep of time, it was Thoreau who spoke as a conservative and a traditionalist. For the first American dream, before the others shoved it rudely aside, had been one not of work but of leisure. In the Western tradition, in fact, Thoreau's vision was the oldest dream of all.

One could begin with Aristotle's claim that leisure was the only fit life for man—the commonplace of a slave society that passed from there into one of the axioms of Western philosophy. Or one might begin with the fact of slavery itself and the social hierarchies that all through the West had set a man's worth and freedom by his exemption from toil and had made gentility synonymous with leisure. Still closer to the common life was speech, where the ache of toil was fashioned into a tangled etymological relationship between the words "labor" and "pain" that remains deeply embedded in the languages of Western Europe. But it was myth that most clearly gathered up and broadcast the painful indignity of work. Classical and Christian alike, the central fables of the West were shot through with longing for a leisured paradise.

The Greek and Roman poets mined the theme through the legend of a lost, workless past, a golden age at the beginnings of human history when the rivers had flowed with wine and honey and men had lived the effortless life of the gods. "All goods were theirs," Hesiod wrote at the head of the tradition, and "the fruitful grainland yielded its harvest to them of its own accord." And yet somehow, whether through punishment or confusion, man had lost that first innocent state. The age of gold had given way to a poverty-saddled age of want, pain, and endless work. Vergil's lament summed up the centuries of mythmaking: "Toil conquered the world, unrelenting toil, and want that pinches when life is hard."

Where the classical poets had clung to the past, Christian mythology captured the same compound of protest and desire in a more complex design—first in the vision of a garden "eastward in Eden" in which all man's wants had been satisfied, and still more hopefully in what Augustine

called the "eternal leisure" of heaven. The biblical tradition was more ambiguous than the classical, and from the beginning it contained seeds of
more positive attitudes toward labor. Adam was no idler in Eden, after all,
but was placed in the garden to watch and to "till" it, while the Judeo-
Christian God himself "worked" and "rested." But Christianity heightened the vision of paradise by pushing it into the reachable future, and
the pattern of the Christian myth—in which men fell out of a bounteous
harmony into a vale of toil and sorrow, to endure until redeemed to permanent, heavenly rest—reverberated no less strongly than the classical fables with the aching pain of labor. By the end of the Middle Ages, popular versions of the two myths were close enough to coalesce, Christian
optimism merging with the sensuousness of the classical golden age as
the paradises fused and fused once more with the palpable milk-and-
honey Edens that, according to European folk legends, lay hidden somewhere at the ends of the earth for an adventurous explorer to regain. It
was a compelling vision, the more so because its roots sank so deeply into
the potent stuff of experience. To work was to do something wearisome
and painful, scrabbling in the stubborn soil. It was the mark of men en-
trapped by necessity and thus of men who were not wholly free. At best
work was an inescapable necessity, a penance for old sins. Surely not this
but leisure was man's first estate, the telltale mark of paradise, the proper
focus of men's longings.

The myths waited only for a land to claim them, and with the discovery of America Europeans eagerly turned the hints the new continent
offered into visions of a world untouched by the age-old curse of work.
Columbus was the first to see the outlines of the ancient fables in the new
world, finally giving up his hopes for a passage to the Indies only to conclude that he had all but reached the gates of Eden itself, perched like the
stem end of a pear somewhere in present-day Venezuela. His report was
but the first of the images of a land of all but workless plenty, soon inex-
tricably intertwined with stores of the fabulous wealth of Mexico and
Peru, which long hovered over the American continents. Exploring the
Carolina coast a century after Columbus, Captain Arthur Barlowe found
himself in the midst of such "incredible" fruitfulness that, seen through
the mists of classical learning and desire, he was certain it was the "golden
age" intact—a land where "the earth bringeth forth all things in abundance,
as in the first creation, without toil or labor." Even farther to the north the
shaping force of desire produced visions only slightly dimmer. Captain
John Smith was a veteran of Virginia's first, starvation years by 1614 when
he undertook a careful mapping of the New England coast. But he came
away convinced that three days' work a week would satisfy any settler in
that fruitful land, much of that spent in the "pretty sport" of fishing.

Soberer, disillusioned adventurers often brought back far less flattering reports of America, bearing tales of native savagery and cannibalism and of a coast that turned to barrens and ice as one penetrated northward. But the European imagination fed on stories such as Barlowe's, on the image of an American paradise where the fruitful earth and innocent men lived in the original leisured harmony. As astute a reader of the explorers' reports as Montaigne concluded that the American natives whiled away their days in dancing in an ease far more perfect than the ancient poets had ever imagined. No cares troubled them, he wrote, no poverty, and "no occupations but leisure ones." "All men idle, all," Shakespeare caught the same hopes in *The Tempest,* his "American fable" in Leo Marx's phrase; but

> *Nature should bring forth,*
> *Of its own kind, all foison, all abundance,*
> *To feed my innocent people.*

Not only for those Europeans who stayed at home but for the Englishmen who came to Virginia and the colonies to the south, that dream of a leisured America was to have a long and stubborn history. Here was a new Eden, they claimed of Virginia, "the paradise of the world," "a land even as God made it."

Yet among those Englishmen who settled the country north of the Chesapeake, nothing was more common than to describe their American paradise as a "wilderness"—as a "howling wilderness" during moments of stress. Disappointment figured in the wilderness cry, most clearly in William Bradford's poignant description of Cape Cod in autumn that stands at the head of the tradition. Theology likewise buttressed the idea, for every Puritan minister knew the Book of the Revelation's promise that when troubles were thickest God would send his church into the "wilderness" for safekeeping. Still, the wilderness image had deeper roots than these, and throughout the seventeenth century, long after the Northern colonists had learned to love their land and prosper in it, it echoed and re-echoed in their writings.

In the end the word "wilderness" served as a shorthand for a sense of self and of mission. Unlike the first new world adventurers, the settlers of Puritan New England and Quaker Pennsylvania came with no hopes for prelapsarian ease. They were laborers for their Lord, straighteners of crooked places, engaged in a task filled with hardship, deprivation, and toil. They did not expect to pluck treasures from the land but planned to civilize and tame it, even as they expected to struggle to civilize and tame the wild places in themselves. At times this amounted to a thirst for affliction, a distrust of idly gotten fortune as a snare and a temptation. God's people "must come into, and go through a vast and roaring Wilderness, where they must be bruised with many pressures, [and] humbled under many overbearing difficulties," Thomas Hooker told his Connecticut flock with the same trust in adversity with which other Puritans warned prospective settlers away from the "overflowing riches" of the West Indies. Such men came ready, if not eager, to work in the sweat of their faces and to see, as William Penn wrote, "what sobriety and industry can do in a wilderness against heat, cold, wants, and dangers." They chose to call America a wilderness because it fit the countervision in their minds' eye that the moral life was a matter of hard work and hard-bitten determination. Out of the American Eden they fashioned a land preoccupied with toil.

During the first half of the nineteenth century, when Europeans began to come in numbers to inspect the new American nation, they marveled at the extent of the transformation. Almost without exception, visitors to the Northern states commented on the drawn faces and frantic busyness of Jacksonian Americans and complained of bolted meals, meager opportunities for amusement, and the universal preoccupation with what Charles Dickens damned as the "almighty dollar." The visitors' assessments of the pace of American life are not to be fully trusted. Moving in the company of business and professional men, few of the Europeans actually entered an American worshop or followed a farmer across his fields. There was, moreover, something of a litany to the repeated complaint about the Northerners' compulsive activity; it became a ritual as much a part of the American tour as the Patent Office or Niagara Falls. Yet the Europeans were genuinely perplexed at the absence of an extensive class devoted to the pursuits of leisure. "In the United States," Tocqueville wrote, "a wealthy man thinks that he owes it to public opinion to devote his leisure to some kind of industrial or commercial pursuit or to public business. He would think himself in bad repute if he employed his life solely in living." After ten years as a resident of Boston, the Viennese immigrant Francis Grund came to the same puzzled conclusion:

> There is, probably, no people on earth with whom business constitutes pleasure, and industry amusement, in an equal degree with the inhabitants of the United States of America. Active occupation is not only the principal source of their happiness, and the foundation of their national greatness, but they are absolutely wretched without it, and instead of the "*dolce far niente,*" know but the *horrors* of idleness. Business is the very soul of an American: he poursues it, not as a means of procuring for himself and his family the necessary comforts of life, but as the fountain of all human felicity . . . it is

as if all America were but one gigantic workshop, over the entrance of which there is the blazing inscription, *"No admission here, except on business."*

It was not the pace of work in America that inspired responses like this so much as its universality, its bewilderingly exalted status, the force of the idea itself.

Yet, on the whole, the objects of these complaints were not disturbed at their ignorance of what another visitor, in a distinctly European phrase, called "the difficult art of being gracefully idle." Mid-nineteenth-century politicians and poets alike in the North dwelled expansively on the dignity of labor and the moral worth of those who worked. "Labor, gentlemen, we of the free States acknowledge to be the source of all our wealth, of all our progress, of all our dignity and value," William Evarts told a campaign audience in 1856, in a conviction that, with slightly altered nuances, could be heard at virtually any lyceum series or political rally— Whig, Democrat, or Republican. Amid the paeans to industry and the disrepute of leisure, it was little wonder the Europeans concluded that the Americans had mortgaged the pleasures of life to the wilderness virtues: business, speculation, work, and action.

Ultimately Penn and Hooker and their heirs assaulted the paradise myths themselves, redrawing their moral to suit their revaluation of toil. Like the Puritans before them, nineteenth-century moralists agreed that Adam had worked in Eden or, if not, that his idleness had been all the worse for him. Over and over again, to anyone who would listen, they insisted that work was not a curse, whatever the hints in the Genesis story. Nor was it merely a painful means to moral health and redeeming grace. Labor was a blessing: not "a burden or a bare necessity . . . [but] a privilege, a glory, and a delight." Among academic moralists, the economists held out against the idea that work was natural to man, clinging, by and large, to the older idea that labor was a fragile, irksome habit grafted onto a human nature as lazy as it dared to be. But the weight of moral thinking was against them. Man was "made to labor," the century's orators asserted. "It is his destiny, the law of his nature," placed there by a creator who was himself, as Henry Ward Beecher—mid-nineteenth-century America's most famous preacher—insisted, the most tireless laborer of all.

In the end, even heaven itself—Augustine's "perpetual sabbath"— fell before the onslaught. The idea of an eternity of rest vexed and troubled many nineteenth-century American Protestants, and their most widely read spokesmen answered that uneasiness with promises of more "palpable" and "useful" tasks than mere praise and singing. "Surely there must be work to do in heaven, / Since work is the best thing on earth we know," the mill girl turned poet, Lucy Larcom, wrote toward the end of the century. New York's flamboyant evangelist DeWitt Talmage claimed more confidently that heaven was "the busiest place in the universe." Shunting aside generations of mythmaking, the moralists succeeded in writing the gospel of work not only on the land but on paradise itself. "God sent you not into this world as into a Play-house, but a Work-house," ran a Puritan reminder. It was, in fact, a choice Northerners made for themselves.

In our day we know that perplexing decision as the "work ethic." It is a simplified label, as inviting to abuse as it is convenient, but it points to an important truth: for the elevation of work over leisure involved not an isolated choice but an ethos that permeated life and manners. It reared its head in the nineteenth and early twentieth centuries in the countless warnings against the wiles of idleness and the protean disguises of the idler. It gave a special reverberation to the word "duty" and set an infectious model of active, conscientious doing. Theodore Roosevelt caught its tenor in his thundering insistence that only the strenuous life was worth living, that "nothing in this world is worth having or worth doing unless it means effort, pain, difficulty." That conviction was by no means Roosevelt's alone. The doctrine of the industrious life pervaded churches and children's storybooks, editorial columns and the stump rhetoric of politics. Not least, it transformed the processes of work themselves, energizing, mechanizing, and systematizing them in ways that made those who cared most about the worth of toil at once immensely proud and profoundly uneasy. But in another sense the phrase is misleading, for the work ethic as it stood in the middle of the nineteenth century, at the threshold of industrialization, was not a single conviction but a complex of ideas with roots and branches.

The taproot, as Max Weber suggested long ago, was the Protestant Reformation. Universalizing the obligation to work and methodizing time, the Reformers set in motion convictions that were to reverberate with enormous consequences through American history. At the heart of Protestantism's revaluation of work was the doctrine of the calling, the faith that God had called everyone to some productive vocation, to toil there for the common good and His greater glory. Paul had said as much centuries before, but the Reformers stripped down the list of admissible callings, lopping off not only the beggars and rascals whose idleness cumbered the land but the courtiers and monks who were no better. The medieval *summum bonum*, a life of contemplation and prayer, suddenly was no vocation at all. "True Godliness don't turn men out of the world" into a *lazy, rusty, unprofitable self-denial*," William Penn insisted, joining the attack on the monasteries; faith set men to work in the occupations of the secular, commonplace world. Nor was their labor there to be seen as an act of penance and mortification, as Christian tradition so long had had it. *Laborare est orare:* work itself was prayer, from the governing duties of kings to the meanest peasant's task. In the end faith, not labor, saved, of course; the Reformers never confused the secular vocation with a believer's primary, spiritual calling. But Protestantism extended and spiritualized toil and turned usefulness into a sacrament. Zwingli's benediction put the point succinctly: "In the things of this life, the laborer is most like to God."

Protestantism tried to turn religion out of the cloisters into the world of work, but it emptied the monasteries only to give everyone the ascetic responsibilities of a monk. This was the side of the Protestant ethic that most interested Weber: the obligation to survey and order the moral life that the Reformation, and English Puritanism in particular, imposed on its adherents. Striking down the Catholic rhythm of sin and confession, folly and remorse, Puritanism required that the believer ceaselessly analyze, rationalize, and forge his life into a systematic service to the Lord. Weber's argument exaggerated the somber, pleasure-destroying side of the Puritans, for they were not nearly the beetle-browed enemies of the spontaneous enjoyment of life he took them for. Even the strictest Calvinist did not object to the "seasonable recreations" that sharpened the wits or exercised the body. But Weber was certainly right in his claim that Puritanism tried to "penetrate . . . [the] daily routine of life with its methodicalness." Puritans methodized the English calendar, throwing out the irregular carnival of saints' days and replacing it with the clocklike rhythm of the weekly Sabbath, when men were to be as tireless and unbending in their rest as they had been during the week at their labors. In the same manner, Puritanism saturated its believers with an acute sense of the dangers of idleness, enjoining them to guard against the misspence of time to improve the passing moments, each of which, in the end, had to be accounted for in heaven. This was an asceticism of a novel sort, worldly and systematic, looking forward to the time-and-profit calculus of industrial life rather than backward to the flesh-denying torments of the desert hermits. Joined with the doctrine of the calling, it demanded not only that all men work but that they work in a profoundly new way: regularly, conscientiously, and diligently.

Puritans and Quakers carried these injunctions to the new world as articles of faith. Long before Isaac Watts solidified the idea in rhyme, New Englanders spoke of time as "precious" and censured those who used it idly and unprofitably. "Abhor . . . one hour of idleness as you would be ashamed of one hour of drunkenness," Thomas Shepard wrote to his son at Harvard. And from every corner ministers like Shepard broadcast the necessity of a calling. "Away to your business," Cotton Mather charged;

"lay out your strength in it, put forth your skill in it." Part of the persistent strength of the work ethic was due to the skill with which the preachers joined the ideal of diligent, productive labor to the demands of faith and gave it the form in which it was to be handed down and the generations in homilies and countless Sunday school tracts and carried west on the efforts of revivalists and home mission societies.

Yet the nineteenth-century work ethic was not simply the Protestant ethic in modern dress. In the first place, by the middle of the nineteenth century a good deal of secularization had taken place. The old ideas never completely died out, but gradually the term "calling" faded from common speech and with it the idea that in work one labored in the first instance for the glory of God. Increasingly the moralists talked instead of usefulness. Benjamin Franklin helped set the new tone in his tireless string of maxims and projects for the public good, and by the era of the American Revolution political writing was saturated with the ideal of public usefulness, the common weal filling the place the Reformers had given to God. The legacy persisted well into the nineteenth century. In one of her short stories of the 1830s, Sarah Hale had her Yankee hero try the elegant leisure of a Saratoga resort and come away to conclude that "this trifling away of time when there is so much to be done, so many improvements necessary in our country, is inconsistent with that principle of being useful, which every republican ought to cherish.

So much to be done. Hale's concerns pointed forward as well as backward, for intruding amid the eighteenth-century phrases she placed the idea that increasingly preoccupied nineteenth-century moralists. Not only did immense projects seem to wait at every hand, but with rising conviction, economists, editors, and preachers insisted that a failure to meet them, a slackening of the pace, would send the nation skidding into poverty and decay. The Victorian concern with scarcity, with the economic necessity of constant doing, was evident well before Darwin's *Origin of Species* made its full impact in America. In phrases foreign to the eighteenth century, mid-nineteenth-century writers castigated businessmen who thought to retire and slip out of harness while there was labor left in them. Economics imposed stricter necessities than this. The moralists were loath to call economic life cruel, but they did insist that it demanded constant effort. William Ellery Channing told a Boston mechanics' group in 1840:

> The material world does much for the mind by its beauty and order; but it does more for our minds by the pains it inflicts; by its obstinate resistance, which nothing but patient toil can overcome; by its vast forces, which nothing but unremitting skill and effort can turn to our use; by its perils, which demand continual vigilance; and by its tendencies to decay.

"Life is a stern, hard service," a contributor to the *Atlantic Monthly* wrote a generation later; "it takes a great deal of hard work to keep this world going on." In sentiments like these scarcity gradually nudged out the common good, just as the ideal of public usefulness had all but nudged out God. Where Puritans had been called to their vocations, nineteenth-century Americans were told that in a world of pressing material demands it was one's social duty to produce.

Working also held one back from the sink of idleness. Despite the gradual dropping away of the theological superstructure of Puritanism, the ascetic injunctions of the Protestant ethic retained and multiplied their force in the midnineteenth century. Looking back on her New England childhood years in the 1830s, Lucy Larcom remembered growing up "penetrated through every fibre of thought with the idea that idleness is a disgrace. It was taught with the alphabet and the spelling-book; it was enforced by precept and example, at home and abroad; and it is to be confessed that it did sometimes haunt the childish imagination almost mercilessly." This harrowing of the imagination was often quite deliberate. In his immensely popular *Seven Lectures to Young Men* of 1844, Henry Ward Beecher described the idle mind as an eerie, abandoned castle:

> Its gates sag down and fall; its towers gradually topple over; its windows, beaten in by the tempest, give entrance to birds and reptiles; and its stately halls and capacious chambers are covered with the spider's tapestry, and feebly echo with mimic shrieks of the bat, blinking hither and thither in twilight sports. The indolent mind is not empty, but full of vermin.

There was nothing in this that Thomas Shepard would not have agreed with; idleness was the parent of all sin, the devil's workshop, the Puritans had insisted. But in Beecher's choice of images—the shrieking bats and slithering reptiles—there is more than a hint of the gathering nervousness that were particular to the nineteenth century. Sexuality was one of these, as the metaphors made clear. The imagination of the idler was rank with weeds, Beecher and his contemporaries warned; it was the haunt of unlawful visitors, a hothouse of "salacious daydreams . . . rosy at first and distant, [which] deepen every day, darker and darker, to the color of actual evil." In what Carlyle called the "purifying fire" of regular labor, midnineteenth-century moralists hoped to consume the sexual passions that seemed increasingly to threaten them. But they hoped for more as well. Work cleared away doubts and vanquished despair; it curbed the animal instincts to violence; it distracted the laborer from the siren call of radicalism; it redeemed the convict prisoner. It did all this in part by character-building, by ingraining habits of fortitude, self-control, and perseverance, and in part by systematic exhaustion. The truly moral man was at once a person of strength and a *perpetuum mobile* of repressing energy, the man "whose days are so crowded full of honest and healthy tasks that he has no room for dreaming." Victorians were somewhat more apt than Puritans to reserve their asceticism for others. But for those who saw their world as beset with temptations and dangers, the sanitizing effects of constant labor offered at once a social panacea and a personal refuge.

The doctrine of usefulness and an intense, nervous fear of idleness were both indirect legacies of the Reformation. The other two ingredients of the mid-nineteenth-century work ethic—the dream of success and a faith in work as a creative act—had other roots and implications. By diligence a man could improve his lot; as the proverbs had it, he could stand before kings. The hope had seeped early into Puritanism, overturning the initially static implications of the "calling." Benjamin Franklin had condensed it into the kind of aphorisms that stuck in one's head and helped shape the axioms of a culture. But none of this was a match for the massive outflow of literature that the nineteenth century produced on behalf of the argument that work was the highroad to independence, wealth, and status. This is a country of "self-made men," where from the humblest beginnings a man with "merit and industry" could rise to the top, Calvin Colton announced in 1844 at the beginning of the flood. Endless repetition—in conduct guides, boys' storybooks, handbooks of business advice, and magazine fillers—ingrained the idea as one of the century's most firmly held commonplaces. In the fluid American economy, hard work, self-control, and dogged persistence were the certain escalators of success. Despite the speculative booms that so conspicuously dotted economic life—despite the financial adventurism and ardent pursuit of the main chance that Twain totted up in *The Gilded Age*—businessmen and moralists stuck to the canon. Even on Wall Street, the "law" of success was "unbending and regular," Matthew Hale Smith wrote in 1873, the year Twain's book appeared: "Industry, honesty, perseverance, sticking to one thing, invariable lead to success." Henry Ward Beecher, who served as the conduit for so many of the presuppositions of mid-nineteenth-century Americans, insisted that the one thing necessary for wealth was "Industry—plain, rugged, brown-faced, homely clad, old-fashioned Industry." By his labor a man worked out the position he deserved on the economic ladder; it was the key to success in the business of living.

Finally, it was urged, through work men impressed something of themselves on the material world. "A small Poet every Worker is," Carlyle wrote. Emerson seconded the idea: "Labor: a man coins himself into his labor; turns his day, his strength, his thoughts, his affection into some product which remains a visible sign of his power." Craft traditions, the legacy of the Renaissance artist-craftsmen, and romanticism all converged on the theme, often with extravagant results. In a poem picked up from the transcendentalist *Harbinger* and passed through the labor papers of the 1840s, Augustine Duganne apotheosized the artisan as "God's high priest," standing "midway / Between the earth and heaven, all things sway / To thy high-working mind!" Perorations of this sort were most common among writers who, like Duganne, stood at the boundary between artisan and literary culture. The more frequent acknowledgment of the creative role of labor was a simpler conviction that "work" was not "drudgery," and that it was room for employment of the mind that told them apart. One stumbles over the distinction again and again. Drudgery was the word the writers recurred to when faced with blind, thoughtless toil—the labor of slaves or the bent, haunting peasant of Millet's famous painting "The Man with the Hoe." In work, they insisted, mind and spirit had a part, transforming "dead" muscle labor into acts of skill. Work was creation. "To become an artist in dealing with tools and materials is not a matter of choice . . . [but] a moral necessity," Hamilton Wright Mabie told the readers of the *Outlook* at the end of the century. "Work is sacred . . . not only because it is the fruit of self-denial, patience, and toil, but because it uncovers the soul of the worker."

Obviously there were tensions within this set of ideals. Work was a creative act and a means of self-repression, a social obligation that paid off in private rewards. The ingredients of the work ethic were not held together by the logical consistency of their premises. The clearest of the tensions lay between the idea of work as ascetic exercise and work as art. The one looks toward system, discipline, and the emerging factor order; the other toward spontaneity, self-expression, and a narrowing of the gulf between work and play. The latter, creative ideal was clearly the weaker of the two in the nineteenth century. For a moment in the 1880s a large number of Americans discarded it altogether and devoured an enormously popular tract entitled "Blessed Be Drudgery," and it was long a half-suspect intruder amid the calls to effort, self-discipline, and ambition.

There was a second, nagging contradiction between the ideals of duty and of success—between the appeal to the dignity of all labor, even the humblest, and the equally universal counsel to work one's way as quickly as possible out of manual toil. Manual workers felt the full force of the contradiction and complained repeatedly of the disjuncture between the grandiloquent rhetoric and the practical disrepute of their occupations. William Dean Howells, who agonized over the point in the 1880s and 1890s, was finally driven to conclude that Americans liked their inconsistencies on a large scale. And yet a man like Beecher, and scores of other writers as well, demonstrably held all these ideas at once: the creative and the ascetic ideals, the rhetoric of an expansive economy and of early Protestantism, a sincere, fervent belief in toil and elitist reservations. The disparate strands all came together to reaffirm the central premise of the work ethic: that work was the core of the moral life. Work made men useful in a world of economic scarcity; it staved off the doubts and temptations that preyed on idleness; it opened the way to deserved wealth and status; it allowed one to put the impress of mind and skill on the material world. At the advent of the factory system, few of the keepers of the Northern moral conscience did not, in some measure, believe in them all.

The Henry Ward Beechers no more spoke for all Northerners, of course, than they spoke for all Americans. There was a sociology to the work ethic as well as an amalgam of ideas. Praise of work in the mid-nineteenth century was strongest among the middling, largely Protestant, property-owning classes: farmers, merchants, ministers and professional men, independent craftsmen, and nascent industrialists. Such groups had formed the backbone of English Puritanism, flinging their gospel of labor at the idle aristocracy and the dissolute mass of laborers that seemed to beset them on either side. The work ethic, too, was largely their creation. The Europeans who marveled at the untiring energy of the Americans were describing not ordinary laborers but their own social counterparts, particularly merchants of moderate means, who in America seemed as hard at work as their junior clerks.

On both ends of the social scale one can readily find other ethics and other styles of life. The ascetic injunctions of Puritanism never penetrated very far into the urban working classes. When Arthur Young wrote that "everyone but an idiot knows that the lower classes must be kept poor or they will never be industrious," he voiced the virtually unanimous conviction of seventeenth- and eighteenth-century English employers. A mass of prejudice obviously entered into statements of this sort, but they were not manufactured wholly out of class bias. In early nineteenth-century America, it is clear that many urban laborers did their best to punctuate work and play in the irregular, clock-defying pattern that is far older than the Protestant ethic. Gambling, rioting, generous drinking habits, and a good deal of boisterous, elbow-shoving, Sabbath-defying amusement played an important part in urban working-class life. If by no means every laborer, journeyman, and apprentice escaped the inner compulsions of the work ethic, enough of them did to make their presence felt in Jacksonian America. Among the very rich, too, the ideal of industriousness met with resistance. Compared with Europe or the American South, in the North the thoroughly idle gentleman was a rarity. The leisured aristocracy there was small, and its resources were relatively limited. But wealthy businessmen like New York City's Philip Hone showed no inclination to chain themselves to their counting tables or to consume their pleasures moderately. Conspicuous leisure was everywhere the identifying mark of the aristocrat, his bastion against the moralistic assaults of the middle classes; and in this regard the North was no exception.

Work was the gospel of the bourgeoisie, above all of the Protestant bourgeoisie, but it was not for that reason simply a subcultural peculiarity. In the American North, as nowhere else in the Western European orbit, the middle classes set the tone and standards for society as a whole. They did so through their hold over the strategic institutions of economics and culture. Business enterprise was theirs. So were the Protestant churches and the myriad agencies of moral reformation they spawned in the nineteenth century to care for the poor, educate the ignorant, and hold the wayward to the path of virtue. So were the institutions of learning: the schools and the colleges, the nation's publishing houses, and the major journals of opinion. It was in the last, in particular, that the ideals of middle-class Protestant respectability were debated, codified, and—with the conservative power of print—preserved. Editors like E. L. Godkin of the *Nation*, J. G. Holland of *Scribner's Monthly*, Howells and Beecher of the *Atlantic* and the *Christian Union*, and Mary Mapes Dodge of the children's *St. Nicholas*—or, after the turn of the century, George H. Lorimer of the *Saturday Evening Post* and Edward Bok of the *Ladies' Home Journal*—oversaw the process with an acute sense of responsibility and self-importance. They opened the pages of the middle-class magazines in a careful and considered way to the organizers of economic and cultural life and to the nation's most prominent writers as well as to a dedicated corps of anonymously conventional scribblers. I have called this interlocking set of persons the "moralists," keepers of their countrymen's moral conscience. They were not the only Northerners who felt keenly about ethics, but, given the institutional structure of their society, their opinions carried uncommon weight and influence.

The work ethic radiated not only from the secular pulpits of journalism but from all the institutional fortresses of the middle class. Campaigns to inculcate the values of industriousness in schoolchildren, and to impose it upon employees and social dependents, gathered and spent their force over and over again in nineteenth-century America, leaving behind a crust of middle-class morality of uncertain but perceptible depth. Still more important, probably, was the subtle contagion of example, aided by the moralists' near-monopoly on the definitions of respectability. In the years after the Civil War, praise of work noisily invaded the South, as its spokesmen turned upon their old "bondage to leisure" to announce their love affair with toil. It officially overrode whatever reservations the bishops of the American Catholic church may have felt about the repressive sobriety of Protestantism and led them, in the midst of the Americanist campaign of the 1880s, to put the weight of their influence behind thrift, industry, temperance, and Protestant Sabbatarianism. Elsewhere, too, potential resistance crumbled. Political aspirants, who presumably knew what they were about, regularly curried the favor of workingmen with orations on the dignity of toil. Frederick W. Taylor's father, a genteel Philadelphia lawyer, retired while still a young man to devote himself to study, public affairs, and the broadening influence of travel; yet the younger Taylor absorbed the work ethic, somehow, into the very marrow of his bones. Over and over again the opposite could be heard, that the old respect for labor was faltering in its paces. But the sense of decay was as indispensable to the moralists' temper as it was to the work ethic itself, a reassurance that there were still urgent tasks to be done and moral wildernesses still to be tamed.

None of the ingredients of the work ethic were unique to America. It was John Locke who announced that all property took its title from labor, Adam Smith who claimed that labor was the ultimate source of wealth, and Henry Bergson who in the phrase *homo faber* made work synonymous with man himself. Samuel Smiles's *Self-Help* dominated nineteenth-century success writing, just as Thomas Carlyle's example loomed over virtually all those in America who wrote in praise of work. But nowhere else than in the American North, with its truncated social structure, was resistance to these claims so limited. The result was an odd creation: a class and sectarian dogma that was at the same time as close to an article of popular faith as the region afforded.

Exactly how busy is a diligent man? It was only after the factories had overrun economic life that Northern industrialists set out to answer that question with any precision and to graft onto their countrymen the time obsession characteristic of modern industrial societies. The work ethic in its mid-nineteenth-century form did not entail a particular pace of activity so much as a manner of thinking, a moral preoccupation with labor. Moreover, the ideas that came together in praise of work took shape and flourished in an era when, by modern standards, time moved at a haphazard gait. First-generation New England ministers might urge their congregations that each moment was precious and that "one grain of time's inestimable sand [was] worth a golden mountain." But in a society in which household clocks were extraordinarily rare and the best of them possessed only a single, marginally accurate hand, such words hardly carried their modern meaning. By the end of the seventeenth century affluent families could purchase pendulum clocks of two and three hands; but large-scale production of brass household clocks did not begin in America until the end of the 1830s, and it was not until the Civil War that the characteristic arbiters of industrial time—cheap, mass-produced pocket watches—began to pour out of the American Watch Company plant at Waltham. "Time is money," Franklin had said, but when so much of time passed by unreckoned it is doubtful that he intended the meanings Frederick W. Taylor was to find in the words two centuries later. There is, in short, a misleading modernity to the phrases of the work ethic. They were rooted in, and creatures of, an economy older than and quite different from that of the factories.

Not only time but work moved in irregular, often leisurely rhythms in preindustrial America. Colonial workers who hired out their labor were generally expected to work the "whole day" six days a week, or from dawn to dusk in winter and from ten to twelve hours a day of actual labor in summer. But work itself was scarcely this even. Farming, the dominant colonial occupation, oscillated between bouts of intense labor and the short, much slower days of winter and was punctuated by country recreations—fishing, horse racing, visiting, and tavern-going—that even in Puritan New England were as much a part of rural life as the aching toil of planting and harvesting. In the same manner, the typical colonial workshop, with its three or four journeymen and apprentices, went through cycles of activity and probably was rarely busy day in and day out. By the early nineteenth century the tempo of economic life had increased perceptibly. In the East, many rural families now filled in the slack periods of farming by turning materials put out to them by nearby wholesale merchants into boot and shoe uppers, woven cloth goods, straw hats, and a variety of other products. The stores and workshops of Jacksonian America were bigger and considerably more bustling than their colonial counterparts. But weather, changes in demand and availability of materials, and poor communication and transportation facilities still conspired to interrupt the steadiness of work. "Incessant toil . . . was not the bane of Philadelphia's antebellum artisans," their most recent historian has concluded, but "the fitful pace of work, the syncopated rhythm of the economy." This context, too, qualified the calls to diligence. For all their intense fears of the idle life, mid-nineteenth-century moralists did not demand that men work with the ceaseless regularity of machines, but merely asked that they keep soberly and steadily to what tasks lay before them. In a world remote from the time clock and the efficiency expert, the work ethic was not a certain rate of busyness but a way of thinking.

Yet the strength of mid-nineteenth-century work ideals was exactly in their mesh with the bustling, irregular economy of the antebellum North. In this regard two characteristics of the antebellum economy were acutely important: its expansive energy and its limited industrial technology. The first is difficult to exaggerate. In the early nineteenth century the North underwent a startling transformation from an essentially agricultural to a commercial economy. Within the generation between 1815 and 1850, Northerners dug a regional transportation system of canals and waterways and started on a railroad network to replace it, dotted the Middle West with new settlements and at the same time burst the institutions of the seaboard cities at the seams, flooded the Patent Office with inventions, and raised the value of manufactures produced severalfold. "Go ahead" was the motto of the age, the European travelers reported, and with good reason.

But, for all the aggressive innovation of the age, as late as 1850 the centers of manufacturing remained the home and the workshop. Home production was not simply a rural phenomenon. The puttingout system flourished in every manufacturing town, employing shoemakers, weavers, tailors, and seamstresses in the traditional hand processes. Moreover, the workshops that threatened the livelihood of the home workers were on the whole far from the factory stage. In Boston, according to a careful enumeration of its factories and workshops in 1832, almost half the workmen were employed in shops of ten or fewer employees, and 80 percent worked in shops of no more than twenty. Philadelphia in the mid-1850s was much further into the industrial revolution, and its two sprawling locomotive works alone employed about 1600 hands. But even in the nation's preeminent manufacturing center 100 employees was enough to rank an establishment as a major enterprise, and the dozens that reach this size were still surrounded by literally hundreds of tiny one- to five-man workshops.

The cotton textile industry was the great exception. Barn-sized, water-powered spinning mills had begun to appear in southern New England as early as the 1790s. It was the founding of Lowell, Massachusetts, in the early 1820s, however, that marked the real beginning of the new industrial order in America. Lowell was the first of the large-scale mill towns, an unprecedented assemblage of machines, bosses, and operatives. Within a decade there were nineteen textile mills in operation in the city, employing an army of 5000 factory hands. With its paternalistic regulations and its boarding houses full of Yankee farm girls turned short-term mill hands, Lowell was the marvel of the nation and an obligatory part of the American tour. By the middle of the century, however, rivals had sprung up at Chicopee, Manchester, Manayunk, a dozen other textile centers. The cotton mills were the first and archetypal factories, set off by their size, discipline, and thorough mechanization. Dwarfing most other enterprises, the largest mid-nineteenth-century textile mills employed a thousand or more workers, operatives for the most part, tied to the power looms and spinning machinery they tended and hemmed in by rigid sets of factory rules. Less dramatically, a few other industries moved in the direction of the cotton mills. Arms manufacturers began extensive use of machinery and subdivision of labor early in the century, ingeniously enough to warrant inspection by an official English delegation in the mid-1850s, which found the same techniques in use in the manufacture of clocks, furniture, and a variety of wood and metal products. In the 1840s iron rolling mills, too, moved swiftly toward factory dimensions. "Stave-machines, planing-machines, reaping-machines, ploughing-machines, thrashing-machines, steam wagons," Walt Whitman chanted in his "Song for Occupations." But this was in 1855, when the shift in manufacturing processes had begun to accelerate rapidly. Outside the textile centers, the home, farm, and workshop still ruled the early nineteenth-century economy. In 1841, in a judgment that comes closer to the truth of the period, a Cincinnati observer claimed: "Our manufacturing establishments, with the exception of a few, . . . are, in the literal sense, manufactures,—*works of the hand*."

This was an economy in the earliest stages of industrialization—expansive yet simple— and it went hand in hand with the intellectual legacies to fashion the mid-nineteenth-century work ethic. The economic matrix reinforced old assumptions about work, stirred up new ones, and held them all together in a way logic could not. Expansion fueled the command to be up and doing and helped turn the ideal of usefulness out of the religious and political spheres and make it an economic obligation. "The busy world angrily shoves aside / The man who stands with arms akimbo set." James Russell Lowell put the phrase in Oliver Cromwell's mouth, but its accents were those of Lowell's own mid-nineteenth-century generation, impressed by the immensity of the enterprises to be undertaken, the goods to be made, the projects to be done.

Expansion likewise took the hope of upward mobility and screwed it to a new pitch. In a world that seemed to have jumped the old restraining ruts—where a Cornelius Vanderbilt could ride the new transportation systems to a fortune and a skillfull Yankee carpenter such as Thomas Rogers could become one of the nation's leading locomotive manufacturers—the dream of success was hardly to be escaped. It rose in close correlation with economic growth, gathering strength in the 1830s and 1840s and turning into a flood after the middle of the century. But if the promise of mobility was virtually inevitable, it was no less inevitable that the moralists should try to control the unleased promises and turn them, by insistent praise of work and self-control, into safe, familiar channels. Exhilaration and nervousness were both part of mid-nineteenth-century life. Enterprises that boomed hopefully also collapsed spectacularly, and the economy itself fell apart disastrously in 1819, again in 1837, and every twenty years thereafter throughout the nineteenth century. If growth fueled dreams of success, the sudden collapses and paralyses ingrained the lessons of scarcity, heightened anxieties over the disorders of commercial and urban life, and added to the Victorian nervousness. In all, it was a paradoxical society—booming yet fragile, engaged in the march of progress yet adrift in flux, inspiring expansive hope even as it reinforced the fears that encouraged the ascetic, nerve-numbing discipline of diligence. On all counts, even in its contradictions, it helped reinforce the primacy of work.

Finally, the economy of the antebellum North was one in which a certain measure of independence and creativity could be taken for granted. No one directly supervised home workers or farmers, and in the shops and small mills supervision was rarely exacting. The heated political arguments that accompanied the making of shoes or cigars were more than a figment of later, nostalgic imaginations. Pick and shovel labor was a matter of another sort, but in general the hand processes of manufacture, the flexible rhythms of labor, and the absence of strict discipline made it possible for most workers to impress some of their idiosyncrasies on their toil, if not always to love it. Intellectuals have long romanticized the state of things before the coming of the factories. Preindustrial America had ample share of hardships, poverty, and pain. In hindsight, in fact, the degradation of the urban craftsman was well under way by 1850, as artisans found themselves increasingly caught in dependency to merchants whose capital enabled them to control the supply of raw materials and the marketing of the finished products. In the 1840s, New Englanders likewise peered under the Lowell mills' attractive facade and debated the merits of the factories. But, in the face of an enormous enthusiasm for technology, little of this penetrated far into the consciousness of middle-class Northerners. They thought their society what it seemed to be: a land of bustling farms and workshops where work told; where indeed it was the core of living.

In the second half of the nineteenth century the factory system invaded the antebellum farm and shop economy, overturning not only the familiar patterns of work but the ways Northerners had been accustomed to think of their labor. The speed of the transition to the factory economy varied widely from industry to industry and from place to place. It was an uneven movement—felt not as a shock, as it has often been described, but as a series of shivers, greatest in years of major labor unrest when the nation suddenly reckoned up the extent of change. But in the end the factory system challenged each of the certainties upon which the work ethic had rested and unsettled the easy equation of work and morality in the minds of many perceptive Americans.

Well after 1850 the economy still presented a patchwork array of contrasts. In Philadelphia, handloom weavers worked in their own homes virtually in the shadow of the mechanized textile mills. In New York City, tiny tenement cigar shops competed with factor establishments of several hundred employees. Rural and urban industrial workers differed, the country factory hands often retaining a degree of community power their urban counterparts had lost. The detailed disciplinary codes of the textile mills contrasted with the haphazard management typical of many other mechanized industries. As late as 1889, David A. Wells, one of the nation's leading economists, could depreciate the importance of the factory system altogether and insist that no more than one-tenth of the gainfully employed were properly described as factory hands. Yet for all the variety and confusion, the drift of change was evident. As the century progressed, the mills grew larger, labor discipline more exacting, and the work processes more minutely subdivided and dependent on machinery.

At times and in places, moreover, the transition to the factory economy took place with wrenching, unsettling speed. The shoe industry was for most nineteenth-century Americans the preeminent example of the rate at which the new could obliterate the old. As late as the 1840s the typical New England shoe shop was a $10' \times 10'$ cottage housing a handful of skilled workers who made shoes by time-honored hand methods according to their personal, often eccentric, notions of size and fit. Some subdivision of tasks set in during that decade under the pressures of the merchants who controlled the trade, but the real revolution in shoemaking came in the 1860s with a rash of inventions, beginning with a sewing machine capable of stitching soles to uppers. Aggressive subdivision of labor, mechanization, and factory building quickly followed. By the 1870s, the shoemaking cottages were empty, and the men who had once been shoemakers now found themselves factory machine operators: beaters, binders, bottomers, buffers, burnishers, channellers, crimpers, cutters, dressers, edge setters, and so on through some thirty or forty subdivided occupations. Glassmaking was another example of the rapid destruction of a craft. In 1896 the entire output of bottles, jars, and window glass was made by gangs of skilled men and boy helpers, who gathered, blew, and shaped the glass by hand. Twenty years later half the jar and bottle blowers were gone, and the window glass workers were rapidly being replaced with automatic or semiautomatic machines. More commonly than this, the foundations shifted under an entire town. In 1850 Paterson, New Jersey, was a small city with a number of modest manufacturing establishments. Twenty-five years later the city boasted three huge locomotive works, fourteen silk mills, and the largest jute, linen, and mosquito netting factories in the country. The number of inhabitants had trebled; the number of saloons had increased almost sixfold.

Size, discipline, and displacement of skill characterized the factories. The physical growth of the workplace was evident at every hand. The Baldwin locomotive works had been a giant among factories in the mid-1850s with 600 employees. Twenty years later there were 3000 factory hands at Baldwin, and by 1900 there were more than 8000. The McCormick reaper plant in Chicago followed the same course, growing from about 150 employees in 1850 to 4000 in 1900. But the manufacturing colossi of the early twentieth century dwarfed even these. By 1916 the McCormick plant had grown to 15,000 workers; and in that year the payroll at the Ford Motor Company works at Highland Park reached 33,000. Workshops of the size that had characterized the antebellum economy, employing a handful or a score of workers, persisted amid these immense establishments. But they employed a smaller and smaller fraction of the workers. By 1919, in the Northern states between the Mississippi River and the Atlantic Ocean, three fourths of all wage earners in manufacturing worked in factories of more than 100 employees, and 30 percent in the giants of more than 1000.

In plants of this size, the informality of the small workshop was an inevitable casualty. From the beginning the great textile mills had laid down extensive regulatory codes and enforced them with heavy fines and the threat of discharge. Other industries adopted such measures more slowly. The Winchester Repeating Arms plant in New Haven, for example, did not begin to insist that employees arrive on time until the 1890s, and in the piecework trades workers clung for a long time to their traditional right to set their own hours of labor. By the 1890s, however, gates were common around factories, supplemented by the exacting eye of the first factory time clocks. Inside the plants the baronial foremen, who had commonly hired, fired, and cajoled the necessary labor out of their workers on their own whim and responsibility, slowly disappeared. In their place the larger factories evolved tighter, more systematic, and more centralized schemes of management. By 1920 personnel departments, rational and precise cost accounting, central planning offices, and production and efficiency engineers had become fixtures of the new factory bureaucracies. Defenders of the new management techniques argued that they were fairer than the old. Certainly by the end of the century there was little to be envied in the lot of the workers left behind in the sweatshops and tenement rooms. But neither qualification lessened the growing distance between a factory hand and his employer or the subordination of the rhythms of work to the increasingly exacting demands of efficiency.

By the same token, skills disappeared in the new factories. Whether owing to such a simple device as the cigar mold—a wooden frame that enabled an untrained worker to bunch cigar tobacco—or the complex, automatic tools of the machine shop, the factories made obsolete a host of carefully preserved hand trades. Tailoring, cabinetmaking, barrel making, felt-hat making, and pottery making all gave way before new inventions and the specialization of labor. The clothing and slaughtering industries were particularly conspicuous examples of the relentless subdivision of tasks. In 1859, less than a decade after the introduction of the sewing machine, a Cincinnati clothing factory had succeeded in dividing the making of a pair of men's pants, formerly the job of a single tailor, into seventeen different occupations. At Smith's packing plant in Chicago at the turn of the century, 150 men, each with his specific mite of butchering to perform, handled each hog on its way from the pen to the cooling room. Dressing the tail of a beef carcass alone occupied the labor of five men: two skinned it, another two cut it off, and a fifth threw the skinned and severed appendage into a box. Nowhere did the pursuit of efficiency go on more aggressively than in the automobile industry, where the jobs were relentlessly morseled before being chained to the assembly line. One of the tasks at Ford's Highland Park plant consisted in joining pistons and rods by driving out, oiling, and replacing a pin, inserting and tightening a screw, and installing a cotter pin. All together the operation took three minutes. The Ford engineers divided the job into four pieces and doubled the output. The automobile had been a triumph of the mechanic's art, but by the second decade of the twentieth century fewer than one job in twelve in the auto plants took more than half a year to learn.

The factories made skills as well as destroyed them. Mule spinners in the textile factories and heaters and rollers in the steel mills worked at highly skilled, factory-created jobs. But the drive toward ever-greater efficiency made every skilled job precarious. A New York City machinist, complaining of the subdivision of labor in his trade in the 1880s, insisted that ten years earlier the machinist had "considered himself a little above the average workingman; he thought himself a mechanic, and felt he belonged to the middle class; but to-day he recognizes the fact that he is simply the same as any other ordinary laborer, no more and no less." Employers did not hesitate to enforce the point. When in 1885 the managers at the McCormick plant found themselves in a dispute with their unionized iron molders, they dismissed the entire force and installed molding machines and unskilled recruits in their places. Despite occasional compensations, all factory jobs increasingly converged toward the semi-skilled; the typical factory hand became a machine operator of fractionated workman, toiling at a single bit of the manufacturing process.

How extensive the new modes of work actually were was a matter of some debate. In 1860, one fifth of the gainfully occupied population of the Northern states worked in what the census defined as a manufacturing establishment; by 1919, when the correlation between factory and "manufacturing establishment" was considerably closer, the proportion had grown to about a third. But the new forms of toil affected not only manufacturing workers but spread out from the factories as well. In the late 1870s, large-scale production methods invaded agriculture in the wake of the rapid mechanization of farm tools. The most famous of the early "food factories," as their critic William G. Moody called them in the 1880s, sprawled over 30,000 acres of Dakota Territory wheat land, and at its peak employed two hundred reapers, thirty steam-powered threshers, and a thousand hands to bring in the crop. Individual bonanza farms like this came and went, and their number grew fairly slowly after the initial spurt of the 1870s. The transformation of coal mining in the early twentieth century was more complete. Between about 1900 and 1910, coal-cutting machinery and subdivision of labor began to enter the bituminous coal mines of the Middle West, remaking the operations and shoving out the hand miners who had once worked at the pit faces virtually as autonomous subcontractors. About the same time the efficiency experts began to turn their attention to the huge new clerical forces employed by firms like Sears and Roebuck. Arrayed behind banks of desks, strictly supervised, paid at times like industrial workers on piecework, many of the new clerical workers differed from factory hands only in status and neatness—just as the big, turn-of-the-century department stores employing several thousand saleswomen and cash girls differed little from fair-sized industrial establishments. In 1850 the job of a clerk or a farmer had been worlds away from that of a mill hand, but slowly, perceptibly, all work grew more and more like factory work.

What industrialization offered in return was a fantastic increase in output. The constantly growing flood of goods impressed and bewildered Northerners. In 1894 Congress instructed the Bureau of Labor to try to compute the savings in time and costs the new methods of manufacture had brought. The two volumes that resulted added nothing to the science of statistics. But the report that the factories were now making ten times as many fine-grade women's shoes and overalls a week as had been possible with the old, hand methods, fourteen times as many hardwood bedsteads, and twenty-two times as many stem-winding watches gave a striking, if impressionistic, suggestion of the economic dividends of the factory system. Modern indexes of production, though they must find approximate ways to equate cotton textile bolts and automobiles, provide a more reliable measure of the change. Between 1860 and 1920, the nation's population a little more than tripled, but the volume of manufactured goods produced increased somewhere between twelve- and fourteenfold. In international terms, the growth of manufactures was just as striking. In 1850 the factor economy was just emerging in America. By the turn of the century the United States had pushed past all other nations in industrial production. By 1910 it had outstripped its nearest rival, Germany, by nearly two to one.

This avalanche of factory-produced goods might have been expected to flow neatly into greater general well-being, but it did not. By the 1880s many businessmen had begun to worry that there were too many factories for the economy to absorb. Excess productive capacity in such diverse industries as steel, stoves, textile machinery, and sewing machines, in fact, troubled the economic waters, driving down prices, encouraging industrial consolidations to jack them up again, and in the process widening still further the gap between the old, workshop economy and the new. Intellectually, too, the phenomenon of more goods than the market could absorb was deeply troubling. Production had long been the chief of the economic virtues, impossible to take to excess. But if the industrial cornucopia could easily spew out far more goods than the nation was able to buy, what then was the place of work?

This was only one of the questions the invasion of the factors posed to those who cared deeply about work. The whole issue was a maze of paradoxes. The industrial economy was in a large part a creature of the intense regional faith in the worth of labor. The work ethic helped impel the restless personal energies of the Northern manufacturers, blessed their enterprises with a sense of mission, and gave them a transcendent sanction. It helped anesthetize employers to the eleven- and twelve-hour days they imposed on their workers and the pace at which the factories drove them. The work ethic provided the language of calculation, system, and diligence into which the efficiency engineers poured their new and stricter meanings, turning the new plants into matchless hives of industriousness. But if the factories were creatures of middle-class work ideals, they devoured those ideals as well. In disturbing ways, the transformation of labor undercut virtually all the mid-nineteenth-century assumptions about the moral preeminence of work.

Industrialization upset the certainty that hard work would bring economic success. Whatever the life chances of a farmer or shop hand had been in the early years of the century, it became troubling clear that the semiskilled laborer, caught in the anonymity of a late-nineteenth-century textile factory or steel mill, was trapped in his circumstances—that no amount of sheer hard work would open the way to self-employment or wealth. Still more rudely, the factory system overturned the equation of work and art. Amid the subdivided and monotonous tasks, the speed, and the discipline of a box factory or an automobile plant, where was the room for mind or for the impress of individual creativity? Even the successes of the industrial transformation unsettled ideas and values. As the factories poured forth an ever-larger volume of goods into the homes of the middle class, the ascetic legacies of the Protestant ethic slowly and steadily eroded, giving way to a noisy gospel of play and, at the fringes of middle-class thought, to a cultivation of a life free of effort itself. As industrialization shook the idea of the permanence of scarcity, as the measure of economic health turned from how much a society produced to how equitably and conscientiously it consumed, it became harder and harder to insist that compulsive activity, work, and usefulness were the highest goals of life.

The moralists did not perceive these troubling questions all at once. When they did there were always the ancient maxims to fall back on. Work, they continued to insist, was what man was made to do—the foundation of happiness, the condition of existence since the days of Adam's husbandry in the garden. But industrialization could not be stopped from wedging into the preserve of ethics. And as the economy was transformed a deeply rooted set of presumptions cracked and shifted.

QUESTIONS TO CONSIDER

1. What were the various sources of the idea that leisure was the ideal condition for humankind?
2. What was the distinctive about the American attitude toward work in the midnineteenth century? What is that attitude called today?
3. How did the Puritan celebration of work as "calling" evolve by the midnineteenth century?
4. How did the gospel of work relate to class in America in the midnineteenth century?
5. What were three significant changes in the shift from antebellum to postwar industrialism?
6. How did the success of the factory system undermine midnineteenth century assumptions about work?

5

The Jacksonians,
the Populists,
and the Governmental Habit*

John F. Hughes

In the 1830s farmers tended to support Andrew Jackson and fought against the growth of government, drawing on Thomas Jefferson's ideals in his struggles against the Federalists in the 1790s. They saw the government as inclined to distort the natural equality of humanity by dispensing corporate charters and other special privileges to the few, and so they called for freedom for anyone to have access to such advantages. This stance ironically helped lead to classic laissez-faire liberalism and a surge in capitalism, industrial development, and a market economy.

By the 1890s classical liberalism was orthodoxy, but many farmers found that they were not faring very well in the market economy. No longer self sufficient yeoman farmers (Richard Hofstadter argued that they had never been "happy yeomen" but always wanted to be part of the market economy, and Hughes wonders how anyone could question its desirability), the Populists had to choose between two ideals: farm prosperity and laissez faire. They opted for the former, and sought government action to ensure it by, among other things, regulating banks and railroads, two critical elements of the economy they perceived as harming their interests. But the Populists never won widespread support even in most farm areas and they failed to enlist industrial workers in their

*Reprinted from *Mid-America: An Historical Review,* Winter 1994, by permission of the publisher, Loyola University of Chicago.

cause. Not until Populism was dead, along with the nineteenth century, would Progressivism finally launch a partially effective challenge to laissez-faire.

John F. Hughes, professor of history at Drake University, explores the relationship between the ideas of the Jacksonians and the Populists, their differing success, and the implications of their views in this 1994 article.

In the *Age of Reform* Richard Hofstadter observed of the Populist movement that "[it] is significant that the leadership of this 'radical' movement included a surprisingly large number of old men born in the Jacksonian era, gray-haired veterans of innumerable Granger, Greenback, and anti-monopoly campaigns." Charles Destler and Norman Pollack also noted the lineage among both leaders and rank-and-file alike among the Granger and Greenback movements of the early 1870s and the Populist movement two decades later. Frank Klement has found an earlier lineage in which Civil War midwestern Copperheadism linked Jacksonian Democracy and Grangerism. Whatever the generational and temporal linkages spanning the half-century between the Jacksonian and Populist movements, comparison of their *weltansicht* with regard to capitalistic economic development reveals four parallels sufficiently striking and comprehensive in nature that we may view the Populist movement as a distant, attenuated aftershock of Jacksonian Democracy.

First, both Jacksonian Democracy and the Populist movement were overwhelmingly agrarian in character. The agrarian nature of the former can be seen clearly in its advocacy of rapid territorial expansion. The Jacksonians believed, correctly, that the huge and bountiful landmass of the North American continent would enable them to forestall the development of the type of economy the Whigs envisioned, and yet maintain their high living standards in the face of population growth. The lack of an effective land constraint made possible replication of traditional economic institutions through territorial expansion without diminishing returns. As for the ideological urban Jacksonians of the East, or Locofocos as they were called, Carl Degler identified them, in an early challenge to the entrepreneurial thesis, as "urban agrarians" who "opposed the metamorphosis of agrarian America into an industrial-commercial nation."

The People's party made an attempt to garner support among urban industrial workers, but was utterly ineffectual. While the Populist movement was almost wholly agrarian in nature, it was able to enlist the support of only a minority of even distressed farmers. In a study of Populist voting patterns James Turner found economic distress to be a necessary, but not sufficient condition for voting Populist. Those farmers who voted Populist also tended to live outside of the social and economic mainstream. Hofstadter noted the deleterious effects this kind of isolation and alienation from the larger society had for the farmer's ability to cope with the impersonal forces and institutions of a modern market economy: "The predominance in American agriculture of the isolated farmstead standing in the midst of great acreage, the frequent movements, the absence of village life, deprived the farmer and his family of the advantages of community, lowered the chances of association and cooperation, and encouraged that rampant, suspicious, and almost suicidal individualism for which the American farmer was long noted. . . "

The Populists seem to have been genuinely bewildered by the rapid changes and the complexities that accompany economic development in a market economy. For example, an editorial in the Populist *Platte County Argus* stated: "We are on the eve of an important election. The classes with their fabulous wealth, debauched newspapers and news monopolies, mysterious and powerful corporations . . . . is arrayed against the industrial masses." But the brashness of Populist rhetoric was belied by a general lack of a sense of self-efficacy that same rhetoric revealed. Populists routinely portrayed themselves as innocent common folk in an aggressive and uncaring world, susceptible to deception and exploitation by the more sophisticated members of society. This self-portrait finds an exact correspondence among the Jacksonians of a half-century before. According to Kohl, "one of the strongest bonds uniting the disparate elements forming the Democratic party was the common perception of living outside society's dominant sources of power and acceptance." The Democrat tended to see himself as an "outsider," fighting against what he perceived to be a mysterious, unjust, and artificial socioeconomic system. Like the Populists, the Jacksonians too, portrayed themselves as innocents at the mercy of those superior in wealth, power, and knowledge. They saw the financial system, merchants, corporations, the professions, and the press as all allied against them. Consequently, both Populist and Jacksonians rhetoric repeatedly proclaimed that human dignity was inherently the province of all, and was not contingent upon personal achievement or acceptance by others. This served in part to assuage the inner anxieties of those sorely in need of reassurance as to their self-worth.

Second, both movements adhered to an extreme form of the labor theory of value that placed little value on entrepreneurship. While the labor theory of value was pervasive in antebellum America, the Jacksonian version distinguished itself in its tendency to devalue nonphysical forms of labor. These included trade, banking, management, and most significantly, entrepreneurship. The outlook of the Jacksonian was shaped by the economic assumptions of a traditional society; he was uncomfortable in the increasingly complex market economy of the 1830s and 1840s, where the value of an individual's labor was determined by the impersonal mechanism of the market. As they did not believe that there were any great differences in the productivity of labor, they had great difficulty accepting that one individual's services could be worth significantly more than those of another. The Jacksonian's adherence to premodern economic assumptions and values led him to believe that wealth could be accumulated only over a long period of time through "patient industry." Having far less appreciation of, or faith in, the growth potential of modern market economy than his Whig counterpart, the rapid accumulation of wealth accorded to entrepreneurship by capitalism struck the Jacksonian as akin to a lottery—for every big winner there had to be a multitude of smaller losers. The Jacksonian exhibited a marked tendency to view the economic interdependence of individuals through the market system as a kind of zero-sum game.

Examination of Populist writings reveals the same world view. Henry Demarest Lloyd, the famous muckraking journalist, and also the most significant intellectual of the Populist movement, wrote in *Wealth Against Commonwealth* that:

> We make ourselves "rich" by appropriating the property of others by methods which lessen the total property of all. . . . Modern wealth more and more resembles the winnings of speculators in bread during famine. . . . What we call cheapness shows itself to be unnatural fortunes for a very few, monstrous luxury for them and proportionate deprivation for the people. . . . The new wealth now administers estates of fabulous extent from metropolitan bureaus, and all the profits flow to men who know nothing of the real business out of which they are made. Red tape, complications, the hired man, conspiracy have taken the place of the watchful eye of the owner, the old-fashioned hand at the plough.

An editorial in the Populist *Alliance-Independent* claimed that: "The men who work for wages must earn their wages and more, that is, a profit for their employers; and if a capitalist stands behind the employer the wage-earner must earn another profit for him." In an 1894 campaign speech the People's Party candidate for governor of Texas stated that: "Wealth acquired in legitimate ways, by the exercise of industry and skill and the investment of capital, cannot hurt either its possessor or the community."

Third, for both Jacksonians and Populists economic and social equality took precedence over economic growth. The constrictive labor theory of value held by the Jacksonians, firmly rooted in a static, premodern conception of economic reality, naturally led them to equate great wealth with exploitation. Accordingly, the concept of equality was preeminent in the

Jacksonian value complex. The Jacksonian tended to assess his economic position in terms of his relationship to others, not with regard to his individual accomplishments. Even when he did admit that economic growth had raised the living standards of the common man, the Democrat insisted that absolute improvements were not sufficient. An 1842 editorial in the *Democratic Review* entitled "White Slavery," acknowledged that economic growth had provided the laborer with wages far exceeding those of earlier ages, but insisted that the greater distance between rich and poor in their age represented an increase in "relative poverty." Yet, while Jacksonians tended toward an essentially static conception of economic reality, they imbued economic inequality with a dynamic nature which actively worked to mold a socioeconomic system in which the many would be locked in permanent dependence upon a wealthy few.

Like the Jacksonians, the Populist conception of a just society placed far greater importance on the relatively equal distribution of wealth than it did on economic growth. Henry Demarest Lloyd's views on the modern mass production technology of the later nineteenth century were characteristic of the Populist mind: "If this be cheapness, it comes by the grace of the seller, and that is the first shape of dearness, for security in society by the grace of the ruler is the first form of insecurity. . . . [The] certain end of all this, if unarrested, unreversed, can be nothing less than a return to chattel slavery. . . . Between our present tolerance and our completed subjection the distance is not so far as that from the equality and simplicity of our Pilgrim Fathers to ourselves."

Finally, the combined force of the Jacksonian and Populist movements' agrarian nature, the low value both placed on entrepreneurship, and their equalitarian ideology acted to engender a world view in which society was dichotomized into victims and victimizers. This *Weltansicht* led Populist orators Mary Elizabeth Lease and John Davis to liken the nation's wage earners to slaves, and Gaspar C. Clemens to claim of his contemporaries that "only a few live in comfort, fewer still have homes and the great majority live constantly in a state of poverty similar to what would be made possible by partial famine!" This outlook received its most memorable statement in the famous Omaha platform of 1892: "[We] meet in the midst of a nation brought to the verge of moral, political, and material ruin. . . . From the same prolific womb of government injustice we breed two great classes—tramps and millionaires. . . . A vast conspiracy against mankind has been organized. . . . " The rhetoric of victimization and oppression, and the tendency to interpret impersonal events in personal terms, was also pervasive in Jacksonian rhetoric: "The standard form of Jacksonian rhetoric was accusatory. . . . it was the collective cry of men who felt the world was not treating them fairly." Adherents of both movements demonstrated a marked tendency to project the source of life's difficulties outward onto society.

This parallel is made manifest by the two movements' common employment of that nineteenth-century bogeyman known as "the money power." For the Jacksonian, "the money power was the ultimate symbol of the forces which threatened [him]. It combined all his fears of the commercial economy and its ties of self-interest with his sense that his freedom was menaced by sinister forces with immense, uncontrollable power. By its very nature the concept of the money power did not lend itself to precise definition. It was a vaguely imagined but tightly organized combination of those who controlled the wealth of the country through their privileged access to the banking system." A Populist congressman wrote in 1895 that "[it] is the fad among certain large daily papers representing the money power to say there is no plutocracy, that it is all a mere hallucination. . . . [Today] the money aristocracy, intoxicated by power, reveling in an excess of wealth, surfeited with a redundancy of money, has grown bold and arrogant in its demands, and asks that the toilers of the nation, those that work with brawn and brain, be made slaves to this libidinous plutocracy."

In dramatic contrast to the Jacksonians, the Whigs were generally comfortable with modern economic processes. They placed a high value on mental labor generally, and on entrepreneurship in particular. For Whigs the legitimate production of wealth was not restricted to the patient industry of farmers, mechanics, and artisans. Ralph Waldo Emerson captured this Whiggish sentiment thusly: "Wealth is in applications of mind to nature; and the art of getting rich consists not in industry, much less in saving, but in a better order, in timeliness, in being at the right spot." To the Whig mind, the principal impediment to the economic advancement of the common man was the low productivity of his labor, something the equalization of existing wealth could not ameliorate. Possessing an implicit faith in what today we call scale economies, Whigs believed that large accumulations of capital would raise the productivity of labor, and hence the living standards of the masses. In this way, Whigs found it impossible to conceive of how one could get rich without also benefiting the poor. For Whigs equality per se was an improper criterion for social justice. Their focus was on raising the living standard of the average citizen and fostering an economic system which provided opportunities for varied human talents. Therefore, the Jacksonian concept of "relative poverty" had no meaning for Whigs; they saw poverty as absolute, not relative in nature. Their criterion for social justice was not relative equality, but improvements in the living standards of the great mass of the populace, and, Whigs believed, a more equal distribution of wealth would only postpone these improvements.

This sentiment is captured perfectly in Edward Everett's observation that if millionaire merchant Stephen Girard's fortune were distributed equally among the population of the country, each individual's share would be of minuscule benefit, but the cost to society significant indeed: "How many ships would have furled their sails, how many warehouses would have closed their shutters, how many wheels, heavily laden with the products of industry, would have stood still, how many families would have been reduced to want, and without any advantage resulting from the distribution."

Seen in this light, it appears classical liberalism was in fact the culmination of a process by which the Whig economic outlook and value system was implicitly accepted by an overwhelming majority of the electorate. John Ashworth writes that "the Whigs were the first political party to offer a mass electorate a viable and appealing conservative programme. Many of these arguments that they employed were to be used, and with considerable success, by later generations. Some retain their force even to this day. The inegalitarian and meritocratic outlook, the idea of limitless upward mobility, the desire for commercial expansion and diversification—these have passed so completely into the mainstream of American life and culture that it is difficult to appreciate that they could ever have been controversial.

The one important area in which the Jacksonians and Populists differed significantly was the proper role for government in the economy. Indeed, the governmental philosophies of the two movements were antipodal. Whereas the Jacksonians espoused an extreme version of laissez-faire, the Populist movement advocated the type of activist interventionist state that anticipated the New Deal. The Omaha platform proclaimed: "We believe that the powers of government—in other words, of the people—should be expanded as rapidly and as far as the good sense of an intelligent people and the teachings of experience shall justify. . . ." If the economic world views of the Jacksonians and Populists were essentially the same, then why did they proffer opposite political responses to capitalist economic development?

In order to posit an answer to this question we must begin by examining the rationale behind Jacksonian laissez-faire and ask the question: If Jacksonian ideology was essentially agrarian and precapitalistic in nature, why was adherence to the free market doctrines of Adam Smith pervasive among Democrats? Central to this question is the Jacksonian distinction between "natural" and "artificial" inequality of wealth. In principal, natural inequality was that which stemmed from innate differences among individuals in "personal vigor, personal activity, superior talent, prudence or enterprise." In practice, however, Jacksonians tended to presuppose a basic similarity among individuals. In turn, this essential similarity in the productivity of labor implied a roughly equal distribution of wealth. Not surprisingly, the sharp increase in the concentration of wealth occurring from the 1820s to the late 1840s documented by Jeffrey Williamson and Peter Lindert, was deeply disturbing to Jacksonians. Williamson and Lindert have also shown that per capita income was increasing during this period, but given the Jacksonians' essentially zero-sum conception of economic processes, this could only mean that wealth was being transferred from the "producing classes" into the hands of "the money power." The exact mechanism of this transfer was cloaked in mystery, but most Jacksonians had no doubt that government was its prime agent. Thus, the solution to the increasing concentration of wealth was to eliminate any kind of special privileges and charters, grant equal rights to all, and limit government to its essential functions. Then, given the fundamental similarities among men, equal treatment would result in a roughly equal distribution of wealth. In this way Adam Smith was conscripted for the defense of a precapitalist, agrarian social order. This was in marked contrast to Britain, where free trade theory was used by a growing capitalist class against entrenched landed interests.

The superficial nature of the Jacksonian attachment to Adam Smith's "natural laws" can be illustrated by an incident involving William Leggett, a prominent political journalist of the 1830s and intellectual leader of the Locofoco movement. A group of merchants in New York City had conspired to raise the price of bread. Leggett's initial response was that "natural law" precluded the possibility that they could permanently maintain artificially high prices. But when confronted with the fact that the poor would likely suffer privation in the interim, Leggett reversed himself, arguing that if a commodity of undoubted necessity was being withheld from the public, the government had a right to seize it (with due compensation). This from a man who had devoted his journalistic career to the service of a most extreme and doctrinaire philosophy of limited government.

It seems natural then, that as American economic development progressed, and especially with the rise of the giant corporation in the late nineteenth century, and laissez-faire failed to promote an equalitarian society, that adherents of the Jacksonian persuasion would abandon it. Indeed, exactly this occurred. In 1891, the Populist *Farmer's Alliance* editorialized that:

> The plutocracy of today is the logical result of the individual freedom which we have always considered the pride of our system. The theory of our government has been and is that the individual should possess the very greatest degree of liberty consistent, not with the greatest good of the greatest number, but with the very least legal constraint compatible with law and order. Individual enterprise was allowed unlimited scope . . . Individualism incorporated has gone wild . . . The corporation has absorbed the community. The community must now absorb the corporation.

And three years later, having been renamed the *Alliance-Independent,* the paper proclaimed that "a reigning plutocracy with the masses enslaved, is the natural development and end of individualism;" and the "only possible permanent democracy is the democracy of unselfish socialism." In 1896, the *Platt County Argus* declared that the rise of the giant corporation had "annulled the natural laws of supply and demand." In 1889, Populist journalist W. Scott Morgan wrote: "Some will contend that competition will correct all inequalities arising in the various conditions of labor. Adam Smith says, 'it is the great regulator of industrial action. It is beneficent, just and equalizing'. . . . This might perhaps be true if we had, or it were possible to have, like competition in all things."

Once this recognition was complete the logical next step was to enlist the powers of the state to bring about a more egalitarian society. Frank Doster, a prominent Kansas Populist and later Chief Justice of the Kansas Supreme Court, declared in a speech on Labor Day, 1894, that "[the] failure to adapt the legislation of the country to the strange conditions which this new life has forced upon us is the cause in greater part of our industrial ills."

The life of Henry Demarest Lloyd provides us with a living link between the Jacksonian and Populist movements. Lloyd's parents were staunch Jacksonian Locofocos, and he wholeheartedly shared his parents' principles, believing that government intervention in the economy was counter to the spread of liberty. Lloyd became prominent in the New York Free Trade League while only in his midtwenties. The leaders of the league were devout disciples of William Leggett, the intellectual leader of Locofocoism. Most important of these was William Cullen Bryant, editor of the *New York Evening Post,* and former colleague of Leggett. In an 1870 lecture for the league, Lloyd "declared that Adam Smith's 'declaration of independence . . . had done more to elevate mankind than the one made by Jefferson and Franklin.'" Yet by the end of the decade Lloyd would part company with Adam Smith. In the words of his biographer: "Actual circumstances diverged too far from Adam Smith's 'law of economic harmonies' and libertarianism, and the assumption of ensuing justice, for the contradictions between them and American practice to be tolerable." As early as 1879, Lloyd wrote in his notebook that "[the] only way to checkmate tendencies of individual selfishness and power, the aggressions of corporations is by a public opinion acting through the provided organ of a public government. . . . A *New Democracy.*" In *Wealth Against Commonwealth* Lloyd declared:

> In all this we see at work a "principle" which will go into the records as one of the historic mistakes of humanity. Institutions stand or fall by their philosophy, and the main doctrine of industry since Adam Smith has been the fallacy that the self-interest of the individual was a sufficient guide to the welfare of the individual and society. Heralded as a final truth of "science" this proves to have been nothing higher than a temporary formula for a passing problem. It was a reflection in words of the policy of the day. . . . Mankind has gone astray following a truth seen only partially, but coronated as a whole truth.

Central to Lloyd's conception was the restoration of democracy's property basis through a redistribution of wealth. For those alienated by late nineteenth century economic changes, Lloyd's views proved to be remarkably influential in the years ahead.

Thus, agrarian radicalism's switch from advocacy of a negative to an interventionist state can be regarded as a change in strategy in response to a change in economic circumstances: the Jacksonians sought to impede the development of a nascent market economy; the Populists sought to control a mature, pervasive, and entrenched market economy.

Historians sympathetic to the Populist movement have seen the phenomenon as an understandable and rational response to the stresses and dislocations inherent in the development of industrial society. Yet it was the Jacksonian protest that was more closely grounded in economic reality. Prior to the transportation revolution which commenced after 1815, the "majority of free Americans lived in a distinctive subsistence culture remote from river navigation and the market world." While subsistence farm families were not wholly self-sufficient, money served as a "specialized commodity," needed only for limited exchanges with the market world, in particular, for paying taxes or purchasing the few store goods that could not be bartered for farm products at the country store. The market was tangential to the lives of these families. As the transportation revolution progressed and reached new areas, household production fell dramatically, with the greatest reductions occurring after 1830. Producing commodities above that required for subsistence, and in turn selling them for cash with which to purchase manufactured goods, required the expenditure of a mere fraction of the labor time necessary for household production of those same goods. Thus, the transportation revolution begat a market revolution which would transform the simple traditional society of the early republic into a modern market economy. By 1860 the system of household production had largely disappeared from the modern states. *How could anyone have not seen this process as mutually beneficial in nature?*

In a re-examination of the question of antebellum Southern exceptionalism, Civil War historian James M. McPherson argued persuasively that it was in fact the rapidly modernizing antebellum North that was exceptional, for the traditional society of the South was broadly typical of most of the societies in the world at the time. One can make the same claim for the partisan battles of the Jacksonian era. Just as the antebellum South looks aberrant, even perverse, when viewed from afar through the lens of modernity, so too do the Jacksonians of the 1830s and 1840s as regards their attitudes toward economic development. Yet a strong case can be made that in fact it was the Whigs who were exceptional, not the Jacksonians.

First, the Jacksonians were not without foundation in believing that they were people who had something to lose. The agrarian society of the colonial period and the early republic was not only exceptionally prosperous by the standards of the day, but when viewed from a global perspective, our day as well. Alice Hanson Jones has estimated that the average per capita income (excluding slaves) in 1774 was between $573 and $995 in 1973 prices. The high estimate is about the same as the Soviet Union in that year, while the low estimate is about that of modern Mexico. Colonial Americans lived well both by the standards of at least half the modern world. Moreover, the economic institutions of colonial America and the early republic provided a level of personal independence unknown in modern economies. If individuals place a positive value on independence, then, ceteris paribus, per capita income in a modern economy must be higher to provide the same level of utility as that in an agrarian one.

Second, no commercial-industrial economy of the type envisioned by the Whigs had yet shown conclusively that it could lift the standard of living of the masses of the populace. As the "great standard of living debate" among European economic historians has demonstrated, the "net beneficence" of the industrial revolution was not manifest in Britain, the most advanced commercial-industrial economy of the time, until after 1850.

Third, Thomas Jefferson bequeathed to the Jacksonians a *Weltschau-*

nung that was deeply suspicious, if not overtly hostile to the type of economy and society the Whigs envisioned. Jefferson's deeply held belief that an agrarian society formed the only sound basis for republican government is exceedingly familiar. Yet this traditional focus on city versus country obscures a deeper issue. Jefferson was deeply suspicious not just of cities per se, but of impersonal market relationships and institutions in general. As Robert Kelley put it: "Jefferson believed, in short, that there are among us, always and everywhere, dishonest men who seek constantly to subvert the proper social order and exploit their fellow men. It was in this fundamental view of society that Jefferson gave to his posterity what has been called his ideology of conflict, his belief that there is an inherent struggle going on constantly in society between the masses and those that would exploit them."

Jefferson's fears seemed to be confirmed by a sharp rise in inequality which was widely noted by contemporaries. Estimates by Williamson and Lindert reveal a sharp increase in the concentration of wealth between 1774 and 1860, with the greatest increase in inequality occurring from the 1820s to the late 1840s. In 1774, the top 1 percent of wealth holders held 12.6 percent of the total assets, while the top decile held just 50 percent. By 1860, Williamson and Lindert found those shares had risen to 29 percent and 73 percent, respectively. This surge in inequality that economic growth in the early stages of industrial development must, to Jeffersonian's ideological scions, have seemed a manifestation of their worst fears. Kelley has noted that the beginning of the age of Jacksonian controversy can be dated from Jefferson's vilification, in 1826, of the newly inaugurated John Quincy Adams' call for a wide variety of federal programs to stimulate the economic and cultural life of the nation. Jefferson's posthumous *Memoirs* became available in 1829 and shortly thereafter the leading Jacksonian newspaper in the West proclaimed them required reading. It has been said that few, if any, publications of the periods had greater impact or importance.

By the time of the Populist revolt it had become clear that while the system of free market capitalism led to great concentrations of wealth, there could be no doubt concerning its ability to raise the living standards of the masses. Fogel and Engerman estimated that per capita real income in the antebellum North increased by 29 percent from 1840 to 1860. For the postbellum era, Simon Kuznets estimated that national per capita real income increased by 59 percent from the decade average of 1869–78 to that of 1884–93.

The Jacksonian movement had been able to garner widespread electoral support. The second party system of the Jacksonian period was characterized by exceptionally high voter participation and party loyalty, with the two parties about evenly matched in strength. Clearly the rhetoric ideology, and programs of both parties resonated deeply held values. To the contrary, the People's party was electorally impotent at the national level, receiving only 8.6 percent of the popular presidential vote in 1892. Most significant was the geographic distribution of those votes: 34 percent came from the impoverished and isolated one-party states of the old Confederacy; the border states of Kentucky and Missouri contributed another 6 percent; 28 percent came from the Great Plains states of Kansas, Nebraska, and the Dakotas; with 15 percent from the mountain and far West states. Thus, only 17 percent of the People's party tally came from the nation's agricultural and industrial heartland. Most telling of Populism's severely limited electoral appeal was its performance in the three lower midwest states of Ohio, Indiana, and Illinois. During the antebellum period the southern half of this region had been settled by migrants from the upland South and had been staunchly Jacksonian. During the Civil War it proved to be fertile ground for the copperhead movement. Yet the People's party received the votes of only 2.6 percent of the electorate of these states in 1892. The lesson of these electoral returns was not lost on the Populists themselves, as they were painfully aware of the powerful hold classical liberalism had on the late nineteenth century body politic. In the first full-scale treatment of the Populist revolt since John D. Hicks' in 1931, an admiring historian called them "[h]eretics in a land of true believers and recent converts;" and in turn noted that "[in] their struggle, Populists learned a great truth: cultures are hard to change." The Populists realized their support had probably peaked in 1894; their fusion with free-silver Democrats two years later was an act of desperation—and even that partnership with one of the major parties was met with crushing defeat.

Two decades ago Anne Mayhew advanced the thesis that the Populist revolt was a response to the commercialization of midwestern agriculture in the late nineteenth century, with commercial agriculture defined as that in which farmers devote most of their time and land to growing crops for market. Mayhew argued that middle western agriculture did not reach this stage until after railroads moved into the region in force after the Civil War. She then claimed the Populists were those farmers who had the most difficulty in making the psychic transition to a world of impersonal market relationships. James Turner's work, referenced above, buttressed Mayhew's argument. Turner found that Populists tended not merely to be rural people, but people who lived outside the orbit of towns and villages. Their ties with the organized life of their society were weak. In Turner's words, "these 'backward' people remained the last outposts of the old America. Their isolation made them, perhaps, fearful and uncertain of the new order."

The Jacksonians were a people swept up in a tidal wave of revolutionary socioeconomic change; whereas the Populists were a relatively small group of people who found themselves standing at the fringes of a world that had passed them by. As stated above, the Populist movement may best be understood by seeing it as a distant, attenuated aftershock of Jacksonian Democracy.

In *The Governmental Habit* Jonathon Hughes asserted that in the Populist movement "American capitalism had somehow spawned a massive opposition that either had to be crushed or accommodated." In underestimating the dissent which greeted American capitalism in its infancy, historians have perhaps overstated the importance of the Populist revolt during American capitalism's unruly adolescence. Historians have rightly stressed the significance of the Populist program for the future development of government intervention, but, as Higgs stresses, that story belongs to the twentieth century, not the nineteenth. Yet, the perception that agrarian radicalism was largely indigenous to the late nineteenth century has obscured the vital and fascinating story of just how the bipartisan ideology of classical liberalism formed out of the deep partisan division of the Jacksonian era.

QUESTIONS TO CONSIDER

1. What four parallels does Hughes see between Populism and Jacksonianism?
2. What were the basic Whig beliefs about the economy?
3. How and why did Jacksonians and Populists differ over the role of government in the economy?
4. What great economic transformation took place in advanced states between 1815 and 1860 and what were its implications?
5. Why does Hughes suggest that the Jacksonians had sound reasons for maintaining their laissez-faire ideal?
6. How does Hughes reduce the Populists to a lower level of significance than the Jacksonians?

6

American Women and Foreign Policy, 1898–1905*

Judith Papachristou

In 1898 the United States fought the Spanish-American War, ostensibly to free Cuba from Spanish rule. In the aftermath of war, however, the nation found itself with colonial possessions (the Philippines, Puerto Rico, Hawaii) and a paternalistic relation to the newly independent Cuba. Further, the Filipinos resisted the American takeover and the United States fought a savage war to suppress the independence movement in the islands. This series of events caused a profound debate within the United States over the nature of the nation and its role in the world.

How, critics asked, could the United States, born in a revolution dedicated to self rule, deny the right to other peoples? What did it imply that the United States had acquired millions of ethnically alien subjects for whom citizenship was not a prospect? The American character, forged in a war for independence, became confused as the nation became what its ideals condemned, an imperial power. The debate would divide Americans often in the twentieth century, most passionately over Vietnam in the 1960s.

In 1898 and the years immediately following, women for the first time played a significant role in debating American foreign policy. Judith Papachristou, professor emerita of history at Sarah Lawrence College, explores the implications of that involvement along with the whole question of the role of gender in diplomatic history in this 1990 article.

*Reprinted by permission from *Diplomatic History*, Fall 1990.

During the decades that framed the end of the nineteenth century the United States made its debut as a world power. Wars in Cuba and the Philippines, the acquisition of overseas territories, and moves toward hegemony in the Caribbean and Central America were unequivocal signs that the United States was assuming a new role in international affairs. At home, this change provoked unprecedented citizen activism, and record numbers of Americans joined a profusion of new groups to demonstrate support for or opposition to government policies.

Touched by this political fever, a handful of determined women attempted to create a female foreign policy constituency out of an existing network of more than a million women who belonged to the popular women's clubs and organizations of the time. In the course of a decade, tens of thousands of women joined male pacifists, peace reformers, and anti-imperialists as foreign policy activists. Never before had American women involved themselves in foreign affairs in such a way and to such an extent.

Historians of American foreign relations have studied the decades before World War I, searching for the roots of the nation's global ambitions in its economy, political life, and culture. In the public debate over American expansionism and the acquisition of overseas territories, they have discerned a profound conflict over the character of the nation itself, a conflict generated by the transition to industrialism, urbanism, and imperialism. Studies of the advocates of imperialism and navalism and the anti-imperialists, pacifists, and peace reformers who opposed them disclose the deep differences in Americans' responses to the changing times. Confronted with the effects of modernization, some felt alienation, regret, and foreboding, while others were enthusiastic about the present and optimistic about the future.

Changes in the peace movement offer a good example of such differences. The peace movement that developed after 1900 consisted of small groups without a mass base. In this respect the organizations were like their nineteenth-century predecessors. In other respects they were very different. The new peace reformers eschewed the uncompromising religious pacifism and moral fervor of the extant peace organizations, the Universal Peace Union (UPU) and the American Peace Society. Members of the forty-five new organizations chose instead to emphasize the role that new structural and legal reforms could play in preventing international conflict. In the minds of the lawyers and businessmen who dominated the twentieth-century movement, peace and war were matters of practicality and reason rather than good and evil.

Although peace researchers have recognized the widespread participation of women in the postbellum peace movement, only a few historians have recognized the nature and extent of female foreign policy activism that took place outside of the new peace movement around the turn of the century. Logically, diplomatic historians have focused on men, for in a society that carefully delineated sex roles and separated the private and domestic concerns of women from the public and political affairs of men, foreign affairs were a male preserve. The few studies of women and foreign policy that do exist have mainly been the work of historians of women, whose research has mainly been concerned with women's role in peace movements, particularly during World War I and after 1945.

In documenting an important episode in female foreign policy activism, this essay builds on the work of both historians of foreign relations and historians of women. Beyond expanding the historical record, it explores a new dimension in diplomatic history where, with few exceptions, historians have ignored or dismissed the relevance of gender in the study of foreign relations. I would like, however, to propose that the gender system that existed at the turn of the century is relevant to a discussion of relations among nations. The idea of gender as a category of historical analysis is new to most historians. But it should not be totally unfamiliar to scholars who are beginning to recognize the role of cognitive biases and ethical codes in shaping public policy as well as those who search for the personal psychological aspects of political behavior.

The women described below differed significantly on foreign policy issues from male policymakers and from male anti-imperialists and peace reformers as well. The women themselves believed that their disagreements with men originated in profound differences between male and female attitudes and moral values. Female foreign policy activists rejected the instrumental view of the state as an entity with a life and ethic of its own that underlay much of the thinking about international relations at the time. Instead, women tended to perceive the state as a collection of individuals, each of whom was morally responsible for his actions. Thus they regarded foreign policy as an expression and reflection of the men in power, men whose values they saw as inimical to their own precisely because they were male values.

The origins of female involvement in foreign policy lie far back in the nineteenth century when women first formed organizations to try to influence public policy, most notably to work for abolition, temperance, and suffrage. They considered these organizations an extension of their domestic responsibilities and described their political activities in the Gilded Age as "home protection" and as a way to extend the superior morality of the home into public life. They contended that women, rooted in home and family, were caring and unselfish, in contrast to men, who functioned in the realm of business and politics, where calculation, competition, and selfishness prevailed. Consequently they were certain that women could make unique contributions to politics and public life.

By 1900, women's organizations of this kind were numerous and disparate although their membership was mainly white, Protestant, and middle class. Most of the women shared a general apprehension about the impact of industrialization and modernization on the family and the moral order, and they supported reforms such as temperance and prohibition as ways to purify and regenerate society. There were, however, important differences among them and their organizations. Some of the groups were conservative and were eager to preserve nineteenth-century institutions. Others supported suffrage, which was still a controversial reform, and a few espoused the radical ideas of Christian socialism or incipient feminism.

The Woman's Christian Temperance Union (WCTU), the largest and most successful women's social purity organization in the nineteenth century, was the first to concern itself with issues of war and peace. Conscious of the powerlessness of wives and children at the hands of abusive husbands and fathers, WCTU members were particularly sensitive to issues of physical violence. As President Frances Willard noted, the WCTU wanted "to bring peace to homes and native land." In 1887 the union established a Department of Peace and International Arbitration, led by an indefatigable organizer, Hannah J. Bailey. A deeply committed pacifist, Bailey exemplified the strong links that existed between women's organizations and the American peace movement. Despite the relatively important role of women in the postbellum peace movement, most women's organizations were not involved with international issues until the end of the century, when events abroad attracted widespread public interest.

A small, diverse group of women (and a few men) consciously set out to interest members of women's organizations in international issues and thereby organize a female foreign policy constituency. They perceived women as a potential force for peace and equated the expansion of women's rights and women's public influence with a moral foreign policy and international harmony. Those who spearheaded this effort included Hannah Bailey of the WCTU, Lucia Ames Mead, and May Wright Sewall, all prominent peace reformers as well as suffrage leaders; Belva Lockwood and Amanda Deyo, officers of the Universal Peace Union; and Henry B. Blackwell, Alice Stone Blackwell, Anna Howard Shaw, and Caroline Severance, well-known figures in the struggle for suffrage and in club activities. Leaders from the peace movement contributed their high principles and moral commitment to the endeavor, along with their knowledge of European politics and peace activities. Mead's main objective was the prevention of international conflict through arbitration, while

Bailey, an unreconstructed pacifist, wanted to eradicate all forms of violence. Those with decades of experience in the temperance and suffrage movements emphasized the role of gender in shaping political ideas and the importance of women's participation in political life. Suffragists like the Blackwells were primarily interested in strengthening the case for the vote.

Many of the women they sought to mobilize were wary of suffrage, hesitant to intrude into male politics, and unfamiliar with foreign policy issues. The success of this small vanguard of activists hinged upon its ability to translate foreign policy issues into the vocabulary of female experience, to reveal the connection between women's concerns and events taking place far beyond the confines of the domestic sphere, and to incite and justify female political activity accordingly.

Their efforts to mobilize women kept pace with international affairs. In 1891, when the United States flexed its muscles in a minor dispute with Chile, both the National Council of Women (NCW) and the Woman's Christian Temperance Union petitioned Congress to avoid war. Four years later the Venezuela boundary dispute elicited strident calls for war with England from both public officials and private citizens. Members of the WCTU and the National American Woman's Suffrage Association (NAWSA) urged Washington to arbitrate the dispute. At NAWSA's annual convention, suffragist Lillie Devereaux Blake deplored the inability of men to settle conflict without violence and scored their willingness to "deluge the world in blood for a strip of land in Venezuela or a gold mine in Africa." Like other leaders, WCTU President Frances Willard accused those calling for war of pursuing selfish goals because the dispute had little to do with American interests.

Events in Cuba proved to be a watershed in the development of a female foreign policy constituency. From the onset of the revolt against Spain, women activists sided with the Cuban insurgents. As suffragist Susan B. Anthony explained "we know what it is to be deprived of our political rights." Nonetheless many female activists opposed war with Spain. As representatives of their organizations, women urged the United States and Spain to settle their differences over Cuba through negotiation and pressed President William McKinley and Congress to avoid violence. When the explosion of the U.S.S. *Maine* in Havana harbor raised the war fever in the United States, officials of the NCW reminded McKinley that more deaths would neither atone for those lives lost on the *Maine* nor defend national honor.

Most women, like men, lost patience with Spain during the spring of 1898 and reluctantly concluded, in the words of Clara Bewich Colby, a lifelong member of the UPU and editor of a suffrage paper, that "peaceful settlement was impossible." Yet not everyone jumped on the bandwagon when Congress declared war in April. Pacifists like Amanda Deyo and Belva Lockwood, bolstered by deep conviction and inured to public disapproval, held their ground. An ongoing debate in the pages of the leading suffrage paper, the *Woman's Journal*, revealed a deep disagreement among suffragists over the nature and purpose of the fight with Spain. The great majority seemed to believe that the war was what the administration claimed it was—an honorable struggle for Cuban independence. Some, however, claimed it was an unnecessary and unjust war for "selfish aggrandizement."

For most Americans, Congress's specific disclaimer of any territorial ambition in Cuba gave credence to the image of a just war. Women's groups rallied to war work with enthusiasm, and throughout the fighting, their publications reported regularly on the military, social, and political aspects of the conflict with Spain.

The talk of annexing the Philippines, Puerto Rico, and even Cuba that quickly followed American victories provoked widespread agitation in the United States. In June 1898, two months before the fighting ended and treaty negotiations began, an "anti-imperialist" meeting was held in Boston's Faneuil Hall to protest "the insane and wicked ambition which is driving the nation to ruin." The meeting heralded the formation of the Anti-Imperialist League. Distinct from the peace movement, the league was concerned about the acquisition of overseas territories, and its spokesmen launched a great public debate over American expansionism that lasted from February 1899 to 1903. The targets of the league's criticism were the proposed treaty with Spain (under which the United States acquired Puerto Rico, Guam, and the Philippines) and later the war to subdue the Philippines.

More than half the audience at the Faneuil Hall meeting was female. And as the controversy over the Philippines intensified, the WCTU's *Union Signal* called on women's organizations to voice their opposition to colonial empire and to support the American commitment to self-government. Many women joined in the activities of the male-run Anti-Imperialist League. Others turned to the women's groups where there was considerable agitation and activity over the Philippines. Speakers excoriated the "present intoxication with the hashish of conquest" in the United States. Letters and editorials in women's journals condemned forcible annexation, and some organizations officially denounced American policy.

Critics of the war frequently portrayed it as a selfish quest "for territory and trade" and denounced "the money power . . . and its greed for gold and territory." Most focused on the injustice and immorality of forcing a government on those who did not want it. Echoing widespread distaste for the war and the brutal methods used to subdue the Filipinos, one woman wrote that only brutes would kill "people who had committed no wrong to this country, and who only were seeking their inalienable right to liberty and self-government." Suffragists openly identified themselves with the Filipinos as people who were governed without their consent. Unlike many anti-imperialists who questioned the wisdom of annexing "backward" peoples, they disputed the contention that native inferiority justified American domination of other peoples. A similar argument, they pointed out, was used to deprive women of their rights. They also noted with irony that if women had had the right to vote the war would not have taken place and the issue of governing the Philippines would never have arisen.

It was clear that there was considerable variation in women's perceptions of government policy in the Philippines. To those who understood the war in terms of political economy, the issue was American aggression and imperialism. To suffragists, both annexation and the war represented a failure of democracy and illustrated above all the injustice of governing without the consent of the governed. Most women in the network of organizations, however, whether or not they were members of social purity organizations like the WCTU, considered the sale of alcohol on army bases and the military's licensing of prostitution to control venereal disease among the troops in the Philippines the most convincing evidence that the war was wrong.

Behind this viewpoint lay the deep conviction that intemperance was the key to the nation's ills. Thus the belief that "nothing increases intemperance like war, and nothing tends toward war like intemperance" gave organization women an unusual perspective on the Philippine war and on American expansionism in general. One WCTU speaker, for example, described the army in Cuba, Puerto Rico, and the Philippines as "intoxicated by unexpected victories and immense acquisition of territory and power." Others linked American torture of the Filipinos and other "monstrous evils" perpetuated by the army directly to the liquor traffic and prostitution.

Social purity organizations rallied to protest the Philippine war and, joined by other women's groups, attempted to change public policy by imposing "women's values" on a male government. They hoped not only to bring an end to the war but also to rectify a broad range of ills. In their articles and speeches they linked moral degradation (exemplified by intemperance and prostitution) with capitalism, commercialism, militarism, and territorial expansion. One critic, for example, warned Americans of the dangers posed by "the domination of material things" and declared that it was time for a new patriotism, based not on "our country right or wrong" but on *real* love of country. What the nation needed was another Declaration of Independence in which the underclasses rejected the growing tyranny of the plutocracy.

The fundamental issue for women in the group network, despite the differences among them, remained the perniciousness of male values. Organization spokeswomen repeatedly interpreted America's role in international affairs in terms of the character of the men who shaped foreign policy. In their view, male aggressiveness and competitiveness begat expansionism and war, and an increasing preoccupation with commerce. They rejected the idea that the state had a life of its own and that men were compelled to serve its needs; they maintained that America's male leaders were morally responsible as individual Christians for their public actions. This viewpoint conditioned women's critique of public policy and their perception of international relations.

Although speakers and writers for the network of women's organizations agreed that women must rein in the champing "steeds of civilization" to control American materialism, militarism, and expansionism, they were not at all certain how to do so. Although some organization women were political veterans, schooled in lobbying, testifying before government committees, and maneuvering among political parties, others still considered these activities unwomanly and were dubious about participating in the political process in order to make their voices heard. Lobbying campaigns against increased naval appropriations, for example, never matched the intensity and breadth of activities against liquor and prostitution in the Philippines, despite widespread opposition to increased military spending among organization members and repeated calls for action from their leadership.

It proved far easier to generate support for worldwide peace reform, which evoked a more elaborate and sustained response from women than any other international issue. Network organizations provided the bulk of public support for The Hague peace conferences in 1899 and 1907. As the *Woman's Tribune* observed, "No movement in this generation has so enlisted the interest of women as this peace conference." Even groups unfamiliar with political agitation, such as Utah's Congress of Mothers and the Woman's Relief Corps (a veteran's organization auxiliary), took up the cause. In 1899, as the conferees met in Holland, women held meetings in more than ninety cities and towns in Utah, for example, from which they cabled support to the American delegates at The Hague. Disappointment with the conference, along with a calmer international atmosphere, dulled interest in the 1907 meeting, however, which attracted far less support than its predecessor.

After 1899, enthusiasm for peace reform through international arbitration and disarmament was diverted toward a homelier yet equally important goal. Leaders called upon organization women to "cultivate a sentiment that will demand a cessation of war, and . . . war spirit." Women viewed the spread of "peace sentiment" as a contest for the hearts and minds of the country and as a momentous struggle against the values and attitudes of the men who shaped public policy. To this end, NCW president Fannie Gaffney exhorted the organization woman "as servator of the human race . . . [to] rouse herself to use every effort to preserve that general balance between things temporal and spiritual which has ever kept the human family from reverting to gross materialism if not brute ferocity. . . . Today there lies great danger that material things will overshadow things essential to the best interests of humanity.

In this struggle for peace, the arena shifted after 1899 from legislative chambers and cabinet offices to schools and other educational forums. The focus of efforts to spread peace sentiment was the celebration of Peace Day on 15 May. Peace Day was essentially an educational device to make people think about issues of war and peace and to teach the interdependence of nations. The observance of Peace Day was also a tactic for mobilizing support for international arbitration and other peace reform. Under Lucia Ames Mead and May Wright Sewall's direction, hundreds of thousands of network women participated in Peace Day activities. They distributed volumes of peace literature to clergymen, teachers, newspaper publishers, editors, and boards of education. They encouraged the establishment of programs about peace issues in religious and educational institutions and sponsored many themselves. For several years the great majority of NCW affiliates reported extensive Peace Day activities. In 1905, for example, the National Woman's Relief Society and the Young Ladies Mutual Improvement Society sponsored fifty-six Peace Day meetings in Utah, Idaho, Washington, and Montana, as well as Alberta, Canada.

Because cultivating peace sentiment in the young was a priority, most Peace Day literature was written for classroom use and children's programs. Women also participated in ongoing efforts to revise textbooks, urging teachers to single out the accomplishments of conciliators and creative persons instead of glorifying military and political heroes of the past.

In cultivating peace sentiment, women inevitably came into conflict with the "widespread revival of the martial ideal" that was preaching love of war and glorifying aggressiveness to receptive audiences at the turn of the century. They were on unfamiliar and hostile territory. When they disparaged masculine aggression and spoke out against the construction of an imperial navy, they challenged popular figures like Theodore Roosevelt, advocate of the strenuous life, symbol of imperial expansion, and ardent champion of a first-class navy.

Spokeswomen for women's groups eagerly accepted the task of challenging the prevailing ethos, and some proposed radically new ideas about the nature of the sexes. Suffragist Anna Howard Shaw claimed that the nation was "teaching the wrong idea of what constitutes manliness." Boys, she insisted, ought to be more like girls. She repudiated the biological basis of sex differences and contended that "nine boys out of ten fight simply because they are cowards. . . . They don't dare not to fight." Such sentiments were not isolated. The assertion that real heroes were to be found on farms, in schools, on sick beds, and in homes, and not on the battlefields, was a frequent refrain among female speakers and writers at this time.

The WCTU, ever-sensitive to issues of physical violence, took the lead in condemning militarism. Union conventions annually registered a protest against "the growing tendency toward militarism in the government [and] the extravagant expenditures of funds on battleships." Other groups passed similar resolutions and petitioned against rising military appropriations although less consistently.

The attack on the nation's arms policy was a skirmish compared with the fight against the spreading practice of staging military drills and forming boys' brigades in public and Sunday schools. Hannah Bailey directed the union's crusade against the proliferating brigades. "We seek to inspire children with a love of peace by making everything of a military nature distasteful to them," she wrote, "but the sham parade, sham battles, sham drills and sham brigadeism tend to undo our work." With support from other organizations, the WCTU fought juvenile military training with all the fervor and intensity it put into its temperance work. Women petitioned, protested, and, with some success, lobbied politicians, school administrators, clergymen, parents, and teachers. They also extended their campaign to military toys, the unlicensed sale of firearms, and boxing.

In confronting militarism, women repeatedly rejected the "pernicious notion . . . that patriotism is somehow necessarily connected with the idea of killing." True patriotism meant "study and understanding of the great issues of the time, not dying young or watching loved ones die without opposition." May Wright Sewall noted that it took "but a moment to be shot," whereas it might take "threescore years and ten to live a patriot's life." In 1907, several organizations publicly condemned the celebrations and festivities surrounding the three-hundredth anniversary of the founding of Jamestown as "the apotheosis of militarism."

After 1904, women's involvement in foreign policy declined. By 1907, the WCTU's *Union Signal* no longer regularly printed international news. Despite frequent displays of U.S. military power in the Caribbean and the rush to manufacture armaments and form alliances in Europe, nothing provoked the American public as much as the wars in Cuba and the Philippines had. The apparent triumph of conventional patriotism and nationalism frustrated efforts to promote international peace, arbitration, and a "new patriotism." Organization leaders in the vanguard of female foreign policy activism were not deterred, however; they lobbied and petitioned against increasing military expenditures and urged women to stay informed and involved. But the great swell of interest and activity that characterized the years between 1899 and 1905 subsided. Only in 1915, with the formation of the Woman's Peace Party, would organized women play a significant, independent role in foreign policy activism again. In the largest sense, the female foreign policy constituency failed, as did the male groups that were organized to curb American expansionism and promote the peaceful resolution of international conflict. Yet their experience offers food for thought for historians and activists alike. The individuals comprising the vanguard of this effort set out to educate American women about foreign policy, to politicize them, and to temper U.S. policy with "female influence." These goals rested on two assumptions that bear further analysis. First was the assumption that there was such a thing as female influence and that women were different from men. The vanguard also assumed that numbers of women could be converted into foreign policy activists despite their unfamiliarity with foreign affairs and the traditional divide between international affairs and women's concerns.

What of the claim to difference that lay at the heart of female foreign policy activism? Were women sufficiently different from men to warrant speaking of male and female perceptions of foreign policy? Recent scholarship about nineteenth-century American women supports the claim, insofar as it identifies and delineates a distinct "female culture" nurtured and enforced by the separation of men and women's roles and experiences. This study, though limited to organization women and their leaders, also confirms the claim to difference but with important reservations discussed below.

Unquestionably, the leaders of women's groups and their constituency were at odds with national policymakers. Less obviously, they differed from their male counterparts as well. Male anti-imperialists, like female activists, regarded the Philippine episode as a threat to American purity; behind the forcible annexation of the Philippines they discerned new values and new forces that would weaken the nation's commitment to self-government and free trade among other principles. Male anti-imperialists, however, were essentially anticolonialists, opposed primarily to the acquisition of overseas territories (and, not incidentally, to the annexation of large numbers of people of color). Unlike female activists, many of them were neither opposed to militarism nor in favor of peace activism.

The new generation of male peace reformers resembled female activists in their dedication to world peace and order, which they hoped to achieve through legal mechanisms like international arbitration. Yet many male peace reformers supported overseas expansion, which was synonymous to them with the extension of Anglo-American institutions and an increase in world stability. Similarly, they believed that the increase of American military strength would help to maintain world order.

Female activists considered expansion, militarism, and issues of war and peace as parts of a whole, rather than separate issues. They considered expansionism and militarism, along with an increase in commercialism and materialism and a decline in national purity, to be the products of a rapidly industrializing society, and they attributed these changes to the character of the men in power. As relatively powerless observers of the dynamic developments of their era, many organization women equated the modernization of America with the triumph of male values and the defeat of their own, with the victory of strength over weakness, selfishness over sacrifice, justice over injustice, vice over morality, promiscuity over chastity, and materialism over faith. And in this way their perspective on foreign policy issues was uniquely female.

Nineteenth-century men and women accepted sex differences as part of the natural scheme of things. Women's rights activists, for example, were untroubled by seeming contradictions between sex differences and their demands for equality. Today, in contrast, questions of equality and difference fuel vigorous discussion among historians of women, feminist theorists, civil rights lawyers, and political activists. Some point out, for example, that the idea of "equality," carried to its conclusion, obliterates the concept of "women" and with it the reason for considering women as a separate category. They remind us that "women" remains an ahistorical concept unless it is grounded in a specific context. Others argue that, without the concept of "women," there can be no women's issues, women's history, or women's movement as such. Moving beyond this debate, historian Joan W. Scott rejects the notion that equality and difference are opposite or incompatible pointing out "the way difference has long figured in political notions of equality," and suggesting that "sameness is [not] the only ground on which equality can be claimed."

In light of this controversy, it is important to clarify what this study reveals about difference. For while it is clear that there are significant gender differences on certain issues and that we can justifiably speak of a "women's perspective" on foreign policy, it is important to note that the views of the women in the vanguard of female activism were not representative of all women, or even of all organization women. Among and within women's organizations there were considerable differences of opinion on foreign policy issues, as evidenced, for example, by the diverse interpretations of and reactions to the Philippine war and by the varied responses to calls for action. Moreover, many "women's" ideas about foreign affairs were not unique to women. Organization women had much in common with nineteenth-century male pacifists, with whom they shared a Christian humanitarianism, a concern for social justice, and an abhorrence of violence. Universal Peace Union President Alfred Love held a place in the vanguard of female foreign policy activism, along with suffragist Henry B. Blackwell, not only because he favored political power for women but also because he tended to perceive international affairs in the same way women leaders did.

These reservations notwithstanding, we can identify a distinct female perspective on foreign policy, a set of ideas and attitudes that were more meaningful and persuasive to women activists than to men at the time. The leaders of network organizations could rely on this distinctive perspective in trying to transform women into foreign policy activists.

This endeavor was very ambitious in light of the mystique that normally surrounded matters of international moment and set them on a plane above public scrutiny and in light of the particular handicaps that separated the disfranchised sex from public policy in general. To accomplish its goals the network leadership had to entice women onto unfamiliar territory, to inform and educate them, and to rebut the perception that international affairs were the affair of men. They attempted to do this by translating foreign policy issues into the language of women's experience, which involved explicating the connections between women's domestic concerns and the nation's foreign policy.

Despite its success in mobilizing large numbers of women, this strategy was problematic. To educate their constituency, leaders utilized women's publications and conventions, assuming that an informed citizenry would defend its interests better than an ignorant one. After education came politicization, a formidable objective in view of the diversity within and among women's organizations. Organization women did agree, however, that the moral order was in danger, and they were also in agreement about prostitution and temperance. Therefore, in trying to arouse and win support from their constituency, network leaders often utilized these social purity concerns and relied on the language of the social purity movement, which tended to oversimplify, sentimentalize, and distort at the same time that it broadened and educated.

Social purity concerns should not be denigrated; women's sentimental and moralistic concerns were not superficial. They were, in fact, realistic responses to real problems. It was farseeing and intelligent to ponder the future of the family, the nature of community life, the quality of daily life, the rise of violence, and the increasing influence of materialism and militarism in the United States. But female activists used the vocabulary of the social purity movement, replete as it was with sentimental and moralistic catchwords, often without venturing beyond rhetoric to substantive issues. Although this technique enlisted recruits, and was remarkably successful during the war in the Philippines, it did not deepen women's understanding of the issues. Neither, as it turned out, did it foster sustained interest in international affairs. Politicization was dependent upon education, and the pioneer citizen activists of this era were unable to combine and synchronize the two effectively.

The leadership of women's organizations used the argument of women's difference and women's ability to make a unique contribution to society to justify and expand women's interests and activities beyond the home. But what was intended to expand could also confine, and the argument that transformed some women locked others into constricted thinking about themselves and the world. In politicizing women, the leadership called on them to play a role in a male arena, but to do so as women. By and large, the women in this study resolved their dilemma by using methods that were indirect and persuasive. In other words, they acted in a womanly way, through the education of children and the moral influence of the home. But did this not reinforce the differences and prejudices that locked women out of the policymaking process in the first place? Although we should not dismiss their contention that the roots of militarism, expansionism, and war lay at home, cultivating "peace sentiment" on the home front was, to say the least, a long-term project. Moreover, their solution rested upon unproved assumptions about the pliability of human nature and the feasibility of eradicating "martial sentiment" through education. In the meantime, outside the home and the classroom, the political process went on, deprived of whatever "female influence" might have been exercised to rein in the "champing steeds."

The truth of the matter is that in nineteenth- and early twentieth-century America, women's foreign policy activism *was* unwomanly behavior, as were women's earlier campaigns to influence public policy, despite the rationalization that such activities were mere extensions of the domestic role. Women activists were, in fact, acting as men were supposed to act, seeking power to shape the society and the world in which they lived. In doing so they were rejecting prevailing notions about sex roles that relegated them to compliance and domesticity.

In this respect, female activists illustrate the dynamic character of the gender system. The women who nineteenth-century Americans knew were changing, and female foreign policy activists heralded the construction of new women. What reciprocal changes were occurring in the nature of men? And what was the relation between these changes and the emergence of the United States as a world power? Questions such as these challenge historians to explore further the place of gender in the study of diplomatic history.

QUESTIONS TO CONSIDER

1. What significant changes occurred in the 1898–1905 period that made foreign policy such an important issue in the United States?
2. Why did many women reject the foreign policy values of the male establishment? What was their rationale for women's activism in the public sphere?
3. On what grounds did women oppose the war in the Philippines? What issue in particular related to women's experience?
4. What was Peace Day?
5. What did the WCTU and others condemn about growing militarism?
6. How were women different enough from men to warrant speaking of male and female perceptions of foreign policy?
7. What does Papachristou conclude about the womanliness of female involvement in foreign policy?

7

What We Lost
in the Great War*

John Steele Gordon

Despite unprecedented prosperity, Americans today are worried
about the future and uneasy about the nation's institutions. To
some extent this reflects a loss of confidence that stems from World
War I. The optimism and expectation that the United States shared
with Europe a century ago seems naive, even foolish, to those of
us who, with the wisdom of hindsight, know that the twentieth century would bring two world wars, the worst depression in American
history, Stalin, Hitler, Pol Pot, and the Holocaust. But for people living at the end of a remarkable century of material and ideological advance, the twentieth century seemed to promise a closer
approach to utopia.

In this article, American Heritage contributing editor John Steele
Gordon explores the reasons for the confidence that pervaded society in 1900, along with some suggestions about why our own century has been such a disappointment. He offers an encouraging
conclusion—that we are rediscovering the keys to the nineteenth
century's development, democracy and capitalism, after flirting
with disastrous alternatives since the Great War.

A few years ago I wrote a book called *The Scarlet Woman of Wall Street*
about a place and a people that flourished in the nineteenth century: the

*Reprinted by permission of *American Heritage* Magazine, a division of Forbes, Inc.
© Forbes, Inc., 1992.

New York City of the 1860s and 1870s. We might call it Edith Wharton's New York. Mrs. Wharton herself wrote late in her life, in the 1930s, that the metropolis of her youth had been destined to become "as much a vanished city as Atlantis or the lowest level of Schliemann's Troy." To those of us who know the modern metropolis—what we might call Tom Wolfe's New York—that city of only a century ago seems today as far away and nearly as exotic as Marco Polo's Cathay.

What happened to Edith Wharton's world? Why does the society our grandparents and great-grandparents lived in seem so very much a foreign country to us today?

To be sure, Edith Wharton's New York was a still-provincial city of horses and gas lamps, Knickerbockers and Irishmen, brownstones and church steeples. Its population was characterized by a few people in top hats and a great many people in rags, for in the 1860s grinding poverty was still thought the fate of the majority of the human race.

In contrast, Tom Wolfe's New York—far and away the most cosmopolitan place on earth—is a city of subways and neon, Korean grocers and Pakistani news dealers, apartments and skyscrapers. If poverty has hardly been expunged, the percentage of the city's population living in want has greatly diminished even while society's idea of what constitutes the basic minimums of a decent life has greatly expanded.

It was constant, incremental change that brought about these differences, a phenomenon found in most societies and all industrial ones. Indeed, one of the pleasures of growing old in such a society, perhaps, is that we come to remember personally—just as Edith Wharton did—a world that has slipped out of existence.

But this sort of change comes slowly and is recognized only in retrospect. As the novelist Andrew Holleran explained, "No one grows old in a single day." Rather, something far more profound than incremental change separates us from Edith Wharton's world, and we look at that world now across what a mathematician might call a discontinuity in the stream of time.

Only rarely in the course of history does such a discontinuity occur and turn a world upside down overnight. When it does happen, it is usually as the result of some unforeseeable cataclysm, such as the volcanic explosion that destroyed Minoan civilization on the island of Crete about 1500 B.C., or the sudden arrival of the conquistadors in the New World three thousand years later.

Edith Wharton's world suffered just such a calamity. The diplomat and historian George Kennan called it "the seminal catastrophe of the twentieth century": the First World War.

Certainly that war's influence on subsequent world events could hardly have been more pervasive. Had there been no First World War, there would, of course, have been no Second, and that is not just playing with numbers, for in geopolitical terms the two wars were really one with a twenty-year truce in the middle.

But for the First World War, the sun might still shine brightly on the British Empire. But for the war, there would have been no Bolshevik coup and thus no Soviet state. But for the war, there would have been no Nazis and thus no genocide of the Jews. And, of course, most of us never would have been born.

Far more important, however, than its effect upon the fate of great nations, and on our own individual existence, was the First World War's influence on the way that we heirs of Edith Wharton came to question, and for a while even to dismiss, many of the basic values of the culture she lived in. Because of the war, the word *Victorian* became a term of opprobrium that extended far beyond the ebb and flow of fashion.

The reason for this is simply that the First World War, more than any other in history, was psychologically debilitating, both for the vanquished and for the victors. Indeed, there really was no victory. No premeditated policy of conquest or revenge brought the war about—although both those aims had clouded the politics of Europe for years. Therefore, no aims, beyond national survival, were achieved.

Indeed, relations among the Great Powers of Europe were better in the early summer of 1914 than they had been for some time. The British and Germans had recently agreed about the Berlin to Baghdad railway and a future division between them of Portugal's colonies. Even the French, still bitter over their ignominious defeat at the hands of Prussia in 1871, were moving to improve relations with Germany, a move that Germany welcomed.

Rather, the war came about because a lunatic murdered a man of feathers and uniforms who had no real importance whatsoever. The politicians, seeking to take advantage of circumstances—as politicians are paid to do—had then miscalculated in their blustering and posturing.

The mobilization of an army when railroads were the only means of mass transportation was a very complex undertaking, one that had to be planned in advance down to the smallest detail. Once a mobilization plan was implemented, it could not be stopped without throwing a country's military into chaos, rendering it largely defenseless. Russia, seeking only to threaten Austria and thus prevent its using the assassination of Archduke Ferdinand to stir up trouble in the Balkans, discovered that it could not move just against Austria. It was general mobilization or nothing. Russia chose to mobilize.

At that point the statesmen realized that the war they had threatened so freely—but which no one, in fact, had wanted at all—had now, suddenly, become inescapable. A fearful, inexorable logic had taken decisions out of human hands.

Once it began, the generals found they had no tactical concepts to deal with the new military realities that confronted them. It had been forty-three years since Great Powers had fought each other in Europe. In those four decades the instruments of war had undergone an unparalleled evolution, and their destructive power had increased by several orders of magnitude.

Railroads, machine guns, and barbed wire made an entrenched defense invulnerable. Stalemate—bloody, endless, gloryless stalemate—resulted. For lack of any better ideas, the generals flung greater and greater numbers of men into the mouths of these machine guns and gained at best mere yards of territory thereby.

In the first day—day!—of the Battle of the Somme in 1916, Great Britain suffered twenty thousand men killed. That was the bloodiest day in the British army's long history. Altogether there were more than a million casualties in this one battle alone. An entire generation was lost in the slaughter of the Somme and other similar battles.

This almost unimaginable destruction of human life, to no purpose whatsoever, struck at the very vitals of Western society. For this reason alone, among the casualties of the First World War were not only the millions of soldiers who had died for nothing, most of the royalty of Europe, and treasure beyond reckoning but nearly all the fundamental philosophical and cultural assumptions of the civilization that had suffered this self-induced catastrophe.

For there was one thing that was immediately clear to all about the Great War—as the generation who fought it called it—and that was that this awful tragedy was a human and wholly local phenomenon. There was no volcano, no wrathful God, no horde of barbarians out of the East. Western culture had done this to itself. Because of the war, it seemed to many a matter of inescapable logic that Western culture must be deeply, inherently flawed.

In four years of blood and smoke and flame, the world of Edith Wharton became the world of W. H. Auden; the Age of Innocence, the Age of Anxiety.

For us, who can see the tragedy that was looming up in what was for them the future, and thus, for them, impenetrable, many of the cultural assumptions of Edith Wharton's world smack of the hubris that is the inevitable progenitor of tragedy. But hubris, like the winner in a horse race, can be much more easily discerned in retrospect. And people cannot live—or, for that matter, bet on horses—in retrospect.

Given their vantage point in history, the inhabitants of Edith Wharton's world had every good reason for their attitudes. Their civilization had, after all, entirely remade the world in the preceding two hundred years.

Consider the facts:

In the year 1700 there had been little to distinguish European culture in terms of power, wealth, and creativity from the other great civilizations on earth. The Ottoman Turks had conquered most of the Muslim world and much of Europe itself in the previous two centuries. The Turkish army had besieged Vienna as recently as 1683.

The Mogul emperor of India, whose father had built the incomparable Taj Mahal, sat on the Peacock Throne, ruling over an empire of a million square miles, and lived in a splendor unmatched even by the Versailles of Louis XIV.

The Chinese Empire was the largest and perhaps the most cultured on earth. It was also the most industrially advanced, running a strong trade surplus with Europe.

But by the year 1700 Europe had already invented a cultural tool of transcendent power called the scientific method. In the eighteenth century this tool was applied to an ever-widening area of inquiry with beneficial results in fields as diverse as agriculture, cloth manufacture, and metalworking. By the close of that century, Europe was clearly the dominant power center of the world and was projecting that power commercially, militarily, and politically over a wider and wider area.

And in 1782 James Watt perfected the rotary steam engine. The Industrial Revolution was under way.

A hundred years later still, at the end of the nineteenth century, any comparison between the West and other cultures bordered on the meaningless, so great had the gap in power and wealth grown. Westerners had projected that power over the entire globe and created the modern world, a world they utterly dominated. The Western people of that world took for granted what seemed to them the manifest superiority of Western technology, governance, and even religion over all others.

To better understand the predominant attitudes of the West before the First World War, consider what it accomplished in the nineteenth century as a result of the Industrial Revolution. Quite simply, the quality of life was miraculously transformed. Indoor plumbing, central heating, brilliant interior lighting, abundant clothing, and myriad inexpensive industrial products from wallpaper to iceboxes gave the middle and upper classes a standard of living undreamed of a century earlier by even the richest members of society.

In 1800 it had required a month to cross the Atlantic in a damp, crowded, and pitching ship. In 1900 vast and luxurious liners made the crossing in a week. Information that once had been limited to the speed of human travel could now circle the entire globe in minutes by telephone, telegraph, and undersea cable.

In the 1830s the lights and shadows of an instant were captured by photography. In the 1870s Edison's phonograph imprisoned sound. To the Victorians it was as though time itself had been tamed.

Newspapers, books, and magazines proliferated by the thousands so that information and entertainment could be quickly and cheaply obtained. Free public libraries spread to nearly every city in the Western world. Andrew Carnegie alone paid for nearly five thousand of them in the United States and Britain.

Physics, chemistry, geology, and biology penetrated farther into the fathomless heart of nature than anyone had thought possible a hundred years earlier. Even the mighty Newton's model of the universe was found to be less than wholly universal when Einstein published his Special Theory of Relativity in 1905.

As the new century began engineers showed the world with the Crystal Palace in London how to enclose vast spaces, with the Brooklyn Bridge in New York how to span great distances, with the Eiffel Tower in Paris how to scale great heights. The automobile, the airplane, the movies, and wireless communication promised still more wonders.

Ever more important than the technological and scientific advances of the age, however, were the economic and political ones.

The nineteenth century is usually perceived as one in which great industrial and commercial fortunes were created in the midst—even because of—the grinding poverty of the masses. This is largely a misperception. To be sure, the absolute number of people living in poverty in the Western world greatly increased in the nineteenth century, but only because the population as a whole greatly increased. Moreover, the movement of workers from agriculture to industry concentrated the poor in highly visible urban areas. But their forebears had been no less poor. The ancestors of those who lived in the unspeakable urban hovels of Dickens's England had inhabited the equally unspeakable rural hovels of Fielding's England. Meanwhile, the percentage of the population living in poverty declined.

In 1800 perhaps 85 percent of the population of Britain—then the richest and most advanced of Western nations—lived in or very near poverty, where 85 percent of the human population had always lived. These people had to work as hard as they could just to get enough to eat and obtain shelter and clothes. They stored up a little in good years, perhaps, in order to survive the bad ones. But luxuries, and even a formal education for their children, were out of the question. For millions, only rum, gin, and other spirits in staggering quantities—often quite literally in staggering quantities—made life endurable.

But by 1900 less than 30 percent of the British population was still at that economic level, and most of the children were receiving at least the rudiments of an education and therefore the hope of a better life. Meanwhile, the per capita consumption of alcohol had fallen sharply. While no one in 1900 thought that 30 percent of the population living in poverty was acceptable, parents and grandparents were there to tell them how far they had come.

In 1800 less than five percent of the British population was allowed to vote for those who represented them in Parliament, and real political power resided in fewer than two thousand families. By 1900 universal male suffrage was taken for granted and women were on the march for equal rights. Democracy, beginning to develop only in the new United States in 1800, was by 1900 the birthright of millions in both the old and new worlds.

In two hundred years Western civilization had made itself rich and powerful and learned while the rest of mankind remained poor, and therefore weak and ignorant. Political and economic power in the West had ceased to be the exclusive possession of a narrow upper class and had spread widely to other levels of society, promoting social stability by giving everyone both a stake in society's institutions and the power to affect those institutions.

It was this dispersal of economic and political power that guaranteed that no one person or segment of society could become too powerful and threaten the rights or the prosperity of others. When heavy industry, in pursuit of economies of scale, conglomerated in the late nineteenth century into huge concerns of unprecedented financial and economic power, many Americans believed they threatened a plutocracy. So society moved to check the potential abuse of power with antimonopoly legislation, such as the Sherman Antitrust Act, and to channel that power into productive, not hegemonic, purposes. This may have been a violent and wrenching process; nevertheless, it happened.

Who can blame the people who accomplished all this for feeling good about themselves? Would we, or anyone, have been any wiser or more humble?

Because of this fantastic record of progress, the people of Edith Wharton's world believed in the inevitability of further progress and the certainty that science would triumph. They believed in the ever-widening spread of democracy and the rule of law. They believed in the adequacy of the present and the bright promise of the future. To be sure, they fought ferociously over the details of how to proceed, but they had no doubt whatever that the basic principles that guided their society were correct.

Then, all at once, the shots rang out in Sarajevo, the politicians bungled, the armies marched, the poppies began to blow between the crosses row on row. The faith of the Western world in the soundness of its civilization died in the trenches of the western front.

Seventy-five years later, richer, more powerful, more learned than ever, the West still struggles to pick up the psychological pieces, to regain its poise, to find again the self-confidence that in the nineteenth century it took entirely for granted.

If the Great War was the result not of deliberate policy but of ghastly accident, we now know it was an accident waiting to happen. Still, like most accidents, it resulted from the concatenation of separate chances, each unlikely. Indeed, it can be reasonably argued that the calamity might well never have come to pass at all if only the imperial throne of Germany had been occupied by someone other than that supreme jerk Kaiser Wilhelm II.

Although highly intelligent, he had been burdened from the start with a withered left arm caused by a difficult and medically mishandled birth. Far worse, Wilhelm had been largely raised by pedantic tutors and sycophantic military aides, for his mother was more interested in Prussian politics than in her children's upbringing.

The result was that an undisciplined, impulsive, deeply insecure neurotic inherited the throne of the greatest military power in Europe. Worse, the constitution of the German Empire gave him a very large measure of control over foreign and military policy.

The consequence was disaster for Germany and the world. And in complex societies, just as in simple ones, when disaster strikes, "the king must die." And not just Wilhelm (who spent the last twenty years of his life in exile). The entire pre-war establishment was everywhere blamed for this purposeless, victorless war. The mainstream politicians who had failed to prevent it, the businessmen who had profited from it, the scientists and engineers who had created its lethal technology—all those, in fact, who had constituted the nexus of power in Edith Wharton's world suffered a grievous loss of prestige.

Those who had been only on the margins of power and influence in the nineteenth century—the Cassandras who are present in all societies, the philosophers, the artists (in short, the intellectuals)—saw their opportunities and seized them. To use Theodore Roosevelt's famous metaphor, power began to move from the players in the arena to the observers in the seats.

In the relatively peaceful 1880s, Gilbert and Sullivan in *The Mikado* had put on the Lord High Executioner's little list of social expendables "the idiot who praises, with enthusiastic tone, / All centuries but this, and every country but his own." After the First World War people listened eagerly to just such philosophers, many of whom thought that only a radical restructuring of Western society and its economic system could prevent a recurrence of the calamity. Not surprisingly, the philosophers had no lack of prescriptions for how to accomplish this and no doubt whatever as to just who should be put in charge of the project. Although many of these ideas turned out to be in Winston Churchill's phrase, "so stupid that only an intellectual could have conceived" them, people were ready to give them a try.

We must now look, briefly, at the philosophical baby that so many intellectuals were ready to toss out with the bath water of war.

At the core of Western thought lies the concept of the importance of the individual human being. It is a uniquely Western idea, with its origins in ancient Israel and Greece (a civilization where the gods themselves were made of all-too-human clay). Later the concept was continued and elaborated on by such Christian philosophers as Augustine, Jerome, and Thomas Aquinas.

In medieval England, safe from foreign invasion behind its watery walls, the emphasis on the importance of the individual resulted in the flowering of the concept of liberty, both political and economic. Individuals, thought the English, were born with rights no one, not even kings, could take away, for the king, like his subjects, was bound by the law. This idea—that the majesty of the law was separate and distinct from the king's own majesty—is today encapsulated in the phrase *the rule of law*. It is one of the most important of Western concepts, for without it the Western achievements of the nineteenth century would not have been possible.

The American Revolution and the economic dominance of Britain in the nineteenth century caused liberty's children—capitalism and democracy—to spread widely through the Western world. The increasing acceptance during the nineteenth century of the individual's right, within an ordered society, to pursue his own concept of happiness—in other words, his self-interest—had, to be sure, many consequences, some of them unpleasant. The Victorians, however, were prepared to accept these consequences. They reasoned that because human beings are social creatures, the betterment of society was, in fact, in almost everyone's self-interest. The people of Edith Wharton's world likewise believed that most of the attributes of their society resulted from the interaction of history with human nature, and that human nature, with all its faults, was a given.

The Victorians certainly thought that mankind could get ever better and ever wiser, and in support of this idea they pointed to their own century as Exhibit A. But they equally believed that the perfection of mankind could come only with the arrival of what Christians call the Kingdom of Heaven on Earth. Until then, they thought, they would just have to make do with what they had.

But Karl Marx reversed this equation. He maintained that human nature was only a result of the society in which people lived. Change society, thought Marx, and you change human nature. Perfect society, and you perfect mankind. To Marx and the "social engineers" who followed him, the intellectual, not the grace of God, would be the redeemer of the human race.

Marx was the quintessential intellectual, remarkably detached from the real world. Although he dedicated his formidable mind to the betterment of the new industrial working class, he knew of that class only what he read in the library of the British Museum. Not once in his life did Marx ever set foot in a factory. Consequently, at the time of his death, in 1883, his grand vision stood no more chance of adoption by the real world than had Sir Thomas More's Utopia three hundred and fifty years earlier.

Further, Marx, deeply influenced by Thomas Malthus's and David Ricardo's gloomy (and erroneous) ideas, made a classic intellectual mistake. He looked at the social and economic universe around him—the early stages of the Industrial Revolution—and assumed that the conditions he saw were permanent and the trends of that era would continue indefinitely. But, of course, trends hardly ever continue indefinitely.

In fact they were rapidly evolving, as they continue to do today. But the followers of Marx regarded his theories about society and economics as the equal of Newton's theory in physics: the universal explainer of all observed phenomena.

And while Marx was only an intellectual, his greatest intellectual successor, Lenin, was much more. Lenin was a political genius. Thanks to the opportunities arising out of the First World War, he was able to seize control of a great nation and proclaim a Marxist dawn for mankind. It was to be a new day in which the perfection of society was the only goal and in which the individual pursuit of happiness, or even the right to hold a contrary opinion, had no place whatever. In the first two years of Lenin's rule, fifty thousand of his political opponents were executed.

In shattered Germany, meanwhile, an already neurotic society slid toward psychosis. United only in 1871, Germany had been a latecomer to the world of Great Power politics and was "born encircled" by the other Great Powers. Lacking a vast colonial empire and a long national history, Germany depended on its economic and military might for its prestige, until its one unquestioned superiority—its incomparable army—was nonetheless defeated.

The draconian, score-settling peace imposed on Germany at the Versailles Conference worsened matters considerably. So did the hyperinflation of the early 1920s, which wiped out whatever economic security middle-class Germans had managed to hang on to. In their humiliation the German people felt a desperate need for scapegoats, and Hitler stood ready to supply Jews, homosexuals, Gypsies, and others to fill that need—in exchange, of course, for total power. Many other countries, including Spain and Italy, also adopted fascism, as these disparate movements were collectively called. Even countries with firm democratic foundations felt the effects of this intellectual assault upon the nineteenth-century world view. Britain and France elected their first socialist governments in 1924, and both had active fascist movements.

The Second World War destroyed fascism as a political doctrine but greatly strengthened the Soviet Union, which sought to export its system to areas occupied by the Red Army and to countries in the so-called Third World. Meanwhile, the democratic left, especially in Western Europe and Britain, but increasingly in the United States as well, sought to replace the old economic and social order with systems of their devising that they genuinely believed would be fairer and more peaceful and more prosperous. In pursuit of these worthy goals, these systems tended to concentrate power, rather than disperse it as the nineteenth century had done. And democratically elected leaders—just like their totalitarian counterparts—often assumed that human nature was only clay to be molded in a noble cause.

But human nature has proved recalcitrant. The nineteenth century, it turns out, had it right to start with. The evidence has been piling up through most of the twentieth century, and it is now overwhelming that people act not as Karl Marx and Lenin thought they would but as Adam Smith and John Stuart Mill predicted.

People pursue their self-interests, perceiving those interests to be bound up with themselves, their families—especially their children—and their society as a whole. Class divisions within a society, by which Marxists seek to explain the human universe, are an intellectual construct, with no real-world analogue. Many of the programs advocated by the social engineers, therefore, failed altogether or had vast, wicked, and entirely unanticipated consequences.

Of all the inventions of the nineteenth century, capitalism and representative democracy turned out to be the greatest. To be sure, they are intellectually untidy—often very untidy indeed: just ask Charles Keating, the Reverend Al Sharpton, or the latest congressman under indictment. Nonetheless, they work, for they are consonant with human nature. As

Churchill explained, "Democracy is the worst form of government except all those other forms that have been tried from time to time." He could have made the same point about capitalism.

Capitalism made the West rich in the nineteenth century, and that wealth was spread ever more widely through society as the century went on. All the alternatives pursued in the twentieth have led only to poverty.

Democracy increasingly empowered the ordinary people in the nineteenth century as literacy, newspapers, and the franchise spread to every level. All the modern alternatives have resulted only in tyrannies far worse than any known to the world of Edith Wharton.

After decades of experiments brought on by the First World War, it is clear that what maximizes human happiness is ordered liberty—the idea that individuals should be free to pursue their political and economic self-interests under the rule of law and within the limits set by a democratic society. During the last decade, as the promises of systems that concentrated power rather than dispersed it collapsed, country after country has moved toward economic and political liberty. Today even the citadel of totalitarianism, the Kremlin itself, has fallen to the essential force of these nineteenth-century ideas.

The nineteenth century even knew the reason why these ideas were so forceful, and indeed, one of the century's greatest political philosophers expressed it as dictum. "Power tends to corrupt," Lord Acton wrote in 1887, "and absolute power corrupts absolutely." Perhaps the cruelest legacy of the First World War is that we have required seventy-five years and untold human pain to learn this truth all over again.

All this is not to say that there was nothing to be learned from the First World War and its terrible consequences, that it was all just a ghastly aberration. I think that we heirs of Edith Wharton have learned at least four vital lessons from the catastrophe.

Before the war Westerners believed not only in the superiority of Western culture but in the innate superiority of the white race over what many, twisting Kipling's meaning, referred to as those "lesser breeds without the Law." Today no one but the hopeless bigot believes that those who could inflict the Battle of Verdun upon themselves are a special creation or the sole repository of human genius. The Great War taught us that all human beings are equally human: equally frail and equally sublime.

The second lesson of the First World War was to hammer home forever the truth first uttered by William Tecumseh Sherman thirty-five years earlier. "I am tired and sick of war," the great general said in 1879. "Its glory is all moonshine. . . . War is hell." At 11:00 A.M., on November 11, 1918, as the guns fell silent after fifty-one months and 8,538,315 military deaths, there was hardly a soul on earth who would have disagreed with him. Nor are there many today. If wars have been fought since, they have been fought by people who suffered few illusions about war's glory.

The third lesson is that in a technological age, war between the Great Powers cannot be won in anything but a Pyrrhic sense. In the stark phraseology of the accountant, war is no longer even remotely cost-effective.

The final lesson is that it is very easy in a technological age for war to become inevitable. The speed with which war is fought has increased manyfold since the Industrial Revolution began. In 1914 the Austrians, the Russians, and the German kaiser rattled one too many sabers, and suddenly, much to their surprise, the lights began to go out all over Europe. This all too vividly demonstrated fact has induced considerable caution in the world's statesmen ever since—if not, alas, in its madmen.

Bearing this in mind, there is one aspect of the First World War for which we might be grateful: If it had to be fought, it was well that it was fought when it was. We learned the lessons of total war in a technological age less than forty years before we developed the capacity to destroy ourselves utterly with this technology. Had the political situation that led to the Great War coincided with the technological possibilities that produced the hydrogen bomb, it is improbable that there would have been a Tom Wolfe's New York—or even any New Yorkers to look back and wonder what happened to Edith Wharton's.

Rather, the great metropolis, a city humming with human life and human genius, would instead be but one more pile of rubble on a vast and desolate plain, poisoned for centuries. If we have truly learned this final lesson, and we must pray that we have, then those millions who lie today in Flanders fields did not die in vain.

QUESTIONS TO CONSIDER

1. Why did World War I so undermine the philosophical and cultural assumptions of western civilization?
2. Why had the West so outdistanced other world cultures between 1700 and 1900?
3. What were the most important advances in the nineteenth century—technological, scientific, cultural, and political?
4. From whom and to whom did power shift in the aftermath of war, according to Theodore Roosevelt?
5. What great nineteenth century thinkers and ideas were undermined by World War I? Who or what replaced them? What was the result of that change?
6. What four lessons of World War I does Gordon suggest?

8

Assimilation in America*
Milton M. Gordon

Milton M. Gordon (1918–), longtime sociology professor at Amherst College, won several awards for his work on the sociology of race. Among his books is *Assimilation in American Life*, an expansion of this 1961 article. In the article he challenges some enduring myths about life in the United States.

The United States is a nation of immigrants. The way in which newcomers are absorbed into the country does much to determine the national character. Since 1975 there has been an upsurge of refugees entering the United States from Indochina. The influx has reawakened traditional American fears about how new arrivals, especially non-Caucasians, can be integrated into American society. Gordon's article provides some sociological and historical insight into the ways in which assimilation has occurred—and has failed to occur—in the past.

Gordon considers three basic theories of assimilation—the melting pot, Anglo-conformity, and cultural pluralism—to see which model best fits the American experience. The melting pot, traditionally viewed as the ideal in that it takes different immigrant groups and forges them into new "Americans," has been honored more in theory than in reality. Anglo-conformity, making over new arrivals in the image of the Anglo-American, has been far more

*"Assimilation in America" reprinted by permission of *Daedalus,* Journal of the American Academy of Arts and Sciences, from the issue entitled *Ethnic Groups in American Life,* Spring 1961, volume 90, number 2.

prevalent in practice. Racially different immigrants, however, have proven difficult to assimilate and have resulted in a third and increasingly relevant model—cultural pluralism. Since Gordon demonstrates that Anglo-Americans are unwilling to socially assimilate many different immigrant groups, an open recognition of the value and legitimacy of different cultural heritages appears to be the best the United States can do to meet her democratic ideals. Rather than a melting pot, cultural pluralism suggests a stew pot.

Three ideologies or conceptual models have competed for attention on the American scene as explanations of the way in which a nation, in the beginning largely white, Anglo-Saxon, and Protestant, has absorbed over 41 million immigrants and their descendants from variegated sources and welded them into the contemporary American people. These ideologies are Anglo-conformity, the melting pot, and cultural pluralism. They have served at various times, and often simultaneously, as explanations of what has happened—descriptive models—and of what should happen— goal models. Not infrequently they have been used in such a fashion that it is difficult to tell which of these two usages the writer has had in mind. In fact, one of the more remarkable omissions in the history of American intellectual thought is the relative lack of close analytical attention given to the theory of immigrant adjustment in the United States by its social scientists.

The result has been that this field of discussion—an overridingly important one since it has significant implications for the more familiar problems of prejudice, discrimination, and majority-minority group relations generally—has been largely preempted by laymen, representatives of belles lettres, philosophers, and apologists of various persuasions. Even from these sources the amount of attention devoted to ideologies of assimilation is hardly extensive. Consequently, the work of improving intergroup relations in America is carried out by dedicated professional agencies and individuals who deal as best they can with day-to-day problems of discriminatory behavior, but who for the most part are unable to relate their efforts to an adequate conceptual apparatus. Such an apparatus would, at one and the same time, accurately describe the present structure of American society with respect to its ethnic groups (I shall use the term "ethnic group" to refer to any racial, religious, or national origins collectivity), and allow for a considered formulation of its assimilation or integration goals for the foreseeable future. One is reminded of Alice's distraught question in her travels in Wonderland: "Would you tell me, please, which way I ought to go from here?" "That depends a good deal," replied the Cat with irrefutable logic, "on where you want to get to."

The story of America's immigration can be quickly told for our present purposes. The white American population at the time of the Revolution was largely English and Protestant in origin, but had already absorbed substantial groups of Germans and Scotch-Irish and smaller contingents of Frenchmen, Dutchmen, Swedes, Swiss, South Irish, Poles, and a handful of migrants from other European nations. Catholics were represented in modest numbers, particularly in the middle colonies, and a small number of Jews were residents of the incipient nation. With the exception of the Quakers and a few missionaries, the colonists had generally treated the Indians and their cultures with contempt and hostility, driving them from the coastal plains and making the western frontier a bloody battleground where eternal vigilance was the price of survival.

Although the Negro at that time made up nearly one-fifth of the total population, his predominantly slave status, together with racial and cultural prejudice, barred him from serious consideration as an assimilable element of the society. And while many groups of European origin started out as determined ethnic enclaves, eventually, most historians believe, considerable ethnic intermixture within the white population took place. "People of different blood" [*sic*]—write two American historians about the colonial period, "English, Irish, German, Huguenot, Dutch, Swedish—mingled and intermarried with little thought of any difference." In such a society, its people predominantly English, its white immigrants of other ethnic origins either English-speaking or derived largely from countries of northern and western Europe whose cultural divergences from the English were not great, and its dominant white population excluding by fiat the claims and considerations of welfare of the non-Caucasian minorities, the problem of assimilation understandably did not loom unduly large or complex.

The unfolding events of the next century and a half with increasing momentum dispelled the complacency which rested upon the relative simplicity of colonial and immediate post-Revolutionary conditions. The large-scale immigration to America of the famine-fleeing Irish, the Germans, and later the Scandinavians (along with additional Englishmen and other peoples of northern and western Europe) in the middle of the nineteenth century (the so-called "old immigration"), the emancipation of the Negro slaves and the problems created by post-Civil War reconstruction, the placing of the conquered Indian with his broken culture on government reservations, the arrival of the Oriental, first attracted by the discovery of gold and other opportunities in the West, and finally, beginning in the last quarter of the nineteenth century and continuing to the early 1920s, the swelling to proportions hitherto unimagined of the tide of immigration from the peasantries and "pales" of southern and eastern Europe—the Italians, Jews, and Slavs of the so-called "new immigration," fleeing the persecutions and industrial dislocations of the day—all these events constitute the background against which we may consider the rise of the theories of assimilation mentioned above. After a necessarily fore-shortened description of each of these theories and their historical emergence, we shall suggest analytical distinctions designed to aid in clarifying the nature of the assimilation process, and then conclude by focusing on the American scene.

ANGLO-CONFORMITY

"Anglo-conformity" is a broad term used to cover a variety of viewpoints about assimilation and immigration; they all assume the desirability of maintaining English institutions (as modified by the American Revolution), the English language, and English-oriented cultural patterns as dominant and standard in American life. However, bound up with this assumption are related attitudes. These may range from discredited notions about race and "Nordic" and "Aryan" racial superiority, together with the nativist political programs and exclusionist immigration policies which such notions entail, through an intermediate position of favoring immigration from northern and western Europe on amorphous, unre-flective grounds ("They are more like us"), to a lack of opposition to any source of immigration, as long as these immigrants and their descendants duly adopt the standard Anglo-Saxon cultural patterns. There is by no means any necessary equation between Anglo-conformity and racist attitudes.

It is quite likely that "Anglo-conformity" in its more moderate aspects, however explicit its formulation, has been the most prevalent ideology of assimilation goals in America throughout the nation's history. As far back as colonial times, Benjamin Franklin recorded concern about the clannishness of the Germans in Pennsylvania, their slowness in learning English, and the establishment of their own native-language press. Others of the founding fathers had similar reservations about large-scale immigration from Europe. In the context of their times they were unable to foresee the role such immigration was to play in creating the later greatness of the nation. They were not at all men of unthinking prejudices. The disestablishment of religion and the separation of church and state (so that no religious group—whether New England Congregationalists, Virginian Anglicans, or even all Protestants combined—could call upon the federal government for special favors or support, and so that man's religious conscience should be free) were cardinal points of the new national policy they fostered. "The Government of the United States," George Washington had written to the Jewish congregation of Newport during his first term as president, "gives to bigotry no sanction, to persecution no assistance."

Political differences with ancestral England had just been written in blood; but there is no reason to suppose that these men looked upon their fledgling country as an impartial melting pot for the merging of the various cultures of Europe, or as a new "nation of nations," or as anything but a society in which, with important political modifications, Anglo-Saxon speech and institutional forms would be standard. Indeed, their newly won victory for democracy and republicanism made them especially anxious that these still precarious fruits of revolution should not be threatened by a large influx of European peoples whose life experiences had accustomed them to the bonds of despotic monarchy. Thus, although they explicitly conceived of the new United States of America as a haven for those unfortunates of Europe who were persecuted and oppressed, they had characteristic reservations about the effects of too free a policy. "My opinion, with respect to immigration," Washington wrote to John Adams in 1794, "is that except of useful mechanics and some particular descriptions of men or professions, there is no need of encouragement, while the policy or advantage of its taking place in a body (I mean the settling of them in a body) may be much questioned; for, by so doing, they retain the language, habits and principles (good or bad) which they bring with them." Thomas Jefferson, whose views on race and attitudes towards slavery were notably liberal and advanced for his time, had similar doubts concerning the effects of mass immigration on American institutions, while conceding that immigrants, "if they come of themselves . . . are entitled to all the rights of citizenship."

The attitudes of Americans toward foreign immigration in the first three quarters of the nineteenth century may correctly be described as ambiguous. On the one hand, immigrants were much desired, so as to swell the population and importance of states and territories, to man the farms of expanding prairie settlement, to work the mines, build the railroads and canals, and take their place in expanding industry. This was a period in which no federal legislation of any consequence prevented the entry of aliens, and such state legislation as existed attempted to bar on an individual basis only those who were likely to become a burden on the community, such as convicts and paupers. On the other hand, the arrival in an overwhelmingly Protestant society of large numbers of poverty-stricken Irish Catholics, who settled in groups in the slums of Eastern cities, roused dormant fears of "Popery" and Rome. Another source of anxiety was the substantial influx of Germans, who made their way to the cities and farms of the mid-West and whose different language, separate communal life, and freer ideas on temperance and sabbath observance brought them into conflict with the Anglo-Saxon bearers of the Puritan and Evangelical traditions. Fear of foreign "radicals" and suspicion of the economic demands of the occasionally aroused working-men added fuel to the nativist fires. In their extreme form these fears resulted in the Native-American movement of the 1830s and 1840s and the "American" or "Know-Nothing" party of the 1850s, with their anti-Catholic campaigns and their demands for restrictive laws on naturalization procedures and for keeping the foreign-born out of political office. While these movements scored local political successes and their turbulences so rent the national social fabric that the patches are not yet entirely invisible, they failed to influence national legislative policy on immigration and immigrants; and their fulminations inevitably provoked the expected reactions from thoughtful observers.

The flood of newcomers to the westward expanding nation grew larger, reaching over one and two-thirds million between 1841 and 1850 and over two and one-half million in the decade before the Civil War. Throughout the entire period, quite apart from the excesses of the Know-Nothings, the predominant (though not exclusive) conception of what the ideal immigrant adjustment should be was probably summed up in a letter written in 1818 by John Quincy Adams, then Secretary of State, in answer to the inquiries of the Baron von Furstenwaerther. If not the earliest, it is certainly the most elegant version of the sentiment, "If they don't like it here, they can go back where they came from." Adams declared:

> They [immigrants to America] come to a life of independence, but to a life of labor—and, if they cannot accommodate themselves to the character; moral, political and physical, of this country with all its compensating balances of good and evil, the Atlantic is always open to them to return to the land of their nativity and their fathers. To one thing they must make up their minds, or they will be disappointed in every expectation of happiness as Americans. They must cast off the European skin, never to resume it. They must look forward to their posterity rather than backward to their ancestors; they must be sure that whatever their own feelings may be, those of their children will cling to the prejudices of this country.

The events that followed the Civil War created their own ambiguities in attitude toward the immigrant. A nation undergoing wholesale industrial expansion and not yet finished with the march of westward settlement could make good use of the never faltering waves of newcomers. But sporadic bursts of labor unrest, attributed to foreign radicals, the growth of Catholic institutions and the rise of Catholics to municipal political power, and the continuing association of immigrant settlement with urban slums revived familiar fears. The first federal selective law restricting immigration was passed in 1882, and Chinese immigration was cut off in the same year. The most significant development of all, barely recognized at first, was the change in the source of European migrants. Beginning in the 1880s, the countries of southern and eastern Europe began to be represented in substantial numbers for the first time, and in the next decade immigrants from these sources became numerically dominant. Now the notes of a new, or at least hitherto unemphasized, chord from the nativist lyre began to sound—the ugly chord, or discord, of racism. Previously vague and romantic notions of Anglo-Saxon peoplehood, combined with general ethnocentrism, rudimentary wisps of genetics, selected tidbits of evolutionary theory, and naive assumptions from an early and crude imported anthropology produced the doctrine that the English, Germans, and others of the "old immigration" constituted a superior race of tall, blonde, blue-eyed "Nordics" or "Aryans," whereas the peoples of eastern and southern Europe made up the darker Alpines or Mediterraneans—both "inferior" breeds whose presence in America threatened, either by intermixture or supplementation, the traditional American stock and culture. The obvious corollary to this doctrine was to exclude the allegedly inferior breeds; but if the new type of immigrant could not be excluded, then everything must be done to instill Anglo-Saxon virtues in these benighted creatures. Thus, one educator writing in 1909 could state:

> These southern and eastern Europeans are of a very different type from the north Europeans who preceded them. Illiterate, docile, lacking in self-reliance and initiative, and not possessing the Anglo-Teutonic conceptions of law, order, and government, their coming has served to dilute tremendously our national stock, and to corrupt our civic life. . . . Everywhere these people tend to settle in groups or settlements, and to set up here their national manners, customs, and observances. Our task is to break up these groups or settlements, to assimilate and amalgamate these people as a part of our American race, and to implant in their children, so far as can be done, the Anglo-Saxon conception of righteousness, law and order, and popular government, and to awaken in them a reverence for our democratic institutions and for those things in our national life which we as a people hold to be of abiding worth.

Anglo-conformity received its fullest expression in the so-called Americanization movement which gripped the nation during World War I. While "Americanization" in its various stages had more than one emphasis, it was essentially a consciously articulated movement to strip the immigrant of his native culture and attachments and make him over into an American along Anglo-Saxon lines—all this to be accomplished with great rapidity. To use an image of later day, it was an attempt at "pressure-cooking assimilation." It had prewar antecedents, but it was during the height of the world conflict that federal agencies, state governments, municipalities, and a host of private organizations joined in the effort to persuade the immigrant to learn English, take out naturalization papers, buy war bonds, forget his former origins and culture, and give himself over to patriotic hysteria.

After the war and the "Red scare" which followed, the excesses of the Americanization movement subsided. In its place, however, came the restriction of immigration through federal law. Foiled at first by presidential vetoes, and later by the failure of the 1917 literacy test to halt the immigrant tide, the proponents of restriction finally put through in the early 1920s a series of acts culminating in the well-known national-origins formula for immigrant quotas which went into effect in 1929. Whatever the merits of a quantitative limit on the number of immigrants to be admitted to the United States, the provisions of the formula, which discriminated sharply against the countries of southern and eastern Europe, in effect institutionalized the assumptions of the rightful dominance of Anglo-Saxon patterns in the land. Reaffirmed with only slight modifications in the McCarran-Walter Act of 1952, these laws, then, stand as a legal monument to the creed of Anglo-conformity and a telling reminder that this ideological system still has numerous and powerful adherents on the American scene.

THE MELTING POT

While Anglo-conformity in various guises has probably been the most prevalent ideology of assimilation in the American historical experience, a competing viewpoint with more generous and idealistic overtones has had its adherents and exponents from the eighteenth century onward. Conditions in the virgin continent, it was clear, were modifying the institutions which the English colonists brought with them from the mother country. Arrivals from non-English homelands such as Germany, Sweden, and France were similarly exposed to this fresh environment. Was it not possible, then, to think of the evolving American society not as a slightly modified England but rather as a totally new blend, culturally and biologically, in which the stocks and folkways of Europe, figuratively speaking, were indiscriminately mixed in the political pot of the emerging nation and fused by the fires of American influence and interaction into a distinctly new type?

Such, at any rate, was the conception of the new society which motivated that eighteenth-century French-born writer and agriculturalist, J. Hector St. John Crèvecoeur, who, after many years of American residence, published his reflections and observations in *Letters from an American Farmer*. Who, he asks, is the American?

> He is either an European, or the descendant of an European, hence that strange mixture of blood, which you will find in no other country. I could point out to you a family whose grandfather was an Englishman, whose wife was Dutch, whose son married a French woman, and whose present four sons have now four wives of different nations. *He* is an American, who leaving behind him all his ancient prejudices and manners, receives new ones from the new mode of life he has embraced, the new government he obeys, and the new rank he holds. He becomes an American by being received in the broad lap of our great *Alma Mater*. Here individuals of all nations are melted into a new race of men, whose labours and posterity will one day cause great changes in the world.

Some observers have interpreted the open-door policy on immigration of the first three-quarters of the nineteenth century as reflecting an underlying faith in the effectiveness of the American melting pot, in the belief "that all could be absorbed and that all could contribute to an emerging national character." No doubt many who observed with dismay the nativist agitation of the times felt as did Ralph Waldo Emerson that such conformity-demanding and immigrant-hating forces represented a perversion of the best American ideals. In 1845, Emerson wrote in his Journal:

> I hate the narrowness of the Native American Party. It is the dog in the manger. It is precisely opposite to all the dictates of love and magnanimity; and therefore, of course, opposite to true wisdom. . . . Man is the most composite of all creatures. . . . Well, as in the old burning of the Temple at Corinth, by the melting and intermixture of silver and gold and other metals a new compound more precious than any, called Corinthian brass, was formed; so in this continent—asylum of all the nations,—the energy of Irish, Germans, Swedes, Poles, and Cossacks, and all the European tribes,—of the Africans, and of the Polynesians,—will construct a new race, a new religion, a new state, a new literature, which will be as vigorous as the new Europe which came out of the smelting-pot of the Dark Ages, or that which earlier emerged from the Pelasgic and Etruscan barbarism. *La Nature aime les croisements.*

Eventually, the melting-pot hypothesis found its way into historical scholarship and interpretation. While many American historians of the late nineteenth century, some fresh from graduate study at German universities, tended to adopt the view that American institutions derived in essence from Anglo-Saxon (and ultimately Teutonic) sources, others were not so sure. One of these was Frederick Jackson Turner, a young historian from Wisconsin, not long emerged from his graduate training at Johns Hopkins. Turner presented a paper to the American Historical Association, meeting in Chicago in 1893. Called "The Significance of the Frontier in American History," this paper proved to be one of the most influential essays in the history of American scholarship, and its point of view, supported by Turner's subsequent writings and his teaching, pervaded the field of American historical interpretation for at least a generation. Turner's thesis was that the dominant influence in the shaping of American institutions and American democracy was not this nation's European heritage in any of its forms, nor the forces emanating from the eastern seaboard cities, but rather the experiences created by a moving and variegated western frontier. Among the many effects attributed to the frontier environment and the challenges it presented was that it acted as a solvent for the national heritages and the separatist tendencies of the many nationality groups which had joined the trek westward, including the Germans and Scotch-Irish of the eighteenth century and the Scandinavians and Germans of the nineteenth. "The frontier," asserted Turner, "promoted the formation of a composite nationality for the American people. . . . In the crucible of the frontier the immigrants were Americanized, liberated, and fused into a mixed race, English in neither nationality nor characteristics. The process has gone on from the early days to our own." And later, in an essay on the role of the Mississippi Valley, he refers to "the tide of foreign immigration which has risen so steadily that it has made a composite American people whose amalgamation is destined to produce a new national stock."

Thus far, the proponents of the melting-pot idea had dealt largely with the diversity produced by the sizeable immigration from the countries of northern and western Europe alone—the "old immigration," consisting of peoples with cultures and physical appearance not greatly different from those of the Anglo-Saxon stock. Emerson, it is true, had impartially included Africans, Polynesians, and Cossacks in his conception of the mixture; but it was only in the last two decades of the nineteenth century that a large-scale influx of peoples from the countries of southern and eastern Europe imperatively posed the question of whether these uprooted newcomers who were crowding into the large cities of the nation and the industrial sector of the economy could also be successfully "melted." Would the "urban melting pot" work as well as the "frontier melting pot" of an essentially rural society was alleged to have done?

It remained for an English-Jewish writer with strong social convictions, moved by his observation of the role of the United States as a haven for the poor and oppressed to Europe, to give utterance to the broader view of the American melting pot in a way which attracted public attention. In 1908, Israel Zangwill's drama, *The Melting Pot,* was produced in this country and became a popular success. It is a play dominated by the dream of its protagonist, a young Russian-Jewish immigrant to America, a composer, whose goal is the completion of a vast "American" symphony which will express his deeply felt conception of his adopted country as a divinely appointed crucible in which all the ethnic divisions of mankind will divest themselves of their ancient animosities and differences and become fused into one group, signifying the brotherhood of man. In the process he falls in love with a beautiful and cultured Gentile girl. The play ends with the performance of the symphony and, after numerous vicissitudes and traditional family opposition from both sides, with the approaching marriage of David Quixano and his beloved. During the course of these developments, David, in the rhetoric of the time, delivers himself of such sentiments as these:

> America is God's crucible, the great Melting Pot where all the races of Europe are melting and re-forming! Here you stand, good folk, think I, when I see them at Ellis Island, here you stand in your fifty groups, with your fifty languages and histories, and your fifty blood hatreds and rivalries. But you won't belong like that, brothers, for these are the fires of God you've come to—these are the fires of God. A fig for your feuds and vendettas! Germans and Frenchmen, Irishmen and Englishmen, Jews and Russians—into the Crucible with you all! God is making the American.

Here we have a conception of a melting pot which admits of no exceptions or qualifications with regard to the ethnic stocks which will fuse in the great crucible. Englishmen, Germans, Frenchmen, Slavs, Greeks, Syrians, Jews, Gentiles, even the black and yellow races, were specifically mentioned in Zangwill's rhapsodic enumeration. And this pot patently was to boil in the great cities of America.

Thus around the turn of the century the melting-pot idea became embedded in the ideals of the age as one response to the immigrant receiving experience of the nation. Soon to be challenged by a new philosophy of group adjustment (to be discussed below) and always competing with the more pervasive adherence to Anglo-conformity, the melting-pot image, however, continued to draw a portion of the attention consciously directed toward this aspect of the American scene in the first half of the twentieth century. In the mid-1940s a sociologist who had carried out an investigation of intermarriage trends in New Haven, Connecticut, described a revised conception of the melting process in that city and suggested a basic modification of the theory of that process. In New Haven, Ruby Jo Reeves Kennedy reported from a study of intermarriages from 1870 to 1940 that there was a distinct tendency for the British-Americans, Germans, and Scandinavians to marry among themselves—that is, within a Protestant "pool"; for the Irish, Italians, and Poles to marry among themselves—a Catholic "pool"; and for the Jews to marry other Jews. In other words, intermarriage was taking place across lines of nationality background, but there was a strong tendency for it to stay confined within one or the other of the three major religious groups, Protestants, Catholics, and Jews. Thus, declared Mrs. Kennedy, the picture in New Haven resembled a "triple melting pot" based on religious divisions, rather than a "single melting pot." Her study indicated, she stated, that "while strict endogamy is loosening, religious endogamy is persisting and the future cleavages will be along religious lines rather than along nationality lines as in the past. If this is the case, then the traditional 'single-melting-pot' idea must be abandoned, and a new conception, which we term the 'triple-melting-pot' theory of American assimilation, will take its place as the true expression of what is happening to the various nationality groups in the United States." The triple-melting-pot thesis was later taken up by the theologian Will Herberg and formed an important sociological frame of reference for his analysis of religious trends in American society, *Protestant-Catholic-Jew*. But the triple-melting-pot hypothesis patently takes us into the realm of a society pluralistically conceived. We turn now to the rise of an ideology which attempts to justify such a conception.

CULTURAL PLURALISM

Probably all the non-English immigrants who came to American shores in any significant numbers from colonial times onward—settling either in the forbidding wilderness, the lonely prairie, or in some accessible urban slum—created ethnic enclaves and looked forward to the preservation of at least some of their native cultural patterns. Such a development, natural as breathing, was supported by the later accretion of friends, relatives, and countrymen seeking out oases of familiarity in a strange land, by the desire of the settlers to rebuild (necessarily in miniature) a society in which they could communicate in the familiar tongue and maintain familiar institutions, and, finally, by the necessity to band together for mutual aid and mutual protection against the uncertainties of a strange and frequently hostile environment. This was as true of the "old" immigrants as of the "new." In fact, some of the liberal intellectuals who fled to America from an inhospitable political climate in Germany in the 1830s, 1840s, and 1850s looked forward to the creation of an all-German state within the union, or, even more hopefully, to the eventual formation of a separate German nation, as soon as the expected dissolution of the union under the impact of the slavery controversy should have taken place. Oscar Handlin, writing of the sons of Erin in mid-nineteenth-century Boston, recent refugees from famine and economic degradation in their homeland, points out: "Unable to participate in the normal associational affairs of the community, the Irish felt obliged to erect a society within a society, to act together in their own way. In every contact therefore the group, acting apart from other sections of the community, became intensely aware of its peculiar and exclusive identity." Thus cultural pluralism was a fact in American society before it became a theory—a theory with explicit relevance for the nation as a whole, and articulated and discussed in the English-speaking circles of American intellectual life.

Eventually, the cultural enclaves of the Germans (and the later arriving Scandinavians) were to decline in scope and significance as succeeding generations of their native-born attended public schools, left the farms and villages to strike out as individuals for the Americanizing city, and generally became subject to the influences of a standardizing industrial civilization. The German-American community, too, was struck a powerful blow by the accumulated passions generated by World War I—a blow from which it never fully recovered. The Irish were to be the dominant and pervasive element in the gradual emergence of a pan-Catholic group in America, but these developments would reveal themselves only in the twentieth century. In the meantime, in the last two decades of the nineteenth, the influx of immigrants from southern and eastern Europe had begun. These groups were all the more sociologically visible because the closing of the frontier, the occupational demands of an expanding industrial economy, and their own poverty made it inevitable that they would remain in the urban areas of the nation. In the swirling fires of controversy and the steadier flame of experience created by these new events, the ideology of cultural pluralism as a philosophy for the nation was forged.

The first manifestations of an ideological counterattack against draconic Americanization came not from the beleaguered newcomers (who were, after all, more concerned with survival than with theories of adjustment), but from those idealistic members of the middle class who, in the decade or so before the turn of the century, had followed the example of their English predecessors and "settled" in the slums to "learn to sup sorrow with the poor." Immediately, these workers in the "settlement houses" were forced to come to grips with the realities of immigrant life and adjustment. Not all reacted in the same way, but on the whole the settlements developed an approach to the immigrant which was sympathetic to his native cultural heritage and to his newly created ethnic institutions. For one thing, their workers, necessarily in intimate contact with the lives of these often pathetic and bewildered newcomers and their daily problems, could see how unfortunate were the effects of those forces which impelled rapid Americanization in their impact on the immigrants' children, who not infrequently became alienated from their parents and the restraining influence of family authority. Were not their parents ignorant and uneducated "Hunkies," "Sheenies," or "Dagoes,"as that limited portion of the American environment in which they moved defined the matter? Ethnic "self-hatred" with its debilitating psychological consequences, family disorganization, and juvenile delinquency, were not unusual results of this state of affairs. Furthermore, the immigrants themselves were adversely affected by the incessant attacks on their culture, their language, their institutions, their very conception of themselves. How were they to maintain their self-respect when all that they knew, felt, and dreamed, beyond their sheer capacity for manual labor—in other words, all that they *were*—was despised or scoffed at in America? And—unkindest cut of all—their own children had begun to adopt the contemptuous attitude of the "Americans." Jane Addams relates in a moving chapter of her *Twenty Years at Hull House* how, after coming to have some conception of the extent and depth of these problems, she created at the settlement a "Labor Museum," in which the immigrant women of the various nationalities crowded together in the slums of Chicago could illustrate their native methods of spinning and weaving, and in which the relation of these earlier techniques to contemporary factory methods could be graphically shown. For the first time these peasant women were made to feel by some part of their American environment that they possessed valuable and interesting skills—that they too had something to offer—and for the first time, the daughters of these women who, after a long day's work at their dank "needletrade" sweatshops, came to Hull House to observe, began to appreciate the fact that their mothers, too, had a "culture," that this culture possessed its own merit, and that it was related to their own contemporary lives. How aptly Jane Addams concludes her chapter with the hope that "our American citizenship might be built without disturbing these foundations which were laid of old time."

This appreciative view of the immigrant's cultural heritage and of its distinctive usefulness both to himself and his adopted country received additional sustenance from another source: those intellectual currents of the day which, however, overborne by their currently more powerful opposites, emphasized liberalism, internationalism, and tolerance. From time to time, an occasional educator or publicist protested the demands of the "Americanizers," arguing that the immigrant, too, had an ancient and honorable culture, and that this culture had much to offer an America whose character and destiny were still in the process of formation, an America which must serve as an example of the harmonious cooperation of various heritages to a world inflamed by nationalism and war. In 1916 John Dewey, Norman Hapgood, and the young literary critic Randolph Bourne, published articles or addresses elaborating various aspects of this theme.

The classic statement of the cultural pluralist position, however, had been made over a year before. Early in 1915 there appeared in the pages of *The Nation* two articles under the title "Democracy *versus* the Melting-Pot." Their author was Horace Kallen, a Harvard-educated philosopher with a concern for the application of philosophy to societal affairs, and, as an American Jew, himself derivative of an ethnic background which was subject to the contemporary pressures for dissolution implicit in the "Americanization," or Anglo-conformity, and the melting-pot theories. In these articles Kallen vigorously rejected the usefulness of these theories as models of what was actually transpiring in American life or as ideals for the future. Rather he was impressed by the way in which the various ethnic groups in America were coincident with particular areas and regions, and with the tendency for each group to preserve its own language, religion, communal institutions, and ancestral culture. All the while, he pointed out, the immigrant has been learning to speak English as the language of general communication, and has participated in the over-all economic and political life of the nation. These developments in which "the United States are in the process of becoming a federal state not merely as a union of geographical and administrative unities, but also as a cooperation of cultural diversities, as a federation or commonwealth of national culture," the author argued, far from constituting a violation of historic American political principles, as the "Americanizers" claimed, actually represented the inevitable consequences of democratic ideals, since individuals are implicated in groups, and since democracy for the individual must by extension also mean democracy for his group.

The processes just described, however, as Kallen develops his argument, are far from having been thoroughly realized. They are menaced by "Americanization" programs, assumptions of Anglo-Saxon superiority, and misguided attempts to promote "racial" amalgamation. Thus America stands at a kind of cultural crossroads. It can attempt to impose by force an artificial, Anglo-Saxon oriented uniformity on its peoples, or it

can consciously allow and encourage its ethnic groups to develop democratically, each emphasizing its particular cultural heritage. If the latter
course is followed, as Kallen puts it at the close of his essay, then,

> The outlines of a possible great and truly democratic commonwealth be-
> come discernible. Its form would be that of the federal republic; its sub-
> stance a democracy of nationalities, cooperating voluntarily and autono-
> mously through common institutions in the enterprise of self-realization
> through the perfection of men according to their kind. The common lan-
> guage of the commonwealth, the language of its great tradition, would be
> English, but each nationality would have for its emotional and involuntary
> life its own peculiar dialect or speech, its own individual and inevitable es-
> thetic and intellectual forms. The political and economic life of the com-
> monwealth is a single unit and serves as the foundation and background
> for the realization of the distinctive individuality of each *nation* that com-
> poses it and of the pooling of these in a harmony above them all. Thus
> "American civilization" may come to mean the perfection of the coopera-
> tive harmonies of "European civilization"—the waste, the squalor and the
> distress of Europe being eliminated—a multiplicity in a unity, an orches-
> tration of mankind.

Within the next decade Kallen published more essays dealing with
the theme of American multiple-group life, later collected in a volume. In
the introductory note to this book he used for the first time the term "cultural pluralism" to refer to his position. These essays reflect both his increasingly sharp rejection of the onslaughts on the immigrant and his culture which the coming of World War I and its attendant fears, the "Red
scare," the projection of themes of racial superiority, the continued exploitation of the newcomers, and the rise of the Ku Klux Klan all served
to increase in intensity, and also his emphasis on cultural pluralism as the
democratic antidote to these ills. He has since published other essays elaborating or annotating the theme of cultural pluralism. Thus, for at least
forty-five years, most of them spent teaching at the New School for Social
Research, Kallen has been acknowledged as the originator and leading
philosophical exponent of the idea of cultural pluralism.

In the late 1930s and early 1940s the late Louis Adamic, the Yugoslav
immigrant who had become an American writer, took up the theme of
America's multicultural heritage and the role of these groups in forging
the country's national character. Borrowing Walt Whitman's phrase, he
described America as "a nation of nations," and while his ultimate goal
was closer to the melting-pot idea than to cultural pluralism, he saw the
immediate task as that of making America conscious of what it owed to
all its ethnic groups, not just to the Anglo-Saxons. The children and grand-

children of immigrants of non-English origins, he was convinced, must be taught to be proud of the cultural heritage of their ancestral ethnic group and of its role in building the American nation; otherwise, they would not lose their sense of ethnic inferiority and the feeling of rootlessness he claimed to find in them.

Thus in the twentieth century, particularly since World War II, "cultural pluralism" has become a concept which has worked its way into the vocabulary and imagery of specialists in intergroup relations and leaders of ethnic communal groups. In view of this new pluralistic emphasis, some writers now prefer to speak of the "integration" of immigrants rather than of the "assimilation." However, with a few exceptions, no close analytical attention has been given either by social scientists or practitioners of intergroup relations to the meaning of cultural pluralism, its nature and relevance for a modern industrialized society, and its implications for problems of prejudice and discrimination—a point to which we referred at the outset of this discussion.

CONCLUSIONS

In the remaining pages I can make only a few analytical comments which I shall apply in context to the American scene, historical and current. My view of the American situation will not be documented here, but may be considered as a series of hypotheses in which I shall attempt to outline the American assimilation process.

First of all, it must be realized that "assimilation" is a blanket term which in reality covers a multitude of subprocesses. The most crucial distinction is one often ignored—the distinction between what I have elsewhere called "behavioral assimilation" and "structural assimilation." The first refers to the absorption of the cultural behavior patterns of the "host" society. (At the same time, there is frequently some modification of the cultural patterns of the immigrant-receiving country, as well.) There is a special term for this process of cultural modification or "behavioral assimilation"—namely, "acculturation." "Structural assimilation," on the other hand, refers to the entrance of the immigrants and their descendants into the social cliques, organizations, institutional activities, and general civic life of the receiving society. If this process takes place on a large enough scale, then a high frequency of intermarriage must result. A further distinction must be made between, on the one hand, those activities of the general civic life which involving earning a living, carrying out political responsibilities, and engaging in the instrumental affairs of the larger community, and, on the other hand, activities which create personal friendship patterns, frequent home intervisiting, communal worship, and communal recreation. The first type usually develops so-called "secondary relationships," which tend to be relatively impersonal and segmental; the latter type leads to "primary relationships," which are warm, intimate, and personal.

With these various distinctions in mind, we may then proceed.

Built on the base of the original immigrant "colony" but frequently extending into the life of successive generations, the characteristic ethnic group experience is this: within the ethnic group there develops a network of organizations and informal social relationships which permits and encourages the members of the ethnic group to remain within the confines of the group for all of their primary relationships and some of their secondary relationships throughout all the stages of the life cycle. From the cradle in the sectarian hospital to the child's play group, the social clique in high school, the fraternity and religious center in college, the dating group within which he searches for a spouse, the marriage partner, the neighborhood of his residence, the church affiliation and the church clubs, the men's and the women's social and service organizations, the adult clique of "marrieds," the vacation resort, and then, as the age cycle nears completion, the rest home for the elderly and, finally, the sectarian cemetery—in all these activities and relationships which are close to the core of personality and selfhood—the member of the ethnic group may if he wishes follow a path which never takes him across the boundaries of his ethnic structural network.

The picture is made more complex by the existence of social class divisions which cut across ethnic group lines just as they do those of the white Protestant population in America. As each ethnic group which has been here for the requisite time has developed second, third, or in some cases, succeeding generations, it has produced a college-educated group which composes an upper middle class (and sometimes upper class, as well) segment of the larger groups. Such class divisions tend to restrict primary group relations even further, for although the ethnic-group member feels a general sense of identification with all the bearers of his ethnic heritage, he feels comfortable in intimate social relations only with those who also share his own class background or attainment.

In short, my point is that, while *behavioral assimilation* or acculturation has taken place in America to a considerable degree, *structural assimilation*, with some important exceptions, has not been extensive. The exceptions are of two types. The first brings us back to the "triple-melting-pot" thesis of Ruby Jo Reeves Kennedy and Will Herberg. The "nationality" ethnic groups have tended to merge within each of the three major religious groups. This has been particularly true of the Protestant and Jewish communities. Those descendants of the "old" immigration of the nineteenth century, who were Protestant (many of the Germans and all the Scandinavians), have in considerable part gradually merged into the white Protestant "subsociety." Jews of Sephardic, German, and Eastern-European origins have similarly tended to come together in their communal life. The process of absorbing the various Catholic nationalities, such as the Italians, Poles, and French Canadians, into an American Catholic community hitherto dominated by the Irish has begun, although I do not believe that it is by any means close to completion. Racial and quasiracial groups such as the Negroes, Indians, Mexican-Americans, and Puerto Ricans still retain their separate sociological structures. The outcome of all this in contemporary American life is thus pluralism—but it is more than "triple" and it is more accurately described as *structural pluralism* than as cultural pluralism, although some of the latter also remains.

My second exception refers to the social structures which implicate intellectuals. There is no space to develop the issue here, but I would argue that there is a social world or subsociety of the intellectuals in America in which true structural intermixture among persons of various ethnic backgrounds, including the religious, has markedly taken place.

My final point deals with the reasons for these developments. If structural assimilation has been retarded in America by religious and racial lines, we must ask why. The answer lies in the attitudes of both the majority and the minority groups and in the way these attitudes have interacted. A saying of the current day is, "It takes two to tango." To apply the analogy, there is no good reason to believe that white Protestant America has ever extended a firm and cordial invitation to its minorities to dance. Furthermore, the attitudes of the minority-group members themselves on the matter have been divided and ambiguous. Particularly for the minority religious groups, there is a certain logic in ethnic communality, since there is a commitment to the perpetuation of the religious ideology and since structural intermixture leads to intermarriage and the possible loss to the group of the intermarried family. Let us, then, examine the situation serially for various types of minorities.

With regard to the immigrant, in his characteristic numbers and socio-economic background, structural assimilation was out of the question. He did not want it, and he had a positive need for the comfort of his own communal institutions. The native American, moreover, whatever the implications of his public pronouncements, had no intention of opening up his primary group life to entrance by these hordes of alien newcomers. The situation was a functionally complementary standoff.

The second generation found a much more complex situation. Many believed they heard the siren call of welcome to the social cliques, clubs, and institutions of white Protestant America. After all, it was simply a matter of learning American ways, was it not? Had they not grown up as Americans, and were they not culturally different from their parents, the "greenhorns"? Or perhaps an especially eager one reasoned (like the Jewish protagonist of Myron Kaufmann's novel, *Remember Me To God*, aspiring to membership in the prestigious club system of Harvard undergraduate social life), "If only I can go the last few steps in Ivy League manners and behavior, they will surely recognize that I am one of them and take me in." But, alas, Brooks Brothers suit notwithstanding, the doors of the fraternity house, the city men's club, and the country club were slammed in the face of the immigrant's offspring. That invitation was not really there in the first place; or, to the extent it was, in Joshua Fishman's phrase, it was a "'look me over but don't touch me' invitation to the American minority group child." And so the rebuffed one returned to the homelier but dependable comfort of the communal institutions of his ancestral group. There he found his fellows of the same generation who had never stirred from the home fires. Some of these had been too timid to stray; others were ethnic ideologists committed to the group's survival; still others had never really believed in the authenticity of the siren call or were simply too passive to do more than go along the familiar way. All could now join in the task that was well within the realm of the sociologically possible— the build-up of social institutions and organizations within the ethnic enclave, manned increasingly by members of the second generation and suitably separated by social class.

Those who had for a time ventured out gingerly or confidently, as the case might be, had been lured by the vision of an "American" social structure that was somehow larger than all subgroups and was ethnically neutral. Were they, too, not Americans? But they found to their dismay that at the primary group level a neutral American social structure was a mirage. What at a distance seemed to be a quasi-public edifice flying only the all-inclusive flag of American nationality turned out on closer inspection to be the clubhouse of a particular ethnic group—the white Anglo-Saxon Protestants, its operation shot through with the premises and expectations of its parental ethnicity. In these terms, the desirability of whatever invitation was grudgingly extended to those of other ethnic backgrounds could only become a considerably attenuated one.

With the racial minorities, there was not even the pretense of an invitation. Negroes, to take the most salient example, have for the most part been determinedly barred from the cliques, social clubs, and churches of white America. Consequently, with due allowance for internal class differences, they have constructed their own network of organizations and institutions, their own "social world." There are now many vested interests served by the preservation of this separate communal life, and doubt-less many Negroes are psychologically comfortable in it, even though at the same time they keenly desire that discrimination in such areas as employment, education, housing, and public accommodations be eliminated. However, the ideological attachment of Negroes to their communal separation is not conspicuous. Their sense of identification with ancestral African national cultures is virtually nonexistent, although Pan-Africanism engages the interest of some intellectuals and although "black nationalist" and "black racist" fringe groups have recently made an appearance at the other end of the communal spectrum. As for their religion, they are either Protestant or Catholic (overwhelmingly the former). Thus, there are no "logical" ideological reasons for their separate communality; dual social structures are created solely by the dynamics of prejudice and discrimination, rather than being reinforced by the ideological commitments of the minority itself.

Structural assimilation, then, has turned out to be the rock on which the ships of Anglo-conformity and the melting pot have foundered. To understand that behavioral assimilation (or acculturation) without massive structural intermingling in primary relationships has been the dominant motif in the American experience of creating and developing a nation out of diverse peoples is to comprehend the most essential sociological fact of that experience. It is against the background of "structural pluralism" that strategies of strengthening intergroup harmony, reducing ethnic discrimination and prejudice, and maintaining the rights of both those who stay within and those who venture beyond their ethnic boundaries must be thoughtfully devised.

QUESTIONS TO CONSIDER

1. What are the three ideologies explaining how the white Anglo-Saxon Protestant (WASP) American society has absorbed immigrants?
2. What does Gordon suggest as the most prevalent ideology of assimilation goals in America throughout history? Define it.
3. What happened in the 1920s to institutionalize the assumptions of Anglo-conformity and the dominance of Anglo-Saxon patterns in the United States?
4. Explain the distinction between "behavioral assimilation" and "structural assimilation."
5. Distinguish between the two levels of structural assimilation.
6. What, then, has been the obstacle to Anglo-conformity and the melting pot?

9

Depression*

William Manchester

William Manchester (1922–   ) brought history alive for countless readers over the past generation. His best-selling histories include the controversial *The Death of a President* (1967), the colorful *American Caesar: Douglas MacArthur, 1880–1964* (1978), and the monumental narrative history of America from 1932 to 1972, *The Glory and the Dream* (1974), from which this selection was excerpted.

The Great Depression permeated all areas of American society in the 1930s and became the terrible nightmare underlying every thought of the people in that grim decade. The human mind possesses a remarkable talent, perhaps necessary for mental health, for filtering out the bad experiences of the past and remembering only the good. So it was with the astounding nostalgia craze of the 1970s—young Americans looked back on the Depression and saw primarily the positive things about it: jobs conscientiously done, neighbor helping neighbor, a nation united in its attempts to defeat the economic catastrophe. Despite their protective filters, however, those who had lived through it regarded such nostalgia as beyond belief. The searing misery of the thirties had scarred their generation, molding its attitudes toward employment, credit, saving, and security in ways that made them incomprehensible to those Americans who grew up in the virtually nonstop prosperity after World War II. In this moving selection, Manchester gives younger readers a chance to understand how the Depression shaped the character of a generation.

In June 1932, Ivy League seniors joined 21,974 other alumni hunting for jobs. By then New York department stores were requiring bachelor degrees for all elevator operators, and that was the best many of them could do, but twenty-year-old Sylvia Field Porter, Hunter '32, was an exception. She switched her major from English to economics because of what she later called "an overwhelming curiosity to know why everything was crashing around me and why people were losing their jobs" and talked her way into an investment counsel firm. At the same time she began a systematic study of the financial world, with the thought that one day she might write a column about it. She then discovered that she was in the middle of a crisis without historical precedent.

Ever since the fiasco of England's South Sea Company in 1720, the phrase "South Sea bubble" had been used to describe a doomed business venture. The bubble had certainly burst; South Sea stock had plunged to 13.5 percent of its highest quotation. Yet it subsequently rallied, and the firm continued to do business for eighty years. By the time of Miss Porter's commencement, however, United States Steel and General Motors had dropped to 8 percent of their pre-Crash prices. Overall, stocks listed on the Big Board were worth 11 percent of their 1929 value. Investors had lost 74 billion dollars, three times the cost of the World War. More than 5,000 American banks had failed—in Iowa City, just across the county line from Hoover's native West Branch, all five banks were shut—and 86,000 businesses had closed their doors. The country's Gross National Product had fallen from 104 billion dollars to 41 billion (in 1973 it would be 2,177 billion). In 1932, 273,000 families were evicted from their homes, and the average weekly wage of those who had jobs was $16.21.

Some enterprises flourished. The contraceptive business was netting a quarter-billion dollars a year, a fact which the youth of that day conveniently forgot after they had become parents. Over half the population was going to the movies once a week (admission was a quarter for adults, a dime for children), and each year saw an increase in the number of cigarette smokers, none of them aware that the habit might be harmful. Kelvinator refrigerators and Atwater Kent radios were moving briskly. Miniature golf courses and circulation libraries were booming. Alfred C. Fuller was doing very nicely with his corps of door-to-door brush salesmen; in the grim month of August 1932 his sales leaped from $15,000 to

$50,000 and grew thereafter at the rate of a million dollars a year. A prodigy named J. Paul Getty was quietly picking up cheap petroleum wells; that February he gained control of 520,000 of the Pacific Oil Corporation's one million shares. Here and there a venture was lucky. In Quincy, Massachusetts, the owner of a curious restaurant with a bright orange roof and pseudo-Colonial architecture was almost bankrupt when a stock company opened across the street. Its first play was Eugene O'Neill's nine-act *Strange Interlude*. Every evening there was an 8:30 intermission for supper, and the restauranteur, Howard Johnson, survived.

But these were exceptions. U.S. Steel, the key to heavy industry, was operating at 19.1 percent of capacity. The American Locomotive Company didn't need much steel. During the 1920s it had sold an average of 600 locomotives a year; in 1932 it sold one. Nor was the automotive industry the big steel customer it had been. Month by month its fine names were vanishing: the Stutz Motor Company, the Auburn, the Cord, and Edward Peerless, the Pierce Arrow, the Duesenberg, the Franklin, the Durant, the Locomobile. One rash man decided to challenge Ford with another low-priced car. He called it the Rockne, lost 21 million dollars, and killed himself. In January an inventive bacteriologist named Arthur G. Sherman had become the sensation of the Detroit Auto Show by exhibiting the first crude, hand-carpentered, wooden trailer. In 1932 he sold just eighty of them. Air transport nose-dived. Airliners then had twelve seats, of which, the Department of Commerce reported, an average of seven were flying empty. And with the exception of the new talkies, most entertainers were foundering. In four years the jazz musician Eddie Condon landed four recording sessions; the phonograph recording industry had dwindled from 50 million dollars a year to a quarter-million. Sally Rand was making a precarious living with her celebrated fans; to a reporter who asked why she did it, she replied, "I never made any money till I took off my pants."

Because poverty was considered shameful, people tried to conceal destitution from neighbors, often with considerable success. One could never be sure about the family across the street. The smartly dressed young lawyer who always left home at the same time each morning may have been off to sell cheap neckties, magazines, vacuum cleaners, pressure cookers, or Two-in-One shoe polish door-to-door in a remote neighborhood. He may have changed his clothes and gone to another part of the city to beg. Or he may have been one of the millions who looked for work day after day, year after year, watching his children grow thinner and fighting despair in the night. There were certain skills developed by men who spent their days in the streets. You learned to pay for a nickel cup of coffee, to ask for another cup of hot water free, and, by mixing the hot water with the ketchup on the counter, to make a kind of tomato soup. In winter you stuffed newspapers under your shirt to ward off the cold; if you knew you would be standing for hours outside an employment office, you wrapped burlap bags around your legs and tied them in place. Shoes were a special problem. Pasteboards could be used for inner soles, and some favored cotton in the heels to absorb the pounding of the concrete. But if a shoe was really gone, nothing worked. The pavement destroyed the cardboard and then the patch of sock next to it, snow leaked in and accumulated around your toes, and shoe nails stabbed your heels until you learned to walk with a peculiar gait.

It was remarkable how ingenious an impoverished, thrift-minded family could be. Men resharpened and reused old razor blades, rolled their own cigarettes or smoked Wings (ten cents a pack), and used twenty-five-watt light bulbs to save electricity. Children returned pop bottles for two cents or stood in line for day-old bread at the bakery. Women cut sheets lengthwise and resewed them to equalize wear, retailored their clothes for their daughters, and kept up a brave front with the wife next door—who may have been doing the same thing on the same meager budget. Families sorted Christmas cards so they could be sent to different friends next year. Sometimes a man would disappear for weeks. All the neighborhood knew was that he had gone on a "business trip." It was a considerate husband who withheld the details of such trips from his wife, for they were often more terrible than anything she could imagine.

He was, of course, looking for work. The legends of job hunting had become folklore by 1932, and some of the unbelievable stories were true. Men *did* wait all night outside Detroit employment offices so they would be first in line next morning. An Arkansas man *did* walk nine hundred miles looking for work. People *did* buy jobs. In Manhattan a Sixth Avenue employment agency *did* have five thousand applicants for three hundred jobs. It is a matter of record that a labor subcommittee of the 72nd Congress heard testimony about men setting forest fires in the state of Washington so they would be hired to put them out. *Business Week* verified the fact that a great many people who no longer loved America either left it or attempted to. Throughout the early Thirties the country's emigration exceeded its immigration. Amtorg, the Russian trading agency in New York, was getting 350 applications a day from Americans who wanted to settle in Russia. On one memorable occasion Amtorg advertised for six thousand skilled workers and a hundred thousand showed up, including plumbers, painters, mechanics, cooks, engineers, carpenters, electricians, salesmen, printers, chemists, shoemakers, librarians, teachers, dentists, a cleaner and dyer, an aviator, and an undertaker.

New York drew countless job seekers from surrounding states

though the city had a million jobless men of its own. A few strangers joined Manhattan's seven thousand nickel shoeshine "boys" or found furtive roles in the bootleg coal racket—10 percent of the city's coal was being sneaked in by unemployed Pennsylvania miners—but most outsiders wound up on one of New York's eighty-two breadlines. If a man had a dime he could sleep in a flophouse reeking of sweat and Lysol. If he was broke he salvaged some newspapers and headed for Central Park, or the steps of a subway entrance, or the municipal incinerator. The incinerator's warmth drew hundreds of men on winter nights, even though they had to sleep on great dunes of garbage.

Returning from such an expedition in or under an empty freight car, a husband would review family assets with his wife and estimate how long they could keep going. Wedding rings would be sold, furniture pawned, life insurance borrowed upon, money begged from relatives. Often the next step was an attempt at a home business, with its implicit confession to the neighborhood that the pretense of solvency had been a hoax. The yard might be converted to a Tom Thumb miniature golf course. The husband might open a "parlor grocery." The wife might offer other wives a wash, set, and manicure for a dollar. In Massachusetts, idle textile workers erected looms in their living rooms; in Connecticut, households strung safety pins on wires, toiling long hours and earning a total of five dollars a week for an entire family.

These last-ditch efforts rarely succeeded; there were so few potential customers with money. Finally hope was abandoned. The father went to the city hall, declared himself penniless, and became a statistic. Because those figures were poorly kept, the precise extent of poverty is unknown. Somewhere between 15 million and 17 million men were unemployed, with most of them representing a family in want. *Fortune,* in September 1932, estimated that 34 million men, women, and children were without any income whatever. That was nearly 28 percent of the population, and like all other studies it omitted America's 11 million farm families, who were suffering in a rural Gethsemane of their own.

During the Nixon presidency, when America's farm population had shrunk to 5.2 percent of the population, it was hard to realize that only forty years earlier 25.1 percent had been living, or trying to live, on the land. They had not shared in New Era prosperity; the Crash merely worsened a situation which had already become a national scandal. By 1932 U.S. farmers had come to remind one reporter of Mongolian peasants seen in the rotogravure sections of Sunday newspapers, and the shadow of imminent famine fell across the plains. Agricultural prices hadn't been so low since the reign of Queen Elizabeth. Farmers were getting less than twenty-five cents for a bushel of wheat, seven cents for a bushel of corn, a dime for a bushel of oats, a nickel for a pound of cotton or wool. Sugar was bringing three cents a pound, hogs and beef two and a half cents a pound, and apples—provided they were flawless—forty cents for a box of two hundred.

Translated into the bitter sweat of rural life, this meant that a wagon of oats wouldn't buy a pair of four-dollar Thom McAn shoes. A wagon of wheat would just do it, but with mortgage interest running at $3.60 an acre, plus another $1.90 in taxes, the wheat farmer was losing $1.50 on every acre he reaped. In cotton fields the strongest and most agile man would toil from "can see" to "can't see"—fourteen hours of daylight— and receive sixty cents for the 300 pounds he had picked. It was cheaper to burn corn than sell it and buy coal. With meat bringing such ruinous prices, a man would spend $1.10 to ship a sheep to market, where it would return him less than $1.00. In Montana a rancher bought bullets on credit, spent two hours slaughtering a herd of livestock, and left it rotting in a canyon. It wasn't worth its feed. Turning away, he muttered to a reporter, "One way to beat the Depression, huh?"

As farm prices caved in, tens of thousands of mortgage foreclosure notices went up on gateposts and county courthouses. It has been esti- mated that one-fourth of the state of Mississippi was auctioned off. William Allen White, the Republican country editor who had pleaded with Hoover to come and see what was happening to the Middle West, wrote, "Every farmer, whether his farm is under mortgage or not, knows that with farm products priced as they are today, sooner or later he must go down." When the farmer did fail, unable to pay the small costs of binder twine, tool repair, and seed, the bank would take title as absentee landlord, and he would rent from it the land his family had owned for generations. Meantime, while ranchers fed mutton to buzzards and warmed their hands over corn fires, millions in the cities could not afford the low prices which were destroying farmers (butter at 39 cents a pound, prime rib roast at 21 cents, two dozen eggs for 41 cents) because so many were idle and those who had jobs were often earning what could only be called starvation wages.

There was no one to protect them. The President disapproved of wage cuts and said so, but he was equally opposed to wage-hour legisla- tion, so that when U.S. Steel made its second big wage slash in the spring of 1932, the workers were helpless. The labor movement was almost ex- tinct; AFL membership had dwindled from 4.1 million in 1920 to 2.2 mil- lion, about 6 percent of the work force. There were strikes of desperation in 1932. All were lost. Miners were paid $10.88 a month, were at the mercy of check-weight men, and were required to buy groceries at inflated prices in the company store; when they rebelled the protest was bloodily suppressed by armed strikebreakers backed by the National Guard. The United Mine Workers were too weak to offer the victims anything but sympathy.

In such New England mill towns as Lynn and Lowell, where only one worker in three was employed, men were treated like serfs; one of them left Manchester, New Hampshire, to apply for a job in New Haven, was arrested, brought before a judge on a charge of vagrancy, and ordered back to his Manchester mill. The immense pool of job seekers tempted employers to slash their wage bills again and again. Department stores paid clerks as little as five dollars a week. An investigation in Chicago disclosed that the majority of working girls were getting less than twenty-five cents an hour; for a fourth of them, it was less than a dime. In 1932 hourly rates had shrunk to ten cents in lumbering, seven-and-a-half cents in general contracting, six cents in brick and tile manufacturing, and five cents in sawmills. Before the Depression, Massachusetts textile mills rarely required skilled operators to be responsible for more than twenty looms eight hours a day. Then the mills introduced speed-ups and stretch-outs, and Louis Adamic saw teen-aged girls running thirty wide looms from before dawn until after sunset.

In the sweatshops of Brooklyn fifteen-year-olds were paid $2.78 a week. Women received as little as $2.39 for a fifty-hour week. In the summer of 1932 the Connecticut Commissioner of Labor reported that there were over a hundred shops in the state paying as little as sixty cents for a fifty-five-hour week. New York City was the worst sweat spot in that state, and its garment industry, employing fifty thousand women, was the most sweated trade. "Unscrupulous employers," *Time* reported, had "battered wages down to the Chinese coolie level." Hat makers crocheted hats for forty cents a dozen; in a week a worker could make two dozen. Apron girls were paid two-and-a-half cents an apron; they earned twenty cents a day. A slipper liner received twenty-one cents for lining seventy-two pairs; if she completed one slipper every forty-five seconds, she took home $1.05 after a nine-hour day. Girl cleaners in a pants factory were paid a half-cent for each garment they threaded and sponged. It was a five-minute operation; their income was six cents an hour. Honest employers could not survive that kind of competition. Welfare rolls grew longer and longer, the President continued to withhold federal help, and as the fourth Depression winter loomed the relief structure began to disintegrate.

When a senator declared the workers simply could not survive on one or two days' wages a week, President J. E. Edgerton of the National Association of Manufacturers said, "Why, I've never thought of paying men on the basis of what they need. I pay for efficiency. Personally, I attend to all those other things, social welfare stuff, in my church work." Doubtless he thought he did. As *Fortune* explained it, the theory was that now, as in the past, private charity and semipublic welfare groups could care for the old, the sick, and the indigent.

It wasn't working. The Depression, while multiplying the demands upon charities, had dried up their sources of contributions. By 1932, private help had dwindled to 6 percent of the money spent upon the needy, leaving some thirty million people to public welfare. Unfortunately, local governments couldn't handle the burden. State and city budgets had been in the red since 1930. About nine-tenths of municipal income came from taxation on real estate, which in terms of the Depression dollar was ludicrously overappraised. Landlords were liable to taxation if they held title to buildings; their inability to realize income from their houses was legally irrelevant, even when their tenants were on municipal relief, which never paid rentals. The landlords tried desperately to get their money. At first, in exasperation, they turned penniless occupants out. In New York there was hardly a block without a daily dispossession, and in Philadelphia so many families were put on the street that little girls invented a doll game called Eviction.

But empty tenements solved nothing; they merely contributed to the unpopularity of men of property while leaving tax bills unpaid. Eventually, as Professor Sumner H. Slichter of the Harvard Business School explained to the Senate Committee on Manufactures, there was "a more or less national moratorium on rents, insofar as the unemployed are concerned." Delinquent tax ratios hovered between 20 and 30 percent in metropolitan areas, and the cities, lacking this revenue, cut services. Roads were unpaved, sidewalks crumbled, streets blocked by winter snow were left unplowed. Chicago, deprived of two years' receipts by a taxpayers' strike, borrowed from the banks—and agonized over its unemployed population of 600,000.

Given the bankruptcy of public treasuries, and the widespread feeling that the poor were somehow responsible for their fate, it was inevitable that admittance to relief rolls would be made extremely difficult. Before applications were even considered, homes and possessions had to be sold, insurance canceled, credit exhausted, and evidence produced that all known relatives were broke. Even then, in many cities no assistance was granted to unmarried people or people without young children. Every possible stigma was attached to aid. In September 1932 Lewiston, Maine, voted to bar all welfare recipients from the polls, a goal already achieved by property requirements in the constitutions of ten states from Massachusetts to Oregon. West Virginia hospitals refused to admit patients unless payment for services was guaranteed; a referring physician suggested to one surgeon that he delay operating upon a child until the parents promised to pay $1000. Two doctors in Royce City, Texas, put the following advertisement in the local paper:

TO WHOM IT MAY CONCERN: If you are expecting the stork to visit your home this year and he has to come by way of Royce City, he will have to bring a checkbook to pay his bill before delivery.

In some communities taxpayer associations tried to prevent welfare children from attending schools, and families receiving public assistance were known to have been excluded from churches.

Even those who surmounted all barriers found that the approval of a welfare application was exceptional. In mill towns, mining communities, and on sharecropper farms, *Fortune* reported, "relief is merely a name." In the cities only 25 percent of qualified families were getting some form of help. The mayor of Toledo said in 1932: "I have seen thousands of these defeated, discouraged, hopeless men and women, cringing and fawning as they come to ask for public aid. It is a spectacle of national degradation." Admittance to the rolls did not end the defeat, discouragement, and hopelessness. In Philadelphia a family of four was given $5.50 a week, which hardly encouraged the debauchery predicted by those who objected to the dole, and Philadelphia was munificent compared to New York ($2.39), Mississippi ($1.50) and Detroit ($0.60). At the most, assistance covered only food and fuel. Since welfare families had often been inadequately clothed before the Crash, their rags three winters later sometimes defied description. It was not uncommon to see the head of a family dressed like a vaudeville tramp, wearing a buttonless suit coat out at one elbow, a pair of trousers out at the knee and in the seat, an old summer cap that had hung for years in some furnace room, worn tennis shoes covered by patched rubbers, a pair of mismatched canvas gloves; the whole covered by a filthy old sheepskin.

Frequently public employees were almost indistinguishable from public wards, since money for both came from the same sources. As a rule community elders found a way to provide their policemen with decent uniforms, for it was a time of anxiety about public safety. This concern did not cover schoolteachers, who more than any other group were victims of local governments' inadequate tax base. At the beginning of the Depression they had been assessed part of their pay to finance soup kitchens. With the school population increasing by over two hundred thousand each year, further economies were inevitable. Desks were set up in corridors, in coal-heated portables, in tin shacks; courses in art and music were stricken from the curriculum; the same textbooks were handed down semester after semester, until they had become dog-eared, dirty, with pages defaced or missing. Classrooms became more and more crowded. Finally, the money to pay the teachers began to disappear.

By 1932, a third of a million children were out of school because of lack of funds. Teachers in Mississippi, northern Minnesota, Idaho, South Dakota, and Alabama managed to eat only by "boarding around" at the homes of parents. In Dayton, Ohio, schools were open only three days a week; in Arkansas over three hundred schools were closed ten months or more. In Kansas, twenty-five-cent wheat meant rural teachers were being paid $35 a month for an eight-month year—$280 a year. In Iowa they were receiving $40 a month, half the income Washington had said was necessary for industrial workers to exist. Akron owed its teachers $300,000, Youngstown $500,000, Detroit $800,000, and Chicago's debts to its teachers were more than 20 million dollars.

The story of the Chicago schools was a great Depression epic. Rather than see 500,000 children remain on the streets, the teachers hitchhiked to work, endured "payless paydays"—by 1932 they had received checks in only five of the last thirteen months—and accepted city scrip to be redeemed after the Depression, even though Chicago bankers would not accept it. Somehow the city found money to invest in its forthcoming World's Fair of 1933, when Sally Rand would gross $6000 a week, but it turned a deaf ear to the Board of Education. A thousand teachers were dismissed outright. Those who remained taught on at immense personal sacrifice. Collectively the 1400 teachers lost 759 homes. They borrowed $1,128,000 on their insurance policies and another $232,000 from loan sharks at annual interest rates of 42 percent, and although hungry themselves, they fed 11,000 pupils out of their thin pocketbooks.

Teachers, welfare workers, and policemen saw hardship at close range. Nobody called cops pigs in the early 1930s. Even when they were used to break strikes, it was widely acknowledged that they were as exploited as the workers. In New York, men on the beat had been distributing food in the most stricken neighborhoods since 1930. The money came from city employees, including themselves, who contributed 1 percent of their salaries; as Caroline Bird pointed out, this was "the first public confession of official responsibility for plain poverty, and it came, not from the top, but from the lowest civil servants, who worked down where the poor people were."

Once more the teachers bore witness to the worst, for the most heartbreaking Depression martyrs were in the classrooms. In October of that terrible year, a month before the presidential election, the New York City Health Department reported that over 20 percent of the pupils in the pub-

lic schools were suffering from malnutrition. In the mining counties of
Ohio, West Virginia, Illinois, Kentucky, and Pennsylvania, the secretary of
the American Friends Service Committee told a congressional committee,
the ratio was sometimes over 90 percent, with deprived children afflicted
by "drowsiness, lethargy, and sleepiness," and "mental retardation." A
teacher suggested that one little girl go home and eat something; the child
replied, "I can't. This is my sister's day to eat." A little boy exhibited his
pet rabbit to a visitor and the boy's sister whispered, "He thinks we aren't
going to eat it, but we are." Lillian Wald, a social worker, asked in anguish,
"Have you ever seen the uncontrolled trembling of parents who have
starved themselves for weeks so that their children might not go hungry?"
A bitter father said, "A worker's got no right to have kids any more," and
a Massachusetts priest said, "One family I know has lived on lentils, nothing but lentils, all this year. They can't afford to buy bread. What is going
to happen to our children?"

"Nobody is actually starving," President Hoover told reporters.
"The hoboes, for example, are better fed than they have ever been. One
hobo in New York got ten meals in one day." In September 1932 *Fortune*
flatly called the President a liar and suggested that "twenty-five millions
in want" might be a fairer description of the nation's economic health.
Cases of starvation were being chronicled by *Fortune,* the *San Francisco
Chronicle,* the *Atlantic,* the *New York Times,* and in congressional testimony.
The New York City Welfare Council reported 29 victims of starvation and
110, mostly children, dead of malnutrition. Hoover simply hadn't seen the
suffering, though he was not to be spared after his departure from the
White House; on a fishing trip in the Rocky Mountains he was led by a
native to a hut where one child had succumbed and seven others were dying of hunger.

Millions stayed alive by living like animals. In the Pennsylvania
countryside they were eating wild weed-roots and dandelions; in Kentucky they chewed violet tops, wild onions, forget-me-nots, wild lettuce,
and weeds which heretofore had been left to grazing cattle. City mothers
hung around docks, waiting for spoiled produce to be discarded and then
fighting homeless dogs for possession of it. After the vegetables had been
loaded on trucks they would run alongside, ready to snatch up anything
that fell off. A cook in a midwestern hotel put a pail of leftovers in the al-
ley outside the kitchen; immediately a dozen men loomed out of the darkness to fight over it. In Long Beach, California, a sixty-six-year-old physician named Francis Everett Townsend glanced out his window while
shaving and saw, among a group of refuse barrels, "three haggard very
old women," as he later called them, "stooped with great age, bending
over the barrels, clawing into the contents." Whole families were seen

plunging into refuse dumps, gnawing at bones and watermelon rinds; a Chicago widow always removed her glasses so she wouldn't see the maggots. At night in New York Thomas Wolfe observed "the homeless men who prowled in the vicinity of restaurants, lifting the lids of garbage cans and searching around inside for morsels of rotten food." He saw them "everywhere, and noticed how their numbers increased during the hard and desperate days of 1932."

It was considered benevolent by well-to-do Americans that year to give your garbage to fellow countrymen who were famished. The Elks of Mount Kisco, New York, and the eating clubs of Princeton University instructed their servants to see that their leftovers reached the needy. The *Brooklyn Eagle* proposed a central depot where edible swill could be sent by charitable citizens and where the poor might apply for portions of it. In Oklahoma City John B. Nichlos, a gas company executive, worked out a plan under which restaurants, civic clubs, and hotel chefs would pack swill in "sanitary containers of five (5) gallons each," to be "labeled 'MEAT, BEANS, POTATOES, BREAD AND OTHER ITEMS.'" The Salvation Army would pick up the cans, the contents of which would then be distributed to jobless men who would first chop wood donated by—of all people—the farmers. "We expect a little trouble now and then from those who are not worthy of the support of the citizens," the gas man wrote Secretary of the Army Hurley, "but we must contend with such cases in order to take care of those who are worthy." Hurley thought it a marvelous idea, and urged the administration to adopt it. It was vetoed by the director of Hoover's Emergency Committee for Employment on the ground that the gesture might be misunderstood.

It never seems to have occurred to Nichlos, the *Eagle*, the Princetonians and the Elks that more dramatic solutions might lie ahead. But already there were those who pondered the contrast between the well-fed rich and the starving multitude, and who thought they saw the dark shadow of things to come. Thomas Wolfe would talk to the tragic men in New York's public toilets until he could not stand their anguish any more. Then he would mount the steps to the pavement twenty feet above and gaze out upon "the giant hackles of Manhattan shining coldly in the cruel brightness of the winter night. The Woolworth Building was not fifty yards away, and a little further down were the silvery spires and needles of Wall Street, great fortresses of stone and steel that housed enormous banks. The blind injustice of this . . . seemed the most brutal part of the whole experience, for there . . . in the cold moonlight, only a few blocks away from this abyss of human wretchedness and misery, blazed the pinnacles of power where a large section of the entire world's wealth was locked in mighty vaults."

QUESTIONS TO CONSIDER

1. What was the popular attitude toward poverty in the Depression?
2. What were some indications that people were eager to find work?
3. Who, according to prevailing theory, was supposed to take care of charity? What was wrong with the theory?
4. Do you see much evidence of people trying to cheat the welfare system?
5. What was President Hoover's response to public hunger?
6. Does the conclusion make you feel you would have been interested in participating in some kind of revolt against the system in 1932? Why or why not? What actually happened in 1932?

10

The Centrality of the Bomb*

Gar Alperovitz and Kai Bird

In 1945 the United States, United Kingdom, and USSR wound up a successful wartime alliance against the axis powers, Germany, Japan, and Italy. By 1950, in a truly Orwellian switch (in fact, George Orwell wrote *1984* during this period), the United States and the United Kingdom counted Germany, Japan, and Italy as allies and condemned the USSR and their erstwhile ally China as enemies. How had this dramatic change occurred? How had the alliances of World War II been transformed into the new alignments of the Cold War? Who, or what, was at fault for the much-anticipated postwar peace giving way to a military arms race between East and West?

In this article, two analysts suggest that the atomic bomb, in particular the American monopoly of the weapon from 1945 to 1949, determined the course of superpower relations in the years after World War II. Possession of the bomb freed President Harry Truman from the need to cooperate with the Soviet Union to ensure peace in Europe and thus led him into much more confrontational policies than would have been the case otherwise.

Gar Alperovitz, president of the National Center for Economic Alternatives and a fellow of the Institute for Policy Studies, wrote *Atomic Diplomacy: Hiroshima and Potsdam* in 1965, advancing

*Reprinted with permission from *Foreign Policy* 94 (Spring 1994). Copyright 1994 by the Carnegie Endowment for International Peace.

the argument that the bomb had been used not primarily to defeat Japan but to influence the Soviet Union's behavior after the
war. That view has won at least partial, grudging acceptance by
many historians. In 1995 he wrote the massive *The Decision to Use
the Atomic Bomb and the Architecture of an American Myth*, further developing his theme. Kai Bird is the author of *John J. McCloy:
The Making of the American Establishment.*

Russia and the United States [have] always gotten along for a hundred and
fifty years history with Russia friendly and helpful. Our respective orbits do
not clash geographically and I think on the whole we can probably keep out
of clashes in the future.

—*Secretary of War Henry Stimson
April 1945*

Before the atom bomb was used, I would have said, yes, I was sure we could
keep the peace with Russia. Now I don't know. . . . People are frightened
and disturbed all over. Everyone feels insecure again.

—*General Dwight Eisenhower
Visiting Moscow, August 1945*

Even though the Cold War's abrupt, peaceful demise rendered useless
most of the assumptions and theories advanced to explain that strange
conflict, orthodox historians have kept on writing about it as if what actually happened had been inevitable. Moreover, they largely avoid the
specific role the atomic bomb played in fueling the Cold War. In fact, the
bomb was a primary catalyst of the Cold War, and, apart from the nuclear
arms race, the most important specific role of nuclear weapons was to rev-
olutionize American policy toward Germany. The bomb permitted U.S.
leaders to do something no American president could otherwise have
contemplated: rebuild and rearm the former Nazi state. That in turn had
extraordinary, ongoing consequences.

The bomb also made the Korean and Vietnam wars possible: Had the
weapon not been available to protect the U.S. global flank in Europe, such
episodes would always have been "the wrong war in the wrong place at
the wrong time," to use General Omar Bradley's words. Finally, those who
believed early on that America and Russia could reach a great power accommodation were probably right—and such an accommodation may
well have been delayed for four decades because the atomic bomb appeared precisely when America and the Soviet Union were beginning to
feel their way to a new post-World War II relationship.

Not only does that explanation of the Cold War offer a good measure
of common sense, but a vast body of new archival research lends power-

ful support to the hypothesis. This is not to say that frictions, rivalries, and areas of conflict would not have existed between the major powers had there been no atomic bomb. What needs to be explained is the extreme militarization of great power relations that came to be called "the Cold War."

Historians like to see patterns, trends, and continuity in long periods of development, but they rarely pause to reflect upon the extreme chanciness of the timing of historically important events. Consider the prehistory of nuclear weapons. Physicist Hans Bethe once observed that it was only very "slowly and painfully, through a comedy of errors, [that] the fission of uranium was discovered."

It was by mere chance, for instance, that Enrico Fermi made his critical 1934 discoveries about the capacity of the atom's nucleus to capture slow neutrons. Fermi's seemingly accidental findings built on a line of development that began with Albert Einstein's famous 1905 papers and continued with subsequent reports and inventions by scientists such as Leo Szilard (in connection with the cyclotron) and James Chadwick (in connection with the existence of the neutron).

Most accounts do not acknowledge that had twentieth-century physics not been moving at the particular rate it did, America would never have gotten to the 1939 Szilard-Einstein letter to President Franklin Roosevelt, the 1941 MAUD Committee report, and then the Manhattan Project—to a sufficiently advanced point, that is, where large sums of money and engineering expertise could have produced an atomic bomb by August 1945. As Bethe's remark suggests and others have noted, events might just as well have moved a decade or two slower or perhaps faster.

With that in mind, it is instructive to reflect on what might have happened (or, more precisely, what probably would not have happened) if the "independent track" of scientific historical development had not reached fruition in 1945. What might the postwar world have looked like in the absence of an early U.S. atomic monopoly?

GERMANY AND THE BOMB

At Yalta, Roosevelt had been quite clear about two fundamentals: First, given the domestic political concerns of a country taught to fear and hate Germany in the course of two world wars, he believed that the former Nazi state simply had to be eliminated as a serious security threat in the postwar period. It was both a strategic and an absolute political requirement. Second, as is well-known, Roosevelt felt that the American people would not permit him to keep American troops in Europe for long after the war. Given strong "isolationist" sentiments that appeared in Congress and the popular press, he was almost certainly correct in his judgment.

Those constraints produced the main requirements of Roosevelt's postwar security policy: He needed a rough agreement with the other dominant military power—the Soviet Union—to control Germany directly, and he needed a concrete way (beyond rhetoric) to weaken Germany's underlying military potential. Exaggerated discussions of "pastoralization" apart, Roosevelt's strategy centered on the notion of "industrial disarmament" to weaken Germany's military-industrial complex—and simultaneously to cement American-Soviet cooperation. Reductions in German industry could also provide the short-term reparations Joseph Stalin desperately sought to help rebuild the war-torn Soviet Union.

Related to that strategy, of course, were implications for Roosevelt's de facto acceptance of a Soviet sphere of influence in Eastern Europe. To the extent Stalin was certain that Germany would not rise again, at least in theory Soviet policy could be more relaxed in Eastern Europe. The Yalta agreement embodied big-power control of Germany, large-scale reparations, and an extremely vague declaration on the status of Eastern Europe.

Often overlooked is that from the American point of view, the advent of nuclear weapons gave Washington an alternative to constructing a European peace in cooperation with the Soviet Union. At Yalta, Washington had essentially agreed to a neutralized Germany, but with the bomb U.S. policymakers realized they could afford the risks of acting unilaterally. The western portion of Germany could safely be reconstructed economically and, later, integrated into a West European military alliance. Only the atomic monopoly permitted that with little fear of German resurgence and without regard to Soviet security interests.

At Potsdam, American leaders explicitly understood that the atomic test the United States had conducted at Alamogordo, New Mexico, had upended the assumptions of policy. Compare, for instance, the views of President Harry Truman's closest adviser, James Byrnes, before and after Alamogordo. On June 6, 1945, six weeks before the blast, the diary of Ambassador Joseph Davies records that Byrnes, about to become secretary of state, "discussed the entire Russian situation at great length":

> It was clear that without Russian cooperation, without a primary objective for Peace, another disastrous war would be inevitable. . . . Nor did he think that our people on sober second thought would undertake fighting the Red Army and Russia for a hopeless cause of attempting to control the ideology or way of life which these various rival groups wished to establish in the various countries.

Although Russian cooperation was needed before the bomb, many scholars now recognize that the successful atomic test gave Truman "an entirely new feeling of confidence," as he put it. It provided Secretary of State Byrnes in particular with what he called "a gun behind the door" that he believed could make Russia "more manageable." One of many similar conversations from the period was recorded by Secretary of War Stimson in his diary shortly after Hiroshima: "Byrnes was very much against any attempt to cooperate with Russia. His mind is full of his problems with the coming meeting of foreign ministers and he looks to having the presence of the bomb in his pocket, so to speak, as a great weapon to get through the thing."

In connection with the U.S. approach to Germany, the atomic bomb altered policy in two quite specific ways that went to the heart of Rooseveltian strategy. Shortly after the atomic test Byrnes simply abandoned the Yalta understanding that had set German reparations at roughly $20 billion (half of which would go to the Soviet Union). Another Davies diary entry on July 28, 1945, shows that he did so explicitly relying on the atomic bomb: "[Byrnes] was having a hard time with reparations . . . , [but the] details as to the success of the atomic bomb, which he had just received, gave him confidence that the Soviets would agree as to these difficulties."

Moreover, according to Davies, the secretary of state was also quite clear about the shift in fundamental power relations in Europe: "Because of the New Mexico development [Byrnes] felt secure anyway." Byrnes suggested that "the New Mexico situation had given us great power, and that in the last analysis it would control." Several American policymakers (notably Benjamin Cohen, an assistant to Byrnes) had believed that international control of the Ruhr industrial heartland might be the key to a compromise approach. In principle, it could achieve security without necessarily weakening the German economic reconstruction effort. But—again, shortly after the report of the successful nuclear test—Byrnes rejected that proposal as well.

Many scholars now understand that the atomic bomb altered the Truman administration's general postwar approach to the USSR. What needs to be grasped is the specific implications the weapon had for the continuing U.S. approach to Germany. That there was a close link between the bomb and the German problem in the minds of U.S. policymakers was made quite explicit again, for instance, in two August 22, 1945, meetings with General Charles de Gaulle. Here Truman and Byrnes together urged that "the German danger should not be exaggerated." De Gaulle, however, continued to emphasize French fears—and, like Roosevelt's advisers and the Russians, urged direct security measures to manage the longer-term German threat (including international control of the Ruhr and severing the west bank of the Rhine from Germany). Finally, Truman and Byrnes—responding explicitly to de Gaulle's concern about Germany—became blunt: "The atomic bomb will give pause to countries which might [be] tempted to commit aggressions."

Although U.S. policymakers still worried about the potential power of a united German state, very early in the postwar period they clearly understood that Germany no longer presented a fundamental military threat. The new nuclear monopoly substantially relieved the Truman administration of the central foreign-policy and military concern of Roosevelt and his advisers. "In the last analysis it would control" as Byrnes said—even if the American people forced the withdrawal of U.S. troops from the Continent, even if American-Soviet cooperation failed, and even if Germany were not disarmed industrially. Put another way, the bomb made it possible to pursue a policy described by scholars in recent years as "double containment"—that is, the division of Germany could be used to contain both the Germans and the Soviets.

SCARING STALIN

The problem was obviously not quite the same from the Soviet point of view. In the first place, the new weapon itself now posed a threat. Generalized fear provoked by the new weapon was only one aspect of the problem: In the fall of 1945 and spring of 1946, American policy moved slowly but steadily away from Roosevelt's approach to Germany. Partly as a result of French obstruction on the Allied Control Council, partly out of understandable fear of economic chaos and political disorder, and partly—but not at the outset—out of frustration with Soviet policy, U.S. policy shifted from industrial disarmament to rebuilding German economic power. A major turning point was probably the decision to stop reparation shipments in May 1946—dramatically followed by the tough speech Byrnes gave that September in Stuttgart.

That shift occurred at the same time that policymakers began to play up the bomb as a strategic factor. The U.S. stockpile of assembled weapons was actually quite small, but the potential of the nuclear monopoly was also obviously extraordinary—as was advertised by the atomic tests in June 1946 at Bikini Atoll in the Pacific. Code-named "Operation Crossroads," the blasts took place at the same time Byrnes and Soviet foreign minister Vyacheslav Molotov were again trying to reach agreement over Germany. *Pravda* took note of the mushroom cloud over Bikini and accused Washington of plotting an atomic war. And as the arsenal grew (50 weapons were available by 1948), the Truman administration steadily found the courage to act more forcefully and unilaterally in Germany.

Reams have been written about the extreme Russian security fears of the German threat. Stalin, in Nikita Khrushchev's judgment, "lived in terror of an enemy attack." The Soviet premier observed in April 1945 that Germany "will recover, and very quickly"—but apparently he initially believed that "quickly" meant as many as 10 or 15 years. Sometime at the end of 1947, as Michael McGwire observes in a recent study, "Stalin shifted focus . . . to the more immediate threat of war within 5–6 years against a capitalist coalition led by the Anglo-Saxon powers."

Recently released Soviet documents offer additional insight. Soviet ambassador to the United States Nikolai Novikov, for instance, painted a deeply disturbing picture of American intentions toward the Soviet Union in 1946. Citing the U.S. "establishment of a system of naval and air bases stretching far beyond the boundaries of the United States" and the "creation of ever newer types of weapons," Novikov believed that Washington was preparing for war. In the heart of Europe, he

> emphasized, America was "considering the possibility of terminating the Allied occupation of German territory before the main tasks of the occupation—the demilitarization and democratization of Germany—have been implemented. This would create the prerequisites for the revival of an imperialist Germany, which the United States plans to use in a future war on its side."

U.S. leaders fully understood Russian fears of Germany. Ambassador Averell Harriman, for instance, later recalled that "Stalin was afraid of Germany, Khrushchev was afraid of Germany, the present people [Brezhnev] are afraid of Germany—and I am afraid of Germany . . . [The Soviets] have a feeling that the Germans can arouse a situation which will involve us and that will lead to a disaster."

Obviously, the critical turning point came with the decision to partition Germany and rearm West Germany. American leaders recognized that the Soviets would view even the restoration of significant German economic power as a threat—and that this would have painful repercussions in Eastern Europe. At a cabinet meeting in late 1947, Secretary of State George Marshall predicted that because of U.S. actions in Germany the Soviets would have to "clamp down completely" on Czechoslovakia, and that when they did, it would be a "purely defensive move."

Was Marshall's basic insight into a critical dynamic feature of the early Cold War correct? Was Soviet policy in Central and Eastern Europe primarily defensive and a reaction to American policy toward Germany?

It is difficult to know, of course, but others also recognized the point early on. In his opinion columns at the time, Walter Lippmann, for instance, regularly pointed out the obvious connection between what happened in Germany and what happened in Eastern Europe. Unless the German problem were settled first, he urged, the Russians were unlikely ever to relax their hold on Eastern Europe. Lippmann believed that Byrnes's strategy of pressing forward on Eastern Europe without simultaneously promoting a reasonable settlement of the German issue was demanding too much. "We must not set up a German government in the two or three Western zones," Lippmann urged the Wall Street lawyer and future secretary of state John Foster Dulles in 1947. "We must not make a separate peace with it."

A steadily expanding body of research and documentary evidence suggests that Marshall's fundamental insight and Lippmann's early judgment offer the most plausible explanation for one of the most dramatic and painful features of the Cold War—Stalin's clampdown on Eastern Europe. The Soviet archives have yet to divulge anything definitive about Stalin's intentions at the end of World War II. However, even Harriman, who is usually portrayed as a hardliner in early postwar dealings with Moscow, thought the Soviet dictator had no firm plan at the outset: "I had a feeling," Harriman observed, "that they were considering and weighing the pros and cons of cooperating with us in the postwar world and getting the benefit of our cooperation in reconstruction."

Recent scholarship has uncovered far more indications of ambivalence—and, indeed, a great deal more caution and cooperation—in Soviet policy during 1945 and 1946 than is commonly recognized. A number of developments helped produce judgments about the Soviet Union like Harriman's:

- General elections in Hungary in the fall of 1945 held under Soviet supervision resulted in the defeat of communist-supported groups.
- In September 1945, Moscow unilaterally withdrew troops from Norway, despite its long-standing claims on Bear Island and Spitzbergen.
- In the wake of the December 1945 Moscow agreements, the government in Romania was enlarged to include noncommunists, after which both the United States and Great Britain recognized it.
- The Soviet military also withdrew from Czechoslovakia at that time, and free elections produced a coalition government of communists and noncommunists committed to keeping the country's doors open to both the East and the West.
- In the spring of 1946, Soviet troops left the Danish island of Bornholm.
- In accord with his "percentage agreement" with Winston Churchill, Stalin abandoned the Greek communists at a critical juncture in their civil war, leaving Greece within the Western sphere of influence.

- In Austria, the Soviet army supervised free elections in their occupation zone and, of course, withdrew after the signing of the Austrian Peace Treaty in 1955.
- The Soviets warned the French communist leader, Maurice Thorez, against attempting "to seize power by force since to do so would probably precipitate an international conflict from which the Soviet Union could hardly emerge victorious." (American intelligence obtained a report on that conversation in November 1946.)
- Despite a short delay, Soviet troops in 1946 did pull out of Iran—a country bordering the Soviet Union—after a brief and, in retrospect, rather modest international dispute.
- Perhaps most revealing, former Soviet officials who had defected to the West documented that important railway lines running from the Soviet Union through Eastern Europe were yanked up in the very early postwar period. The working assumption appeared to be that since there would be only a short occupation, Soviet forces should hurry to remove as much useful material as possible.
- Nor did Stalin pursue an aggressive policy in the Far East during the early years. Indeed, for a good period of time Stalin supported Nationalist Chinese leader Chiang Kaishek—much to the lasting chagrin of Chinese communist leaders. And Red Army troops departed Manchuria in May 1946.

Many historians now accept that substantial evidence exists that Stalin neither planned nor desired the Cold War. Finland and Austria—neutral but free states—serve as alternative models for border-area countries that the Soviet Union might have accepted had a different dynamic been established after World War II.

Of course, Soviet policy in Eastern Europe was to shift dramatically, especially after 1947 and 1948. Along with the announcement of the Truman Doctrine, the Marshall Plan also appears to have been far more threatening to Stalin than was previously understood: It suggested the creation of a powerful "economic magnet" to draw Eastern Europe into the Western orbit. Once it was clear that Germany was to be rebuilt and later rearmed, the crackdown in Eastern Europe became irrevocable.

That interpretation returns us to a central point, namely that the U.S. decision to rearm West Germany was made possible only by the atomic bomb. Modern writers often forget the degree of concern in the U.S. foreign policy establishment and elsewhere about the former Nazi state in the early postwar years. Even after the outbreak of the Korean War—and even with the atomic bomb—Truman's high commissioner in Germany, John McCloy, initially opposed the creation of a German national army. So too did his successor, James Conant. And when they changed their minds, both men had to deal with the unrelenting opposition of the French. As late as August 1950, the State Department declared it "opposed, and still strongly opposes, the creation of German national forces."

Further, Truman himself was deeply worried about the Germans—again, even with the bomb. Among many indications of Truman's worry was a memo to Secretary of State Dean Acheson in June 1950:

> We certainly don't want to make the same mistake that was made after World War I when Germany was authorized to train one hundred thousand soldiers, principally for maintaining order locally in Germany. As you know, that hundred thousand was used for the basis of training the greatest war machine that ever came forth in European history.

Truman also recognized that he faced very powerful domestic political opposition to rearming a nation that had so recently caused the deaths of so many American boys. "From today's perspective, the rearmament of Germany seems natural and almost inevitable," writes historian Frank Ninkovich in a recent study.

> To achieve it, however, American policy makers had to clear a long series of hurdles, including self-doubts, widespread European reluctance, and Soviet obstructionism. . . . The amazing thing, then, is not that rearmament took place with such enormous difficulty, but that it happened at all.

Amazing, indeed! All but unimaginable in the absence of nuclear weapons or popular support for maintaining major conventional forces. As Roosevelt had forecast, the American people overwhelmingly demanded rapid demobilization after the war. In June 1945, the United States had more than 12 million men and women under arms, but one year later the figure was only 3 million, and by June 1947 demobilization had left the armed services with no more than 1.5 million personnel. Congress defeated universal military training in 1947 and in 1948; defense spending in general declined rapidly during the first postwar years. Such domestic political realities left U.S. policymakers empty-handed: They did not have sufficient conventional forces to hold down the Germans.

Given such realities—and considering the extraordinary difficulty of achieving German rearmament even with U.S. possession of the atomic bomb—it is all but impossible to imagine the early rearmament of the former Nazi enemy had there been no atomic bomb. Put another way, had the scientific-technical track of development that yielded the knowledge required to make an atomic weapon not chanced to reach the point it had by 1939, the central weapon in America's postwar diplomatic arsenal would not have existed.

There is a further reason why we believe this hypothesis explains the early Cold War dynamic: German rearmament and the U.S. Cold War conventional buildup, many scholars recognize, probably could not have happened without the dramatic U.S. decision to enter the Korean War. That decision, in turn, was made possible only by the atomic bomb—and, hence, the train of subsequent events is difficult to imagine in the absence of the bomb.

Even with the atomic bomb virtually every important American military leader was extremely skeptical about a land war in Asia. The Korean peninsula, of course, had been arbitrarily divided in 1945 by Moscow and Washington, and both powers were well aware that their client regimes in Pyongyang and Seoul were committed to unifying the country under their own flags. Each regime had guerrilla units operating in the other's territory in what amounted to a simmering civil war. (Washington was actually restricting the supply of offensive weapons to the Syngman Rhee regime in South Korea for fear that they would be used in an invasion of the North.)

By late 1949, as is well known, Truman's National Security Council (NSC) advisers had concluded that Korea was of little strategic value to the United States and that a commitment to use military force in Korea would be ill-advised. Early in 1950, both Acheson and the chairman of the Senate Foreign Relations Committee, Tom Connally, had publicly stated that South Korea lay outside the perimeter of U.S. national security interests.

Most important, to pledge troops to a land war in Asia would expose the American "European flank," since moving troops to Asia would weaken the American presence on the Continent. As General Bradley recounted in his memoirs, "We still believed our greatest potential for danger lay in Soviet aggression in Europe." And, "to risk widening the Korean War into a war with China would probably delight the Kremlin more than anything else we could do." The famous Bradley comment quoted earlier summarized the general view within the Joint Chiefs of Staff: Fighting in Korea would involve the United States "in the wrong war, at the wrong place, at the wrong time, and with the wrong enemy." When an invasion of the South did occur in June 1950, the Truman administration's decision to intervene amounted to an astonishing policy reversal.

If, even with the atomic bomb, U.S. military leaders hesitated to pledge land forces to the defense of Korea, then without the atomic bomb—which to the generals would have meant a totally exposed European "flank"—a decision to protect South Korea would have been practically impossible.

And again, very few would disagree with the proposition that the Korean War, in turn, provided a crucial fulcrum upon which the Cold War pivoted. Most scholars accept that NSC-68, the document outlining a massive rebuilding of the U.S. military, was going nowhere in early 1950; the defense budget was being cut, not raised. The political drama surrounding the Korean War permitted an extraordinary escalation both in Cold War hysteria and in military spending. Before Korea such spending was around 4 percent of gross national product (GNP); during the war it peaked at nearly 14 percent. After Korea it stabilized to average roughly 10 percent of GNP during the 1950s—an unimaginable extravagance before that time. (The buildup, in turn, established a structure of forces and political attitudes without which the subsequent intervention in Vietnam is difficult to imagine.)

Most important, Germany almost certainly could only have been rearmed in the domestic political atmosphere that accompanied the chaotic Korean conflict, along with the qualitative political shift in Cold War tensions that the war brought. The entire scenario depended ultimately upon the odd historical timing that put nuclear weapons in American hands at a particular moment in the twentieth century.

What of "the Cold War" per se—the larger, overarching dynamic? Recall that the issue is not whether the usual tensions between great powers would or would not have existed. The issue is whether the relationship would have had to explode into the extremely militarized form it took.

Recently declassified archival materials from both sides should destroy the traditional assumption that the Soviet army at the end of World War II offensively threatened Western Europe. In 1945, roughly half the Soviet army's transport was horse-drawn, and it would remain so until 1950. Moreover, Soviet troops demobilized massively and dramatically in the early postwar period. Soviet documents suggest that Stalin's army shrank from 11,365,000 in May 1945 to 2,874,000 in June 1947.

While there is debate about how widely such information was known or heeded by top U.S. officials, a number of scholars have recently cited evidence suggesting that U.S. policymakers fully understood that the Soviet Union had neither the intention nor the capability to launch a ground invasion of Western Europe. In December 1945, for instance, the State Department circulated an intelligence estimate concluding that for at least five years "the United States need not be acutely concerned about the current intentions of the Soviet Union [and has] considerable latitude in determining policy toward the USSR." A Joint Chiefs of Staff report at the end of 1948 estimated the Soviets might be able to marshal only some 800,000 troops for an attack force. Two years later, the CIA used the same figure in its intelligence estimate. Similarly, documents recapped in

Frank Kofsky's recent *Harry S. Truman and the War Scare of 1948* provide devastating proof that American military intelligence estimates consistently concluded that the Soviets could not and did not want to wage war. One illustration is a high-level briefing given directly to Truman in late 1948:

> The Russians have dismantled hundreds of miles of railroads in Germany and sent the rails and ties back to Russia. There remains, at the present time . . . only a single track railroad running Eastward out of the Berlin area and upon which the Russians must largely depend for their logistical support. This same railroad line changes from a standard gage going Eastward, to a Russian wide gage in Poland, which further complicates the problem of moving supplies and equipment forward.

George Kennan, for one, "never believed that they [the Soviets] have seen it as in their interests to overrun Western Europe militarily, or that they would have launched an attack on that region generally even if the so-called nuclear deterrent had not existed."

Credible documentation has also emerged from the Russian archives that Stalin repeatedly rejected North Korean leader Kim Il-Sung's requests for support of an invasion of South Korea. As one scholar, Kathryn Weathersby, has explained in a recent working paper, Stalin reluctantly "approved the plan only after having been assured that the United States would not intervene." Even then he apparently did so because Kim Il-Sung would otherwise have pursued the war anyway with support from the communist Chinese. As Weathersby concludes, "it was Soviet weakness that drove Stalin to support the attack on South Korea, not the unrestrained expansionism imagined by the authors of NSC-68."

Moreover, Bruce Cumings's sweeping, two-volume history, *The Origins of the Korean War*, demonstrates that the U.S. command in South Korea knew at the time that South Korean irregular army units had been provoking the North Koreans for months. A once clear-cut case of communist aggression is now seen by most knowledgeable historians as a complicated civil war that dated back at least to 1945.

The Russian archives also show that often neither Stalin nor his successors could control the regimes in Eastern Europe, Cuba, China, North Korea, or North Vietnam. "It's a big myth that Moscow directed a unified monolith of socialist states," argues Deborah Kaple of Columbia University's Harriman Institute. Newly uncovered documents, for instance, make it clear that the Sino-Soviet split existed almost from the day Mao Tse-tung seized power. And other recent archival discoveries suggest that East Germany's Walter Ulbricht largely initiated the Berlin crisis of

1958–1961, forcing a reluctant Khrushchev to engage in brinkmanship diplomacy.

All of these events suggest a broadly defensive post-World War II Soviet foreign policy that on occasion accommodated American security interests. The monolithic enemy of Cold War fame, many now agree, existed mainly in the imaginations of America's ardent anticommunist cold warriors. At the very least, these events suggest Stalin appeared willing to cut a deal with Washington in the critical early postwar years.

This analysis does not suggest that the American-Soviet relationships could have been a tranquil sea of cooperation. But the unusual and dangerous over-militarization of foreign policy during the Cold War demands an explanation on its own terms—and the atomic bomb is the first item in that lexicon.

This essay has not attempted to untangle the many factors that led to the end of the Cold War. One related issue, however, may be noted: The advent of nuclear weapons (and the U.S. nuclear monopoly in particular) upset the balance of power in general and especially in Europe, where from the Soviet point of view the critical issue was Germany. However, once the Soviet Union had its own nuclear weapons and a credible way to deliver them—and Germany had no such weapons—then the implicit balance of power in general and in Europe, too, was essentially restored, albeit at a higher level.

Before that time the Soviets kept Germany relatively weak by occupation, reparations, and tight control of the invasion routes. After the Soviet Union had secured nuclear weapons (and once the implications were digested and fought out by policy elites), Soviet policy could relax all three prongs of its earlier strategy. Old military and foreign policy *apparatchiks* did not easily abandon traditional assumptions, as the crackdown in Czechoslovakia in 1968 suggests. The preconditions for ending the Cold War, however, were established only after the basic power relationship between the Soviet Union and the United States was rebalanced.

Might history have taken a different course? Many high-level Western policymakers believed an accommodation with the Soviet Union was a reasonable possibility in the early postwar years. The United States was also in a position to encourage Soviet cooperation with the lure of desperately needed long-term economic aid. Indeed, had the United States lacked a nuclear weapons monopoly—and given the rapid pace of U.S. demobilization and Congress's rejection of universal military training— such an approach might well have been the only acceptable option from the U.S. point of view.

All of this, of course, is "counter-factual" history. As the late philosopher Morris Cohen observed in 1942, however, "we cannot grasp the full significance of what happened unless we have some idea of what the situation would have been otherwise." But in a sense all history is implicitly counter-factual—including, above all, the counter-factual orthodox theory that had the United States not taken a tough stand after World War II, there would have been no "long peace" and disaster would inevitably have befallen the Continent, the world, and the United States.

In *A Preponderance of Power*, Melvyn Leffler concludes that because of its enormous strength the United States must also bear a preponderance of responsibility for the Cold War. That important judgment, like Stimson's rejected 1945 plea for an immediate, direct, and private effort to cut short what became the nuclear era, brings into focus the question of just how wise were the "wise men" who crafted America's Cold War policies at the moment when the two great tracks of twentieth-century scientific and global political development converged. At the very least, they failed to find a way to avoid one of history's most costly and dangerous—indeed, literally world-threatening—struggles.

QUESTIONS TO CONSIDER

1. What events do the authors suggest the bomb made possible?
2. How did possession of the bomb affect American policy toward Germany?
3. How did George Marshall and Walter Lippmann link the German issue to Eastern Europe in late 1947?
4. Besides the bomb, what American policies in 1947 and 1948 do the authors suggest made the Soviet Union crackdown on Eastern Europe irrevocable? Why?
5. How did the bomb affect American decisionmaking in Korea and what were the implications of the Korean War for development of the Cold War?
6. What evidence do the authors advance that communism was not a monolith with the Soviet Union directing it?
7. How did Soviet nuclear weapons ease the basic East-West tensions in Europe?

11

Civil Religion in America*

Robert N. Bellah

Harvard-educated Robert N. Bellah (1927–   ) served as professor of sociology at the University of California for most of his distinguished career. He won his greatest acclaim as the principal author of *Habits of the Heart: Individualism and Commitment in American Life* (1985), a penetrating look at the contemporary American character. Bellah's expertise on world religions and comparative studies gives him a broad perspective and scholarly background for his observations on civil religion in the United States.

In this 1967 article, Bellah explains how civil religion has come from Judeo-Christian traditions without being explicitly either Jewish or Christian. The dogmas of civil religion—the existence of God, the life to come, the reward of virtue and the punishment of vice, and the exclusion of religious intolerance—derive from the eighteenth-century French philosopher Jean-Jacques Rousseau. While not incompatible with Christianity or Judaism, these dogmas and their application are in fact more Unitarian. Bellah notes that although all presidents have mentioned God in their inaugural addresses, none, not even born-again Jimmy Carter, has mentioned Christ; God is a general term that each hearer can fill with his or her own meaning. In its American manifestation, civil religion was launched during the revolutionary period and was shaped and

*Reprinted by permission of *Daedalus,* Journal of the American Academy of Arts and Sciences.

profoundly deepened by the Civil War. Bellah argues that civil religion has substantially affected American public policy and that
their religious consciousness should chasten and guide Americans
in exercising their power as a nation.

    This article should lead you to question the assumption that the
United States is a Christian nation. In terms of those ideas on which
most Americans agree, the country might be more aptly described as Unitarian.

While some have argued that Christianity is the national faith, and others
that church and synagogue celebrate only the generalized religion of "the
American Way of Life," few have realized that there actually exists alongside of and rather clearly differentiated from the churches an elaborate
and well-institutionalized civil religion in America. This article argues not
only that there is such a thing, but also that this religion—or perhaps better, this religious dimension—has its own seriousness and integrity and
requires the same care in understanding that any other religion does.

THE KENNEDY INAUGURAL

Kennedy's inaugural address of 20 January 1961 serves as an example and
a clue with which to introduce this complex subject. That address began:

> We observe today not a victory of party but a celebration of freedom—sym-
> bolizing an end as well as a beginning—signifying renewal as well as
> change. For I have sworn before you and Almighty God the same solemn
> oath our forebears prescribed nearly a century and three quarters ago.
>   The world is very different now. For man holds in his mortal hands the
> power to abolish all forms of human poverty and to abolish all forms of hu-
> man life. And yet the same revolutionary beliefs for which our forebears
> fought are still at issue around the globe—the belief that the rights of man
> come not from the generosity of the state but from the hand of God.

And it concluded:

> Finally, whether you are citizens of America or of the world, ask of us the
> same high standards of strength and sacrifice that we shall ask of you. With
> a good conscience our only sure reward, with history the final judge of our
> deeds, let us go forth to lead the land we love, asking His blessings and His
> help, but knowing that here on earth God's work must truly be our own.

These are the three places in this brief address in which Kennedy mentioned the name of God. If we could understand why he mentioned God,

the way in which he did it, and what he meant to say in those three references, we would understand much about American civil religion. But this is not a simple or obvious task, and American students of religion would probably differ widely in their interpretation of these passages.

Let us consider first the placing of the three references. They occur in the two opening paragraphs and in the closing paragraph, thus providing a sort of frame for the more concrete remarks that form the middle part of the speech. Looking beyond this particular speech, we would find that similar references to God are almost invariably to be found in the pronouncements of American presidents on solemn occasions, though usually not in the working messages that the president sends to Congress on various concrete issues. How, then, are we to interpret this placing of references to God?

It might be argued that the passages quoted reveal the essentially irrelevant role of religion in the very secular society that is America. The placing of the references in this speech as well as in public life generally indicates that religion has "only a ceremonial significance"; it gets only a sentimental nod which serves largely to placate the more unenlightened members of the community, before a discussion of the really serious business with which religion has nothing whatever to do. A cynical observer might even say that an American president has to mention God or risk losing votes. A semblance of piety is merely one of the unwritten qualifications for the office, a bit more traditional than but not essentially different from the present-day requirement of a pleasing television personality.

But we know enough about the function of ceremonial and ritual in various societies to make us suspicious of dismissing something as unimportant because it is "only a ritual." What people say on solemn occasions need not be taken at face value, but it is often indicative of deep-seated values and commitments that are not made explicit in the course of everyday life. Following this line of argument, it is worth considering whether the very special placing of the references to God in Kennedy's address may not reveal something rather important and serious about religion in American life.

It might be countered that the very way in which Kennedy made his references reveals the essentially vestigial place of religion today. He did not refer to any religion in particular. He did not refer to the Catholic Church. In fact, his only reference was to the concept of God, a word which almost all Americans can accept but which means so many different things to so many different people that it is almost an empty sign. Is this not just another indication that in America religion is considered vaguely to be a good thing, but that people care so little about it that it has lost any content whatever? Isn't Eisenhower reported to have said, "Our government makes no sense unless it is founded in a deeply felt religious faith—and I don't care what it is," and isn't that a complete negation of any real religion?

These questions are worth pursuing because they raise the issue of how civil religion relates to the political society, on the one hand, and to private religious organizations, on the other. President Kennedy was a Christian, more specifically a Catholic Christian. Thus, his general references to God do not mean that he lacked a specific religious commitment. But why, then, did he not include some remark to the effect that Christ is the Lord of the world or some indication of respect for the Catholic Church? He did not because these are matters of his own private religious belief and of his relation to his own particular church; they are not matters relevant in any direct way to the conduct of his public office. Others with different religious views and commitments to different churches or denominations are equally qualified participants in the political process. The principle of separation of church and state guarantees the freedom of religious belief and association, but at the same time clearly segregates the religious sphere, which is considered to be essentially private, from the political one.

Considering the separation of church and state, how is a president justified in using the word *God* at all? The answer is that the separation of church and state has not denied the political realm a religious dimension. Although matters of personal religious belief, worship, and association are considered to be strictly private affairs, there are, at the same time, certain common elements of religious orientation that the great majority of Americans share. These have played a crucial role in the development of American institutions and still provide a religious dimension for the whole fabric of American life, including the political sphere. This public religious dimension is expressed in a set of beliefs, symbols, and rituals that I am calling the American civil religion. The inauguration of a president is an important ceremonial event in this religion. It reaffirms, among other things, the religious legitimation of the highest political authority.

Let us look more closely at what Kennedy actually said. First he said, "I have sworn before you and Almighty God the same solemn oath our forebears prescribed nearly a century and three quarters ago." The oath is the oath of office, including the acceptance of the obligation to uphold the Constitution. He swears it before the people (you) and God. Beyond the Constitution, then, the president's obligation extends not only to the people but to God. In American political theory, sovereignty rests, of course, with the people, but implicitly, and often explicitly, the ultimate sovereignty has been attributed to God. This is the meaning of the motto, "In God we trust," as well as the inclusion of the phrase "under God" in the pledge to the flag. What difference does it make that sovereignty belongs to God? Though the will of the people as expressed in majority vote is carefully institutionalized as the operative source of political authority, it is deprived of an ultimate significance. The will of the people is not itself the criterion of right and wrong. There is a higher criterion in terms of which this will can be judged; it is possible that the people may be wrong. The president's obligation extends to the higher criterion.

When Kennedy says that "the rights of man come not from the generosity of the state but from the hand of God," he is stressing this point again. It does not matter whether the state is the expression of the will of an autocratic monarch or of the "people"; the rights of man are more basic than any political structure and provide a point of revolutionary leverage from which any state structure may be radically altered. That is the basis for his reassertion of the revolutionary significance of America.

But the religious dimension in political life as recognized by Kennedy not only provides a grounding for the rights of man which makes any form of political absolutism illegitimate, it also provides a transcendent goal for the political process. This is implied in his final words that "here on earth God's work must truly be our own." What he means here is, I think, more clearly spelled out in a previous paragraph, the wording of which, incidentally, has a distinctly Biblical ring:

> Now the trumpet summons us again—not as a call to bear arms, though arms we need—not as a call to battle, though embattled we are—but a call to bear the burden of a long twilight struggle, year in and year out, "rejoicing in hope, patient in tribulation"—a struggle against the common enemies of man; tyranny, poverty, disease and war itself.

The whole address can be understood as only the most recent statement of a theme that lies very deep in the American tradition, namely the obligation, both collective and individual, to carry out God's will on earth. This was the motivating spirit of those who founded America, and it has been present in every generation since. Just below the surface throughout Kennedy's inaugural address, it becomes explicit in the closing statement that God's work must be our own. That this very activist and noncontemplative conception of the fundamental religious obligation, which has been historically associated with the Protestant position, should be enunciated so clearly in the first major statement of the first Catholic president seems to underline how deeply established it is in the American outlook.

Let us now consider the form and history of the civil religious tradition in which Kennedy was speaking.

THE IDEA OF A CIVIL RELIGION

The phrase *civil religion* is, of course, Rousseau's. In Chapter 8, Book 4, of *The Social Contract*, he outlines the simple dogmas of the civil religion: the existence of God, the life to come, the reward of virtue and the punishment of vice, and the exclusion of religious intolerance. All other religious opinions are outside the cognizance of the state and may be freely held by citizens. While the phrase *civil religion* was not used, to the best of my knowledge, by the founding fathers, and I am certainly not arguing for the particular influence of Rousseau, it is clear that similar ideas, as part of the cultural climate of the late-eighteenth century, were to be found among the Americans. For example, Franklin writes in his autobiography,

> I never was without some religious principles. I never doubted, for instance, the existence of the Deity; that he made the world and govern'd it by his Providence; that the most acceptable service of God was the doing of good to men; that our souls are immortal; and that all crime will be punished, and virtue rewarded either here or hereafter. These I esteemed the essentials of every religion; and, being to be found in all the religions we had in our country, I respected them all, tho' with different degrees of respect, as I found them more or less mix'd with other articles, which, without any tendency to inspire, promote or confirm morality, serv'd principally to divide us, and make us unfriendly to one another.

It is easy to dispose of this sort of position as essentially utilitarian in relation to religion. In Washington's Farewell Address (though the words may be Hamilton's) the utilitarian aspect is quite explicit:

> Of all the dispositions and habits which lead to political prosperity, Religion and Morality are indispensable supports. In vain would that man claim the tribute of Patriotism, who should labour to subvert these great Pillars of human happiness, these firmest props of the duties of men and citizens. The mere politician, equally with the pious man, ought to respect and cherish them. A volume could not trace all their connections with private and public felicity. Let it simply be asked where is the security for property, for reputation, for life, if the sense of religious obligation *desert* the oaths, which are the instruments of investigation in Courts of Justice? And let us with caution indulge the supposition, that morality can be maintained without religion. Whatever may be conceded to the influence of refined education on minds of peculiar structure, reason and experience both forbid us to expect that National morality can prevail in exclusion of religious principle.

But there is every reason to believe that religion, particularly the idea of God, played a constitutive role in the thought of the early American statesmen.

Kennedy' inaugural pointed to the religious aspect of the Declaration of Independence, and it might be well to look at that document a bit more closely. There are four references to God. The first speaks of the "Laws of Nature and of Nature's God" which entitle any people to be independent. The second is the famous statement that all men "are endowed by their Creator with certain inalienable Rights." Here Jefferson is locating the fundamental legitimacy of the new nation in a conception of "higher law" that is itself based on both classical natural law and Biblical religion. The third is an appeal to "the Supreme Judge of the world for the rectitude of our intentions," and the last indicates "a firm reliance on the protection of divine Providence." In these last two references, a Biblical God of history who stands in judgment over the world is indicated.

The intimate relation of these religious notions with the self-conception of the new republic is indicated by the frequency of their appearance in early official documents. For example, we find in Washington's first inaugural address of 30 April 1789:

> It would be peculiarly improper to omit in this first official act my fervent supplications to that Almighty Being who rules over the universe, who presides in the councils of nations, and whose providential aids can supply every defect, that His benediction may consecrate to the liberties and happiness of the people of the United States a Government instituted by themselves for these essential purposes, and may enable every instrument employed in its administration to execute with success the functions allotted to his charge.
>
> No people can be bound to acknowledge and adore the Invisible Hand which conducts the affairs of man more than those of the United States. Every step by which we have advanced to the character of an independent nation seems to have been distinguished by some token of providential agency. . . .
>
> The propitious smiles of Heaven can never be expected on a nation that disregards the eternal rules of order and right which Heaven itself has ordained. . . . The preservation of the sacred fire of liberty and the destiny of the republican model of government are justly considered, perhaps, as *deeply as finally*, staked on the experiment intrusted to the hands of the American people.

Nor did these religious sentiments remain merely the personal expression of the president. At the request of both Houses of Congress, Washington proclaimed on October 3 of that same first year as president that November 26 should be "a day of public thanksgiving and prayer," the first Thanksgiving Day under the Constitution.

The words and acts of the founding fathers, especially the first few presidents, shaped the form and tone of the civil religion as it has been maintained ever since. Though much is selectively derived from Christianity, this religion is clearly not itself Christianity. For one thing, neither Washington nor Adams nor Jefferson mentions Christ in his inaugural address; nor do any of the subsequent presidents, although not one of them fails to mention God. The God of the civil religion is not only rather "unitarian," he is also on the austere side, much more related to order, law, and right than to salvation and love. Even though he is somewhat deist in cast, he is by no means simply a watchmaker God. He is actively interested and involved in history, with a special concern for America. Here the analogy has much less to do with natural law than with ancient Israel; the equation of America with Israel in the idea of the "American Israel" is not infrequent. What was implicit in the words of Washington already quoted becomes explicit in Jefferson's second inaugural when he said: "I shall need, too, the favor that Being in whose hands we are, who led our fathers, as Israel of old, from their native land and planted them in a country flowing with all the necessaries and comforts of life." Europe is Egypt; America, the promised land. God has led to his people to establish a new sort of social order that shall be a light unto all the nations.

This theme, too, has been a continuous one in the civil religion. We have already alluded to it in the case of the Kennedy inaugural. We find it again in President Johnson's inaugural address:

> They came here—the exile and the stranger, brave but frightened—to find a place where a man could be his own man. They made a covenant with this land. Conceived in justice, written in liberty, bound in union, it was meant one day to inspire the hopes of all mankind; and it binds us still. If we keep its terms, we shall flourish.

What we have, then, from the earliest years of the republic is a collection of beliefs, symbols, and rituals with respect to sacred things and institutionalized in a collectivity. This religion—there seems no other word for it—while not antithetical to and indeed sharing much in common with Christianity, was neither sectarian nor in any specific sense Christian. At a time when the society was overwhelmingly Christian, it seems unlikely that this lack of Christian reference was meant to spare the feelings of the tiny non-Christian minority. Rather, the civil religion expressed what those who set the precedents felt was appropriate under the circumstances. It reflected their private as well as public views. Nor was the civil religion simply "religion in general." While generality was undoubtedly seen as a virtue by some, as in the quotation from Franklin above, the civil religion was specific enough when it came to the topic of America. Precisely because of this specificity, the civil religion was saved from empty formalism and served as a genuine vehicle of national religious self-understanding.

But the civil religion was not, in the minds of Franklin, Washington, Jefferson, or other leaders, with the exception of a few radicals like Tom Paine, ever felt to be a substitute for Christianity. There was an implicit but quite clear division of function between the civil religion and Christianity. Under the doctrine of religious liberty, an exceptionally wide sphere of personal piety and voluntary social action was left to the churches. But the churches were neither to control the state nor to be controlled by it. The national magistrate, whatever his private religious views, operates under the rubrics of the civil religion as long as he is in his official capacity, as we have already seen in the case of Kennedy. This accommodation was undoubtedly the product of a particular historical moment and of a cultural background dominated by Protestantism of several varieties and by the Enlightenment, but it has survived despite subsequent changes in the cultural and religious climate.

CIVIL WAR AND CIVIL RELIGION

Until the Civil war, the American civil religion focused above all on the event of the Revolution, which was seen as the final act of the Exodus from the old lands across the waters. The Declaration of Independence and the Constitution were the sacred scriptures and Washington the divinely appointed Moses who led his people out of the hands of tyranny. The Civil War, which Sidney Mead calls "the center of American history," was the second great event that involved the national self-understanding so deeply as to require expression in the civil religion. In 1835, De Tocqueville wrote that the American republic had never really been tried, that victory in the Revolutionary War was more the result of British preoccupation elsewhere and the presence of a powerful ally than of any great military success of the Americans. But in 1861 the time of testing had indeed come. Not only did the Civil War have the tragic intensity of fratricidal strife, but it was one of the bloodiest wars of the nineteenth century; the loss of life was far greater than any previously suffered by Americans.

The Civil War raised the deepest questions of national meaning. The man who not only formulated but in his own person embodied its meaning for Americans was Abraham Lincoln. For him the issue was not in the first instance slavery but "whether that nation, or any nation so conceived, and so dedicated, can long endure." He had said in Independence Hall in Philadelphia on 22 February 1861:

> All political sentiments I entertain have been drawn, so far as I have been able to draw them, from the sentiments which originated in and were given to the world from this Hall. I have never had a feeling, politically, that did not spring from the sentiments embodied in the Declaration of Independence.

The phrases of Jefferson constantly echo in Lincoln's speeches. His task was, first of all, to save the Union—not for America alone but for the meaning of America to the whole world so unforgettably etched in the last phrase of the Gettysburg Address.

But inevitably the issue of slavery as the deeper cause of the conflict had to be faced. In the second inaugural, Lincoln related slavery and the war in an ultimate perspective:

> If we shall suppose that American slavery is one of those offenses which, in the providence of God, must needs come, but which, having continued through His appointed time, He now wills to remove, and that He gives to both North and South this terrible war as the woe due to those by whom the offense came, shall we discern therein any departure from those divine attributes which the believers in a living God always ascribe to Him? Fondly do we hope, fervently do we pray, that this mighty scourge of war may speedily pass away. Yet, if God wills that it continue until all the wealth piled by the bondsman's two hundred and fifty years of unrequited toil shall be sunk, and until every drop of blood drawn with the lash shall be paid by another drawn with the sword, as was said three thousand years ago, so still it must be said "the judgments of the Lord are true and righteous altogether."

But he closes on a note if not of redemption then of reconciliation—"With malice toward none, with charity for all."

With the Civil War, a new theme of death, sacrifice, and rebirth enters the civil religion. It is symbolized in the life and death of Lincoln. Nowhere is it stated more vividly than in the Gettysburg Address, itself part of the Lincolnian "New Testament" among the civil scriptures. Robert Lowell has recently pointed out the "insistent use of birth images" in this speech explicitly devoted to "these honored dead"; "brought forth"; "conceived," "created," "a new birth of freedom." He goes on to say:

The Gettysburg Address is a symbolic and sacramental act. Its verbal quality is resonance combined with a logical, matter of fact, prosaic brevity. . . . In his words, Lincoln symbolically died, just as the Union soldiers really died—and as he himself was soon really to die. By his words, he gave the field of battle a symbolic significance that it had lacked. For us and our country, he left Jefferson's ideals of freedom and equality joined to the Christian sacrificial act of death and rebirth. I believe this is a meaning that goes beyond sect or religion and beyond peace and war, and is now part of our lives as a challenge, obstacle and hope.

Lowell is certainly right in pointing out the Christian quality of the symbolism here, but he is also right in quickly disavowing any sectarian implication. The earlier symbolism of the civil religion had been Hebraic without being in any specific sense Jewish. The Gettysburg symbolism (". . . those who here gave their lives, that that nation might live") is Christian without having anything to do with the Christian church.

The symbolic equation of Lincoln with Jesus was made relatively early. Herndon, who had been Lincoln's law partner, wrote:

For fifty years God rolled Abraham Lincoln through his fiery furnace. He did it to try Abraham and to purify him for his purposes. This made Mr. Lincoln humble, tender, forbearing, sympathetic to suffering, kind, sensitive, tolerant; broadening, deepening and widening his whole nature; making him the noblest and loveliest character since Jesus Christ. . . . I believe that Lincoln was God's chosen one.

With the Christian archetype in the background, Lincoln, "our martyred president," was linked to the war dead, those who "gave the last full measure of devotion." The theme of sacrifice was indelibly written into the civil religion.

The new symbolism soon found both physical and ritualistic expression. The great number of the war dead required the establishment of a number of national cemeteries. Of these, the Gettysburg National Cemetery, which Lincoln's famous address served to dedicate, has been overshadowed only by the Arlington National Cemetery. Begun somewhat vindictively on the Lee estate across the river from Washington, partly with the end that the Lee family could never reclaim it, it has subsequently become the most hallowed monument of the civil religion. Not only was a section set aside for the Confederate dead, but it has received the dead of each succeeding American war. It is the site of the one important new symbol to come out of World War I, the Tomb of the Unknown Soldier; more recently it has become the site of the tomb of another martyred president and its symbolic eternal flame.

Memorial day, which grew out of the Civil War, gave ritual expression to the themes we have been discussing. As Lloyd Warner has so brilliantly analyzed it, the Memorial Day observance, especially in the towns and smaller cities of America, is a major event for the whole community involving a rededication to the martyred dead, to the spirit of sacrifice, and to the American vision. Just as Thanksgiving Day, which incidentally was securely institutionalized as an annual national holiday only under the presidency of Lincoln, serves to integrate the family into the civil religion, so Memorial Day has acted to integrate the local community into the national cult. Together with the less overtly religious Fourth of July and the more minor celebrations of Veterans Day and the birthdays of Washington and Lincoln, these two holidays provide an annual ritual calendar for the civil religion. The public-school system serves as a particularly important context for the cultic celebration of the civil rituals.

THE CIVIL RELIGION TODAY

In reifying and giving a name to something that, though pervasive enough when you look at it, has gone on only semiconsciously, there is risk of severely distorting the data. But the reification and the naming have already begun. The religious critics of "religion in general," or of the "religion of the 'American way of Life,'" or of "American Shinto" have really been talking about the civil religion. As usual in religious polemic, they take as criteria the best in their own religious traditions and as typical the worst in the tradition of the civil religion. Against these critics, I would argue that the civil religion at its best is a genuine apprehension of universal and transcendent religious reality as seen in or, one could almost say, as revealed through the experience of the American people. Like all religions, it has suffered various deformation and demonic distortions. At its best, it has neither been so general that it lacked incisive relevance to the American scene nor so particular that it has placed American society above universal human values. I am not at all convinced that the leaders of the churches have consistently represented a higher level of religious insight than the spokesmen of the civil religion. Reinhold Niebuhr has this to say of Lincoln, who never joined a church and who certainly represents civil religion at its best:

> An analysis of the religion of Abraham Lincoln in the context of the traditional religion of his time and place and of its polemical use of the slavery issue, which corrupted religious life in the days before and during the Civil War, must lead to the conclusion that Lincoln's religious convictions were

superior in depth and purity to those, not only of the political leaders of his day, but of the religious leaders of the era.

Perhaps the real animus of the religious critics has been not so much against the civil religion in itself but against its pervasive and dominating influence within the sphere of church religion. As S. M. Lipset has recently shown, American religion at least since the early nineteenth century has been predominantly activist, moralistic, and social rather than contemplative, theological, or innerly spiritual. De Tocqueville spoke of American church religion as "a political institution which powerfully contributes to the maintenance of a democratic republic among the Americans" by supplying a strong moral consensus amidst continuous political change. Henry Bargy in 1902 spoke of American church religion as *"la poesie du civisme."*

It is certainly true that the relation between religion and politics in America has been singularly smooth. This is in large part due to the dominant tradition. As De Tocqueville wrote:

> The greatest part of British America was peopled by men who, after having shaken off the authority of the Pope, acknowledged no other religious supremacy: they brought with them into the New World a form of Christianity which I cannot better describe than by styling it a democratic and republican religion.

The churches opposed neither the Revolution nor the establishment of democratic institutions. Even when some of them opposed the full institutionalization of religious liberty, they accepted the final outcome with good grace and without nostalgia for an *ancien regime.* The American civil religion was never anticlerical or militantly secular. On the contrary, it borrowed selectively from the religious tradition in such a way that the average American saw no conflict between the two. In this way, the civil religion was able to build up without any bitter struggle with the church powerful symbols of national solidarity and to mobilize deep levels of personal motivation for the attainment of national goals.

Such an achievement is by no means to be taken for granted. It would seem that the problem of a civil religion is quite general in modern societies and that the way it is solved or not solved will have repercussions in many spheres. One need only to think of France to see how differently things can go. The French Revolution was anticlerical to the core and attempted to set up an anti-Christian civil religion. Throughout modern French history, the chasm between traditional Catholic symbols and the symbolism of 1789 has been immense.

American civil religion is still very much alive. Just three years ago we participated in a vivid re-enactment of the sacrifice theme in connection with the funeral of our assassinated president. The American Israel theme is clearly behind both Kennedy's New Frontier and Johnson's Great Society. Let me give just one recent illustration of how the civil religion serves to mobilize support for the attainment of national goals. On 15 March 1965 President Johnson went before Congress to ask for a strong voting-rights bill. Early in the speech he said:

> Rarely are we met with the challenge, not to our growth or abundance, or our welfare or our security—but rather to the values and the purposes and the meaning of our beloved nation.
> The issue of equal rights for American Negroes is such an issue. And should we defeat every enemy, and should we double our wealth and conquer the stars and still be unequal to this issue, then we will have failed as a people and as a nation.
> For with a country as a person, "What is a man profited, if he shall gain the whole world, and lose his own soul?"

And in conclusion he said:

> Above the pyramid on the great seal of the United States it says in Latin, "God has favored our undertaking."
> God will not favor everything that we do. It is rather our duty to divine His will. I cannot help but believe that He truly understands and that He really favors the undertaking that we begin here tonight.

The civil religion has not always been invoked in favor of worthy causes. On the domestic scene, an American-Legion type of ideology that fuses God, country, and flag has been used to attack nonconformist and liberal ideas and groups of all kinds. Still, it has been difficult to use the words of Jefferson and Lincoln to support special interests and undermine personal freedom. The defenders of slavery before the Civil War came to reject the thinking of the Declaration of Independence. Some of the most consistent of them turned against not only Jeffersonian democracy but Reformation religion; they dreamed of a South dominated by medieval chivalry and divine-right monarchy. For all the overt religiosity of the radical right today, their relation to the civil religious consensus is tenuous, as when the John Birch Society attacks the central American symbol of Democracy itself.

With respect to America's role in the world, the dangers of distortion are greater and the built-in safeguards of the tradition weaker. The theme of the American Israel was used, almost from the beginning, as a justification for the shameful treatment of the Indians so characteristic of our history. It can be overtly or implicitly linked to the idea of manifest destiny which has been used to legitimate several adventures in imperialism since the early nineteenth century. Never has the danger been greater than today. The issue is not so much one of imperial expansion, of which we are accused, as of the tendency to assimilate all governments or parties in the world which support our immediate policies or call upon our help by invoking the notion of free institutions and democratic values. Those nations that are for the moment "on our side" become "the free world." A repressive and unstable military dictatorship in South Viet-Nam becomes "the free people of South Viet-Nam and their government." It is then part of the role of America as the New Jerusalem and "the last hope of earth" to defend such governments with treasure and eventually with blood. When our soldiers are actually dying, it becomes possible to consecrate the struggle further by invoking the great theme of sacrifice. For the majority of the American people who are unable to judge whether the people in South Viet-Nam (or wherever) are "free like us," such arguments are convincing. Fortunately President Johnson has been less ready to assert that "God has favored our undertaking" in the case of Viet-Nam than with respect to civil rights. But others are not so hesitant. The civil religion has exercised long-term pressure for the human solution of our greatest domestic problem, the treatment of the Negro American. It remains to be seen how relevant it can become for our role in the world at large, and whether we can effectively stand for "the revolutionary beliefs for which our forebears fought," in John F. Kennedy's words.

The civil religion is obviously involved in the most pressing moral and political issues of the day. But it is also caught in another kind of crisis, theoretical and theological, of which it is at the moment largely unaware. "God" has clearly been a central symbol in the civil religion from the beginning and remains so today. This symbol is just as central to the civil religion as it is to Judaism or Christianity. In the late eighteenth century this posed no problem; even Tom Paine, contrary to his detractors, was not an atheist. From left to right and regardless of church or sect, all could accept the idea of God. But today, as even *Time* has recognized, the meaning of the word *God* is by no means so clear or so obvious. There is no formal creed in the civil religion. We have had a Catholic president; it is conceivable that we could have a Jewish one. But could we have an agnostic president? Could a man with conscientious scruples about using the word *God* the way Kennedy and Johnson have used it be elected chief magistrate of our country? If the whole God symbolism requires reformulation, there will be obvious consequences for the civil religion, consequences perhaps of liberal alienation and of fundamentalist ossification that have not so far been prominent in this realm. The civil religion has been a point of articulation between the profoundest commitments of the Western religious and philosophical tradition and the common beliefs of ordinary Americans. It is not too soon to consider how the deepening theological crisis may affect the future of this articulation.

THE THIRD TIME OF TRIAL

In conclusion it may be worthwhile to relate the civil religion to the most serious situation that we as Americans now face, what I call the third time of trial. The first time of trial had to do with the question of independence, whether we should or could run our own affairs in our own way. The second time of trial was over the issue of slavery, which in turn was only the most salient aspect of the more general problem of the full institutionalization of democracy within our country. This second problem we are still far from solving though we have some notable successes to our credit. But we have been overtaken by a third great problem which has led to a third great crisis, in the midst of which we stand. This is the problem of responsible action in a revolutionary world, a world seeking to attain many of the things, material and spiritual, that we have already attained. Americans have, from the beginning, been aware of the responsibility and the significance our republican experiment has for the whole world. The first internal political polarization in the new nation had to do with our attitude toward the French revolution. But we were small and weak then, and "foreign entanglements" seemed to threaten our very survival. During the last century, our relevance for the world was not forgotten, but our role was seen as purely exemplary. Our democratic republic rebuked tyranny by merely existing. Just after World War I we were on the brink of taking a different role in the world, but once again we turned our back.

Since World War II the old pattern has become impossible. Every president since Roosevelt has been groping toward a new pattern of action in the world, one that would be consonant with our power and our responsibilities. For Truman and for the period dominated by John Foster Dulles that pattern was seen to be the great Manichaean confrontation of East and West, the confrontation of democracy and "the false philosophy of Communism" that provided the structure of Truman's inaugural address. But with the last years of Eisenhower and with the successive two presidents, the pattern began to shift. The great problems came to be seen as caused not solely by the evil intent of any one group of men, but as stemming from much more complex and multiple sources. For Kennedy, it was not so much a struggle against particular men as against "the common enemies of man: tyranny, poverty, disease and war itself."

But in the midst of this trend toward a less primitive conception of ourselves and our world, we have somehow, without anyone really intending it, stumbled into a military confrontation where we have come to feel that our honor is at stake. We have in a moment of uncertainty been tempted to rely on our overwhelming physical power rather than on our intelligence, and we have, in part, succumbed to this temptation. Bewildered and unnerved when our terrible power fails to bring immediate success, we are at the edge of a chasm the depth of which no man knows.

I cannot help but think of Robinson Jeffers, whose poetry seems more apt now than when it was written, when he said:

> *Unhappy country, what wings you have! . . .*
> *Weep (it is frequent in human affairs), weep for*
> *terrible magnificence of the means,*
> *The ridiculous incompetence of the reasons, the*
> *bloody and shabby*
> *Pathos of the result.*

But as so often before in similar times, we have a man of prophetic stature, without the bitterness or misanthropy of Jeffers, who, as Lincoln before him, calls this nation to its judgment:

> When a nation is very powerful but lacking in self-confidence, it is likely to behave in a manner that is dangerous both to itself and to others.
>
> Gradually but unmistakably, America is succumbing to that arrogance of power which has afflicted, weakened and in some cases destroyed great nations in the past.
>
> If the war goes on and expands, if that fatal process continues to accelerate until America becomes what it is not now and never has been, a seeker after unlimited power and empire, then Vietnam will have had a mighty and tragic fallout indeed.
>
> I do not believe that will happen. I am very apprehensive but I still remain hopeful, and even confident, that America, with its humane and democratic traditions, will find the wisdom to match its power.

Without an awareness that our nation stands under higher judgment, the tradition of the civil religion would be dangerous indeed. Fortunately, the prophetic voices have never been lacking. Our present situation brings to mind the Mexican-American war that Lincoln, among so many others, opposed. The spirit of civil disobedience that is alive today in the civil rights movement and the opposition to the Viet-Nam war was already clearly outlined by Henry David Thoreau when he wrote, "If the law is of such a nature that it requires you to be an agent of injustice to another, then I say, break the law." Thoreau's words, "I would remind you countrymen that they are men first, and Americans at a late and convenient hour," provide an essential standard for any adequate thought and action in our third time of trial. As Americans, we have been well favored in the world, but it is as men that we will be judged.

Out of the first and second times of trial have come, as we have seen, the major symbols of the American civil religion. There seems little doubt that a successful negotiation of this third time of trial—the attainment of some kind of viable and coherent world order—would precipitate a major new set of symbolic forms. So far the flickering flame of the United Nations burns too low to be the focus of a cult, but the emergence of a genuine trans-national sovereignty would certainly change this. It would necessitate the incorporation of vital international symbolism into our civil religion, or, perhaps a better way of putting it, it would result in American civil religion becoming simply one part of a new civil religion of the world. It is useless to speculate on the form such a civil religion might take, though it obviously would draw on religious traditions beyond the sphere of Biblical religion alone. Fortunately, since the American civil religion is not the worship of the American nation but an understanding of the American experience in the light of ultimate and universal reality, the reorganization entailed by such a new situation need not disrupt the American civil religion's continuity. A world civil religion could be accepted as a fulfillment and not a denial of American civil religion. Indeed, such an outcome has been the eschatological hope of American civil religion from the beginning. To deny such an outcome would be to deny the meaning of America itself.

Behind the civil religion at every point lie Biblical archetypes: Exodus, Chosen People, Promised Land, New Jerusalem, Sacrificial Death and Rebirth. But it is also genuinely American and genuinely new. It has its own prophets and its own martyrs, its own sacred events and sacred places, its own solemn rituals and symbols. It is concerned that America be a society as perfectly in accord with the will of God as men can make it, and a light to all the nations.

It has often been used and is being used today as a cloak for petty interests and ugly passions. It is in need—as is any living faith—of continual reformation, of being measured by universal standards. But it is not evident that it is incapable of growth and new insight.

It does not make any decision for us. It does not remove us from moral ambiguity, from being, in Lincoln's fine phrase, an "almost chosen people." But it is a heritage of moral and religious experience from which we still have much to learn as we formulate the decisions that lie ahead.

QUESTIONS TO CONSIDER

1. How does Bellah define American civil religion?
2. What did Rousseau define as the four elements of civil religion?
3. What is the difference between civil religion and Christianity?
4. How did the Civil War provide parallels with Christianity? What document most captures the parallel?
5. How has civil religion distorted America's role in the world?
6. How has this article affected your view of the relationship between the United States and Christianity?

12

Cracks in the Mold*

Sara Evans

Sara Evans (1943–), educated at Duke and the University of North Carolina and now a professor of women's history at the University of Minnesota, is the author of the highly regarded *Born for Liberty: A History of Women in America* (1989). She first won acclaim in 1979 when her autobiographical account *Personal Politics* was published. The book provided a professional scholar's firsthand exploration of the intersection of the church, the civil rights movement, the New Left, and the feminist movement. A preacher's kid who got into the civil rights movement through the church, Evans found it to be as sexist as the establishment against which it was revolting. She discovered a striking parallel with women in the abolitionist movement 130 years earlier. They had found the oppression of slaves not dissimilar to their own second-class status and launched the first women's movement in 1848 at Seneca Fall, New York. Women in the modern civil rights movement also found many similarities between black grievances and their own condition, and the radical women's movement was born.

In this selection, the prologue to her book, Evans explains how many women in the 1950s recognized that they were limited to functioning as wives and mothers but were not finding fulfillment in those roles. Her thorough analysis of the condition of women and

---

*Reprinted from *Personal Politics*, by Sara Evans, by permission of Alfred A. Knopf, Inc. Copyright © 1979 by Sara Evans.

their emancipation when Betty Friedan wrote her best-selling *The Feminine Mystique* in 1963 merits close attention from students of the American character. But even though women came out of the closet after 1963, Evans explains the essential conservatism of the career women who organized the National Organization for Women. It was left to younger women, energized by the civil rights and New Left movements, to take the feminist movement in more radical directions, challenging not only the male monopoly of the mainstream, but the nature of the mainstream itself. The character of American women, neatly constricted by a "cult of true womanhood" in the nineteenth century and a similar "feminine mystique" after World War II, has emerged into an ongoing state of redefinition.

> Of the accomplishments of the American woman, one she brings off with the most spectacular success is having babies.
>
> —*Life* magazine, December 24, 1956

In the mid-1950s Betty Friedan wrote and edited articles entitled "Millionaire's Wife," "I Was Afraid to Have a Baby," and "Two Are an Island" for *Cosmopolitan, McCall's,* and *Mademoiselle.* Robin Morgan was a child-actress playing Dagmar on the popular TV series "I Remember Mama." Thousands of other future feminists lived in middle-class homes, growing up to be bright, popular, and good. Everything appeared to promise them a future of happy domesticity. Who would have guessed that within a decade they would rise up to challenge that promise, to name it fraud, and to demand fundamental changes in American society under the banner of women's liberation? Feminism had been dead for over thirty years. Even the word had become faintly embarrassing. Feminists were seen as unfulfilled, neurotic, grasping women.

When *Life* magazine produced a special issue on women in December 1956, Mrs. Peter Marshall charged in her introduction that "many of woman's current troubles began with the period of her preoccupation with her 'rights.'" She advised women to turn instead to the most satisfying and "completely fulfilling" moments of their lives: the first formal dance, the first embrace, the first baby. In the same issue Cornelia Otis Skinner denounced the "shrill ridiculous war over the dead issue of feminism." "Ladies," she appealed, "we have won our case, but for heaven's sake let's stop trying to prove it over and over again."

The odor of embarrassment surrounding women's changing roles lingered as a reminder of the acrid attack that had been launched more than a decade before when Philip Wylie had blamed "Mom" for all the evils of American society. Modern industrialization, the critics argued, had undermined the basic functions of the traditional home. Such changes induced severe neurosis in women, they said. According to Wylie, it transformed them into narcissistic "Moms" who devoured their sons and husbands, robbing them of independence and ego strength. Freudians like Marynia Farnham and Ferdinand Lundberg pointed to another "pathological" response in modern women: feminism. They recommended massive use of psychotherapy, government propaganda and awards for good motherhood, cash payments to mothers, and the restoration of such traditional home tasks as cooking, preserving, and decorating. Only through a return to the traditional home, "a social extension of the mother's womb," could "women's inner balance" be reclaimed and the level of hostility in the world reduced.

By the midfifties such worries seemed a bit misplaced. Women were marrying younger, having three and four children, and apparently loving it. The vast majority of American women identified themselves as housewives whether they worked outside the home or not. Although growing numbers of them attended college, educators assured the public that they were simply preparing to be better mothers and wives, nothing more. If pickling and preserving had become the province of automated canneries, the work of the suburban housewife expanded in other ways. *Life* described a "typical" housewife under the banner: "Busy Wife's Achievements: Marjorie Sutton is Home Manager, Mother, Hostess, and Useful Civic Worker." No longer a household drudge, Marjorie the housewife had became a glamorized "superwoman" whose husband made $25,000 a year. Married at sixteen, she managed her household with the help of a full-time maid, worked with the Campfire Girls, the PTA, did charity fund raising, and sang in the choir. She cooked, sewed clothes for her four children, entertained 1500 guests a year, and exercised on a trampoline "to keep her size 12 figure."

While alternative images of womanhood never disappeared altogether, for most people they scarcely existed. The mass media proclaimed the triumph of domesticity. Women's magazines displayed "feminine" fashions with cinched waists, billowing petticoats, and accented bustlines. The movie industry promoted blond, buxom, sexy-but-innocent stars like Marilyn Monroe and Jayne Mansfield. Advertisers peddled a host of new appliances and household products to improve the housewife's ability to serve her family with cleaner, whiter clothes, odor-free kitchens, and "Poppin' Fresh" breads. The family as firmament of a stable social order received a stream of paeans from noted figures who encouraged women to center their energies in the home. Adlai Stevenson, liberal hero and two-time Democratic Party nominee for president, exhorted Smith College graduates in 1955 to remember that marriage and motherhood gave them a unique political duty. A woman could "inspire in her home a vision of the meaning of life and freedom . . . help her husband find values that will give purpose to his specialized daily chores . . . [and] teach her children the uniqueness of each individual human being." Studies indicated that most young women intended to do just that.

How, then, shall we explain the fact that by the early 1960s Betty Friedan had issued her famous denunciation of the "feminine mystique"—her term for the identification of womanhood with the roles of wife and mother? Or that Robin Morgan would grow up to organize a demonstration against Miss America in 1968 and use her powerful skills as writer and poet to proclaim herself a radical lesbian feminist in the early 1970s? Or that newspapers would be filled with news of a revival of feminism while feminist organizations and projects sprouted in every city in the country? The feminist resurgence in the 1960s and the 1970s makes sense only when one looks deeper under the surface of the apparent placidity of the 1950s, for there lay a dramatically changed reality for women, one that the old ideologies about women's place could not explain. The "feminine mystique" in operation offered a modernized version of the Victorian notion of women's sphere sharply separated from the public (male) realms of paid work, politics, and "historic" action. As an ideology it shaped women's and men's perceptions of reality, but its life was limited at the outset.

This undercurrent of change provoked Wylie's rage and Farnham and Lundberg's assault. And it prompted Adlai Stevenson to preface his remarks about the political power of homemakers with an acknowledgment that many women in that role "feel frustrated and far apart from the great issues and stirring debate for which their education has given them understanding and relish. Once they wrote poetry. Now it's the laundry list." The reassertion of domesticity and its apparent hegemony in the 1950s constituted an attempt to ignore and contain the altered conditions of the twentieth century that had begun to culminate in new life patterns for women. But women's lives could no longer be encompassed by the older definitions of a "woman's place."

Within the home women with more and more education found that they had less and less to do. Despite the baby boom, their families were smaller than their grandmothers' had been. Technology abbreviated the physical labor of housework while consumer items complicated and, in effect, expanded it again. Laundry could be done by an automatic machine, but it required the appropriate detergents, bleaches, and rinses to meet changing standards of cleanliness. Children spent their days in school and afternoons at the playground, but a model mother had to be constantly available, both physically—to drive car pools, lead Scout troops, entertain bored children—and emotionally to avoid inflicting irreparable psychic damage. The suburban supermom, as illustrated by Marjorie Sutton, fulfilled a complex round of community activities and enhanced her husband's career opportunities with her well-kept home and lavish entertaining. Other women attempting a similar burden with less money and no full-time maid felt anxious, guilty, and inadequate. For all their busyness, little of what they did felt like work. Women's function in the home had shifted from producing food and clothing for family use to maintaining the family as an emotional community, making sure that everyone was healthy and above all happy. Led to fantasize that marriage would provide them with total emotional and intellectual fulfillment, more and more women experienced acute disappointment and then guilt when it fell below the mark. In particular, educated suburban housewives, the women who attempted to live out the mystique in its fullest form, found that their goal had become a trap.

Large numbers of them now attended college, where they performed to intellectual standards that made no allowances for sex. Although educators defensively proclaimed that they were educating women to be better wives and mothers, they nonetheless offered women essentially the same training as that which prepared men for future careers in professions and business. Thus women entered marriage with heightened expectations of companionship and fulfillment and with a growing knowledge of their own diverse capabilities. Yet they arrived to find that suburbia had become a female ghetto. Their husbands worked miles away; parents and relatives lived in other cities. The social isolation of modern housewives and the automation of housework, combined with a rising awareness of what they were missing "out there," produced, inevitably, a high degree of loneliness and boredom. Life seemed to be passing them by: shopping trips became forays into the outside world, and husbands, who had less and less time to spend with their families, were now their major link to the public realm.

Even more important than these changes in the home was the fact that many housewives were also leaving home for up to eight hours a day to shoulder additional jobs as secretaries, social workers, teachers, sales clerks, stewardesses, and waitresses. These were not the dreaded "career women." They had jobs, not professions. But the fact that most of them were older, married women shattered the notion that work outside the home was a male preserve, to be shared only with young, single women filling in a gap between childhood and marriage. Furthermore, they were not all victims of grinding poverty. Throughout the fifties women from middle-income families entered the labor force faster than any other group in the population.

If Harvard seniors in 1955 were concerned to limit the boundaries of their future wives' aspirations, then they had reason to worry. "She can be independent on little things, but the big decisions will have to go my way," said one. "The marriage must be the most important thing that ever happened to her." Another would permit his wife to work until she had children, after which she must stay home. A third wanted an "Ivy League type," who "will also be centered in the home, a housewife." Writers like Ashley Montagu bemoaned women's failure to understand that home-making was the world's most important occupation and exhorted them to look to the model of European women, who focused their lives on the happiness of their husbands and children. Such women, he noted wistfully, "seem to behave as if they love their husbands." The fear of female competition with men had become a thread running through contemporary fiction, while the funny pages featured strong-minded Blondies married to foolish, ineffectual Dagwoods.

Yet few of the women entering the labor force saw themselves engaged in a challenge to tradition. They were simply doing what they could to help their families. And the jobs open to them were generally accepted as appropriate "women's work," requiring attributes similar to those expected of women at home. A changing economy created new jobs in such fields as health care, education, child care, clerical work, social work, and advertising—many of them labeled "female" from the beginning. If there were not enough young single women available for them, employers would have to relinquish their prejudices against married women and women with children. And they did. Thus millions of families achieved their "middle-class" status in the surge of postwar prosperity because of the additional income brought in by women. By 1956, 70 percent of all families in the $7,000 to $15,000 annual income range had at least two workers in the family, and the second was most often a woman.

Such participation in the labor force widened women's horizons. It gave them new skills and a paycheck that enhanced their role in family decisionmaking. But the blessing was a mixed one. A woman's work was likely to be threatening to her husband. It implied that he was not being a "good provider." Her guilt required that she avoid planning, training, or high aspirations. As a result she could not challenge discrimination according to sex. The only jobs logically open to most women were repetitious and boring. This structural inability to take oneself seriously induced a deep insecurity and a negative self-image. The lack of seriousness with which women and their employers viewed their work reflected itself in their paychecks. In 1966 women received a smaller income relative to men than in 1939; and as the percentages of women in certain occupations rose, their incomes relative to men in the same occupations fell.

In this context it seems logical that between 1940 and 1960, while the overall percentage of women working outside the home was climbing rapidly, there should have been a "slight but persistent decline in the proportion of professional, technical, and kindred workers that were female." Professional women could not pretend that their work was secondary and inconsequential. They pursued their careers with drive and determination.

These professional women were the most unmistakably "deviant," and often harbored among themselves the few remnants of feminism left in the 1950s. Many found it difficult to accept their performance of formerly "male" roles and went out of their way to assure themselves and others that they were still truly "feminine." A study of female executives found that all of the women surveyed placed home and family ahead of business, but felt that they could do both jobs, "if they want to badly enough." Frances Corey, a senior vice-president at Macy's, argued that women were "equal-but-special." "My attitude is that I can contribute something as a woman," she said. "My reaction is much more emotional—and emotion is a necessary commodity. There are places where I can't fill the bill as well as a man and I don't try."

The next generation, daughters of the fifties, grew up with the knowledge that their identifying roles should be those of wife and mother, but they knew that they would probably have a job at some point as well. They frequently observed their mothers shouldering the double burden of work outside the home and continuing responsibility for housework. Many knew that their mothers worked hard and were good at what they did—running day-care centers and shops, working in factories or offices, as lawyers or musicians. But their pay stayed low and their jobs offered few independent rewards. The feminine mystique had not obliterated the reality of working women. Rather, it had absorbed them. In 1956, alongside its "typical housewife," *Life* magazine included six pages of pictures bearing the title: "Women Hold ⅓ of U.S. Jobs." The accompanying photographs showed masses of women in various occupations. None of the jobs was portrayed as inviting; none seemed in the pictures to imply creativity or excitement. For example, hundreds of nurses in identical uniforms sat in a large auditorium listening to a male doctor; 104 middle-aged teachers stared impassively into the face of a man lecturing them on mental tests given to girl students; a typing pool of 450 pounded away in one enormous room. The only lively picture of the lot showed scantily clad chorus girls. This dulling mosaic contrasted sharply with other articles describing the "rich experience" of having a baby, the "achievements" of the busy housewife, and the glistening kitchen of a "Housewife's House."

Both in the home and outside it, women experienced themselves in new ways, discovering their capacities; yet they remained enclosed in the straitjacket of domestic ideology. To challenge it openly would be too frightening. In a rapidly changing world, clouded with the threat of nuclear warfare and the early brushfires of racial discontent and urban decay, where corporate behemoths trained their bureaucrats into interchangeable parts, few were ready to face the unnerving necessity of reassessing the cultural definitions of femaleness and maleness. If the world was changing, at least men could know that they were men and women were women. But that could happen only if women continued to maintain the home as a nurturing center, a private enclave, symbol of security and stability.*

Yet even in that most intimate arena, newly recognized female potentials generated tremors. Alfred Kinsey let the cat out of the bag in 1953. A sexual revolution had been going on for most of the twentieth century. Women, it turned out, had orgasms; they masturbated, engaged frequently in heavy premarital petting and not uncommonly in premarital intercourse; they committed adultery; they loved other women, and as Kinsey pointed out "heterosexual relationships could . . . become more satisfactory if they more often utilized the sort of knowledge which most homosexual females have of female sexual anatomy and female psychology." One commentator noted that "the criticism here implied of hetero-

---

*The resurgence of domestic ideology in the 1950s had complex roots. In the broadest context it meshed with a national mood that denied change in all aspects of American life. In foreign policy the rhetoric of the cold war held out the threat of nuclear annihilation as the price for violation of the status quo. Domestically McCarthyism was only the most extreme form of "rooting out subversion from within," as even moderate arguments for change in areas like race relations, labor, and education were treated as serious threats. The permission granted by government leaders and mass media to ignore or deny threatening changes was received gratefully by the American middle class, which after a generation of depression and war wanted nothing more than security and stability. And nothing represented these more clearly than home and family.

In addition, the feminine mystique may have represented the projected needs of middle-class men unable to accept their own changing roles. Within the burgeoning corporate and governmental bureaucracies, the work of these "organization men" had become increasingly technical, specialized, rationalized, and separated from any tangible "product." Bureaucracy suppressed emotion and passion, training its members into "interchangeable parts." Bureaucratic values emphasized "female" traits of cooperation, passivity, and security. "Getting along" and being well-liked became new life goals. Yet the older definitions of masculinity remained, and few could recognize the contradictory fact that what one part of their consciousness valued, another part judged unmanly. Thus, if women would stay within their traditional role, men could receive reassurance both that the emptiness in their own lives would be cared for and that their "manhood" had not changed. In one last realm, the home, the man could maintain the illusion of control.

sexual relationships on the average in our society is, to say the least, devastating to the male ego." Now the "togetherness" of the home required achievement of the simultaneous orgasm as proof of its felicity.

However, this too could be contained, at least temporarily. The romantic fantasy life fostered by popular culture reemphasized passivity rather than power in female sexuality. The seductive but innocent woman remained a child. Beauty pageants stressed the competitive display of women's bodies and jealously guarded the purity of the chosen queens. *Life* preceded its "typical housewife" and working women with a thirteen-page display on "The American Girl at Her Beautiful Best." Yet most of the ten "girls" were married and over twenty. Advertisements made sex itself a commodity and women's bodies the medium for an array of beauty-enhancing products. Titillation and suggestion were "in," but direct discussion of sexuality remained a (faltering) taboo.

The entire special issue of *Life* provides an interesting study in the contrasts and blandly unresolved ambivalences of the midfifties. In praising beauties and babies, the primacy of sex-stereotyped roles went largely unquestioned. Beyond the "housewife's house," however, lay an article entitled "My Wife Works and I Like It." Here a multitude of commentators examined, defended, and criticized women's status. Emily Kimbrough, prolific writer of witty travelogues and former editor for the *Ladies' Home Journal*, defiantly challenged those who urged women to return to the home. "All the Canutes in the world, lined up shoulder to shoulder, could not turn back this tide now." *Life* staff writer Robert Coughlan railed at length against that "fatal error" of feminism, "that common urban phenomenon known as the 'career woman.'" He found hope, however, in the reappearance of the three- to five-child family in upper- and upper-middle-class suburbs. This somewhat more optimistic replay of Farnham and Lundberg appeared in a magazine whose cover was graced by the profiles of a young mother and a five-year-old child, gazing fondly into each other's eyes. The caption read: "Working Mother."

Clearly the feminine mystique was already in the process of erosion, even as it reached its zenith. Emily Kimbrough was correct. The traditionalists could not win. But their temporary hegemony in the continuing domination of the feminine mystique laid the basis for the more explosive readjustment of a feminism reborn. The dilemma went underground and gathered force. It did not disappear.

Eventually the conflicts could no longer be contained. The feminine mystique's promise of "fulfillment" raised the expectations of middle-class women. Yet the social role of housewife as it shaped women's work both in the home and in the paid labor force generated disappointment as expectations continually fell short, and strain as large numbers of bored and restless women strove to meet the growing emotional demands placed upon them. Such pervasive unhappiness could not remain hidden. The illusion of the "happy housewife" began to crack along with the rest of the illusory equilibrium of the 1950s. Its solidity was undermined as on every level changing realities came crashing through old assumptions to expose the uncertainty and anxiety that lay beneath. Internationally, the upsurge of third world nationalism undermined the earlier cold war certainty of American superiority and "goodness." Domestically, a few Beatnik young people with disheveled lifestyles and writings on the problem of "meaninglessness" challenged the lives and dreams of middle Americans. Invisible to the general public, a much larger mass of affluent youth yearned for something they couldn't define, a purpose and goal beyond the material security their parents had achieved. More visibly, black Americans began to express their discontent with the barriers to full participation in the "mainstream." Signs of racial unrest began to multiply: in 1956 the Montgomery Bus Boycott; in 1957, Little Rock; and then early in 1960, the sit-in movement, which was to initiate directly that mass protest reverberating through the decade.

The election of John Fitzgerald Kennedy in 1960 marked a shift in the public mood. Change became a positive rather than a negative value. Together with the southern civil rights movement, programs like the Peace Corps and VISTA sparked a resurgence of idealism and active involvement in social change. The child-mother no longer fit the times. She was too static, too passive, maybe even too safe. A rising number of voices in the late 1950s urged the abandonment of outmoded myths, though usually with a qualifying clause about the importance of mothers to very young children and the primacy of the family. Many social scientists moved from using "role conflict" as an argument for women to refuse outside work, to a more realistic appraisal of the problems of the "working wife," who could not and would not evade such conflicts by returning to the home. Thus, such observers had finally achieved the level of adjustment to changing reality accomplished already by millions of American families. Jobs for women were becoming legitimate as extensions of the housewife role.

With the growing public acceptance of women's work outside the home, the mass media suddenly discovered the "trapped housewife." Betty Friedan pointed out that in 1960 the housewife's predicament was examined in *The New York Times, Newsweek, Good Housekeeping, Redbook, Time, Harper's Bazaar,* and on CBS Television. *Newsweek* entitled a Special Science Report and cover story: "Young Wives with Brains: Babies, Yes— But What Else?" The editors reported that the American middle-class woman "is dissatisfied with a lot that women of other lands can only dream of. Her discontent is deep, pervasive, and impervious to the superficial remedies which are offered at every hand." Both seriously and superficially, most articles in the issue treated women's problems of boredom, restlessness, isolation, over-education, and low esteem.

Educators also responded to the changing mood. Beginning in about 1960, a series of educational experiments and innovations appeared to meet the newly recognized malaise of the middle-class housewife. The "continuing education movement" focused on shaping the educational system to meet the demands of women's "dual role." Educational and career interruptions due to marriage and children were presumed inevitable. The problem, therefore, was to allow middle-class educated women to reenter the work force either full or part time without being forced into low-skilled, low-paid work.

Even the federal government began to treat women's roles as a public issue and to explore public policy alternatives to meet changing conditions. On December 14, 1961, President Kennedy established the President's Commission on the Status of Women, chaired by Eleanor Roosevelt. The purpose, in fact, may have been to quell a growing pressure for an Equal Rights Amendment, but unwittingly the government organized its own opposition. The existence of the commission and in subsequent years of state commissions on the status of women provided a rallying point for professional women. Such commissions constituted a tacit admission that there was indeed a "problem" regarding women's position in American society, that the democratic vision of equal opportunity had somehow left them out. Furthermore, they furnished a platform from which inequities could be publicized and the need for women's rights put forth. The President's Commission's report, entitled *American Women* and published in 1963, was moderate in tone. Yet despite obeisance to the primacy of women's roles within the family, it catalogued in great detail the inequities in the lives of women, the discrimination women faced in employment, and the need for proper child-care centers.

The importance of the report and the commission itself lay less in the specific changes they generated directly than in the renewed interest in "women's place in society" which they reflected. The following year women's rights advocates gained a crucial legal victory in the passage of Title VII of the Civil Rights Act, which prohibited discrimination by private employers, employment agencies, and unions on the basis of sex as well as race, color, religion, and national origin. Though introduced by a southern senator in a facetious gesture of hostility to the entire act, Title VII provided women with a legal tool with which to combat pervasive discrimination in hiring and promotion in all aspects of the economy.

The renewed discussion and activism took place primarily among professional women, who did not see themselves as housewives. Precisely because these professional women thought their work important and because they resented being patronized as if they had fled housework to get a little excitement, they felt even more acutely the discrimination leveled against them. Having openly admitted a certain level of drive and ambition, they were far more likely to experience discriminatory hiring, training, promotion, and pay rates as unfair. Other women could justify their unwillingness to fight against such barriers by saying, "I wouldn't be here if I didn't have to be," or "I'm only doing this for my family, not for myself." But for professional women, long-term careers were involved. Discrimination could close off opportunities they had invested years of training and hard work to attain. And it could deny them the positive reinforcement of respect from their colleagues. Since they took their work seriously, they were more vulnerable to the contempt that underlies patronage.

In general such women embraced the American ideology of equal opportunity, believing in advancement according to individual merit and achievement. Between 1940 and 1960, while the numbers of professional women declined relative to men, they also grew in absolute numbers by 41 percent. With more and more women in professional jobs, there were more examples to prove that women could excel at any occupation they chose. The individual professional woman was not a fluke or a freak of nature. On the other hand, there were also multiplying examples of blatant discrimination as their salaries and promotions increasingly lagged behind those of men with the same training and experience.

The new public attention to women's roles finally generated an overtly feminist position in 1963 in Betty Friedan's book, *The Feminine Mystique.* In a brilliant polemic she declared that housework was intrinsically boring, that the home had become a "comfortable concentration camp" which infantilized women. She took dead aim at the educational establishment, Freudians, women's magazines, and mass advertising, which she believed had combined to limit women's horizons and to force them back into the home. More academic but equally critical reassessments of women's traditional roles soon followed.

By the mid-sixties these angry professional women were developing an oppositional ideology and a strong network within governmental commissions on the status of women. As participants and consultants, they articulated the discrepancy between the ideals of equal opportunity and the actual treatment of women by employers. They mobilized to press for the passage of Title VII and then for its enforcement. A growing circle of women, including Friedan, Rep. Martha Griffiths, and the lawyers Mary Eastwood and Pauli Murray, urged the creation of an action group to pressure a government that continued to issue provocative reports but showed little sign of taking effective action. When, at a national conference of state commissions on the status of women in 1965, activists were informed that they could pass no resolutions and take no action in their capacity as state commissioners, a group broke away to resolve to found the National Organization for Women (NOW). These women had become convinced that, for real change to occur, a new civil rights group must be formed that could pressure the government to enact and enforce laws against sexual discrimination. Thus NOW became the "women's rights" branch of a renewed feminism.

In general, the professional women who created NOW accepted the division between the public and private spheres and chose to seek equality primarily in the public realm. Betty Friedan's devastating critique of housewifery ended up with a prescription that women, like men, should be allowed to participate in both realms. In effect she urged women to do it all—to be superwomen—by assuming the dual roles of housewife and professional. She made no serious assault on the division of labor within the home. For Friedan it was easier to imagine a professional woman hiring a "professional housewife" to take her place in the home than to challenge the whole range of sex roles or the division of social life into home and work, private and public, female and male domains.

In contrast, however, the oppression of most American women centered on their primary definition of themselves as "housewife," whether they worked solely inside the home or also outside it. Although they could vote, go to college, run for office, and enter most professions, women's primary role identification created serious obstacles both internally and in the outside world. Within themselves, women were never sure that they could be womanly when not serving and nurturing. And such doubts were reinforced by a long series of experiences: the advice and urging of high school and college counselors; discrimination on the job; pressure from family and friends; a lack of social services such as child care; and social expectations on the job that continually forced women back into traditional roles. Somehow women in every position from secretary to executive all too often ended up making the coffee.

At the same time that women acknowledged the social judgment that their work counted for very little—by accepting lower pay and poor jobs outside the home, or describing themselves as "just a housewife"— they also felt uncomfortable in any role other than that of the housewife. To admit discontent was to face a psychic void. The choices were there in a formal sense, but the price they exacted was a doubled workload and loss of both self-approval and public approval. Thus, though the *Newsweek* article on "Young Women with Brains" generated a storm of response from women, many who responded in writing denied the existence of a problem altogether. Others advised volunteer work and hobbies to fill the time, or else criticized women for their unhappiness. Only a few women echoed the article and discussed their distress.

If women found housewifery unfulfilling, they also on some level believed it was their own fault, thus turning their guilt and anger back in upon themselves. In a culture that offered no support for serious alternatives, women clung to the older definitions. If such roles did not reflect changing options or their real desires, at least they were familiar.

The tenacity of traditional roles and their internalization by most women meant that any successful revolt that drew on women's discontent would finally neither accept a traditional view of "female nature" as particularly suited to home and motherhood nor restrict itself simply to a critique of inequities in the public realm. For this reason, the emergence of the National Organization for Women did not provoke a massive grass-roots feminist movement. As a civil rights lobbying group, it could and did raise the public policy issues of discrimination in education, employment, and media in accordance with its stated purpose:

> to take action to bring women into full participation in the mainstream of American society *now,* exercising all the privileges and responsibilities thereof in truly equal partnership with men.

But while the professional women in NOW's constituency militantly demanded equality in the public realm, they were not prepared to question the mainstream itself, nor to carry their critique into the operation of sex roles in every aspect of life.

Yet the initiation of a mass movement required that the problem be addressed at its core. The pressures on most women were building up not on the level of public discrimination but at the juncture of public and private, of job and home, where older structures and identities no longer sufficed but could not simply be discarded either. The growing emotional strains of providing nurture for others with nowhere to escape to oneself, of rising expectations and low self-esteem, of public activity and an increasingly private, even submerged, identity required a radical—in the literal sense—response. A new movement would have to transform the privacy and subjectivity of personal life itself into a political issue.

Once such issues were raised by the radical young feminists in the late sixties, the challenge to traditional roles penetrated the mainstream of American society within a few years. Outrageous assaults on such cultural icons as Miss America, motherhood, and marriage caught the attention of the mass media. Americans were both shocked and intrigued by the sudden questioning of fundamental assumptions. As ever-widening circles of women joined in the process, a range of institutions—from corporations to families—began to experience angry insurgency from within. The *Ladies' Home Journal*, its offices seized by female journalists, agreed to print in August 1970 a special section written and produced by feminists; soon afterwards, women at *Newsweek* and *Time* staged their own rebellions. No institution, it seemed, was sacred or safe. Nuns organized within the Catholic Church; female seminary students began to agitate for full equality within Protestant churches. In 1975 they wracked the Episcopal Church with controversy, when eleven women defiantly joined in an unauthorized ordination service. And in the privacy of thousands of bedrooms and kitchens across the country, revolutions over housework, child care, family decisionmaking, and sexuality raged on or reached quiet resolution.

The young are prominent in most revolutions. In this case in particular it seemed logical and necessary that the initiative should come from young women who did not have marriages and financial security to risk or years invested in traditional roles to justify. Within the context of cultural unrest and the attack on tradition made by women like Friedan, the catalyst for a profounder criticism and a mass mobilization of American women proved to be the young female participants in the social movements of the 1960s. These daughters of the middle class had received mixed, paradoxical messages about what it meant to grow up to be women in America. On the one hand, the cultural ideal—held up by media, parents, and school—informed them that their only true happiness lay in the twin roles of wife and mother. At the same time they could observe the reality that housewifery was distinctly unsatisfactory for millions of suburban women and that despite the best efforts of *Ladies' Home Journal*, most American women could expect to work outside the home a substantial part of their lives. Furthermore, having grown up in an era that commoditized sexual titillation while it reasserted repressive norms, they found themselves living on the ambiguous frontiers of sexual freedom and self-control opened up by the birth control pill. Such contradictions left young, educated women in the 1960s dry tinder for the spark of revolt.

The stage was set. Yet the need remains to unravel the mystery of how a few young women stepped outside the assumptions on which they had been raised to articulate a radical critique of women's position in American society. For them, a particular set of experiences in the southern civil rights movement and parts of the student new left catalyzed a new feminist consciousness. There they found the inner strength and self-respect to explore the meaning of equality and an ideology that beckoned them to do so. There they also met the same contradictory treatment most American women experienced, and it spun them out of those movements into one of their own.

QUESTIONS TO CONSIDER

1. Define the "feminine mystique." How and when did the term originate?
2. What was the role of education in creating anxiety in women?
3. Describe women's work in the 1950s.
4. How did *Life*'s special issue on women in 1956 reinforce the feminine mystique?
5. How did the feminine mystique relate to the Cold War and the organization man?
6. What events in the 1961–1964 period stimulated the emergence of women?
7. How did NOW differ from radical feminism in its critique of society?

13

The Politics of Prophecy:
Martin Luther King, Jr.*
Alonzo Hamby

One of the enduring questions in history is whether the individual makes the times or the times make the individual. Probably a combination of the two provides the best answer: a significant leader can emerge if the times are right, but it doesn't always happen. Martin Luther King, Jr., provided critical leadership to the civil rights movement, personified civil rights in the minds of much of the nation, and pursued a strategy that astutely drew upon northern white liberal support by his nonviolent approach to fighting injustice. Though recent scholarship has begun to focus on the many local leaders who made a difference in their communities during the civil rights era, King unquestionably was the preeminent national figure in the movement. He called on the better side of the American character by dramatizing the ills of segregation as a simple case of justice against injustice, and in so doing mobilized public opinion to support the most important popular movement of the century. He is today the only American with a national holiday in his honor.

Alonzo Hamby (1940–), since 1975 a professor of history at Ohio University, earned his Ph.D. from the University of Missouri. His area of special interest is the United States since World War II, and he has published three major books dealing with the topic: *Beyond the New Deal: Harry S Truman and American Liberalism* (1973); *Liberalism and Its Challengers: FDR to Reagan* (1985), from which this selection is taken; and *Man of the People: A Life of Harry S Truman* (1996), an outstanding biography.

Roosevelt and the important leaders who followed him frequently engaged in vehement political combat, representing the interests and philosophies of competing groups in American life. Nevertheless, they generally functioned within a loose consensus that stressed political accommodation and a broad spectrum of white middle-class values and assumptions. It was a consensus that became strongly perceived and widely celebrated in the post-World War II atmosphere, deeply embedded as it was in the American historical experience and given a beneficent aura by economic prosperity. Even so, it could not provide satisfaction and justice for all. The greatest segment of the population it effectively excluded was black, largely impoverished, socially and economically segregated, and disfranchised in the Southern states. It is surprising that black protest stayed for so long within the boundaries established by the political and legal system and hardly amazing that it eventually moved in other directions.

Martin Luther King, Jr., was the type of leader who has frequently emerged when relatively powerless, ill-treated people turn to direct action to help themselves. Widely—and correctly—perceived as an agitator who attempted to alter the political system from the outside, he was also a religious leader standing in a long tradition of millenarian Protestantism that throughout the history of Western civilization has possessed a special appeal to the oppressed. A theological scholar of extensive learning, he was first and foremost a preacher who adopted the role of a moral-religious prophet determined to awaken the conscience of America by exposing its racial sins. His mastery of the techniques of political communication was as thorough as that of any public man of his generation. His values appealed to a large and influential portion of the white population as well as to American blacks. In the end, his reach, like that of all millennial prophets, exceeded his grasp, but he did more than any other individual to change the racial consciousness of America in the fifties and sixties. In doing so, he proved that the agitator with a just cause and a sure sense of the imperatives of his time could wield effective leadership from outside the political establishment.

As a student, King's intellectual quest appears to have been for a meaningful synthesis of the interests and influences that had engaged him in earlier years: sociology and social activism, Daddy King's fundamentalist ministry with its emphasis upon personal redemption and salvation, and the speculative philosophy and theology to which he had been introduced at Morehouse. The theologian who appealed to him most was Walter Rauschenbusch, the central figure of the early-twentieth-century social gospel. Rauschenbusch, he later admitted, had made some mistakes—he had been too much a believer in automatic progress, too optimistic about human nature, too close to identifying the Kingdom of God itself with earthly social justice. Nevertheless, Rauschenbusch had performed an important service by giving the Christian churches a theological basis for social concern; by demonstrating the relationship between spiritual well-being and material well-being, he had shown that the church must deal with the whole person, not just with the soul.

If Rauschenbusch provided a basis for social reform, Thoreau and Gandhi provided a technique. Thoreau had excited King ever since his freshman days at Morehouse. He became thoroughly acquainted with the ideas of Gandhi while a theological student, devoured his works, and developed a deep attraction to the Indian leader's concept of *Satyagraha*, which convinced him that nonviolent resistance to injustice could be undertaken in a strong, forceful manner. Gandhi, he later wrote, had been the first great historical figure "to lift the love ethic of Jesus above mere interaction between individuals to a powerful and effective social force on a large scale."

Rauschenbusch and Gandhi were unquestionably the dominant intellectual forces in King's life; his allegiance to them was tempered only a bit by his reading of Reinhold Niebuhr. Like Rauschenbusch and Gandhi, Niebuhr combined theology with social thought and social reformism; unlike them, he was profoundly pessimistic about human nature and institutions. For Niebuhr, democracy and social justice were means of ameliorating the human condition and of checking the power of sin in the world; but sin was too pervasive, too integral a part of human nature ever to be eliminated. Again and again, he criticized reformers who overlooked the enduring presence of sin in man and pridefully believed that their efforts could lead to utopia or, in theological terms, the establishment of the Kingdom of God on earth.

Niebuhr's critique of pacifism, a response to the rise of aggressive totalitarianism in the 1930s, followed naturally and was even more disturbing to the young theological student, for it established a conflict that could not be papered over with a few qualifications. Pacifism, Niebuhr declared, was ultimately a form of utopianism, based on an optimistic view of man's nature and denying man's sinful qualities; its latent perfectionism was yet another demonstration of the errors of the radical social gospel, and its practitioners frequently exhibited a self-righteousness that seemed to assert that they somehow had transcended the sin that stained all persons. Tactically, pacifism could be successful only in a very special situation—when used to confront oppressors who themselves had a highly developed moral conscience. It was for that reason alone that Gandhi had enjoyed a measure of success against the British. But nonviolent resistance in other situations would be at best futile if it ended only in maintenance of the status quo, and at worst immoral if it facilitated the spread of evil and injustice.

King's response was to draw a distinction between *Satyagraha*—active, if nonviolent, resistance to evil—and the pacifism that Niebuhr decried, passive nonresistance to evil. He refused to join pacifist organizations as such, but Gandhi's concepts continued to be compelling. His answer was, in truth, more an evasion than a resolution.

Niebuhr was nonetheless important to King. No modern Protestant theologian of equal stature came as close to the old-time fundamentalist Protestant faith in which King had been reared. The concept of God at which King arrived was similar to Niebuhr's: it was a personal God offering personal salvation, not a theological abstraction. Niebuhr's strictures about sin also stayed with King, preparing him for the determined resistance he was soon to meet leading the children of light against the children of darkness, whom he would find strong, determined, and convinced of their own righteousness. If nothing else, Niebuhr gave him the intellectual equipment to shed a mistaken optimism that might have broken an individual unprepared for the enormity of the forces arrayed against him.

King's emergence as a national figure came with accidental suddenness in December 1955, when a black seamstress on the way home from work refused to surrender her bus seat to a white passenger in accordance with Montgomery law. Although she was an antisegregation activist, Rosa Parks acted upon impulse with no grand design in mind; as she later put it, "I was just plain tired, and my feet hurt." Promptly arrested, she was convicted of violating the local segregation ordinances and fined $10. There in earlier days the episode would have ended and soon would have been forgotten, but coming a year and a half after the *Brown* decision and involving a woman of dignity and character, it ignited a will to resist within the Negro community.

The initiative came from the Women's Political Council and the local NAACP, two local black organizations that had been awaiting an opportunity to strike a blow against segregation. Primarily middle-class, they were especially sensitive to the social insult of segregation. But in choosing the transit system as the focus of protest, they had hit upon an issue that affected the daily lives of the disadvantaged bulk of the local black population in an especially grating way. Montgomery blacks not only had to sit at the rear of the bus; they were also obligated to give up even those seats to standing white passengers. Within the black community, one heard countless stories of abuse and physical violence by white bus drivers. Abundant latent mass support existed for a blow against the bus company; all that was needed was the right weapon and the right leadership.

The weapon was obvious—the boycott, a technique that blacks had occasionally employed in similar situations. One of King's friends, Rev. Theodore Jemison, had successfully led such an effort in Baton Rouge, Louisiana, two and a half years earlier. The boycott was perhaps the only way in which an impoverished, nonvoting black population could apply substantial leverage against the bus company; Negroes, after all, constituted 75 percent of the ridership.

The question of leadership was trickier. The two instigators of the campaign were both unable to serve: Jo Ann Robinson of the Women's Political Council was apparently deemed ineligible because of her sex; and E. D. Nixon, the head of the local NAACP, was a working Pullman porter frequently absent from the city. The movement, which took the name Montgomery Improvement Association (MIA), made King its president for the most mundane reasons. As a minister, he was a prominent young member of the black leadership class; and, unlike many of his colleagues, he had involved himself in movements for social change. As a relatively new person on the Montgomery scene, he was acceptable to all factions of the organized Negro community. Finally, his youth and lack of roots in Montgomery would make it easy for him to pull up stakes if the movement was crushed; older, established black leaders understood better than he the wrath a spokesman would face from the white population.

If King's leadership was accidental, his swift rise to national prominence was not. No other American black in public life possessed so superb a combination of gifts for the leadership of a mass movement. Working eighteen to twenty hours a day, he was at first involved in excessive organizational detail. He later recalled: "The phone would start ringing as early as five o'clock in the morning and seldom stopped before midnight."

At the same time, he had to present his case in a credible and appealing manner to the public, both black and white, across the country. As a minister, he had customarily spent fifteen hours a week polishing his sermons. Now he proved himself a gifted extemporaneous speaker, capable of the grandiose in his rhetoric and objectives, yet without a trace of the ridiculous in his speech or bearing. Almost immediately, he became a deeply inspirational figure to the black community and to white liberals throughout the country.

The flavor of the movement and of King's leadership was established with his first address to Montgomery blacks after being named president of the MIA. With no time for preparation, knowing only that somehow he wanted to combine in his exhortation militance and moderation, he found himself facing an enthusiastic overflow crowd of some five thousand at the Holt Street Baptist Church, a large structure located in the heart of the black community.

> There comes a time when people get tired. We are here this evening to say to those who have mistreated us so long, that we are tired. Tired of being segregated and humiliated; tired of being kicked about by the brutal feet of oppression.
>
> We have no alternative but to protest . . . our actions must be guided by the deepest principles of our Christian faith. Love must be our regulating ideal. Once again we must hear the words of Jesus echoing across the centuries: "Love your enemies, bless them that curse you, and pray for them that despitefully use you." If we fail to do this our protest will end up as a meaningless drama on the stage of history, and its memory will be shrouded with the ugly garments of shame. In spite of the mistreatment that we have confronted we must not become bitter and end up by hating our white brothers. As Booker T. Washington said, "Let no man pull you so low as to make you hate him."
>
> If you will protest courageously, and yet with dignity and Christian love, when the history books are written in future generations, the historians will have to pause and say, "There lived a great people—a black people—who injected new meaning and dignity into the veins of civilization." This is our challenge and our overwhelming responsibility.

The ovation was thunderous and prolonged. The oration, King realized, had evoked more response than any speech or sermon he had ever delivered. With astuteness and passion, he had spoken both to the pride and anger of his own people and to the conscience of a broader national and international public. . . .

In Montgomery, however, he met only resistance so bitter that it is scarcely possible to comprehend from the perspective of three decades. The initial demands of the MIA were modest: (1) courteous treatment by bus drivers; (2) passengers to be seated on a first-come, first-served basis, *Negroes sitting from the back of the bus toward the front, whites from the front toward the back;* and (3) the eventual employment of black drivers for predominantly black routes. The entire package amounted to little more than a request for a more polite form of segregation; its suggested seating arrangements were already in effect in some other Southern cities, including Nashville, Atlanta, and Mobile. (But the MIA was also appealing the conviction of Rosa Parks to the federal courts in the hope of obtaining a ruling that would outlaw segregated seating.)

The bus company, city officials, and the white population of Montgomery were unyielding. As the hard-line attorney for the bus company put it, "If we granted the Negroes these demands, they would go about boasting of a victory they had won over the white people; and this we will not stand for." Every member of the city commission soon took up membership in the local White Citizens' Council.

King, who had expected a quick settlement, despondently chided himself for his foolish optimism. He had learned, he later wrote, two important lessons. First, those who were privileged were unlikely to surrender their privileges—no matter how reasonable and moderate the requests of the other side—without strong resistance. Second, the real purpose of segregation was not simply to separate the races but to oppress and exploit the segregated; thus justice and equality for the Negro could come only with the elimination of segregation.

King's employment of nonviolent resistance was a brilliant tactic. It avoided bloodshed that surely would have caused death and injury to many more blacks than whites. It united the black community as never before; "big Negroes," who owned Cadillacs and Buicks, arose with the sun to provide rides for black maids and laborers whom they previously had scorned. Segregation embittered blacks of all classes; King's methods drew the entire community together and gave every person in it a chance to become actively involved in a way that would not have been possible if the battle had been exclusively a courtroom affair. The result was to bring black pride and morale to their highest point in Montgomery since Reconstruction. Moreover, King had captured the imagination of white liberals across the country. From the beginning, it appears that the majority of his contributions came from white sources. His entire philosophy invited white participation, and while the number of whites active in the Montgomery effort was relatively small, the total would grow with each new crusade.

No one could doubt the depth and sincerity of King's personal commitment to nonviolence. After his own home was bombed with his wife and infant child narrowly escaping injury, his intervention prevented an angry, armed black crowd from lynching white policemen, city officials, and reporters who had come to the scene. Realizing from then on that his own life was in danger, he was determined to continue, no matter what the outcome. At a mass meeting, he declared, "If one day you find me sprawled out dead, I do not want you to retaliate with a single act of violence." In the first days of bus desegregation, after a rash of violent incidents and nighttime bombings, he addressed another rally: "Lord, I hope no one will have to die. . . . Certainly I don't want to die. But if anyone has to die, let it be me."

King's assault against segregation and his devotion to nonviolence captured the imagination of secular humanists, but neither he nor almost any mortal could have sustained himself in such impossible circumstances without the reassurance of a mystical, millennial commitment. There was always more of Rauschenbusch than of Niebuhr in King's makeup, and in the bitter environment of the Deep South it was nearly inevitable that a nonviolent crusade against segregation would have a touch of the utopian about it. It was also nearly inevitable that a religious leader under the pressure that King endured could find the will to go on only by coming to believe that he was a prophet of the Lord.

Several weeks into the boycott, his nerves strained to the breaking point by countless threats and obscene phone calls, King had been on the verge of quitting. Late one night, in a state of exhaustion after receiving a telephoned death threat, he prayed for guidance:

> At that moment I experienced the presence of the Divine as I never had experienced Him before. It seemed as though I could hear the quiet assurance of an inner voice saying: "Stand up for righteousness, stand up for truth; and God will be at your side forever." Almost at once my fears began to go. My uncertainty disappeared. I was ready to face anything.

King was henceforth convinced that he was a prophet of God, speaking the words of the Lord in the manner of an Isaiah or an Amos. He fully expected the persecution that came to all prophets who spoke unpalatable truths. It was a commitment that reflected not some messianic impulse but a combination of religious faith and leadership duty. He had given much thought to the nature and obligations of prophecy. Not every Christian minister could be a prophet, he wrote, but "some must be prepared for the ordeals of this high calling and be willing to suffer courageously for righteousness." To this burden he was now intellectually and emotionally reconciled.

The eventual victory of the MIA movement seemed to vindicate its tactics. The denouement in fact verged on the miraculous. Just as King and his fellow leaders were facing a state court injunction against their car pool operation, the U.S. Supreme Court sustained a lower federal ruling that the Alabama bus segregation laws were unconstitutional. "God Almighty has spoken from Washington," declared an excited black man.

A sober observer might also have taken the events as defining the limitations of direct action. Although the MIA had endured for a year, lifted the spirits of the black community, and brought the bus company to the verge of bankruptcy, it had failed to win a single concession and was on the brink of a court-ordered dissolution when it was saved by legal tactics handled by the NAACP. Far from converting or redeeming white sinners, it had demonstrated their recalcitrance; most successful in awakening blacks and white sympathizers, it nevertheless had to rely ultimately upon traditional approaches.

All the same, Montgomery unleashed a surge of militance, idealism, and great expectations, especially among young reformminded intellectuals of both races. By employing nonviolent means and articulating his rationale so compellingly, King had laid the basis for an era of protest all over the South, conducted by zealous idealists to whom compromise was anathema. Few activists fully possessed King's theological outlook or religious mentality, but most of those who actually put their bodies on the line were more prone than he to believe they could achieve millennial results. Consequently, the new civil rights movement contained a considerable built-in potential for disillusionment.

King's public adulation carried the movement along. In the wake of Montgomery, he had become a world figure, admired and hated with great passion. In 1957, he took his first trip overseas, primarily as an honored guest at the independence celebration of the new African state of Ghana. The NAACP made him the youngest recipient ever of its esteemed Spingarn Medal. He was one of the featured speakers at a largely forgotten but nonetheless important Prayer Pilgrimage, a thirty-seven-thousand-strong demonstration held in Washington in May 1957 at the Lincoln Memorial to support the token civil rights bill that Lyndon Johnson was moving through Congress. In many respects, the pilgrimage anticipated the far larger demonstration of 1963, not least in the way that King's speech, his first national address, captured the enthusiasm of the crowd and overshadowed the efforts of the older Negro luminaries.

By this time also, King had taken the lead in founding the Southern Christian Leadership Conference (SCLC), whose head he became. Primarily an embodiment of King's personal philosophy in its assumptions and tactics, the SCLC existed in an increasingly uneasy relationship with the NAACP. The establishment of its headquarters in Atlanta eventually required King to leave Montgomery in 1960 and take up his father's standing offer to become co-pastor of the Ebenezer Church.

He also had become the object of intense hatreds. In Montgomery, while he was waiting for an associate in the lobby of the courthouse, policemen roughed him up and charged him with disobeying an officer. The state of Alabama prosecuted him for tax fraud, asserting that he had misappropriated MIA contributions and had failed to report them as income.

The results were ironic. The Montgomery police commissioner felt compelled to pay King's fine on the first charge rather than undergo the embarrassment of jailing him; an all-white jury acquitted him on the second charge.

The freedom rides illustrated the dilemmas that faced both King and the movement as a whole. Initiated in 1961 by a CORE-SNCC coalition, they were efforts by biracial groups to ride through the South on chartered Greyhound and Trailways buses with the objective of integrating terminals. Although he had no effective control over the drive, King agreed to serve as chairman of its coordinating committee. The riders themselves did not meet violence at every stop, but their reception in Alabama was fully deserving of the adjective *explosive*—in Anniston, a mob burned one of the buses; in Birmingham and Montgomery, thugs savagely beat the passengers, including a Justice Department observer; when King went to Montgomery to address a rally in a black church, an angry white crowd surrounded the building, pelted it with missiles, and threatened to overwhelm a thin force of federal marshals that provided its only protection. Having once again become the target of the hatred of white segregationists, King now also took substantial criticism from those forces he supposedly led. When he counseled a cooling-off period and attempts at negotiation, he encountered open hostility from many younger activists, some of whom caustically denounced him for having failed to put his own body on the line as they had.

In the end, however, this division and discord was overshadowed by some substantial success. By evoking a sense of national outrage, by appealing to the better instincts of a liberal president, by utilizing the visibility and moral prestige of King, the freedom riders achieved their immediate objectives, even if they did not change the predominant attitude of the white South. The Kennedy administration provided them federal protection and prodded the Interstate Commerce Commission into issuing strong antisegregation rules for interstate terminals. After protracted negotiation and some litigation, desegregated bus stations became the rule in at least the large and medium-size cities of the South.

The year-and-a-half SNCC-led effort to desegregate Albany, Georgia, however, served only to demonstrate the limits of nonviolent direct action. A bastion of segregationist traditionalism, Albany nevertheless had a white leadership determined to avoid open violence. Its chief of police, Laurie Prichett, refused to use brutality against demonstrators. He bowed his head in prayer along with them, politely requested a dispersal, and only then made peaceful arrests. By one subterfuge or another, the city resisted integration at every turn; its well-behaved policemen excited little indignation in the North and provided no excuse for federal intervention. Thoroughly covered by the news media, Albany developed into a national bore rather than a catalyst of change. King himself, despite an arrest and two-week jail term, became again an object of criticism from young activists, disgruntled by his preference for moderation and conciliation, by his inability to devote exclusive attention to the Albany situation, and by his decision to cease demonstrations when the city obtained a federal court injunction against them. Albany had demonstrated that direct action could be smothered to death.

David Garrow has argued that Albany marked a turning point in the development of King's tactics. He had begun his career as an activist dedicated to the concept of nonviolent persuasion, hoping to convert his bitterest enemies through moral example. Neither in Montgomery nor in Albany had he done so; in the former instance, the intervention of the federal courts had given him victory nonetheless; in the latter case, he had presided over a near-total failure. He and those around him, Garrow asserts, began to rethink nonviolence. They developed a theory of nonviolent coercion, aimed not at converting the oppressor but at displaying his oppressions at their ugliest. They sought confrontations with some of the most vicious representatives of the white Southern establishment, hoping to use the national news media to dramatically display the fascistic qualities of segregationism. Albany and Laurie Prichett clearly were inappropriate targets for nonviolent coercion. King needed the opposition of violent political primitives; he turned to Birmingham.

Perhaps the most segregated and repressive urban center in the South, Birmingham, Alabama, had long been dominated by diehard racist politicians led by Commissioner of Public Safety Eugene "Bull" Connor. A substantial portion of the black population was cowed or apathetic. Birmingham was also much more visible nationally than Albany. It thus provided a nearly ideal setting for a confrontation politics that would display suffering and oppression.

The SCLC's preparation for the Birmingham campaign took shape shortly after the Albany movement had sputtered to a close. For months, SCLC staffers familiarized themselves with legal questions, organized logistical support, raised money across the country, trained local volunteers in the philosophy and tactics of nonviolence, and mapped out demonstration areas with military precision. King and his associates vowed at the beginning to avoid what they had come to perceive as one major mistake of the Albany effort—an attempt to eliminate segregation everywhere in one swoop. They decided instead to concentrate upon segregation and discrimination in Birmingham's major business establishments, especially the exclusion of Negroes from lunch counter service and their relegation to menial jobs. In focusing upon the business community, the SCLC singled out a white leadership group that was among the less resistant to change and the most vulnerable to an economic boycott. Demonstrations were scheduled to coincide with the Easter season of 1963 not just for symbolic reasons but because that time of the year was a peak retail buying period.

The Birmingham movement began on April 3, 1963, with a low-key series of sit-ins and peaceful arrests at downtown lunch counters. At the end of the first week and a half, four or five hundred demonstrators had been arrested; some three hundred were still in jail. Surprisingly, Birmingham's police carted away demonstrators with unexpected gentleness, and the SCLC's pool of volunteers remained thin, despite the progress in arousing enthusiasm. As a result, King found himself pushed toward two important decisions.

The first and least difficult was to have himself arrested. There can be little doubt that he sincerely felt a moral imperative to share in the fate of those he had exhorted to disobedience.

The most significant aspect of "Letter from Birmingham Jail" was its prophetic quality; it expressed King's conviction that he was the trustee of a God-given mission to attack un-Christian institutions wherever they might exist. Responding to an "Appeal for Law and Order" issued by eight prominent white Birmingham clergymen, he began by rejecting the implication that he was an "outsider." Could not the same have been said of the prophets of the eight century B.C. or of the Apostle Paul?

In the prophetic tradition, he challenged his critics to reach a higher state of moral awareness. They expressed concern about disorder, yet they displayed little interest in the conditions that had brought about and ultimately justified that disorder. He devoted most of his denunciation not to the Bull Connors of the South but to those more "respectable" elements that counseled order and patience. They preferred a negative peace, the absence of tension, to a positive peace, the presence of justice; they paternalistically believed they could set the timetable for the freedom of others. Perhaps most dismaying of all was the failure, with only a few exceptions, of Southern white clergymen to throw themselves into the struggle for justice. Some churchmen had been outright opponents; "all too many others have been more cautious than courageous and have remained silent behind the anesthetizing security of stained-glass windows." Like prophets throughout the ages, King employed denunciation as a tool to awaken those whom he considered not servants of the Antichrist, but morally insensitive. Like numerous prophets before him, he assailed the institutional church as corrupt and formalistic.

It was true enough, he conceded, that the SCLC demonstrations broke laws against trespass and parading without a permit. But there were two types of laws—those that were just and those that were unjust; moral man had a duty to obey the first and disobey the second. Man-made laws, in order to be legitimate, had to be in harmony with the law of God. Specifically, "Any law that uplifts human personality is just. Any law that degrades human personality is unjust." All segregation statutes hence were unjust; otherwise just laws, such as the trespass or parade statutes, could rightly be considered unjust when used to defend segregation. Civil disobedience, when undertaken to arouse the conscience of the community, amounted to respect for law, not contempt for it. . . .

"Letter from Birmingham Jail" captured the spirit and motivation of the Southern Negro revolution of the early sixties. The movement had attracted many followers strictly on the humanistic merits of its objectives, and not all its adherents were devoted to nonviolence. Nevertheless, its driving force came from the religious commitment that King personified and articulated so well; the result was a sense of mission and an inspirational aura that secular rationalism alone never could have imparted. Along with this intense dedication, however, there also was inevitably a certain degree of inflexibility and self-righteousness; at times also, there was a tendency to assume that within limits the end justified the means.

It was this cast of mind that figured in King's second decision—the use of children ranging in age from six to sixteen as demonstrators. Apparently forced by the SCLC's inability to turn up reliable adult demonstrators in massive numbers, this move was morally ambiguous. King and other SCLC figures argued that the youngsters had a right to fight for their freedom, but critics might justly retort that few children of any race had minds mature enough to comprehend the commitment they were making or to assess the risks they faced.

Those risks became quickly and terribly apparent. By the time King emerged from jail, the tense weeks of demonstrations had worn away the veneer of civility that had characterized the beginning of the Birmingham campaign. On one or two occasions, black bystanders had pelted police with rocks and bottles; the police, in turn, had brought out attack dogs and fire hoses. As the campaign moved into its fifth week with a seemingly inexhaustible supply of young marchers, the authorities shed their restraint and created the intense crisis that King had sought. In full view of national television cameras, police sprayed marchers with fire hoses powerful enough to peel the bark off trees, released snarling, biting canines, and openly clubbed those whom they apprehended.

The outcome, of course, was more than the movement had dared hope for. By bringing business in downtown Birmingham to a near halt, by raising the specter of full-scale racial rioting even as the movement itself remained nonviolent, King managed to achieve a local settlement that resulted in substantial desegregation and enhanced job opportunities for blacks. The agreement itself, however, was less important than the sympathetic national attention King achieved. The federal government intervened, sending high Justice Department officials to act as mediators. Most importantly, the Kennedy administration rearranged its priorities drastically. Previously convinced that civil rights legislation was a losing proposition, the president made a dramatic call for a sweeping civil rights bill and threw all the strength of his office behind it. Kennedy's untimely death several months later deepened support for the legislation and paved the way for an even more effective effort by his successor, Lyndon Johnson. Before Birmingham, presidents had lent support to the cause of civil rights but never in so fervent a fashion. They did so now not simply out of a personal conversion but because King and the SCLC had created a broad non-Southern majority in favor of strong federal action.

The embodiment of that new consensus was the March on Washington on August 28, 1963. The realization of A. Philip Randolph's old dream, the march was sponsored by a dozen or so civil rights and liberal organizations and planned by Randolph's protégé, Bayard Rustin. It drew a quarter of a million participants, nearly one hundred thousand of whom were white; never before in American history had the integrationist ethic been demonstrated on so vast a scale. The meeting found its aspirations most powerfully expressed in King's address; the closing speech of the day, it reinvigorated a crowd drained by emotional music and oratory and captured the essence of the event so perfectly that it overshadowed every singer and speaker who had gone before. After it was over, the national memory of the March on Washington was of Martin Luther King standing in the shadow of the Lincoln Memorial and speaking for a new day in race relations. . . .

He began to speak extemporaneously, drawing upon other recent addresses and upon all the skills of oratory he had nurtured over the years. "I have a dream . . ." that someday in the red hills of Georgia the offspring of slaves and slaveowners could sit together at the table of brotherhood . . . that even Mississippi could become an oasis of freedom and justice . . . that his four children might someday be judged on the basis of their character and not the color of their skin . . . that someday freedom would ring throughout America . . . that all of God's children, black and white, Jews and Gentiles, Protestants and Catholics could join together in the old Negro spiritual, "Free at last! Free at last! Great God A-mighty, we are free at last!"

That the speech was magnificent and inspired is beyond dispute; its larger influence, along with that of the entire event, is harder to pinpoint.

Although many observers seemed to find it somehow remarkable and impressive that so many Negroes could hold an orderly demonstration, it is doubtful that the march contributed appreciably to the passage of the Kennedy civil rights bill in 1964. It did create a moment of national uplift that reminded the country of its best values. It also helped maintain the considerable momentum the movement had achieved and made indelible King's standing as the symbol of the aspirations of the American Negro. No other black leader had spoken so effectively to the sensibilities of both liberal white America and the liberal democratic cultures of Western Europe. *Time* magazine recognized his importance by naming him man of the year, but that notice was rendered trivial in October 1964 by the announcement that he had been named recipient of the Nobel Peace Prize. . . .

[S]o long as the Negro revolution maintained its momentum, King's optimism could remain alive. Southern resistance and violence did much to sustain the broad national consensus in favor of black civil rights. Episodic bombings of homes and churches and assassinations of civil rights activists served only to deepen the commitment of the movement and to enhance the aura of martyrdom that enveloped it. By using nonviolent tactics to create a crisis, by urging his followers to accept suffering, King had achieved major civil rights legislation. Throughout the Deep South, however, blacks still faced insuperable barriers to voting. It was to meet this affront that at the start of 1965 King mounted a major crusade in the inhospitable northern counties of Alabama around the town of Selma.

Selma itself possessed a professional, relatively moderate police chief, Wilson Baker; but county and state authorities, personified by Sheriff Jim Clark and Highway Patrol Colonel Al Lingo, made even Bull Connor seem a bit pale by comparison. This seems to have been the reason for choosing Selma. Moreover, vigilantes were an even more constant danger than in Birmingham. King himself was momentarily attacked by a local racist while registering as the first black patron of the town's leading hotel, and a black demonstrator was shot and killed by state troopers in the nearby town of Marion. On March 7, 1965, after two months of parades, arrests, and sporadic brutality, troopers and a mounted sheriff's posse broke up a planned protest march from Selma to Montgomery. Before television cameras and newsmen from across the country, troopers immersed the demonstrators in thick clouds of tear gas; then the posse attacked with clubs, cattle prods, and bullwhips. Seen in millions of living rooms, the episode created a situation similar to that of Birmingham. Four days later, the national sense of outrage was deepened when racist thugs clubbed a white Unitarian minister to death.

The result was to bring swarms of white liberals to Selma and give an unstoppable impetus to a new civil rights bill with near-ironclad procedures to facilitate black voting. President Lyndon Johnson identified himself with the cause more emotionally and personally than had even Kennedy. The march itself finally took place under federal protection and produced another martyr, a white woman shot after its completion. Whatever its symbolic importance, the march was less important than the passage of the Voting Rights Act of 1965, a bill that in effect admitted Southern blacks to the most basic right of free citizenship, changed the character of the Southern electorate, and laid the basis for a quiet political revolution in several states. It also concluded most of the work that King could do to meet the special problems of the Southern Negro and encouraged him to broaden the scope of his mission.

The most difficult of King's new challenges, both personally and tactically, was to define his relationship to the black militance that erupted in the mid-sixties. Occasionally violent in deed, always angry in rhetoric, usually vocally antiwhite, and frequently downright separatist, black militance threatened all the values King had preached and posed a serious danger to his moral leadership of the American Negro community. Because of the need to maintain a facade of black unity, it was necessary to downplay disagreements. Because of the need to understand the causes—both material and psychological—of the new mood, King had to reorient his thinking and move on to new issues. Yet his public persona was too sharply defined for him to abandon the prophetic role in which he had cast himself.

By Selma, the revolutionary spirit that King had done so much to awaken among blacks was overflowing the rather narrow channels of nonviolence and civil rights within which he had attempted to confine it. The black Muslims, a long-established but little-noticed sect, grew rapidly and won national attention in a white community at first stunned by their racial bitterness. By then also, urban ghetto riots were becoming an annual summer event. They arose from conditions and impulses that King grasped intellectually, but he never had experienced them himself, nor had he yet addressed his efforts to them. After the upheaval in Watts, he attempted to tour the slum and was taken aback by the number of blacks who did not recognize him and in some instances professed never to have heard of him.

Once considered an upstart by the older national black establishment, King now found himself upstaged by younger, more vehement figures such as Floyd McKissick of CORE and Stokely Carmichael, the new president of SNCC. All the latent tensions came out in 1966 when King, McKissick, and Carmichael led a march into Mississippi, a continuation of one begun by the enigmatic James Meredith, who had been shot and wounded by a white assailant. Carmichael and, at first, McKissick argued unsuccessfully for the exclusion of whites from the march; then Carmichael captured the attention of the nation by leading his followers in the chant "Black Power," a phrase that had a great many harmless meanings but that under the circumstances took on connotations of black racism.

The new militance shocked and angered some white liberals, especially those whose support of the movement had involved personal sacrifice. On the whole, however, the arresting thing about the new black militance was the way in which the white liberal intellectual community not only accepted it but fairly embraced it. The alienation of the militants appealed to the alienation of the intellectuals. The militant eagerness to deliver verbal floggings provided an easy release for white guilt feelings. The militant affectation of a hip ghetto style contrasted favorably in the minds of many white intellectuals with the uptight, bourgeois morality that King represented.

King's response was equivocal. Carmichael, McKissick, and other black militants said in their own way many of the same things he had been saying. On numerous occasions, most vividly in the Birmingham jail letter, King had lectured white liberals and moderates; moreover, he had consistently given his white support scant recognition in his own accounts of Montgomery and Birmingham. He always had been prone to appeal to black pride and self-help, just as did the militants. He also wanted to pull American blacks out of their state of relative powerlessness. He agreed that whites were collectively guilty of countless injustices and that some sort of compensatory action was long overdue.

His disagreements were equally important. He was convinced that black power militance was dangerous tactically—what good, he asked, could come of advocating black violence in rural Mississippi? Nor did he have any wish to indict whites in an angry, personal manner; his condemnations were those of the minister preaching to sinners he hoped to convert. Philosophically, he was repelled by racial separatism and violence, both of which violated Christian ideals of love and brotherhood.

By early 1967, King, convinced that the peace movement was a matter of deep urgency, committed himself to it with the same wholeheartedness as to domestic reform. His rationale was both practical and moral, both intellectual and deeply emotional. The war was drawing thirty billion dollars a year from the struggle against poverty. It was being fought largely by the poor, especially by poor blacks. America, King charged, was "taking black young men who had been crippled by our society and sending them eight thousand miles away to guarantee liberties in Southeast

Asia which they had not found in southwest Georgia and East Harlem." Blacks and whites were integrated for destruction in the U.S. Army but still largely segregated in the peacetime society at home. Among the poor, moreover, the effect of the war was to spread a contagion of violence. The national use of military force as an instrument of policy had undermined his own effort to preach nonviolence to the militant black underclass. It had made him realize that he "could never again raise my voice against the violence of the oppressed in the ghettos without having first spoken clearly to the greatest purveyor of violence in the world today: my government."

His mission, he believed required him to come to grips with all major moral questions: "I have worked too long and hard now against segregated public accommodations to end up segregating my moral concerns." His new role was dictated by his position as a Nobel Peace Prize winner and a minister of Christ with a prophetic function. He had to strive for realization of the SCLC motto—"To save the soul of America." He had to be a spokesman "for the weak, for the voiceless, for the victims of our nation, and for those it calls enemy." . . .

For King, Vietnam was a case study of the latent racism of American diplomacy. It was a product "of comfort, complacency, a morbid fear of Communism, and our proneness to adjust to injustice." The modern Western nations, once the spreaders of the revolutionary spirit, had become the archreactionaries of the world community. He made no effort to conceal his sympathy for the Vietcong insurgency, implying that it was akin to the American Revolution and citing Ho Chi Minh as a great national leader. In siding with Ngo Dinh Diem, the United States had supported "one of the most vicious modern dictators," an ally of extortionist landlords and a ruthless oppressor of the peasants. America was destroying Vietnamese society, both physically and morally, creating orphans, prostitutes, and hordes of uprooted refugees. "If we continue, there will be no doubt in my mind and in the mind of the world that we have no honorable intentions in Vietnam. It will become clear that our minimal expectation is to occupy it as an American colony, and men will not refrain from thinking that our maximum hope is to goad China into a war so that we may bomb her nuclear installations." . . .

During the last two years of his life, he was almost exclusively concerned on the domestic scene with economic deprivation. Like many white liberals and many other black leaders, he sought to spread the mantle of civil rights over the problem of poverty. On its surface, the move appeared timely, coming in a period of heightened national consciousness about the extent of poverty in the United States. Yet poverty was never amerable to the tactics and mood of the civil rights movement. If its existence was undeniable, its roots were obscure. To the extent that it was a result of discrimination, legal remedies had been established. To the extent that it stemmed from some inner deficiency within the poor, such as a lack of skills or motivation, self-improvement was the answer, perhaps with government help. To the extent that it was the fault of white society in some general sense, any remedy was vague.

King and most crusaders against poverty posited that white society was responsible for the plight of the poor and had a duty to help them through programs designed to increase their opportunities, develop their skills, relieve them of burdens, and better their material lot. By the time he focused his efforts in this direction, however, he was doing little more than joining a crusade that Lyndon B. Johnson had brought to national respectability. From the beginning, he found himself in the position of berating a president who had devoted more attention than any chief executive before him to the problem of hard-core poverty and who had established scores of programs to deal with it. To most disinterested observers it was evident that the antipoverty effort required a time of testing in which its assumptions could be examined, costs measured against benefits, and ineffective components weeded out. But from King's perspective, the war against poverty was no more than tokenism; the only answer was a quantum increase in almost every experiment the administration was undertaking.

It was even more difficult to pursue poverty as a civil rights issue, and on this point King displayed considerable confusion. Manifestly, as he acknowledged, poverty was not just a black phenomenon; yet he advocated preferences in jobs and housing for blacks as a mode of national atonement. When pressed about the apparent contradiction, he might assert that the only real solution was the creation of adequate employment opportunity and good housing for all, but such answers were evasions rather than resolutions. Quite consciously, King was preaching a message of collective guilt to a liberal culture that traditionally had assumed guilt to be individual and specific. Few of his white admirers were fully prepared for what he had to say; that so many of them would go so far toward accepting it was a tribute to his eloquence.

The Poor People's Campaign underscored a shift in King's social vision away from an emphasis upon integration and toward a more class-oriented critique of the American social structure. The elements of the new approach, however, were solidly rooted in King's theology. Far from undergoing a conversion from bourgeois liberalism to Marxian radicalism, he was expressing more clearly than ever—in his calls for massive aid to the poor, for a new spirit of Christian brotherhood, for the salvation of American society—the Christian socialism of Walter Rauschenbusch that had so long captured his imagination. While he appears to have increasingly valued his black identity and understood his special role as a leader of his people, the wider reformism of the social gospel, integrationist by definition, remained his deepest inspiration. It carried him into courses that went beyond the more immediate and tangible needs of American blacks and that were consequently more difficult to navigate.

King's death had contradictory results for the movement he had led. In the short run, it delivered a substantial gain: the Civil Rights Act of 1968 was a gesture of expiation designed to facilitate minority access to better housing. In the long run, however, it was a severe blow to a drive that had lost its most effective spokesman. No one remotely approaching his stature emerged to take King's place. The fate of the Poor People's Campaign demonstrated the depth of the loss. Its prospects had been dubious during King's life; they became hopeless with his death. Carried on by the SCLC, it attracted little sympathetic attention. Its shanties, regarded as disruptive eyesores rather than symbols of conscience, eventually were battered down by federal bulldozers.

Yet the same events might have occurred under King's leadership. At the time of his death, he was clearly on the decline, and there is no reason to assume that his eclipse was only temporary. Martyrdom may have ensured his historical reputation just as it enhanced the memory of Lincoln or FDR. Death, which overtook all three men close to the point of their supreme achievements, made it possible to believe that they would have gone on to even more impressive heights and obscured serious obstacles that lay ahead of them.

King had taken the helm of what had been the civil rights movement and had made it into a Negro revolution by utilizing the tools of leadership more effectively than any other leader of his generation. Using all the communications media, he projected an inspirational personality and set of values to a wide constituency, ranging from unlettered evangelical blacks to sophisticated white liberal intellectuals. More importantly, he aligned himself with an urgent social issue whose time had come. Among political figures of the middle third of the twentieth century, only Franklin D. Roosevelt had so thoroughly mastered the imperatives of public leadership.

The difficulties that King encountered after Selma were manifold, but they stemmed heavily from the limitations of his self-defined role as a prophet. Having won the simple moral issues, he brought the prophetic style to more difficult and ambiguous causes. The various struggles against segregation and disfranchisement in Alabama from Montgomery to Selma, with their jailings, bombings, killings, and meanspirited segregationist white officials, lent themselves to a politics of moral prophecy at the most elemental level. The struggle against poverty presented no such easily dramatizable situation and led to a dissipation of King's moral authority.

This difficulty was compounded by King's inability to deal with the rising tide of black militance and separatism as what had been called the Negro revolution began to be designated the black revolution. Anxious to life black pride, King was nevertheless unprepared for the antiwhite sentiment that developed along with the so-called black power movement. It was to his credit that he refused to swim with the tide. But while he never abandoned the integrationist ethic, neither did he find convincing means of dealing with separatism nor with the growing trend toward violent protest. Increasingly, observers noted a tendency among King's own black followers to drop the phrase "black and white together" from renditions of "We Shall Overcome." The disintegration of the last march he headed in Memphis was a sad revelation of the problems he and his staff faced in maintaining control even of an effort they had put together.

It is hard to imagine that King's standing and authority would have been enhanced had he lived to witness the next phase of the black political experience—the movement from militance to affirmative action. One suspects that like the black leaders who survived him, he would have supported affirmative action efforts. His fundamentalist upbringing and biblical training disposed him to accept the concept of collective guilt and the requirement that the current generation atone for the sins of those that preceded it. At the same time, one may speculate that his support of the program would have been as ambiguous and self-contradictory as his support of the theory during his life.

If events had indeed passed King at the time of his death, that in no way should diminish his historical reputation. In a dozen years, he established himself as the greatest figure in American black history, as the American Gandhi, and as the most profound moral leader of his time. Any fair evaluation must consider him within the limits of the role to which he felt he had been called, that of the religious prophet attempting to save his nation, not that of the politician unable to afford the luxury of pure morality and cognizant that good and evil often coexist uneasily in man and his institutions. To engage in prophecy is to state simple, elemental truths, not to negotiate complex solutions for social evils. In the end, King's lasting greatness arose not from what he prescribed but from what he was.

QUESTIONS TO CONSIDER

1. Who were the three major intellectual influences on King and what ideas did each contribute?

2. How did King become the leader of the Montgomery Improvement Association?

3. How did King's experience in Albany, Georgia, force him to adapt his nonviolent tactics?

4. Why was the "Letter from Birmingham Jail" such an effective prophetic force? How did it and the Birmingham campaign change the movement?

5. Why did black militants emerge in 1965 as challengers to King's leadership? How did he respond to them?

6. How and why did King get involved in the antiwar movement?

7. How did King's stance as a prophet succeed in desegregation and voting but not in his antipoverty struggle?

14

The Key
to the Warren Report*

Max Holland

Americans are fascinated by conspiracies. No matter what the evidence, the paranoids will find a way to doubt it. If the government investigates flying saucers and publicizes the act, believers will see evidence of the seriousness of their beliefs; if the government finds nothing but keeps the investigation secret to avoid legitimizing popular fears, it is accused of hiding something. It is a no-win situation, one exacerbated by the decline of confidence in the government's integrity in the wake of the Vietnam War and the Watergate scandal. The American character has, in a very real sense, lost its innocence in the past few decades, and regaining it is a difficult task.

The most widely held and persistent conspiracy belief holds that the Kennedy assassination was the result of some kind of elaborate plot—leftists, right wingers, Cubans, Russians, the CIA, the military-industrial complex, or someone was behind it. Lee Harvey Oswald could not have acted alone. The popularity of Oliver Stone's woefully misleading movie "JFK" has added to the paranoia and made it more difficult for serious scholars to win attention to their endeavors. Gerald Posner's 1993 book *Case Closed* did a solid job of explaining why and how Oswald acted alone. In this article, Max Holland, working on a full-scale treatment of the Warren Commis-

*Reprinted by permission of *American Heritage* Magazine, a division of Forbes, Inc. ©Forbes, Inc., 1995.

sion due out in 1996, shares some of his key insights. Most important, he shows how evidence of government cover-ups related to the killing form an understandable pattern of self-protection by persons and agencies without undermining the fundamental and crucial bottom line: Lee Harvey Oswald acted alone and there was no conspiracy to kill Kennedy.

In September 1994, after doggedly repeating a white lie for forty-seven years, the Air Force finally admitted the truth about a mysterious 1947 crash in the New Mexico desert. The debris was not a weather balloon after all but wreckage from Project Mogul, a top-secret high-altitude balloon system for detecting the first Soviet nuclear blasts halfway across the globe.

During the half-century interim, flying-saucer buffs and conspiracy theorists had adorned the incident with mythic significance, weaving wisps of evidence and contradictions in the Air Force's account into fantastic theories: Bodies of extraterrestrial beings had been recovered by the Air Force; the government was hiding live aliens; death threats had been issued to keep knowledgeable people from talking. Such fictions had provided grist for scores of book, articles, and television shows.

In retrospect the Air Force had obviously thought the Cold War prevented it from revealing a project that remained sensitive long after the Soviet Union exploded its first atomic bomb. And such surreptitiousness was certainly not isolated. Might it provide a model even for understanding that greatest alleged government cover up, the assassination of President John F. Kennedy? Indeed our understanding of the assassination and its aftermath may, like so much else, have been clouded by Cold War exigencies. It may be that the suppression of a few embarrassing but not central truths encouraged the spread of myriad farfetched theories.

Admittedly there are Americans who prefer to believe in conspiracies and cover-ups in any situation. H. L. Mencken noted the "virulence of the national appetite for bogus revelation" in 1917, and more than a century after the Lincoln assassination skeptics were still seeking to exhume John Wilkes Booth's remains. The Columbia University historian Richard Hofstadter definitively described this syndrome in his classic 1963 lecture "The Paranoid Style in American Politics," later published as an essay. "Heated exaggeration, suspiciousness, and conspiratorial fantasy" are almost as old as the Republic, Hofstadter observed, as evinced by the anti-Masonic movement of the 1820s, the anti-Catholicism of the 1850s, claims about an international banking cartel in the early 1900s, and Sen. Joe McCarthy's "immense conspiracy" of the 1950s. But a recurring syndrome is not to be confused with a constant one, Hofstadter argued. Paranoia fluctuates according to the rate of change sweeping through society, and varies with affluence and education.

In the case of the Kennedy assassination, unprecedented belief in all kinds of nonsense, coupled with extraordinary disrespect for the Warren Commission, has waxed in good times and bad and flourishes among remarkable numbers of otherwise sober-minded people. Even the highest level of education is not a barrier, to judge from the disregard for the Warren Report that exists in the upper reaches of the academy. In April 1992 the professional historians' most prestigious publication, the *American Historical Review,* published two articles (out of three) in praise of Oliver Stone's movie *JFK.* The lead piece actually asserted that "on the complex question of the Kennedy assassination itself, the film holds its own against the Warren Report." In a similar vein, in 1993, *Deep Politics and the Death of JFK,* by an English professor named Peter Dale Scott, a book conjuring up fantastic paranoid explanations, was published by no less respected an institution than the University of California Press.

The Warren Commission's inquiry occurred at what we now know was the height of the Cold War, and it must be judged in that context. Perhaps with its history understood, the Warren Commission, instead of being an object of derision, can emerge in a different light, battered somewhat but with the essential integrity of its criminal investigation unscathed. The terrible events that began in Dallas are not an overwhelming, unfathomable crossroads; they are another chapter in the history of the Cold War.

In September 1964, when seven lawyers filed into Lyndon Johnson's White House to deliver their 888-page report on the most searing national event since the attack on Pearl Harbor, the transmogrification of the commission into a national joke would have seemed impossible. Collectively, the commission represented one hundred and fifty years' experience—at virtually every level of American government, from county judge to director of Central Intelligence. Chief Justice Earl Warren's reputation was nearly impeccable after more than twenty-five years of public service, and the influence of Georgia's senator Richard Russell in Washington, so the cliché went, was exceeded only by the President's, given Russell's power over intelligence matters, the armed forces, and the Senate itself. Two other panel members, Allen W. Dulles and John J. McCloy, were singularly well versed in the most sensitive national matters, Dulles having served as CIA director from 1953 to 1961 and McCloy as an Assistant Secretary of War from 1940 to 1945.

For several months the commission appeared to have accomplished its mission of assuring the public that the truth was known about Kennedy's death. The American people seemed to accept that JFK's sole assassin was Lee Harvey Oswald, and the report won almost universal praise from the news media. Prior to its release, a Gallup poll found that only 29 percent of Americans thought Oswald had acted alone, afterward 87 percent believed so.

Long before the report came out, of course, nearly everyone had his or her own explanation for the events in Dallas. It was natural to try to invest the tragedy with meaning. And humans being what they are, individual biases determined people's theories. Even as the President was being wheeled into Parkland Memorial Hospital, anguished aides insisted that unspecified right-wingers were responsible, since uppermost in their minds was the rough reception Adlai Stevenson had gotten in Dallas a few weeks earlier, when the U.N. ambassador was booed, jostled, and spat on by right-wing demonstrators. Dallas's long-time reputation as the "Southwest hate capital of Dixie" only reinforced liberals' inclination to blame "refined Nazis." Even Chief Justice Earl Warren, before his appointment to the commission, could not resist issuing a "blunt indictment of the apostles of hate."

But for the officials whose instincts were honed by national-security considerations, the Soviet-American rivalry loomed over what had happened and dictated what immediately needed to be done. The overwhelming instant reaction among these officials was to suspect a grab for power, a foreign, Communist-directed conspiracy aimed at overthrowing the U.S. government.

The assassination might be the first in a concerted series of attacks on U.S. leaders or the prelude to an all-out attack. Newly installed intercontinental ballistic missiles were capable of reaching their targets in fifteen minutes; whose finger was on the nuclear button now that the President was dead? Both the President and Vice President had traveled to Dallas, and the fact that six senior cabinet members happened to be aboard an airplane headed for Japan suddenly acquired an awful significance. The Washington-area telephone system suffered a breakdown thirty minutes after the shots were fired, and sabotage was suspected. Attention fixed on the Soviet Union, China, and Cuba as the only governments that could possibly undertake and benefit from such a heinous plot.

When Maj. Gen. Chester Clifton, JFK's military aide, arrived at Parkland Hospital, he immediately called the National Military Command Center and then switched to the White House Situation Room to find out if there was any intelligence about a plot to overthrow the government. The Defense Department subsequently issued a flash warning to every U.S. military base in the world and ordered additional strategic bombers into the air. Gen. Maxwell Taylor issued a special alert to all troops in the Washington area, while John McCone, director of Central Intelligence, asked the Watch Committee to convene immediately at the Pentagon. The committee, an interdepartmental group organized to prevent future Pearl Harbors, consisted of the government's best experts on surprise military attacks.

Back in Dallas, Rufus Youngblood, head of Johnson's Secret Service detail, told the President-to-be, "We don't know what type of conspiracy this is, or who else is marked. The only place we can be sure you are safe is Washington." A compliant LBJ slouched below the windows in an unmarked car on the way to Love Field, where Air Force One was waiting. Despite special security precautions, it seemed possible to those on the tarmac that the presidential jet could be raked by machine-gun fire at any moment. When the plane was finally airborne, it flew unusually high on a zigzag course back to Washington, with fighter pilots poised to intercept hostile aircraft. During the flight, Johnson kept in touch with the Situation Room, manned by the national security adviser, McGeorge Bundy, for any sign that the Communist bloc might be exploiting the situation. Waiting for Johnson at Andrews Air Force Base was JFK's national security team— or as much of it as could be assembled.

As minutes and then hours passed uneventfully and overburdened telephone exchanges began working again, fears about a surprise attack receded. Conspiracies like the one being imagined rely on surprise and speed for success, and nothing suspicious had occurred after the assassination. Very soon the thought of a master plot seemed irrational, as William Manchester records in *The Death of a President*: "Hindsight began early. Within the next three hours most of those who had considered the possibility began trying to forget it. They felt that they had been absurd." Still, for hours the U.S. military stood poised to deliver an overwhelming counterstrike.

Within hours the Dallas police arrested a twenty-four-year-old Communist sympathizer named Lee Oswald, a bundle of possibilities and seeming contradictions. Now many liberals showed a reluctance to shift the blame from right-wingers to a self-styled Marxist; a liberal President being assassinated by a Marxist seemed to make no sense. Jacqueline Kennedy's reaction upon being told of Oswald's background was to feel sickened because she immediately sensed it robbed JFK's death of a greater meaning. "He didn't even have the satisfaction of being killed for civil rights," she said, according to Manchester. "It's—it had to be some silly little communist."

For security-conscious officials, however, Oswald's arrest meant replacing one Cold War scenario with another, and the second script filled them with no less dread than the first. Undersecretary of State George Ball ordered a search of federal files as soon as the networks broadcast Os-

wald's capture. Dallas authorities found pro-Soviet and pro-Castro literature in Oswald's boardinghouse room, and frantic searches of FBI, CIA,
and State Department records revealed Oswald's defection to the Soviet
Union, his recent contacts with the Soviet Embassy in Mexico City, and his
one-man Fair Play for Cuba committee in New Orleans. Top officials
working through the night to assemble all the pieces had to wonder if the
KGB had transformed a onetime defector into an assassin or if Castro had
used an overt sympathizer to retaliate against an administration plotting
his downfall. As Ball told the *Washington Post* in 1993, "we were just scared
to death that this was something bigger than just the act of a madman."

The government's leading experts on the Soviet Union doubted it.
Llewellyn Thompson, a well-regarded former ambassador to Moscow, argued that the assassination lacked the earmarks of a Soviet plot. Moscow
might kill defectors but not heads of state, he insisted, and would never
set such a precedent. Averell Harriman, another experienced Soviet hand,
agreed that Oswald was not a likely instrument of the KGB and questioned his professed Marxism. The assassination, utterly inconsistent with
recent Soviet behavior, just made no sense. What could the Soviets possibly hope to achieve through such a rash act in a nuclear-tipped world?
Nor was there evidence of any effort to advance Soviet interests in the
wake of the assassination. As for Cuba, even the mercurial Castro was unlikely to engage in such madness. He had to know that it would put the
existence of his regime, if not his revolution, in extreme danger. But past
history and common sense were not sufficient to banish all thoughts of
Communist complicity. More hard evidence was desperately needed to
rule it out.

Over the next two days, while a nation mourned, the entire intelligence community worked to learn everything it could about Oswald and
his murky, superficially contradictory activities. New intelligence reports
from Mexico City suggested a link between Oswald and the Cuban government. The supersecret National Security Agency and allied eaves-
dropping agencies went into overdrive to decipher intercepted conversations, cable traffic, radio, and telephone communications at the highest
levels of the Soviet and Cuban governments, looking especially for unusual messages between Moscow and the Soviet Embassy in Washington
and between Moscow and Havana.

In about forty-eight hours the intercepts showed beyond a reasonable doubt that both the Soviet and Cuban governments had been as
shocked as anyone by the news from Dallas. "They were frightened," says
one knowledgeable source, "and we knew that." Indeed, Moscow was so
uneasy over its remote link to Oswald that the Foreign Ministry voluntarily gave the State Department a KGB account of his every movement

inside Russia. Not only was Castro's surprise genuine (he was being interviewed by a French journalist when the news came), he was panic-stricken. He believed that President Johnson would send in the Marines if LBJ decided the Cuban government was connected to the assassination.

That Oswald was not the instrument of a foreign power was an intelligence coup of the first order and of incalculable interest to an unsettled public. Late on Saturday, November 23, the State Department issued a public statement declaring that there was no evidence of a conspiracy involving a foreign country. Yet revealing the intelligence sources and methods that had helped form this determination was out of the question. Cold War–era communications intercepts were as prized as World War II feats of decryption, and the NSA's capabilities were—and are—the most highly guarded of secrets. And because content reveals methodology, certain specifics of what had been learned were equally protected. The American public was told the truth but not the whole truth. It would not be the last time.

With fears of foreign involvement ebbing, a third Cold War worry began to dominate thinking among high officials—that given Oswald's extreme views, the assassination might stir dangerous anti-Communist emotions within the body politic. Anyone who had lived through the McCarthy era knew of the domestic dangers of untrammeled anti-Communism. It could threaten the mild détente achieved since the Cuban missile crisis; indeed, the public might even demand that President Johnson retaliate with a show of force. Already an LBJ aide had squelched language in the original indictment charging Oswald with killing the President "in furtherance of a communist conspiracy." And the U.S. ambassador to Moscow, Foy Kohler, had cabled Washington on Saturday expressing his own concern over the "political repercussions which may develop if undue emphasis is placed on the alleged 'Marxism' of Oswald . . . I would hope, if facts permit, we could deal with the assassin as 'madman' . . . rather than dwell on his professed political convictions."

This mostly domestic problem appeared manageable. But then Jack Ruby, prey to rash impulses and a murderous temper, decided to exact proper revenge. Oswald's death abruptly renewed the note of mystery and suspicion: Had he been killed to suppress something? Top officials considered, but eventually discarded, the notion of an elaborate conspiracy involving Ruby; if there had been one, why was Oswald allowed to live for forty-eight hours, let alone be captured? Meanwhile the need to assuage public anxiety only intensified. Johnson considered releasing detailed results from the FBI investigation ordered the night of November 22, but then dismissed the idea as insufficient. The FBI investigation itself had to be validated, though J. Edgar Hoover fumed at the suggestion. Instead an idea advocated by Nicholas Katzenbach, the deputy Attorney General, gathered support within and without the administration.

Katzenbach, deeply concerned over the appearance of a relationship between the Soviets and Oswald, wanted LBJ to impanel a group of prestigious citizens to investigate the assassination, to develop and control information with possible international repercussions, and ultimately to choke off all talk about a Communist conspiracy. Johnson, keenly aware of the South's sensitivity over states' rights, at first wanted an all-Texas investigation. But long-time Washington hands and friends, including the columnist Joseph Alsop, persuaded him that a state inquiry would be considered tantamount to a whitewash. This argument struck a chord in Johnson; Texas was his home state, and the Soviet-bloc press was charging that a leftist was being made a scapegoat for what was actually a right-wing Texas conspiracy in a decadent, violent country.

The motivation for the formation of the Warren Commission, on November 29, is made clear in transcripts of 275 recently declassified presidential telephone conversations from late 1963. They show that Johnson recruited the members of the panel by repeatedly invoking the need to cut off "explosive" and "dangerous" speculation about a Communist plot. Preventing World War III might have been typical Johnson hyperbole, but the concern was real, and there were still contradictory allegations that needed to be checked out, especially Oswald's mysterious September trip to Mexico City, where he had met a KGB agent doubling as a Soviet consular officer. As Johnson told Chief Justice Warren and Senator Russell—both were reluctant to serve—"This is a question that has a good many more ramifications than on the surface, and we've got to take this out of the arena where they're testifying that Krushchev and Castro did this and did that and check us into a war that can kill 40 million Americans in an hour."

Even the commission's enlistment of such respected anti-Communists as Russell and Rep. Gerald Ford did not immediately stanch the mischief and pressure Johnson feared from the right. On December 6 the House Republican Policy Committee issued a statement decrying liberals' claims that "hate was the assassin that struck down the President," saying the true criminal was the "teachings of communism." Republican senator Milward Simpson of Wyoming took the floor that same day to attack those who were seeking "political advantage from warping the uncontestable truth." The senator added that the murderer "was a single kill-crazy communist."

When Earl Warren welcomed the assembled commission staff on January 20, he admonished them, "Truth is our only client here," and that phrase became the commission's unofficial motto. Ultimately, the group's massive undertaking yielded two essential conclusions: that Oswald fired all the shots that killed JFK and wounded John Connally and that there was no evidence of a conspiracy. Reaching these simple findings required a prodigious effort by many dedicated people, and it is no small accomplishment that after more than thirty years the first conclusion remains proven beyond a reasonable doubt and the second has never been challenged by any hard, credible evidence.

The only other politically sensitive question facing the commission was that of Oswald's motive and how it might be connected to his Communist beliefs and activities. How did the commission treat Oswald's politics? It's hard to recreate an earlier time and problem, but it is extraordinarily revealing to do so.

The main difficulty in divining Oswald's motive was of course the fact that Jack Ruby had murdered him before he could confess and explain. During twelve hours of questioning Oswald had fallen silent or lied, with that arrogance and air of fantasy peculiar to sociopaths, whenever confronted with hard evidence tying him to the assassination. No, he wasn't the man holding the Mannlicher-Carcano rifle in that picture; someone had altered the photograph to superimpose his face on another body. No, he had never been in Mexico City. No, he was in the lunchroom when Kennedy was shot. Often Oswald appeared to be baiting his interrogators and "was so smug in the way he dealt with the questions," the Dallas assistant district attorney later recalled, that "at times I had to walk out of the room, because in another few minutes I was going to beat the shit out of him myself." One of Oswald's few requests was that he be represented by John J. Abt, a New York lawyer known for his defense of leading Communist-party figures since 1949.

Lacking a confession or hard evidence like a note, the commission ultimately decided not to ascribe to Oswald "any one motive or group of motives." This nonconclusion was sound and sensible for several reasons. First, the commission viewed itself as akin to a judge at a criminal trial, with the job simply of determining Oswald's culpability and the conspiracy issue; motive was less important. Second, the issue seemed a bottomless pit. In a moment of dark humor one staff member, Norman Redlich, wrote a spoof titled the "Washing Machine Theory of the Assassination," describing how Marina Oswald's rejection of her husband's offer to buy her a washing machine had triggered Oswald's sense of failure and his need to prove his mettle by assassinating a President. There was a serious purpose in Redlich's spoof: He wanted to show that there was simply no way to pick one motive from all the possibilities. The chances of achieving unanimity among the commissioners were slim to nil, and anyway a consensus was bound to subject the report to valid, as opposed to irresponsible, criticism. Consequently the report listed a few possibilities and concluded that "others may study Lee Oswald's life and arrive at their own conclusions as to his possible motives."

However reasonable and sound this nonconclusion was, what is striking in retrospect is how a very plausible motive was buried. Ample details about Oswald's extraordinary political activities were provided, but in a detached and clinical manner; the avalanche of facts tended to obscure a salient one. Whenever Oswald actually took violent action, whenever he set free his internal demons, it was on a political stage. This was true when he attempted suicide in 1959, after the Soviets initially refused his defection, and again in April 1963, when he stalked a right-wing retired general named Edwin A. Walker. Walker and Kennedy had one thing in common in Oswald's eyes: their anti-Communism, especially their antipathy to the "purer" Cuban Revolution that had captured Oswald's imagination. (Walker had called for "liquidating the scourge that has descended on Cuba.") The November murder was first of all an act of opportunity by a bent personality, but Kennedy was not in all likelihood a random victim of Oswald.

How did this de-emphasis occur? The most important factor was the cautiousness described above. The commission's task was not to promote speculation and theorizing, no matter how plausible. Another significant, if perhaps less conscious, element was the dominant role lawyers played on the commission and in writing the report. In the most trenchant criticism of the Warren Report ever to appear, a 1965 *Esquire* article, the critic Dwight Macdonald accepted the commission's conclusions but called the report a prosecutor's brief that failed to meet its overarching purpose, which was to produce an objective account of what happened in Dallas. Because the report was written by lawyers, Macdonald said it had a telling defect: "omnivorous inclusiveness. . . . [the] prose is at best workmanlike but too often turgidly legalistic or pompously official. It obscures the strong points of its case, and many are very strong, under a midden-heap of inessential facts. . . . Its tone is that of the advocate, smoothing away or sidestepping objections to his 'case' rather than the impartial judge or the researcher welcoming all data with detached curiosity." Oswald's seriousness about his politics was buried under a "midden-heap" of facts.

Yet there was also a political tinge to the depiction of Oswald. The same Cold War imperative that had led to the formation of the commission persisted as an undercurrent throughout the investigation, and it ultimately detached Oswald from the politics that had animated him. At the commission's first executive session in December, former Director of Central Intelligence Allen Dulles, one of the members most sensitive to Cold War considerations, gave each of his colleagues a book on the history of presidential assassinations in America. Nearly every killer, would-be or successful, had been a lone psychopath. Dulles suggested to his colleagues that Oswald fitted the historical pattern; a disturbed nonentity, in other words, purchased a mail-order rifle and used it to murder the President of the United States. Later Dulles wrote what he hoped would be an appendix to the report on the topic of presidential assassins.

The manner in which the report described Oswald's preferred legal counsel is also revealing. That Oswald had wanted to retain John Abt, or a lawyer who "believes as I believe" and would "understand what this case is all about," was a sure indication that Oswald had intended to exploit his upcoming trial as a megaphone for his peculiar brand of politics. But the report drew no meaning at all from Oswald's clear preference. All three references to Abt simply describe him as a "New York attorney" (or lawyer), not mentioning his ties to Communist-party figures. The commission's inclination to de-emphasize Oswald's politics was mightily reinforced by another external Cold War imperative. As the staff, to its great chagrin, learned a decade later, the CIA limited its cooperation with the investigation according to its own internal rules. The agency had no intention of volunteering information about American subversion of Castro's regime, including proposed assassination plots that stretched back to the Eisenhower administration, even though Oswald may have suspected the worst about U.S. policy and been motivated by its hostility. And there was no clue that the CIA was holding back, for it did readily share some highly classified secrets, like the communications intercepts. Suspicion of the FBI actually ran far higher, because of J. Edgar Hoover's well-known predilection for holding himself above the law.

When the CIA's omissions were finally revealed in the mid-1970s, the agency was roundly pilloried by Congress and in the news media. Nothing was more devastating to the Warren Commission's reputation, nothing more "weakened the credibility of the Warren Report," CBS's anchorman Walter Cronkite observed. The commission's staff had grown used to bogus "new" revelations by conspiracy buffs, but this genuinely distressed and even angered them. And most Americans, unschooled in the niceties of compartmented information and the need to know, found incomprehensible the notion that the CIA had dissembled in the midst of a national trauma. Could the CIA ever be counted on to tell the whole truth about the assassination? And if the government could so lie to itself—let alone to the public—what wasn't possible?

This revelation made the Warren Commission into a national joke. For a few citizens, of course, the supposed inadequacy of the commission's investigation had been manifest as early as 1966; others had gone through a more gradual disillusionment that reflected their declining faith in government after Vietnam and Watergate. But for most the investigation had never before come under such a cloud, except during a passing controversy over the President's autopsy that had been fairly easily resolved. Now doubts were such that even Congress felt compelled to revisit the entire matter, after fourteen years of self-restraint unprecedented for that publicity-hungry body.

When the House Select Committee on Assassinations issued its final report, in 1979, it castigated the CIA for withholding information. Yet some members of the commission must have pretty well known the CIA wasn't being entirely open. Allen Dulles had extensive knowledge about CIA workings and U.S. efforts to overthrow Castro since March 1960, including proposed assassination plots. John McCloy, chief negotiator during the Cuban missile crisis, was quite familiar with the governmentwide effort to subvert Castro's regime. And two other commissioners, Richard Russell and Gerald Ford, sat in on closed-door unminuted congressional hearings about CIA budgets, policies, and covert activities. Ford confirmed that in 1963–64 he was aware of agency efforts to subvert Castro, with the exception of proposed assassination plots. And Russell, who dominated congressional involvement in intelligence matters, was a stout believer in covert activities. Far from being an inquisitive, troublesome overseer, "Mr. Senate" acted as the CIA's protector and advocate on Capitol Hill. There is no indication that he viewed his role on the commission any differently. Not one of these four—out of seven—commissioners shared whatever special insight he had with the staff, nor is that really surprising. These men were steeped in the Cold War and in what sometimes had to be done to wage it.

Consider, too, the actions of those officials outside the commission who had the standing and power to bring any relevant information to Warren's attention had they chosen to do so. In particular, consider the role of Attorney General Robert Kennedy. He played a unique part: Not only was he the brother of the slain President, but he had virtually unrivaled knowledge about anti-Castro activities. Indeed, more than any other official, the thirty-eight-year-old Kennedy embodied the harsh political, institutional, and personal dilemmas that existed in the assassination's wake. Any reconsideration of the Warren Commission must address RFK's role directly. His response is a Rosetta stone.

The standard explanation for RFK's seeming uninterest in the commission, as put forward in biographies and memoirs by friends, is that he simply found the subject too painful. Although kept fully apprised of the commission's progress, he emotionally recused himself from the investigation. As RFK told close associates, Jack was dead and nothing he could do would bring him back. In *The Death of a President* William Manchester writes that many of the Kennedy clan who were crushed by the assassination managed to right themselves after the funeral—but not RFK. During the spring of 1964 a "brooding Celtic agony . . . darken[ed] Kennedy's life." He was nonfunctional for hours at a time and to those closest to him seemed almost in physical pain.

What genuinely sent RFK reeling may have been what the historian Robert Jay Lifton calls "survivor guilt," a feeling that he should have died instead of the President. In the end, the raw probability, after all conspiracies were ruled out, was that the administration's obsession with Castro had inadvertently motivated a politicized sociopath. Oswald had seen embodied in President Kennedy all American opposition to Castro, but it was Robert Kennedy, more than his brother, who had played the driving role in the anti-Castro subversion. RFK's involvement had begun just two days after the inauguration, when at the new President's behest the new Attorney General had been included in the first of seven CIA briefings on the plans to invade Cuba. Attorneys General had never before participated in such deliberations, but that was only the beginning.

After the Bay of Pigs debacle, in April 1961, the President ordered RFK to help Gen. Maxwell Taylor poke around the Agency and find out what had gone wrong. Operating with his usual zeal, Robert Kennedy immersed himself in Agency affairs over the next two months, and the more he understood of the CIA's capabilities, the more ardent a champion he became. Precisely because the Bay of Pigs was such a catastrophe, the Kennedys grew more determined than ever to see Castro deposed.

While Castro erected a sign near the invasion site that read WELCOME TO THE SITE OF THE FIRST DEFEAT OF IMPERIALISM IN THE WESTERN HEMISPHERE, the Kennedy administration resumed plotting against him in earnest. By November 1961 another covert plan, code-named Mongoose, was moving into high gear. This time the operation aimed to destabilize Castro's regime rather than overthrow it. In concert with overtly hostile diplomatic and economic policies, every possible covert tactic would be brought to bear, including sabotage, psychological warfare, and proposed assassination plots; and the President installed his brother as czar over the entire, governmentwide operation. As Sen. Harris Wofford (then a White House aide) wrote in his 1980 memoir, *Of Kennedys & Kings,* "The Attorney General was the driving force behind the clandestine effort to overthrow Castro. From inside accounts of the pressure he was putting on the CIA to 'get Castro,' he seemed like a wild man who was out-CIAing the CIA."

For the first nine months of 1962, Mongoose was the administration's top covert priority, and Castro next to an obsession for Robert Kennedy. RFK's single-minded micro-management extended to almost daily telephone conversations with Richard Helms, deputy director of the CIA, during which calls the volatile Attorney General applied "white heat" pressure. As Helms told *Newsweek* in 1993, "We had a whip on our backs. If I take off my shirt, I'll show you the scars." It was abundantly clear that Castro was to be gotten rid of.

In 1962 the Attorney General even decided the Mafia could be useful in Mongoose operations. He ordered the CIA to assign a case officer to meet with Mafia figures. "It was Bobby and his secretary (Angie Novello) who called the officer on what used to be called at the Agency a secure line, [to] give him a name, an address, and where he would meet with the Mafia people," recalls Samuel Halpern, a retired CIA official involved in Mongoose. The ensuing conversations contradicted almost every rule for clandestine operations the CIA had, and to add insult to injury, nothing useful ever developed from them. "We thought it was stupid, silly, ineffective, and wasteful," says Halpern. "But we were under orders, and we did it."

The CIA pursued Mongoose with determined vigor until the Cuban missile crisis put the United States and the Soviet Union at the brink of nuclear war. After that some advisers got Kennedy to take tentative steps toward trying to wean Castro from the Soviets, because the Cuban leader was smarting over the Russian "betrayal." But the dominant U.S. policy remained intensely hostile. "Our interest lies in avoiding the kind of commitment that unduly ties our hands in dealing with the Castro regime while it lasts," wrote Secretary of State Dean Rusk in a 1962 document only recently declassified. Ultimately, a more modest program of covert subversion was reintroduced by mid-1963. As before, it included the tactic of "neutralizing" Castro.

Despite the manifest relevance of these activities to the Warren inquiry, Robert Kennedy studiously avoided sharing any information about them with the commission—even when Earl Warren specifically asked him to. As David Belin, a counsel to the Warren Commission, recounts in *Final Disclosure*, Warren informed RFK of the commission's progress, in a letter dated June 11, 1964, and asked him if he was aware of any "additional information relating to the assassination of President John F. Kennedy which has not been sent to the Commission." Warren emphasized in particular the importance of any information suggesting a "domestic or foreign conspiracy."

Kennedy wrote in response that "all information . . . in the possession of the Department of Justice" had been sent to the commission. He added that he had "no suggestions to make at this time regarding any additional investigation which should be undertaken by the Commission prior to the publication of its report."

Several accounts make it clear that Robert Kennedy's immediate instinct after the assassination was to look for a Cuban connection to Oswald, among either pro-Castro elements or Bay of Pigs veterans repatriated from Havana in December 1962. He asked McCone if Agency-connected persons had killed JFK "in a way that [McCone] couldn't lie to me, and [McCone replied] they hadn't." Through close associates, RFK also made other discreet inquires about perceived administration enemies right after the assassination: What was Jimmy Hoffa's reaction? Were Chicago mobsters involved?

Small wonder that in the black months after the murder Robert Kennedy became absorbed by the work of the Greek tragedians. He apparently found solace in one passage from Aeschylus, for he underlined it: "All arrogance will reap a harvest rich in tears. God calls men to a heavy reckoning for overweening pride." Belin also tells of a 1975 conversation he had with McCone after news of the proposed assassination plots finally surfaced along with the fact that Robert Kennedy had overseen those plans. As Belin describes it, "McCone replied that for the first time he could now understand the reactions of Kennedy right after the assassination when the two of them were alone. McCone said he felt there was something troubling Kennedy that he was not disclosing. . . . [It was McCone's] personal belief that Robert Kennedy had personal feelings of guilt because he was directly or indirectly involved with the anti-Castro planning."

In the case of RFK, of course, the national security that dictated silence was reinforced by a very personal imperative. As the reputation of the slain President soared, Robert Kennedy bore the burden of protecting that reputation and carrying its legacy. Already he had sought to insulate his brother from debacles (the Bay of Pigs) and turn near catastrophes into triumphs of calibrated, statesmanlike policy (the Cuban missile crisis). Full disclosure surely would have threatened the emerging Camelot view of the Kennedy Presidency and, it must be said, RFK's fortunes as well. His own political stock was skyrocketing after the assassination.

On the first occasion when he spoke directly about Oswald, Kennedy said exactly what the Warren Commission would eventually report. He told a student questioner in Poland in June 1964, "I believe it was done by a man . . . who was a misfit in society. . . . [He] felt that the only way to take out his strong feelings against life and society was by killing the President of the United States. There is no question that he did it on his own and by himself. He was not a member of a right-wing organization. He was a confessed Communist, but even the Communists would not have anything to do with him."

Even if other officials did not know as much as RFK or share his need to keep the Kennedy image burnished, their personal and institutional loyalties likewise determined the extent of their cooperation with the commission. Anyway, if, as the communications intercepts proved, there was no link between Oswald and the Soviet or Cuban government, then Warren had no need to know about past and ongoing covert operations directed against Cuba, regardless of how relevant they were to Oswald's internal equation. Not a few officials and Cold War operatives had an interest in leaving the assassin a crazed loner, acting on some solitary impulse. To put it another way, officials in the know faced a genuine dilemma only if they had information pointing to someone other than Oswald. The Warren Commission could not deliver to the American people and the world a false conclusion—that might well affect the stability of the government or shake important institutions to their foundations—but there was every reason not to spill secrets that merely echoed the finding that Oswald acted alone. The commission, though denied important supporting information, would still publish the correct conclusion, and the U.S. government could keep its deepest secrets. It was a convenient act of denial and dismissal, but also one perceived as necessary in the midst of the Cold War. Complete candor would not have changed the report's two essential conclusions at all—though it might have done a great deal to prevent its slide into disrepute later.

Full disclosure might have helped the commission explain the political element in Oswald's motive by putting his pro-Castro activities in a new dimension, but the price was considered to be too high. The CIA, especially, had every reason to dread a no-holds-barred investigation into the events of November 22. An uncontrolled investigation would have had serious repercussions for ongoing covert operations. Beyond the inevitable exposure of Mongoose, possibly the largest covert operation that had ever been mounted, the revelations would have given the Communist bloc an undreamed-of propaganda windfall that would have lasted years. There would have followed strong condemnations by the international community and intense investigations of the CIA and administration officials who had directed anti-Castro efforts. Such investigations could conceivably have destroyed the CIA, and it was surely not LBJ's intention to blunt his Cold War weapons when he announced the commission's formation. Altogether, there simply was no contest between these risks and the potential damage that silence might inflict on the Warren Commission's reputation should the withheld information ever leak out.

In time the Warren Commission will be seen for what it truly was. It was not a fiendish cover-up, nor was it designed to anesthetize the country by delivering a political truth at odds with the facts. It was a monumental criminal investigation carried to its utmost limits and designed to burn away a fog of speculation. It did not achieve perfection, and in the rush to print (there was no rush to judgment) the language on pivotal issues, such as the single bullet, was poorly crafted. In retrospect, forensic and scientific experts should have been put on the lawyer-dominated panel. But the commission indisputably achieved its main goal: to determine what happened in Dealey Plaza on November 22, 1963. That was the one thing that needed to and could be proved beyond a reasonable doubt. And the accuracy of the report's essential finding, holding up after three decades, is testimony to the commission's basic integrity. Indeed, as a British reviewer once put it, the best tribute to the solidity of the report is the deviousness of its critics.

The commission did not conduct its work in a political vacuum, nor could it. In fact the Warren Commission reflects a view common during the Cold War, one Gerald Ford explained in general terms during his vice-presidential confirmation hearings in 1973, that government officials have the right, if not the duty, to tell the truth but not necessarily the whole truth when an issue involves national-security matters. Some Americans erroneously believe that secrets per se contradict official verdicts; just as often, if not more often, they buttress conclusions, as the case here shows.

Was parceling out truths an outrageous act or a necessary one during the forty-five years of the Cold War? It depends on one's perspective. There is no doubt it was done here. Secrets considered inessential to the inquiry were kept secret even from the commission. Those considered essential were shared with the commission but not the public. No doubt referring to the communications intercepts, Earl Warren told the press shortly after the report's publication that there were "things that will not be revealed in our lifetime." Or as former President Ford now acknowledges, "Judgments were made back then that seemed rational and reasonable. Today with the totally different atmosphere those judgments might seem improper." The Warren Commission's investigation cut across the entire national-security apparatus during the height of the Cold War, when even a national trauma could not be allowed to disturb the inner workings and unalterable logic of that struggle.

Was this instance of holding back some of the truth one of the great misjudgments in American history? Enduring, perhaps ineradicable controversy over the assassination has helped helped foster deep alienation and cynicism and a loss of respect among the American people for their government and the citizens who serve in it. That is perhaps the most lasting and grievous wound inflicted by Lee Harvey Oswald.

QUESTIONS TO CONSIDER

1. What factors affect national bouts of paranoia, according to Richard Hofstadter? Why is the Kennedy assassination distinctive?

2. What signs at the time of the assassination suggested a possible foreign plot to national security personnel? How long did that suspicion last?

3. Why were details of National Security Agency findings that Russia and Cuba were unconnected to the assassination not revealed to the public?

4. What motivated LBJ to create the Warren Commission just a week after the assassination? What were the commission's two essential conclusions?

5. For what reasons did the Warren Commission avoid getting into Oswald's political motives?

6. What revelations in the midseventies most undermined the credibility of the Warren Commission? Why should the members of the commission not have been surprised by the CIA's behavior?

7. What motives shaped RFK's failure to fully cooperate with the Warren Commission? Why was this significant?

8. Why did the Warren Commission not reveal secrets about relations with Cuba? Did that decision affect the accuracy of its report? What was the long-term impact of the decision?

9. What is your response to the article?

15

The American Environment*

John Steele Gordon

Americans are prone to become caught up in crusades. In the late fifties and well into the sixties, civil rights dominated the nation's crusading spirit. Then, as the movement for black equality became less focused and more divisive, the drive to halt the war in Vietnam replaced it as the preeminent cause. But by 1973 the Americans were out of Vietnam and a new crusade was underway, one that would have much greater staying power—the environmental movement. The environment became the big issue of the seventies, and well beyond.

The movement was based in the grass roots, with politicians re-acting to the public's concerns rather than leading the way. As John Steele Gordon, the author of an earlier article, "What We Lost in the Great War," suggests, the nation had become far more re-ceptive to the environmental message in a century. In 1864 George Perkins Marsh had published *The Earth as Modified by Hu-man Action* to no effect whatsoever. Yet almost a hundred years later, Rachel Carson published *Silent Spring* in 1962, and her book launched Americans into a major readjustment of their behavior. In effect, she began a transformation of the American character. Historically, Americans had disposed of waste by throwing it over "the nearest stone wall" and forgetting about it because there was an apparently infinite amount of land out there. Technologi-

*Reprinted by permission of *American Heritage* Magazine, a division of Forbes, Inc. ©Forbes, Inc., 1993.

cal advance, however, had made it possible to transform even that much land, and pollute endless water, and undermine the quality of life of the nation. Earth Day in 1970 launched the modern environmental movement and Congress created the Environmental Protection Agency and passed the Clean Water Act and the Clean Air Act. The results of the movement have been heartening, as Gordon points out in this 1993 article.

The Cuyahoga River died for our sins. In 1796 the Cuyahoga, which promised easy transportation into the wilderness of the Ohio country from Lake Erie, prompted the city of Cleveland into existence. Over the next 170 years a primitive frontier town grew into a mighty industrial city, one that stretched for miles along the banks of its seminal river.

By the midtwentieth century, however, the river no longer served as a major artery of transportation, having been superseded by railroads and highways. Now, instead of carrying the products of civilization into the vast interior, it carried the effluent of a far more technically advanced civilization out into the lake. The once crystalline waters of the river had become turbid and rank with its new cargo of chemicals and sewage. Its once abundant wildlife had long since fled, leaving only a few carps and suckers to eke out a living in the foul sullage on its bottom, testifying thereby to the very tenacity of life itself.

Finally, late in the morning of June 22, 1969, the Cuyahoga could no longer bear the burden humankind had placed upon it. In a sort of fluvial *cri de coeur*, the river burst into flames.

The fire was no will-o'-the-wisp flickering over a transient oil slick. Rather, it roared five stories into the sky, reduced wooden railroad trestles to ruins, and demonstrated to the people of Cleveland and the nation as no scientific study or news report ever could that the burden being placed on the environment was reaching limits that could be crossed only at the peril of the future.

Less than a year later, on April 22, 1970, Earth Day was held, one of the most remarkable happenings in the history of democracy. Fully 10 percent of the population of the country, twenty million people, demonstrated their support for redeeming the American environment. They attended events in every state and nearly every city and county. American politics and public policy would never be the same again.

Today, nearly a quarter-century after the fire, sunlight once more sparkles off the surface of the Cuyahoga. Boaters cruise its waters for pleasure, and diners eat at riverside restaurants. Mayflies—so characteristic of a Great Lakes spring—once more dance in the air above it in their millions while their larvae provide food for at least twenty-seven species of fish that have returned to its waters.

The Cuyahoga is not pristine, and barring an alteration in human priorities and circumstances beyond anything now imagined, it will not become so. But it has changed greatly for the better and continues to improve. It is once more a living river.

The Cuyahoga and its history is a microcosm of the American environment. For the history of that environment is the story of the interaction between a constantly changing, ever-more-powerful technology and an only slowly shifting paradigm of humankind's proper relationship with the natural world.

Human beings evolved in the Old World, a fact that more than once would have sudden and drastic consequences for the New.

The beginning of the Upper Paleolithic period was marked by a dramatic technological development as humans acquired tools and weapons that were far more sophisticated than any known before and became the most formidable hunters the world has ever known. In the Old World both our prey and our competitors, evolving alongside, quickly learned to treat the emerging biological superpower with the greatest respect, and most were able to adapt successfully. But the New World lay in innocence while human hunters perfected their newfound skills in the Old.

When the land bridge that was a temporary consequence of the last ice age allowed humans to migrate into it, the results were swift and devastating: much of the North American Pleistocene fauna went extinct. Horses, camels, mastodons, mammoths, true elephants, several species of deer, bison, and antelope, ground sloths, glyptodonts, and giant beavers vanished, as did their associated predators such as saber-toothed cats, giant lions, and cheetahs.

It cannot be known for sure to what extent the arrival of human hunters affected this great extinction, but there is little doubt that it was an important, perhaps fundamental, factor. But the evolutionary equilibrium that had been shattered by the arrival of the superhunters eventually returned, for the human population of the New World, limited by numerous other factors besides food supply, remained low. And the surviving among the species they had encountered quickly adapted to the new conditions.

Thus the next human culture that appeared in the New World, the Europeans, found it to possess a biological abundance and diversity of, to them, astounding proportions. But these newcomers failed almost entirely to appreciate this aspect of the New World, for hunting in their culture had been reduced to, at most, a secondary source of food.

They were heirs to the agricultural revolution that began in the Old World at the end of the last ice age. It, too, was marked by a profound leap in technology. In turn the more settled conditions of agricultural communities allowed the development of still more elaborate technologies as well as social and political organizations of unprecedented complexity. The result was what we call civilization.

But the early civilizations were acutely aware that they were small islands surrounded by vast seas of wilderness from which savage beasts, and savage men, might come at any time and wipe them out. Thus their inhabitants came to look on the wilderness as an alien place, separate and apart. Not surprisingly under these circumstances, the religions that developed in the Near East in the wake of the agricultural revolution reflected this worldview, sanctioned it, and codified it. Because it became, quite literally, Holy Writ, it persisted unquestioned for centuries.

The Book of Genesis, in fact, could hardly be more direct on the subject, "God said unto [man], Be fruitful, and multiply, and replenish [i.e., fill up] the earth, and subdue it: and have dominion over the fish of the sea, and over the fowl of the air, and over every living thing that moveth upon the earth."

Over the next more than two thousand years, humans operating with this worldview in mind transformed the continent of Europe, and by the time they began to expand overseas, wilderness had disappeared from all but the margins of that continent.

Thus the world they encountered in North America was unlike anything they had ever seen. The greatest temperate forest in the world, teeming with life, stretched almost unbroken from the Atlantic seaboard to well west of the Mississippi. The grasslands that filled the Great Plains in the rain shadow of the Rocky Mountains also abounded with animal life as millions of bison, pronghorn antelope, elk, white-tailed and mule deer roamed it, as did their associated predators, the wolf, the mountain lion, the bear, and the jaguar.

Farther west still, the forests of the Northwest and the deserts of the Southwest reached to the Pacific.

When the new settlers arrived, they did not see the beauty or abundance of the wilderness that greeted them. Far from it; they regarded it as barren and threatening because the ancient paradigm that dated to the dawn of civilization still molded their thinking. Thus they regarded their first task in the New World to be a re-creation of what they had known in the Old, an environment shaped by the hand of man, for man's benefit.

But while they sought, as nearly as possible, to re-create the Europe they had left behind, converting the "remote, rocky, barren, bushy, wildwoody wilderness" into a "second England for fertilness," there was one way in which the New World was utterly unlike the Old: it possessed an abundance of land so great that it seemed to the early settlers, and to their descendants for many generations, to verge upon the infinite. "The great happiness of my country," wrote the Swiss-born Albert Gallatin, Jefferson's Secretary of the Treasury, "arises from the great plenty of land."

Because the supply seemed without end, the value placed on each unit was small. It is only common sense to husband the scarce and let the plentiful take care of itself. Caring for the land, an inescapable necessity in Europe, was simply not cost-effective here. After all, the settlers could always move on to new, rich land farther west. For three hundred years they did exactly that, with ever-increasing speed.

Americans also developed other habits in the early days that stemmed directly from the wealth of land and scarcity of the population. Today, when American archaeologists investigate a site, they know that the place to look for the garbage dump is on the far side of the fence or stone wall that was nearest to the dwelling. In Europe that was likely to belong to a neighbor; in America it was often wilderness and thus beyond the human universe. This out-of-sight-out-of-mind attitude would have no small consequences when technology increased the waste stream by orders of magnitude.

The early settlers, while they greatly altered the landscape of the Eastern seaboard, clearing whole stretches of the primeval forest and converting the land to fields, pastures, and meadows, did not greatly diminish the biological diversity. They opened up the best land for farming but left untouched the steep or rocky areas as well as, to a great extent, the wetlands and mountains. Indeed in some ways the early settlers increased the diversity by expanding habitat for such grassland species as bluebirds, ground hogs, and meadowlarks. The ecosystem as a whole remained intact.

Only in the South, where plantation agriculture became the rule in areas to which it was suited, did monocultural husbandry greatly diminish the fertility and texture of the soil. Virginia, the largest and, thanks to its tobacco exports, most powerful of the colonies, found its yields declining sharply toward the end of the eighteenth century as the best land was exploited and exhausted. Erosion became an increasing problem. As early as the 1780s Patrick Henry thought that "the greatest patriot is he who fills the most gullies."

Meanwhile, as a new civilization was being built out of the wilderness of North America, new attitudes toward wilderness itself were emerging in Europe. The ancient paradigm that had gripped Western thinking since Genesis was beginning, partially, to shift at last.

In the seventeenth century, wilderness had been universally regarded as at best a waste, if not an evil. In the eighteenth, however, it began to be seen for the first time as a thing of beauty. Mountains came to be viewed as majestic, not just as an impediment to travel or a barrier against invasion.

In Britain the aristocracy began to lay out gardens, such as those by Capability Brown, that were highly stylized versions of nature itself, rather than the direct refutation of it that seventeenth-century gardens, like those at Versailles, had been.

Biology became a systematic science (although the word itself would enter the language only in the early nineteenth century). Linnaeus studied the relationships of plants and animals. Georges Cuvier, William Smith, and others began to examine fossils and to sense, for the first time, a history of the earth that was at variance with the account given in Genesis.

The new attitude toward wilderness soon came to this country and contributed to the growing American sense of uniqueness. James Fenimore Cooper's novels and Thoreau's essays displayed a love of wilderness that would have been inconceivable a century earlier.

Of course, in Europe wilderness was largely an abstraction. In America it was just down the road. At the end of the Revolution, it nowhere lay more than a few days on horseback from the Atlantic shore, and Thomas Jefferson, no mean observer, thought it would be "a thousand years" before settlement reached the Pacific.

Jefferson was wrong. He did not realize—no one could have—that a third technological revolution was just getting under way, one that would give humankind the power to transform the world far beyond anything provided by the first two. It had taken millennia to reshape the face of Europe to human ends. North America would be transformed in less than a century. But there would be a vast price to pay for this miracle.

The steam engine and its technological successors allowed energy in almost unlimited quantity to be brought to bear on any task. So forests could be cut, fields cleared, dams built, mines worked with unprecedented speed. As a result, in less than a single human lifetime an area of eastern North America larger than all Europe was deforested. Virtually uninhabited by Europeans as late as 1820, the state of Michigan by 1897 had shipped 160 billion board feet of white pine lumber, leaving less than 6 billion still standing.

But the new engines needed fuel. At first waste wood supplied much of it, and later coal and then oil. The by-products of this combustion were dumped into the atmosphere as they had always been, but now their quantity was increasing geometrically. In 1850 Americans were utilizing more than eight million horsepower, animal and mechanical. By 1900 nearly sixty-four million, almost all mechanical, was being used by what economists call prime movers.

The factory system and mechanization brought many commodities within the financial reach of millions, while new transportation systems created national markets and made economies of scale both possible and necessary. This, in turn, caused the demand for raw materials to soar. The great mineral wealth that was being discovered under the American landscape was exploited with ever-increasing speed. Again the waste products were dumped at the lowest possible cost, which meant, in effect, on the far side of the nearest stone wall.

Increasing wealth and the new technologies allowed cities to bring in fresh, clean water for their rapidly increasing populations. This water was used to flush away the dirt and sewage of human existence, but only into the nearest body of water. The quality of life in the human environment was immeasurably improved by this, as the squalor that had characterized the urban landscape since Roman times disappeared. But the quality of the nation's waterways sharply deteriorated.

The new technology allowed us to turn more and more of the landscape to human use. The old-fashioned moldboard plow, in use since medieval times, could not deal easily with the rich, heavy soils and deep sod of the American Midwest. The steel plow invented by John Deere in 1837 quickly opened up what would become the breadbasket of the world. Wetlands could now be drained economically and made productive. Millions of acres vanished, and their vast and wholly unappreciated biological productivity vanished too.

So rapid an alteration of the landscape could only have a severe impact on the ecosystem as a whole. The loss of so much forest caused runoff to increase sharply, eroding the land and burdening the waters with silt, destroying more wetlands. Many animals' habitats disappeared. And because the ancient biblical notion that humans had dominion over the earth still held, others vanished entirely.

The beautiful Carolina parakeet, North America's only native parrot, proved a major agricultural pest. Because it lived in large, cohesive flocks, it made an easy target for farmers with the shotguns that the Industrial Revolution made cheap. It was extinct in the wild by the turn of the century; the last known specimen died in the Cincinnati Zoo in 1914.

Another avian casualty was the passenger pigeon, one of the great natural wonders of America, as amazing as Niagara Falls or the Grand Canyon. The passenger pigeon almost certainly existed in larger numbers than any other bird in the world. Moreover, it was concentrated in flocks of unbelievable immensity. Audubon reported one flock that took a total of three days to pass overhead and estimated that, at times, the birds flew by at the rate of three hundred million an hour.

The passenger pigeon nested in heavily forested areas in colonies that were often several miles wide and up to forty miles long, containing billions of birds. Trees within the colony each had hundreds of nests, and limbs often broke under the weight. The squabs, too heavy to fly when abandoned by their parents at the end of the nesting season, were easy prey. With railroads able to ship the fresh-killed birds to the great Eastern cities quickly, hunters slaughtered them in the millions to meet the demand.

Unfortunately it turned out that passenger pigeons needed the company of huge numbers of their fellows to stimulate breeding behavior. Once the size of the flocks fell below a certain very large minimum, the birds stopped reproducing, and the population crashed. Just as with the Carolina parakeet, the last passenger pigeon died in the Cincinnati Zoo in 1914.

The herds of the Great Plains also fell to hunters. It is estimated that upward of thirty million bison roamed the grasslands of North America in the middle of the nineteenth century. By the dawn of the twentieth, less than a thousand remained alive.

As early as the 1850s it was clear to the more thoughtful that something precious and irreplaceable was rapidly disappearing. The wilderness that had helped define the country seemed ever more remote. It was now recognized the natural world could provide refreshment whose need was becoming more and more keenly felt.

Urban parks, such as New York City's incomparable Central and Prospect parks, were intended to provide the population with a taste of nature that many could now obtain no other way. But these parks were, like the aristocratic gardens created in eighteenth-century Britain, wholly manmade and no more truly natural than a sculpture is a rock outcropping.

Movements began to take hold to preserve portions of the fast-vanishing wilderness itself. As early as the 1830s the painter George Catlin put forward the idea of a wild prairie reservation, a suggestion that, alas, was not implemented before nearly all of the country's prairie ecosystem was destroyed. But the movement took root, and in 1864 the first act of preservation was undertaken when ownership of the Yosemite Valley and a stand of sequoias was transferred from the public lands of the United States to the state of California.

In 1872 the first national park in the world was created when reports of the splendors of Yellowstone were delivered to Congress. James Bryce, British ambassador to the United States, called the national parks the best idea America ever had. Certainly they have been widely copied around the world. Today American national parks protect 47,783,680 acres, an area considerably larger than the state of Missouri.

States, too, began to set aside land to protect what was left of the wilderness. New York turned five million acres—15 percent of the state's land area—into the Adirondack Park and Forest Preserve, to remain "forever wild."

In the 1870s Carl Schurz, Secretary of the Interior, began moving for the preservation of federally owned forests. Born in Europe, where forests had long since become scarce and thus precious, and where forest-management techniques were far more advanced than those in this country, Schurz and many others helped create a new concern for America's fast-dwindling woodlands. By the end of Theodore Roosevelt's Presidency, almost sixty million acres were in the forest reserve system.

Today hundreds of millions of acres in this country enjoy various levels of protection from development, and more are added every year. But while the parks and reserves created by this movement are national treasures that have greatly enriched the quality of life, their creation was predicated on the part of the ancient paradigm that still survived. That part held that the natural world and the human one were two separate and distinct places. And it was still thought that each had little effect on the other.

It was George Perkins Marsh, lawyer, businessman, newspaper editor, member of Congress, diplomat, Vermont fish commissioner, and lover and keen observer of nature, who first recognized the folly of this unexamined assumption. Growing up in Vermont, he had seen how the clearcutting of the forests and poor farming practices had degraded the state's environment.

In 1864 he published *Man and Nature,* which he expanded ten years later and published as *The Earth as Modified by Human Action.* Individual instances of human effect on the natural world had been noted earlier, but Marsh, like Darwin with evolution, gathered innumerable examples together and argued the general case. He decisively demonstrated that the impress of humankind on the whole world was deep, abiding, and, because it was largely unnoticed, overwhelmingly adverse. "Man is everywhere a disturbing agent," he wrote. "Wherever he plants his foot, the harmonies of nature are turned to discords."

Recognizing that technology, energy use, population, food production, resource exploitation, and human waste all were increasing on curves that were hyperbolic when plotted against time, he feared for the future. "It is certain," he wrote, "that a desolation, like that which overwhelmed many once beautiful and fertile regions of Europe, awaits an important part of the territory of the United States . . . unless prompt measures are taken."

Darwin's book *On the Origin of Species* provoked a fire storm of controversy in the intellectual world of his time when it was published in 1859. It changed humankind's perception of the world profoundly and immediately. But *Man and Nature* changed nothing. Published only five years later, it met with profound indifference, and its author sank into the undeserved oblivion of those who are out of sync with their times. As late as 1966, when the science of ecology he was instrumental in founding was already well developed, so commodious a reference work as the *Encyclopaedia Britannica* made no mention of him whatever.

Perhaps the difference was that Darwin's ideas had only philosophical, religious, and scientific implications. Marsh's ideas, on the other hand, had profound economic consequences. An America rapidly becoming the world's foremost industrious power did not want to hear them, even though as early as 1881 the mayor of Cleveland could describe the Cuyahoga River as "an open sewer through the center of the city."

In fact, the seeds of the country's first great man-made ecological disaster were being planted even as Marsh wrote.

In the 1860s railroads pushed across the Great Plains and opened them up to settlement by connecting them to Eastern markets. On the high plains toward the Rockies, as hunters slaughtered bison and pronghorns by the millions, ranchers replaced them with cattle, which overgrazed the land. Then farmers began moving in.

World War I greatly increased the demand for wheat, while the tractor made plowing the tough, deep sod of the high plains a more practical proposition. The number of farms in the area east of the Rocky Mountains burgeoned in the 1920s, taking over more and more of the ranchland.

The mean annual rainfall in this area varied between ten and twenty inches, not enough for crop farming except in the best of years. But the early decades of the century happened to see many such years. Then, in the late twenties, the rains slacked off, and drought swept the plains.

This had happened hundreds of times in the past, and the plants and animals that had evolved there were adapted to it. Wheat and cattle were not. Worse, over the last few years, the sod, the deep net of grass roots that had bound the soil together, had been broken over millions of acres by the farmers with their plows. The topsoil, without which no plant can grow nor animal live, now lay exposed to the ceaseless, drying winds.

In 1933 no rain fell for months in western Kansas, and little elsewhere. The crops withered, the livestock died of thirst or starvation, and the dust, bound by neither sod nor moisture, began to blow. On November 11 a howling, rainless storm sprang up. "By midmorning," a reporter wrote of a farm in South Dakota, "a gale was blowing cold and black. By noon it was blacker than night, because one can see through the night and this was an opaque black. It was a wall of dirt one's eyes could not penetrate, but it could penetrate the eyes and ears and nose. It could penetrate to the lungs until one coughed up black. . . .

"When the wind died and the sun shone forth again, it was on a different world. There were no fields, only sand drifting into mounds and eddies that swirled in what was now but an autumn breeze. There was no longer a section-line road fifty feet from the front door. It was obliterated. In the farmyard, fences, machinery, and trees were gone, buried. The roofs of sheds stuck out through drifts deeper than a man is tall."

The dust of this storm, uncountable millions of tons of topsoil, darkened the skies of Chicago the following day and those of Albany, New York, the day after that. Terrible as it was, the storm proved but the first of many that ravaged the high plains in the next several years, as the drought tightened its grip and the unforgiving winds blew and blew. In the middle years of the 1930s, they laid waste thousands of square miles of what had been, just a few years earlier, a vibrant ecosystem. It was now the Dust Bowl. Upward of two hundred thousand people were forced to abandon their farms and trek westward in desperate search of the necessities of life itself.

The rains finally came again, and in the 1940s the discovery of the Oglala aquifer, a vast reservoir of water that underlies much of the Midwest, rescued the farmers who remained. Tapped by ever-deeper wells, the aquifer is now seriously depleted. And economics is slowly rescuing the land as the price of water increases every year.

It was always marginal for farming, and so it remains. Even with many, though mostly ill-conceived, federal programs, the farmers on the high plains are finding it ever harder to compete in world markets. Every year more and more farms are abandoned, and the land reverts to what in a perfect world it would never have ceased to be—shortgrass prairie.

The technological leap that had begun in Jefferson's day only accelerated in the twentieth century. The burdens that had been placed on the environment in the nineteenth century by such things as fuel use and sewage disposal increased sharply as the population expanded and new technologies spread across the land.

The limits of the ability of the environment to cope with the load were being reached more and more often. In October 1947 a thermal inversion settled over Donora, Pennsylvania. The town is set in a natural basin and was home to much heavy industry. The layer of cold air trapped the effluent of that industry and of the cars and furnaces of the population. By the time the inversion ended, four days later, twenty people were dead and six thousand ill enough to require treatment.

To an astonishing extent—at least as viewed from today's perspective—the people of the time accepted such happenings as the price of the Industrial Revolution that had brought them so much wealth and material comfort. A *New Yorker* cartoon of the day showed a woman sitting at a table set for lunch in the garden of a New York brownstone. "Hurry, darling," she calls to her unseen husband, "your soup is getting dirty."

New burdens were also added. The chemical industry grew quickly in this century, fueled by an explosion in knowledge. The disposition of chemicals was, as always, over the nearest stone wall: into a landfill or convenient body of water.

Agriculture became more businesslike as farms grew in size, became much more mechanized, and increasingly specialized in one or two crops. Of course, even Patrick Henry had known, two centuries earlier, that monocultural farming depletes the soil and is vulnerable to insects and other pests. But now the chemical industry could overcome this, thanks to synthetic fertilizers and pesticides.

Such chemicals as DDT were greeted as miracles of modern science when they first became available, and their use spread rapidly. In 1947 the United States produced 124,259,000 pounds of chemical pesticides. Only thirteen years later, in 1960, production was up to 637,666,000 pounds of often far more potent pesticides.

Diseases such as malaria and agricultural pests such as the boll weevil were declared on the verge of eradication. And the "control of nature," the final realization of the dominion enjoined by Genesis, was said to be at hand. DDT and other pesticides sprayed from airplanes blanketed vast areas, to kill gypsy moths, budworms, and mosquitoes.

But there were troubling signs for the few who looked. The pesticides were nondiscriminatory; they killed all the insects they touched. Honeybees, essential for the pollination of many crops and innumerable natural plants, were often wiped out by spraying programs aimed at other insects. Beekeepers began to fight back with lawsuits. "It is a very distressful thing," one beekeeper wrote, "to walk into a yard in May and not hear a bee buzz."

More than two hundred new pesticides were introduced in the years following World War II. The reason was that the older ones became increasingly ineffective. Many species of insects go through numerous generations a year and can evolve very rapidly, especially when a severe pressure such as a new pesticide is applied. In a monument to the vigor with which life clings to existence, they did exactly that.

And birdwatchers noticed a troubling decline in the numbers of some species, especially the large raptors that lived at the top of the food chains. Charles Broley, a retired banker, banded bald eagles in Florida beginning in 1939 as a hobby. He usually banded about a hundred and fifty young birds a year on the stretch of coast he patrolled. Beginning in 1947, more and more nests were empty or held eggs that had failed to hatch. In 1957 he found only eight eaglets, the following year only one.

But these troubling events were scattered, knowledge of them dispersed over a huge country and many scientific disciplines. They were no match for the chemical companies. But these, it turned out, were no match for a frail middle-aged woman named Rachel Carson.

Rachel Carson was trained as a marine biologist, but she was a born writer. In 1952 her book *The Sea Around Us* was published with a very modest first printing. To everyone's astonishment—most of all hers—it became a titanic bestseller that made its author famous across America. Ten years later she published *Silent Spring*. It changed the world.

Again a huge bestseller, *Silent Spring* detailed in lucid, often poetic, and always accessible prose how pesticides were playing havoc with the air, land, and water of the country and how their uncontrolled use was doing far more harm than good. Further, it introduced millions of Americans to the concept that the natural world was an intimately interconnected web. This web, Carson made clear, included humans quite as much as every other living thing that shared planet Earth. What killed insects would, if not handled carefully, one day kill us too. George Perkins Marsh had said much the same thing a hundred years earlier. This time the people read and believed.

The ancient paradigm from the dawn of civilization, when man was frail and nature omnipotent, was dead at last. Dead with it was what had been in theory a dream and in fact a nightmare—the control of nature. It had been, Rachel Carson wrote on the last page of *Silent Spring*, "a phrase conceived in arrogance."

Within a few years the public demand for action in behalf of the environment became irresistible, and it caught a complacent government by surprise. John C. Whitaker, Nixon's cabinet secretary, later recalled that "we were totally unprepared for the tidal wave of public opinion in favor of cleaning up the environment."

Earth Day cleared up any lingering doubts about the public's opinion on the matter. Federal government agencies such as the Environmental Protection Agency were created, and goals and timetables for air and water quality were established. We Americans set out on a crusade to rescue the land from ourselves. In many ways we shared the fervor with which the medieval world had set out to rescue the Holy Land from the infidel.

Today, nearly a quarter-century after the crusade to the new Jerusalem of a clean environment began, there is vast progress to report. In 1959, 24.9 million tons of particulate matter—soot—were emitted into the air in the United States. By 1985, 7.2 million were, and less every year. In 1970, 28.4 million tons of sulfur oxides, a prime contributor to smog, were released by power plants and automobiles. In 1990, 21.2 million tons were, a drop of nearly 25 percent. Carbon monoxide emission has fallen by 40 percent since 1970, and lead has been eliminated as an additive to gasoline.

Cars being manufactured in the 1990s emit only a fifth as much pollution as those made before 1975. Thus 80 percent of all automobile pollution today is generated by just 10 percent of the cars on the road. In the next few years, as these clunkers end up on the scrap heap, automobile pollution will decrease sharply.

Already the number of days per year when the air quality is below standards in most of the country's cities has fallen significantly, by 38 percent in the 1980s alone. Even Los Angeles, the smog capital of the country thanks to its geography and automobile-oriented infrastructure, has enjoyed a 25 percent decline in smog-alert days.

In 1960 only about 50 million Americans were served by municipal sewage plants that provided secondary or tertiary treatment. Today more than half the population is. As a result, many urban waterways are now cleaner than they have been since the early 1800s. New York used to dump the sewage of eight million people into the Hudson, Harlem, and East rivers. Today, in a development that would have stunned turn-of-the-century New Yorkers, there is an annual swimming race around Manhattan Island.

Rural rivers too have greatly benefited. Most of the Connecticut River's four-hundred-mile length was declared "suitable only for transportation of sewage and industrial wastes" in the 1960s. Today 125 new or upgraded water treatment plants, costing $900 million, have transformed it. Fishing and swimming are now allowed almost everywhere, and wildlife such as ospreys, bald eagles, blue crabs, and salmon has returned in numbers.

The sludge that is the end product of sewage treatment was until very recently dumped in the ocean or into landfills. Now it is increasingly being sought by farmers as a cheap fertilizer and soil conditioner. New York City produces 385 tons a day, all of it once dumped beyond the continental shelf. One hundred tons of that is being used by farmers in Colorado and Arizona. Initially skeptical, fifty of those farmers recently sent New York's mayor a letter asking for more. He's likely to oblige. Boston sludge now fertilizes Florida citrus groves. And because sewage sludge not only fertilizes but improves soil quality, it is displacing chemical fertilizers.

As old factories reach the end of their productive lives and are replaced by new ones built under stringent controls, the non-sewage pollution of the waterways is also steadily declining. The violation rate (the percentage of tests where the amount of pollutants was found to be above standards) for lead and cadmium fell to less than one percent. Dissolved oxygen is an important measure of a water body's biological viability. The percentage of times it was found to be below standard fell 60 percent in the 1980s.

Many bodies of water, such as Lake Erie, declared dead in the 1970s, have bounded back with the improved situation and with the help of life's ferocious determination to go on living. The amounts of pesticides being used every year fell by more than a quarter in the 1980s, and those in use today are far less persistent and far less toxic than most of those in widespread use in the 1960s. The level of DDT present in human fatty tissue, a fair measure of its presence in the environment, was 7.95 parts per million in 1970. By 1983 it had fallen to 1.67 parts per million. Today, ten years later, no one even bothers to gather the statistic.

The land, too, has improved. In the eastern part of the United States, the area of forest land has been increasing for more than a century, as clearcut areas have been allowed to regenerate. It will be another hundred years, at least, before they reach the climax stage, but they are on their way. And today 28 percent of all farmland is no longer plowed at all, and the percentage is growing quickly. Conservation tillage is used instead; the method sharply reduces erosion and improves soil quality while slashing costs, producing crops for as much as 30 percent less.

Programs to reduce the use of chemical fertilizers are being tried in more and more areas as farmers learn new techniques. In Iowa in 1989 and 1990 a joint EPA-state program helped farmers cut their use of nitrogen fertilizer by four hundred million pounds without sacrificing crop yields. Because agricultural fertilizers and pesticides now account for more than 65 percent of all water pollution (factories account for only 7 percent), this trend has no small implication for the future.

Wildlife is on the mend in many ways. To be sure, the number of species on the endangered list has grown sharply in the last two decades, but that is much more an artifact of increased knowledge than of a stilldeteriorating situation.

Many species have rebounded sharply, thanks in some cases to protection and in others to the explosion of biological and ecological knowledge that has so marked the last twenty-five years. To give just two examples, alligators, once hunted mercilessly for their skins, are no longer on the list at all. And peregrine falcons, almost extirpated in the Eastern United States by DDT, have been with infinite care and effort put on the road to recovery. Today there is a pair nesting on the Verrazano Bridge at the entrance to New York's Upper Bay, and there is even a pair nesting on the top of the Met Life (formerly Pan Am) building in midtown, exploiting the distinctly unendangered local pigeon population.

Nor has public interest in rescuing the environment slackened. *The New York Times Index* for 1960 needed less than 19 inches to list all the references to air pollution that year, and only 15 for water pollution. In 1991 the two subjects required 87 and 107 inches, respectively. Local organizations monitoring local situations have multiplied across the country. Many hire professionals, such as the Hudson River Fisherman's Association, whose "riverkeeper" patrols the Eastern seaboard's most beautiful waterway.

And public opinion has become a powerful force. In the fall of 1992 the governor of Alaska proposed culling the number of wolves in the state in order to increase the number of moose and caribou for human hunters. It was not long before he wished he hadn't. The state, heavily dependent on tourist dollars, was soon backpedaling furiously before the onslaught of intensely negative public reaction.

So is the American environment once more pristine? Of course not. Many pollutants have proved unexpectedly stubborn and persistent. Many businesses have resisted changing their ways. In most cities the storm and waste sewers are still one and the same, and sewage overflows in bad weather. It will take many years and billions of dollars to correct that. An unknowable number of species are still threatened by human activity.

But the nation's water, air, land, and wildlife all are better, in many respects, than they have been in a century, and they continue to improve. To put it another way, if the task of cleaning up the American environment were a journey from Boston to Los Angeles, we would be well past the Appalachians and might even have the Mississippi in sight.

Then why is the impressions so widespread that we are, at best, entering Worcester, if not actually marching backward somewhere in Maine? There are many reasons, and as so often happens, human nature lies at the root of all of them.

A first reason is that environmental bureaucrats, like all bureaucrats, want to maximize the personnel and budgets of their departments. So from their point of view, it simply makes good sense to highlight new problems and to minimize news about the old ones that have been successfully addressed. Similarly, environmental organizations live and die by fundraising. The-sky-is-falling stories are simply far more effective in getting someone to reach for a checkbook than are things-are-looking-up stories. And environmental bureaucrats and lobbyists alike know that they must struggle hard to maintain their constituencies and budgets to fight the serious problems that do persist. They fear, not without reason, that if they don't play up the troubles that endure, they may lose the ability to address them at all—and we might lose much of what we've won.

A second reason is that the media have often failed to evaluate environmental stories with scientific competence and sometimes even honesty. As in fundraising, bad news sells better than good news.

As a result, tentative data have often been presented as irrefutable fact, and short-term or local trends have been extrapolated into global catastrophes. In the 1970s there were many stories about the coming ice age. Ten years later global warming was destined to extinguish civilization.

A third reason that things often seem to be getting worse here at home is extremists. Extremists are always present in great reform movements, and the goal of environmental extremists is not a clean environment but a perfect one. They are few in number, compared with the legions now dedicated to cleaning the American environment, but like many extremists, they are often gifted propagandists and they are willing to use ignoble means to further noble ends.

Consider the support given by some environmental organizations to the Delaney Clause. The law, passed in 1958, requires that even the slightest residue of pesticides that have been shown to cause cancer in laboratory animals may not be present in processed foods. The Delaney Clause made some sense in the 1950s, when our ability to detect chemicals was limited to about one part in a million and our knowledge of carcinogenesis rudimentary at best. Today it is nothing short of ludicrous, for we can now detect chemicals in amounts of one part in a quintillion. To get some idea of what that means, here is the recipe for making a martini in the ratio of 1:1,000,000,000,000,000,000: Fill up the Great Lakes—all five of them—with gin. Add one tablespoon of vermouth, stir well, and serve.

As a result, to give just one example, propargite, a nonpersistent pesticide that controls mites on raisins, can't be used because it has been shown to cause cancer when fed to rats in massive doses. But a human being would have to eat eleven tons of raisins a day to ingest the amount of propargite needed to induce cancer in laboratory rats. Had it been available in the 1950s, propargite's use would have been perfectly legal because the infinitesimal residue would have been completely undetectable.

Every first-year medical student knows it is the dosage that makes the poison. Yet many environmental organizations are adamantly against any revision of the Delaney Clause for reasons that amount to nothing less than scientific know-nothingism. They are wasting time, money, and, most important, credibility on the chimera of perfection.

But time, money, and most of all credibility are precious commodities. For even if we are at the Mississippi on the journey to clean up the American environment, we still have two thirds of the journey to go. And it will be the most difficult part.

For as we proceed, the problems will become more and more intractable, and thus more and more expensive to deal with. For instance, it was easy to get a lot of lead out of the atmosphere. We simply stopped adding it to gasoline as an antiknock agent, virtually the sole source of atmospheric lead. But getting the fertilizers and pesticides out of agricultural runoff—now far and away the greatest source of water pollution in the country—will be another matter altogether, especially if we are to keep the price of food from rising sharply.

Part of the problem is the iron law of diminishing returns. Getting, say, 90 percent of a pollutant out of the environment may be easy and relatively cheap. But the next 9 percent might cost as much as the first 90, and so might the next .9 percent, and so on. At some point we have to say, "That's clean enough." Where that point will be, in case after case, is going to have to be decided politically, and democratic politics requires give and take on all sides to work.

Another part of the problem is that, increasingly, environmental regulations have been impinging on private-property rights. In the early days, the environmental movement was largely about cleaning up the commons—the air and water that belong to us all. The rule of thumb was easy: He who pollutes—whether the factory owner or the commuter in his automobile—should bear the cost of cleaning up now and of preventing that pollution in the future. Today, however, new regulations are more likely to affect the ways in which someone can use his or her own property and thus gravely affect its economic value.

There is a genuine clash of basic rights here. One is the individual right to hold, enjoy, and profit from private property. The other is the general right to pass on to our children a healthy and self-sustaining environment.

To give just one specific example of how these rights can clash, a man in South Carolina bought beachfront property in the 1980s for $600,000. The property was worth that much because it consisted of two buildable lots. He intended to build two houses, one for himself and one to sell. But the state then changed the regulations, to protect the delicate shoreline ecosystem, and his property became unbuildable. Its value plummeted from $600,000 to perhaps $30,000.

Not surprisingly, the owner sued for the economic loss he had suffered. But the state ruled that it was merely regulating in the public interest and that no compensation was due as it was not a "taking": the property still belonged to the owner. The property owner argued that the regulations, however valuable a public purpose they served, had indeed effected a taking, because the state had sucked the economic value out of his property, leaving him the dried husk of legal title.

This case is still in the courts, and cases like it are multiplying. A general acknowledgment of the validity of both sides' rights and motives is necessary if difficult matters such as these are to be resolved successfully.

Still a third problem is that, increasingly, environmental issues are global issues, beyond the reach of individual sovereign states. Worse, scientists have been studying the earth as a single, interlocking ecosystem for only the last few decades. Global weather and ocean temperature data nowhere stretch back more than a hundred and fifty years and usually much less. The amount of data we possess, therefore, is often insufficient to allow for the drawing of significant conclusions. Has the recent increase in atmospheric carbon dioxide caused an increase in average temperatures, or has a normal cyclical increase in temperature caused an increase in carbon dioxide? We just don't know the answer to that question. But billions, perhaps trillions of dollars in spending may depend on the answer.

Another issue is growth versus the environment. Many feel that economic growth and increased pollution are two sides of the same coin, that it is impossible to have the one without the other. Others feel that economic growth is the very key to cleaning up the environment because it alone can provide the wealth to do so.

Obviously, in some absolute sense, the more production of goods and services, the more waste products that must be dealt with. But if the wealth produced greatly exceeds the pollution produced, the pollution can be dealt with while standards of living continue to rise. Certainly among the world's densely populated countries, the correlation between wealth and environmental quality is striking. People cannot worry about the problem of tomorrow's environment if the problem of tonight's supper looms large. It is landless peasants, more than timber barons, who are cutting down the Amazon rain forest.

So far there has been no flagging of the pace or weakening of the spirit on the crusade to a clean American environment. The commitment of the American people is firm. Doubtless it will remain firm, too, if, in the midst of the ferocious political debates sure to come, we all keep in mind the fact that honorable people can disagree about means without disagreeing about ends; that there is more than one road to the New Jerusalem; and, especially, that cleaning up the American environment is far too important to be left to bureaucrats, activists, journalists, and fanatics. This is our crusade.

QUESTIONS TO CONSIDER

1. When and for what purpose was the first Earth Day?
2. How had European civilization and religion traditionally regarded wilderness? How did that affect their treatment of America?
3. What development made possible the rapid transformation of North America in the nineteenth century? What was its impact?
4. How did the United States, beginning in the 1860s, begin to try to preserve the natural habitat?
5. What was the country's first great man-made environmental disaster? How did it happen?
6. What does Gordon mean by "the nearest stone wall?" Give several examples.
7. What are some evidences of improvements in the environment since 1970?
8. Why is there limited perception of environmental progress, in Gordon's view?

16

Whatever Happened to the Monroe Doctrine?*

Gaddis Smith

Gaddis Smith, Larned Professor of History at Yale, specializes in the history of American diplomacy. He has written several books in the field, including *Morality, Reason, and Power: American Diplomacy in the Carter Years, American Diplomacy During the Second World War, 1941–1945,* and a biography of *Dean Acheson.* This selection is the opening chapter of his book *The Last Years of the Monroe Doctrine, 1945–1993.*

Since its proclamation in 1823, the Monroe Doctrine has been one of the cornerstones of American foreign policy. Though its injunction against the United States getting involved in wars outside the hemisphere lost its force after 1917, the treatment of the Americas as a sphere of influence for the United States to be protected against malign outside forces persisted almost down to the present day. Smith explains how it has finally lost its status as holy writ in this thoughtful, provocative assessment.

In December 1923, on the one hundredth anniversary of President James Monroe's message to Congress containing the doctrine bearing his name, millions of American schoolchildren sat through a reading of the famous text. New Yorkers heard it declaimed over the pioneer radio station

WEAF. A full-page advertisement in the *New York Times* quoted Mary Baker Eddy, founding mother of the Christian Science Church: "I believe strictly in the Monroe Doctrine, in our Constitution and in the laws of God." The original doctrine in which Mrs. Eddy so strictly believed announced three imperatives for American foreign relations: the American continents were closed to further colonization by European powers, the United States must not involve itself in the wars of Europe, and—the heart of the doctrine—the United States would view any attempt by a European power to extend its political system to "any portion of this hemisphere as dangerous to our peace and safety."

The Monroe Doctrine's warning against foreign intrusion in the Americas remained alive and vigorous after its centennial. President Franklin D. Roosevelt before and during the Second World War staunchly invoked the doctrine as the first principle of hemispheric defense against totalitarian threat, although he obviously buried the old prohibition against American entanglement in the political affairs of Europe and Asia. Victory over Nazi Germany and Japan in the Second World War was in part a victory for the Monroe Doctrine.

The Cold War followed the Second World War almost without pause. Historians, understandably drawn to the great collisions of Soviet and American power in Europe and Asia, ceased to inquire about the Monroe Doctrine. In so doing, as this book argues, they missed a significant chapter in the history of how Americans thought about the place of the United States in the world and the nature of national security. Especially for the men—and they were all men—whose adult involvement in the conduct of foreign affairs began before the Second World War, the Monroe Doctrine remained a powerful cluster of ideas. The United States succeeded in writing the Charter of the United Nations in a manner which seemed to assure an American capacity to exclude the UN from political involvement in the Western Hemisphere, thus protecting the Monroe Doctrine. Americans justified support for brutal but anti-Communist regimes in Latin America as required under the Monroe Doctrine and then used the doctrine as cover for the overthrow of the elected President of Guatemala in 1954.

During the crisis over Soviet missiles in Cuba in 1962, the halls of Congress echoed with sentiments that would have warmed the heart of Mary Baker Eddy. Listen, for example, to Congressman John J. Rhodes of Arizona: "The Monroe Doctrine, which every Member of this body was taught as a child in school is as sacred to the American tradition as the Constitution and the Declaration of Independence . . . is not dead. And it will not die unless we ourselves kill it." But Congressman Rhodes and the scores of congressmen and senators who on that occasion invoked the old text were to be disappointed. President John F. Kennedy refused to use the doctrine as explicit justification for action during the Cuban crisis. Although the Soviet Union removed its nuclear weapons from Cuba and promised not to return them, Cuba became a Soviet protectorate and Communist state within the legendary "ninety miles" of American shores.

The year 1962 thus would appear to mark the death of the Monroe Doctrine as an absolute mandate for the conduct of American foreign policy. But the ideas and emotions evoked by the words "Monroe Doctrine" continued for another generation to influence the thinking and behavior of American leaders, especially in the administrations of Presidents Lyndon B. Johnson, Richard M. Nixon, and Ronald Reagan. American leaders simultaneously accepted the Soviet presence in Cuba and reaffirmed the principles of the Monroe Doctrine. They resolved the contradiction by defining the Cuba of Fidel Castro as an alien body no longer belonging to the American continents. They sought, in effect, to expel Cuba from the Western Hemisphere. For those Presidents the Monroe Doctrine meant preventing another Cuba. To that end they intervened in Brazil, the Dominican Republic, El Salvador, Nicaragua, and Grenada.

No post-1945 President was more enamored of the idea of the Monroe Doctrine than Ronald Reagan. He presided over a prolonged covert and often violent effort to assert American will in Latin America: the proxy war to drive the Sandinista government of Nicaragua from power and sustain the repressive government of El Salvador. In the absence of broad congressional and public support for these objectives, the Reagan Administration turned to secrecy, lying, defiance of domestic law, and contempt for international opinion and legal norms. This behavior, however, provoked ever greater opposition within the United States. The frustration of Reagan's advisers is well captured in the sarcastic comment of Robert M. Gates, deputy director of the CIA, in December 1984: "The fact is that the Western Hemisphere is the sphere of influence of the United States. If we have decided totally to abandon the Monroe Doctrine, if in the 1980s taking strong actions to protect our interests . . . is too difficult, then we ought to save political capital in Washington, acknowledge our helplessness and stop wasting everybody's time."

Within less than a decade the United States did, in fact, abandon the Monroe Doctrine. The reasons touch the themes of this book. First and most obviously, the last years of the Monroe Doctrine are inseparable from the Cold War. The more serious the perceived threat to American security from the Soviet Union, the more emphatically the concept of the Monroe Doctrine was applied to policy and the selling of policy to the public. For almost half a century after 1945 the makers of American foreign policy subordinated relations of the United States with Latin America to the overarching purpose of "frustrating the Kremlin design," perceived as a coherent, implacable effort to undermine the security of the "free world" everywhere and in every way. The Soviet threat to American security in the hemisphere was sometimes real, as during the Cuban missile crisis. More often it existed largely in the American imagination and in the propensity to attribute every instance of instability in Latin America, every criticism of the United States as something ordered in Moscow.

A second theme is the pervasive lack of knowledge about or concern by high American officials for Latin America on its own terms. Because the attention of those officials during the Cold War years was dominated by events in Europe, Asia, and the Middle East, they knew almost nothing about Latin American conditions. For example, Secretary of State Dean Acheson, notwithstanding high service in the Department of State since 1941, told his staff in 1950 that he was "rather vague" about Latin America. "He wanted to know whether they were richer or poorer, going Communist, Fascist or what?" Presidents, other Secretaries of State, and their immediate advisers were no better informed than Acheson. The result was a sporadic, crisis-ridden approach: long periods of ignoring Latin America alternating with moments of frantic obsession—for example, over Communists in Guatemala in 1954, over the Soviet presence in Cuba in the 1960s and after, over the Sandinistas in Nicaragua in the 1980s. Latin American governments and people were seen as pawns, not as autonomous actors with self-generated hopes, fears, and policies. If a Latin American government did not endorse and act on the world view of Washington, then it was perceived as an actual or potential puppet of the Soviet Union and thereby a threat to the Monroe Doctrine.

A third theme flows from the first two: the modification of the principles of the Monroe Doctrine to the Cold War philosophy of secrecy, covert action, and the defiance of legal and constitutional restrictions on the conduct of foreign policy. Any means was acceptable, therefore, to maintain compliant, anti-Soviet regimes and undermine those who were uncooperative. James Monroe in 1823 had contrasted American principles of candor, self-government, and respect for national independence with the devious, autocratic, imperial ways of Europe. The doctrine was proclaimed as protection of the first against the second. The abandonment after 1945 of its original ideals made the last years of the Monroe Doctrine a history of moral degradation. Sometimes the words and principles of the Monroe Doctrine were embraced openly, enthusiastically, and with complete candor. More often they were muffled in secrecy, tainted by lies, and in conflict with the public creed of democracy and human rights.

Moral degradation interacted with the fourth theme: the increasing political partisanship of the doctrine. Before 1945 the doctrine had been involved on occasion in domestic politics, but in its final years it was invoked to damage political opponents at home more than to clarify the needs of foreign policy. Previously it had been embraced equally by Republicans and Democrats. After 1945 it became the favored instrument of Republicans and Cold War conservatives of both parties. The Monroeites saw themselves standing for patriotism, strength, and a prideful unwillingness to tie American interests to the constraints of international cooperation, especially in the United Nations. They castigated domestic critics as naïve, liberal exponents of weakness. Critics in turn were unpersuaded that the principles of the Monroe Doctrine justified the covert war in Nicaragua or support for the notoriously brutal government of El Salvador.

The end of the Cold War marked the end of the Monroe Doctrine. Even perfervid wavers of the doctrine had difficulty finding a threat from beyond the hemisphere to the nation's security in Latin America when the Soviet Union unilaterally withdrew from confrontation with the West, accepted the independence of Eastern Europe under non-Communist governments, allowed the unification of Germany on Western terms, abandoned all pretense of influence in the Third World including Latin America, and then ceased to exist itself. Thus, in the early 1990s the doctrine passed into history.

The Monroe Doctrine was fundamentally the assertion of an American sphere of influence. That concept, however, has taken many shapes through history and in different parts of the world. To adopt the terminology of John P. Vloyantes, there are hard spheres of influence and soft ones. A hard sphere edges toward annexation and usually involves the direct use of military force and direct control of the political and economic life of the people within the sphere. Whatever self-government exists within a hard sphere in entirely at the sufferance of the controlling power. There may or may not be local collaborators. The population within a hard sphere exercises no self-determination on the question of whether they wish to belong or withdraw. That is why in the idealist rhetoric of American thought about international relations the evil of spheres of influence and the glory of self-determination are always linked. The rights of outside countries within a dominant power's hard sphere of influence are slight to nonexistent. Other governments may be prohibited from having diplomatic relations with the sphere and their citizens may be barred from trade and travel. Examples of hard spheres are those exercised by Britain over Egypt from the 1880s to the 1950s, by Japan over "independent" Manchukuo, that is, Manchuria, between 1932 and 1945, and by the Soviet Union over Eastern Europe during the Cold War. Soviet action in

Hungary in 1956 and Czechoslovakia in 1968 is the essence of using force to maintain a hard sphere of influence.

A soft sphere, in contrast, involves no overt coercion. Its political rhetoric speaks of community of interest, shared visions of the world, and mutual benefit through voluntary association. The large power in a soft sphere does not dictate with whom the smaller powers can trade or maintain diplomatic relations—although it applies nonviolent pressure, offers positive inducements, and makes clear its preferences. It never interferes overtly in the smaller countries' internal affairs, and it is tolerant when those within the sphere pretend there is no sphere at all.

The sphere of influence which the United States sought but only partially achieved over Latin America in the years after 1945 was both hard and soft. Publicly American policymakers pretended that the sphere was a gathering of like-minded equals to advance democratic values and exclude alien totalitarianism from the American continents. That line fooled few. In practice the policymakers preferred soft methods to hard. When hard methods were employed, they preferred the covert and deniable to the open and blatant application of force. But when soft methods failed to create the conditions they desired, they moved with little hesitation to various forms of coercion.

The blend of hard and soft, open and covert, is easier to illustrate by noting the specific tools and methods applied by the American government toward Latin America than by abstract generalization. Beneath the statements of high policy and the episodic involvement of Presidents, Secretaries of State, and other luminaries were thousands of diplomats, intelligence agents, and military personnel trying every day to make reality conform with the principles of the Monroe Doctrine. Let us take brief note of the nature of this daily activity, the continuing background to the moments of crisis around which this book is organized.

With the exception of the Soviet missiles in Cuba, the perceived immediate threat to the Monroe Doctrine after 1945 was not military, but distant worst-case scenarios ultimately involving traditional military security concerns. Thus, the Rio pact of 1947 was a collective response to the threat of attack on the American continents from beyond the hemisphere. But there was almost no mechanism for coordinating the effort. The Inter-American Defense Board was a sleepy committee, meeting occasionally, an assignment on the American side for offices on the slow track. The United States shared no useful information with the board in the belief that "information passed on to twenty countries in a body of this kind would, in many cases, find its way into the wrong hands."

During the Cuban missile crisis the United States relied on its own nuclear and conventional power to persuade the Soviet Union to withdraw its missiles. On all other occasions American perceptions of a military threat were based on imaginative projection, a set of "what if" questions leading to a fearful outcome at some very distant unspecified time. The first question was what if Latin American governments equipped their armed forces with weapons from a country other than the United States? Beginning during the Second World War and for two decades thereafter, the American military sought to make the United States the sole supplier of arms and professional training for Latin America, thereby replacing a half century of European influence. Weapons, training, organization, and doctrine were all to be standardized to the American model. The goal was publicly justified as necessary for effective hemispheric cooperation and defense. But there were obvious other reasons. Governments completely dependent on the United States for weapons and parts could easily be influenced and constrained from using military equipment in ways disapproved by the United States. By withdrawing or threatening to withdraw the supply of arms, the United States had a useful sanction. Conversely, regimes would gain considerable freedom of action if they had alternative suppliers. The British, French, or Swedes as arms suppliers would be bad enough—but arms from the Soviet bloc would be a serious threat to the principles of the Monroe Doctrine and the security of the United States.

Thus, a 1947 report by a State, War, and Navy interdepartmental committee urged generous supplying of American weapons lest Latin American nations turn to the Soviet Union and its satellites, thereby according the Soviet Union "a political leverage potentially dangerous to U.S. security interests." The report also said that the American defense industry would benefit by having more orders than the U.S. armed forces alone could provide. The U.S. Army also stressed the "benefits of permanent United States military missions and the continued flow of Latin American officers through our service schools. Thus will our ideals and ways of life be nurtured in Latin America to the eventual exclusion of totalitarianism and other foreign ideologies." The United States never came close to achieving this goal. For the first decade after 1945 there was either no legislative framework for transferring U.S. armaments to Latin America or, during the emergency of the Korean War and European rearmament, the United States had few arms to spare. Until the Korean War both the State Department and many members of Congress thought there were more liabilities than advantages in supplying arms: Latin American countries might use them for unwarranted repression or to threaten each other; since direct defense of the hemisphere was an American responsibility, the acquisition of heavy armaments by Latin American governments was a foolish waste of resources; the United States would have to take on a commitment of unpredictable dimensions or be constantly causing ill feeling by saying no.

After the outbreak of the Korean War, American weapons were in short supply, costly, and not available on favorable credit terms. The U.S. military was annoyed at the increasing volume of British sales, especially of jet aircraft, but the National Security Council decided British sales should not be actively opposed. The British, however, believed Americans were blocking them on the principle that the Monroe Doctrine gave the United States "the exclusive right on advising and equipping South American countries with aircraft." The gap between the American aspiration of exclusive supplier and reality was enormous. Europeans provided almost all jet aircraft and new naval vessels from the beginning. By 1960 the United States was still supplying 75 percent of all arms, but the figure dropped to 20 percent in 1970, and was only 7 percent in 1980.

Although the United States reluctantly accepted the growing reliance of the Latin American military on weapons from Western Europe and later Israel, the acquisition of arms from the Communist bloc was ritualistically denounced as a violation of the principles of the Monroe Doctrine and conclusive evidence that a regime was itself Communist or soon would be. It made no difference that the United States might have closed off non-Communist sources, as with Guatemala in the early 1950s. As late as December 1984, Secretary of Defense Caspar Weinberger, while explaining the threat of Soviet weapons in Nicaragua, said that a principle of the Monroe Doctrine "was that there should be no interference, no sponsorship of any kind of military activity in this hemisphere by countries in other hemispheres."

The Korean War, and especially the perilous phase following the intervention of the People's Republic of China, induced the United States to dream of using Latin American military manpower around the world. The U.S. military services thought small, miscellaneous Latin American contingents would be more trouble than they were worth—but the State Department pressed on because of large imagined political advantages. If Latin American troops participate, said a State Department memorandum, "the nationalism and patriotism of the Latin American people will be aroused in support of the entire UN action against Communist aggression"; and that, in turn, would stimulate governments to deal more effectively with Communism within their own borders. A later memorandum said, "There is no better way to effectively incorporate Latin America into the free world than by permitting Latin America to share in the sacrifices." Ivan White, a State Department official, let his imagination dwell on a large inter-American military force "with a portion available to combat current aggression and the balance available for overseas operations in case of a widening of hostilities, this force would constitute a new factor in the world balance of power." Only Colombia welcomed this opportunity to "share in the sacrifices," sending a battalion and a frigate to Korea. All the other Latin American governments, despite heavy arm twisting from Washington, declined not only the short-term requests to help in Korea but a long-term proposal to commit trained manpower to possible global war. Americans, using language drawn from the Monroe Doctrine, could argue that in order to defend the hemisphere it was necessary to meet the enemy along the 38th parallel in Korea, or in Germany, or later in Vietnam. Latin Americans were not persuaded.

The dream of mobilizing Latin American manpower for a global struggle faded after the armistice in Korea. By the 1960s Washington's thinking focused almost entirely on the role of the military in maintaining internal security in Latin America. With U.S. military missions in almost every Latin American country and thousands of officers and enlisted men receiving training every year in the United States or the Panama Canal Zone, American policy makers convinced themselves that a new type of officer had emerged in Latin America. The old political type had been overweight, overdressed, self-decorated, corrupt, cruel, unprincipled, and without a vision of society's larger purposes. The new was envisioned as lean, mentally alert, well educated, professionally competent, honest, and above all dedicated to the welfare of the people—in short, an officer similar to the flattering image American counterparts had of themselves. The contrast was overdrawn and based on two stereotypes, but it was fervently believed and led during the 1960s and 1970s to an uncritical American faith in the capacity of military leadership to transform Latin American society by combating terrorism, stamping out corruption, building schools and roads, improving health.

Enthusiasm for the military did not apply equally to all countries. It was the greatest toward Brazil. Lincoln Gordon, U.S. ambassador to Brazil under Kennedy and Johnson, was the most articulate of civilian advocates for supporting the military. Brazilian military, he said, "are not an aristocratic caste separate from the general public"; they are "moderately nationalist but not anti-United States, anti-Communist but not Fascist, prodemocratic constitutionalist. The military not only have the capability of suppressing possible internal disorders but also serve as moderators on Brazilian political affairs [and an] . . . important source of trained administrators for government civil enterprises." Four weeks after that fulsome appraisal, Gordon's military paragons overthrew the leftist elected government of João Goulart. Gordon was delighted.

The difficulty in the Lincoln Gordon approach came, as we shall see, when various military government groups failed to meet the idealized stereotype—by invading the colony of America's closest ally, as Argentina did in the Falklands; by murderous treatment of political opposition—death squads, disappearances, torture, etc.—as did the Argentine junta, the Pinochet regime in Chile, and the American-supported military in El Salvador. American hardliners argued that such behavior was distasteful but inevitable in the different political culture of Latin America. But the cries of the victims of military brutality reached the United States. The outrage in Congress and among the American public was then so great that no administration could persist in giving unqualified support to repression—Monroe Doctrine or no.

U.S. military forces were employed openly in Latin America in several ways. They backed up invasions by exile groups against Guatemala and Cuba. They mounted large-scale military maneuvers to demonstrate power and supposedly intimidate leftist regimes in Cuba, Nicaragua, and Grenada. Their planes and ships collected intelligence. On occasion they went openly into combat: the Dominican Republic in 1965, Grenada in 1983, Panama in 1989. Special Forces (Green Beret) units worked to train and accompany counterparts in counterinsurgency campaigns. Covert paramilitary activity under the direction of the Central Intelligence Agency figured prominently and repeatedly during the last years of the Monroe Doctrine: the successful overthrow of the Arbenz government of Guatemala, the failure at the Bay of Pigs, the long war by U.S.–maintained "contra" forces against the government of Nicaragua, and considerable sabotage with explosives, fire, and marine mines.

If public rhetoric reflected reality, the principal instrument for defending the American continents against alien forces would have been the Organization of American States. But the OAS was barely more than a paper organization as far as the larger political objectives of the United States were concerned. It could be useful in dealing with relatively minor issues, or as a fig leaf for American unilateralism. The United States frequently, but with decreasing success, sought OAS validation for American action after the fact. But never was the U.S. government willing to let its own course be determined by an OAS vote. Presidents paid little attention. Secretaries of State had to attend meetings from time to time—but found it a burden.

Political action in defense of the principles of the Monroe Doctrine included ordinary diplomatic efforts to win support from Latin American governments for U.S. policies and constant lecturing on the need for every country to be more concerned about the internal threat. Although the United States had maintained diplomatic relations with the Soviet Union continuously since 1934, Washington opposed relations between Latin American countries and Moscow. When those relations were established, the act was seen as potentially unfriendly. When a new regime broke relations, as did Brazil in 1964 or Chile in 1973, the State Department applauded. Similarly the United States favored the outlawing of the Communist Party in Latin American countries, although it was legal in the United States. The American government also urged limitations on the right of travel for suspected Communists and their sympathizers, which went beyond what courts in the United States would tolerate.

The United States devoted considerable attention to the threat from the left within Latin American labor unions. This involved quasi-covert funneling of CIA funds to local anti-Communist labor activities through the American Institute of Free Labor Development (AIFLD), an affiliate of the American Federation of Labor, and the Inter-American Regional Organization of Workers (ORIT). On the more covert side, the CIA subsidized pro-American newspapers, supported some candidates for office, and worked to discredit others. The CIA did its best to uncover Soviet agents. It gathered information on the views and activities of thousands of people and paid government officials for inside information. All of this involved hundreds of people in the field and back in Washington.

Before the 1960s the United States government offered precious little in the way of economic incentives to influence the behavior of the Latin American republics. Washington repeated with liturgical monotony that Latin America's path to economic well-being lay exclusively through private investment in free-market enterprise. Government-to-government aid, said Secretary of the Treasury George Humphrey in 1956, did nothing but build up "little imitations of the Soviet Union." Thus, the United States barred aid to state-owned activities such as the petroleum companies of Mexico or Brazil, Pemex and Petrobras, and complained endlessly of restrictions on American business. The nationalization of American property without prompt and adequate compensation produced growls and snarls—including a congressional restriction, the Hickenlooper Amendment, barring U.S. aid to any government taking American private property without adequate compensation.

But even where aid was minuscule, Washington often used the withdrawal of that aid as a stick—for example, in suspending support for the Rama road, an extension of the Inner-American Highway, in Guatemala during the Arbenz regime. The Eisenhower Administration, much given to spelling out its policies in elaborate memoranda, put it this way: "If a Latin American state should establish with the Soviet bloc close ties of such a nature as seriously to prejudice our vital interests, be prepared to diminish governmental economic and financial cooperation with that country and to take any other political, economic or military actions deemed appropriate." A much more powerful stick to use toward countries producing sugar, such as Cuba, was to reduce or end the quota on sugar imported into the United States.

In the extreme situations where the United States was waging quasi-war against a regime, the stick of an embargo on trade was employed—as with Cuba under Castro, Nicaragua under the Sandinistas, and Panama at the end of the Noriega regime. Trade embargoes were usually accompanied by efforts to induce other countries to stop or limit their trade with the target of American ire. Because these third countries were often allies—for example, Britain, Canada, Italy—it was difficult for the United States to go beyond persuasion to the use of sanctions against them.

The Eisenhower Administration in its last two years began to extend economic aid for Latin American development, but this reached significant levels only with the Alliance for Progress announced by President John F. Kennedy in a famous speech on March 13, 1961. He said: "For the first time we have the capacity to strike off the remaining bonds of poverty and ignorance—to free our people for the spiritual and intellectual fulfillment which has always been the goal of our civilization." The rhetoric of Monroeism was almost totally absent as he outlined "a plan to transform the 1960s into a historic decade of democratic progress." To call the Alliance for Progress an instrument for fulfilling the principles of the Monroe Doctrine is too great a stretch. Only one sentence sounded the old alarm: "Yet at this very moment of maximum opportunity, we confront the same forces which have imperiled America throughout its history—the alien forces which once again seek to impose the despotisms of the Old World on the people of the New."

The Alliance's grand objective was nothing less than the reordering of Latin America's political, economic, and social structure through land reform, rapid economic growth, the distribution of political power on a democratic basis, and the elimination of poverty, illiteracy, and disease. All this was to be achieved through $20 billion in public aid and private investment over ten years. At last the United States would be responding to human needs in Latin America on a scale comparable to the Marshall Plan for Europe in the 1940s.

The Alliance fell far short of its goals. Economic growth was largely offset by soaring population. Politically Latin America in the 1960s moved away from democracy to military regimes supported by oligarchies with no taste for fundamental socioeconomic reform. Those regimes, encouraged by the United States, focused on the issue of internal security. U.S. aid went increasingly to support police forces and train the military in counterinsurgency. The dominant cliché by the mid-1960s was that there could be no social progress until the threat of rural and urban guerrillas was contained. But neither the Latin American regimes nor their American paymasters made much effort to distinguish between political dissent and hardcore subversion. In theory the Alliance for Progress was a repudiation of Washington's propensity to support repressive regimes; in practice the two were too often complementary. The 1970 conclusion of Jerome Levinson and Juan de Onis remains sound: "Between the overambitious idealism of its development goals and the pointless obsessiveness of its concern for security, the United States really undermined the Alliance before it could get started."

Had all the military, political, and economic tools employed by the United States in Latin America worked to perfection, the region would have been as tied to the international political policies of the United States as a state of the American union. In some respects Latin American governments would have had even less freedom than one of the fifty states, since the U.S. Constitution puts some limit on federal authority over the states. All Latin American military and police forces would have been trained by Americans and equipped with American arms. Individuals and organizations on the "far left" (as defined by the United States) would be outlawed. Governments would be strong, above all. If they could be strong and democratic, well enough, but first they must be strong and not shrink from using whatever methods were required to maintain a stable society. Latin American economies would be prosperous, open to U.S. private investment, and based on free-market principles. Latin American governments would speak with one voice, that of the United States, in the OAS. In the UN they would support American world policies while excluding the UN from any involvement in hemispheric disputes. The only thing missing in this fantasy was a national holiday in every American republic on December 2, the anniversary of James Monroe's message.

The story of the last years of the Monroe Doctrine concerns the widening gap between this fantasy and reality. At times high American officials believed they could close the gap by acts of will and a dose of force. They were wrong, and often self-defeating in their delusions. By the 1980s public and congressional support for the fantasy had rapidly evaporated. At that moment the end of the Cold War and the dissolution of the Soviet Union removed the indispensable enemy.

QUESTIONS TO CONSIDER

1. What were the three key precepts of the Monroe Doctrine?
2. What four themes does Smith suggest in treating the last years of the Monroe Doctrine?
3. Distinguish between hard and soft spheres of influence. Which does Smith feel best characterizes the U.S. sphere in Latin America since 1945?

4. How did sales of military weaponry to Latin America show the elasticity of the Monroe Doctrine?
5. What was the flaw in supporting "modern," United States-trained military forces in Latin America?
6. What examples of a double standard does Smith note in contrasting American politics and those urged on Latin America?

17

E Pluribus Unum?*

Arthur Schlesinger, Jr.

Arthur Schlesinger, Jr. (1917–   ) served as an aide in the Kennedy White House and subsequently wrote the award-winning 1965 treatment of JFK's presidency, *A Thousand Days.* A Harvard professor prior to his Washington service, Schlesinger has held the Albert Schweitzer chair in the Humanities at City University of New York since 1966. One of the most gifted writers among eminent historians, he has written many other noteworthy books, including *The Age of Jackson* (1945), *The Age of Roosevelt* (3 vols., 1957–60), *The Imperial Presidency* (1973), and *Robert F. Kennedy and His Times* (1978). He has been an outspoken and articlulate defender of modern liberalism.

The clash of cultures has been a theme in the forging of the American character, beginning with the encounter of Columbus with the American natives, going through bouts of nativism in the 1850s and the 1920s, and re-emerging in the rise of ethnicity in the past few decades. As Milton Gordon suggested in "Assimilation in America," three models of assimilation have dominated the nation's past: the melting pot, Anglo-conformity, and cultural pluralism. In this selection, taken from the introduction and conclusion of his 1991 book *The Disuniting of America: Reflections on a Multicultural Society,* Schlesinger makes an impassioned argument for the melting pot as the ideal that has held a disparate nation together.

*Reprinted by permission of the author.

Full of common sense responses to the flaws in multiculturalism, he provides some solid food for thought about the nature of the United States and the national character as the country approaches the third millenium.

At the beginning America was seen as a severing of roots, a liberation from the stifling past, an entry into a new life, an interweaving of separate ethnic strands into a new national design. "We have it in our power," said Thomas Paine for the revolutionary generation, "to begin the world all over again." The unstated national motto was "Never look back." "The Past is dead, and has no resurrection," wrote Herman Melville. ". . . The Past is the text-book of tyrants; the Future the Bible of the Free."

And the future was America—not so much a nation, Melville said, as a world. "You can not spill a drop of American blood without spilling the blood of the whole world. On this Western Hemisphere all tribes and people are forming into one federated whole. . . ." For Ralph Waldo Emerson too, like Crèvecoeur, like Melville, America was the distillation of the multifarious planet. As the burning of the temple at Corinth had melted and intermixed silver and gold to produce Corinthian brass, "a new compound more precious than any," so, Emerson wrote in his journal, in America, in this "asylum of all nations, the energy of Irish, Germans, Swedes, Poles, & Cossacks, & all the European tribes—of the Africans, & of the Polynesians, will construct a new race . . . as vigorous as the new Europe which came out of the smelting pot of the Dark Ages. . . ."

Melville was a novelist, Emerson an essayist; both were poets. But George Washington was a sternly practical man. Yet he believed no less ardently in the doctrine of the "new race." "The bosom of America," Washington said, "is open . . . to the oppressed and persecuted of all Nations and Religions." But immigrants who nestled as clannish groups in the national bosom retained the "Language, habits and principles (good or bad) which they bring with them." Let them therefore settle as individuals, prepared for "intermixture with our people." Then they would be "assimilated to our customs, measures and laws: in a word, soon become *one people.*"

John Quincy Adams, another sternly practical man, similarly insisted on the exclusiveness of the new American identity. When a German baron contemplating emigration interviewed Adams as secretary of state, Adams admonished his visitor that emigrants had to make up their minds to one thing: "*They must cast off the European skin, never to resume it. They must look forward to their posterity rather than backward to their ancestors. . . .*"

But how could Crèvecoeur's "promiscuous breed" be transformed into a "new race"? How was Emerson's "smelting pot" to fuse such disparate elements into Washington's "one people"? This question preoccupied another young Frenchman who arrived in America three quarters of a century after Crèvecoeur. "Imagine, my dear friend, if you can," Alexis de Tocqueville wrote back to France, "a society formed of all the nations of the world . . . people having different languages, beliefs, opinions: in a word, a society without roots, without memories, without prejudices, without routines, without common ideas, without a national character, yet a hundred times happier than our own." What alchemy could make this miscellany into a single society?

The answer, Tocqueville concluded, lay in the commitment of Americans to democracy and self-government. Civic participation, Tocqueville argued in *Democracy in America*, was the great educator and the great unifier.

> How does it happen that in the United States, where the inhabitants have only recently immigrated to the land which they now occupy, and brought neither customs nor traditions with them there; where they met one another for the first time with no previous acquaintance; where, in short, the instinctive love of country can scarcely exist; how does it happen that every one takes as zealous an interest in the affairs of his township, his country, and the whole state as if they were his own? It is because everyone, in his sphere, takes an active part in the government of society.

Immigrants, Tocqueville said, become Americans through the exercise of the political rights and civic responsibilities bestowed on them by the Declaration of Independence and the Constitution.

Half of a century later, when the next great foreign commentator on American democracy, James Bryce, wrote *The American Commonwealth*, immigration had vastly increased and diversified. Bryce's European friends expected that it would take a very long time for America to assimilate these "heterogeneous elements." What struck Bryce, on the contrary, was what had struck Tocqueville: "the amazing solvent power which American institutions, habits, and ideas exercise upon newcomers of all races . . . quickly dissolving and assimilating the foreign bodies that are poured into her mass."

A century after Tocqueville, another foreign visitor, Gunnar Myrdal of Sweden, called the cluster of ideas, institutions, and habits "the American Creed." Americans "of all national origins, regions, creeds, and colors," Myrdal wrote in 1944, hold in common "the *most explicitly expressed* system of general ideals" of any country in the West: the ideals of the essential dignity and equality of all human beings, of inalienable rights to freedom, justice, and opportunity.

The schools teach the principles of the Creed, Myrdal said; the churches preach them; the courts hand down judgments in their terms. Myrdal saw the Creed as the bond that links all Americans, including non-white minorities, and as the spur forever goading Americans to live up to their principles. "America," Myrdal said, "is continuously struggling for its soul."

The American Creed had its antecedents, and these antecedents lay primarily in a British inheritance as recast by a century and a half of colonial experience. How really new then was the "new race"? Crèvecoeur's vision implied an equal blending of European stocks, and Emerson's smelting pot generously added Cossacks, Africans, and Polynesians. In fact, the majority of the population of the 13 colonies and the weight of its culture came from Great Britain.

Having cleared most of North America of their French, Spanish, and Dutch rivals, the British were free to set the mold. The language of the new nation, its laws, its institutions, its political ideas, its literature, its customs, its precepts, its prayers, primarily derived from Britain. Crèvecoeur himself wrote his book not in his native French but in his acquired English. The "curse of Babel," Melville said, had been revoked in America, "and the language they shall speak shall be the language of Britain."

The smelting pot thus had, unmistakably and inescapably, an Anglocentric flavor. For better or worse, the white Anglo-Saxon Protestant tradition was for two centuries—and in crucial respects still is—the dominant influence on American culture and society. This tradition provided the standard to which other immigrant nationalities were expected to conform, the matrix into which they would be assimilated.

But as the nineteenth century proceeded, non-Anglo immigration gathered speed. European peasants who may never have dared go twenty miles from their birthplaces now undertook the unimaginable adventure of a journey across perilous seas to a strange land in search of a new life. The land was indeed strange; and they could not but feel a need for reassurance and security. So at first they tended to cling to their compatriots and to the language, schools, churches they brought with them. These ethnic enclaves served as staging areas for regrouping and basic training before entry was made into the larger and riskier American life.

These immigrants came principally from western and northern Europe. The Anglos often disliked the newcomers, disdained their uncouth presence, feared their alien religions and folkways. Germans and Scandinavians were regarded as clannish in their fidelity to the language and customs of the old country. The German fondness for beer gardens and jolly Sundays excited puritanical disapproval. The Irish were regarded as shiftless and drunken; moreover, they were papists, and their fealty to Rome, it was said, meant they could never become loyal Americans. They were subjected to severe discrimination in employment and were despised by genteel society. W. E. B. Du Bois, the black scholar, testified that when he grew up in Great Barrington, Massachusetts, in the 1870s, "the racial angle was more clearly defined against the Irish than against me."

As the flow of immigrants increased, so did resentment among the old-timers. By the 1850s immigrants made up half the population of New York and outnumbered native-born Americans in Chicago. Nativist organizations sprang up, like the Supreme Order of the Star-Spangled Banner and its political front, the American Party, calling for a lengthened naturalization process and curtailment of the political rights of the foreign-born. They were referred to as Know-Nothings because members of the Supreme Order, when asked about their secret oaths and rituals, would reply, "I know nothing."

In 1856 the Know-Nothings even ran a former president, Millard Fillmore, as their presidential candidate. "Our progress in degeneracy appears to me to be pretty rapid," observed Abraham Lincoln. "As a nation, we began by declaring that *'all men are created equal.'* We now practically read it 'all men are created equal, *except negroes.'* When the Know-Nothings get control, it will read 'all men are created equal, except negroes, *and foreigners, and catholics.'*"

But the Know-Nothing party fell as quickly as it rose. In the century and a half since, despite recurrent xenophobic outbursts, no nativist political party has appeared to take its place. However prejudiced white Anglo-Saxons were in practice, they were ashamed to endorse nativism in principle. Equally important, an expanding economy in an underpopulated country required a steady influx of new hands. Immigration alleviated the labor shortage, and economic need overpowered moral and aesthetic repugnance.

The pre-Civil War immigrants steadily turned into Americans. "The frontier," in the words of its great historian, Frederick Jackson Turner, "promoted the formation of a composite nationality. . . . In the crucible of the frontier the immigrants were Americanized, liberated, and fused into a mixed race, English in neither nationality nor characteristics." In the crucible of the cities too assimilation proceeded apace. Even "the Irish immigrant's son," Bryce reported in 1888, "is an American citizen for all other purposes, even if he retain, which he seldom does, the hereditary Anglophobia."

After the Civil War came the so-called "new" immigration from southern and eastern Europe. Over 27 million arrived in the half-century from Lee's

surrender at Appomattox to America's entry into the First World War—
more than the total population of the country in 1850. The new immigrants—Italians, Poles, Hungarians, Czechs, Slovaks, Russians, Jews—
settled mainly in the cities, where their bizarre customs, dress, languages,
and religions excited new misgivings.

Yet the old faith in the power of Bryce's "amazing solvent" to fulfill
Washington's conception of Americans as "one people" held fast. However much they suffered from social prejudice, the newcomers were not
barred from civic participation, and civic participation indoctrinated
them in the fundamentals of the American Creed. They altered the ethnic
composition of the country, but they preserved the old ambition to become Americans.

The fastidious Henry James, revisiting his native land in 1904 after
many years abroad, was at first dismayed by the alien bustle of Ellis Island. But he soon understood and appreciated "the ceaseless process of
the recruiting of our race, of the plenishing of our huge national *pot-au-
feu,* of the introduction of fresh . . . foreign matter into our heterogeneous
system." Though he wondered at times what immigration would do to
Americans "ethnically, and thereby physiognomically, linguistically, *personally,*" though he saw at times "the 'ethnic' apparition" sitting like a
skeleton at the feast, he was more impressed by the "colossal" machinery
that so efficiently converted the children of immigrants into Americans—
the political and social habit, the common school, the newspaper, all so
reliably producing what James called "the 'ethnic' synthesis." He
spoke with something like awe about "the cauldron of the 'American'
character."

New race, one people, smelting pot, *pot-au-feu,* cauldron—the original faith received its most celebrated metaphor a few years after James's
visitation. In 1908 a play by Israel Zangwill, an English writer of Russian
Jewish origin, opened in Washington. *The Melting-Pot* tells the story of a
young Russian Jewish composer in New York. David Quixano's artistic
ambition is to write a symphony expressing the vast, harmonious interweaving of races in America, and his personal hope is to overcome racial
barriers and marry Vera, a beautiful Christian girl. "America," David
cries, "is God's crucible, the great Melting-Pot where all the races of Europe are melting and reforming! . . . Here you stand in your fifty groups,
with your fifty languages . . . and your fifty blood hatreds. . . . A fig for
your feuds and vendettas! Germans and Frenchmen, Irishmen and Englishmen, Jews and Russians—into the Crucible with you all! God is making the American."

The climatic scene takes place on the roof garden of a lower-Man-
hattan settlement house. In the background the Statue of Liberty gleams
in the sunset. The composer, alone with Vera, gestures toward the city:

There she lies, the great Melting-Pot—listen! Can't you hear the roaring and the bubbling? Ah, what a stirring and a seething! Celt and Latin, Slav and Teuton, Greek and Syrian,—black and yellow—

VERA *(softly nestling to him):*   Jew and Gentile—

DAVID: Yes, East and West, and North and South, the palm and the pine, the pole and the equator, the crescent and the cross. . . . Here shall they all unite to build the Republic of Man and the Kingdom of God. Ah, Vera, what is the glory of Rome and Jerusalem where all nations and races come to worship and look back, compared with the glory of America, where all races and nations come to labour and look forward! . . . *(Far back, like a lonely, guiding star, twinkles over the darkening water the torch of the Statue of Liberty. From below comes up the softened sound of voices and instruments joining in 'My Country, 'tis of Thee.' The curtain falls slowly.)*

When the curtain fell in Washington and the author walked onstage, President Theodore Roosevelt called from his box: "That's a great play, Mr. Zangwill, that's a great play." "I'm not a Bernard Shaw man or Ibsen man, Mrs. Zangwill," T. R. later told the playwright's wife. "No, *this* is the stuff." Zangwill subsequently dedicated the printed play to Roosevelt. *The Melting-Pot* played before rapt audiences across the country. Jane Addams of Hull-House in Chicago observed that Zangwill had performed "a great service to America by reminding us of the high hopes of the founders of the Republic."

Yet even as audiences cheered *The Melting-Pot,* Zangwill's metaphor raised doubts. One had only to stroll around the great cities, as Basil March did in William Dean Howell's *A Hazard of New Fortunes,* to see that the melting process was incomplete. Ethnic minorities were forming their own *quartiers* in which they lived in their own way—not quite that of the lands they had left but not that of Anglocentric America either: Little Italy, Chinatown, Yorkville, Harlem, and so on.

Nor was the WASP culture showing great inclination to ease their access into Anglo-America. And when it did, when barriers fell, when new immigrants gained acceptance through money or celebrity, there loomed the prospect of intermarriage. In having his drama turn on marriage between people of different races and religions, Zangwill, who had himself married a Christian, emphasized where the melting pot must inexorably lead: to the submergence of separate ethnic identities in the new American race.

Was such a result desirable? Many immigrants doubtless thought so. In the early twentieth century, most of their children certainly did. But soon ethnic spokesmen began to appear, moved by real concern for distinctive ethnic values and also by real if unconscious vested interest in the preservation of ethnic constituencies. Jewish reviewers castigated Zang-will: "All the worse for you and me, brother," wrote one, "who are to be cast into and dissolved in the crucible." Even some of Anglo-Saxon descent deplored the obliteration of picturesque foreign strains for the sake of insipid Anglocentric conformity.

The impression grew that the melting pot was a device to impose Anglocentric images and values upon hapless immigrants—an impression reinforced by the rise of the "Americanization" movement in response to the new polyglot immigration. Americanization programs, benign in intent, sought to expedite assimilation by offering immigrants special education in language, citizenship, and American history. The outbreak of war in 1914 gave Americanization a more coercive edge. Even presidents as friendly to immigrants as Theodore Roosevelt and Woodrow Wilson worried whether in crisis "hyphenated" Americans might not be more loyal to the old country than to their adopted land.

Three days after a German submarine sank the *Lusitania,* Wilson addressed an audience of recently naturalized citizens in Philadelphia. "You cannot become thorough Americans," he told them, "if you think of yourselves in groups. America does not consist of groups. A man who thinks of himself as belonging to a particular national group in America has not yet become an American."

"We can have no 'fifty-fifty' allegiance in this country," Theodore Roosevelt said two years later. "Either a man is an American and nothing else, or he is not an American at all." He condemned Americans who saw the world from the standpoint of another nation. "We Americans are children of the crucible," T. R. said. "The crucible does not do its work unless it turns out those cast into it in one national mould."

"One national mould"? Not everyone agreed. In 1915 Horace Kallen, a Jewish-American philosopher, wrote an essay for *The Nation* entitled "Democracy Versus the Melting-Pot." The melting pot, Kallen argued, was valid neither as a fact nor as an ideal. What impressed him was, on the contrary, the persistence of ethnic groups and their distinctive traditions. Unlike freely chosen affiliations, Kallen said, the ethnic bond was both involuntary and immutable. "Men may change their clothes, their politics, their wives, their religions, their philosophies, to a greater or lesser extent: they cannot change their grandfathers. Jews or Poles or Anglo-Saxons, in order to cease being Jews or Poles or Anglo-Saxons, would have to cease to be. . . ."

Ethnic diversity, Kallen observed, enriches American civilization. He saw the nation not as one people, except in a political and administrative sense, but rather "as a federation or commonwealth of national cultures . . . a democracy of nationalities, cooperating voluntarily and autonomously through common institutions . . . a multiplicity in a unity, an orchestration of mankind." This conception he came to call "cultural pluralism."

Kallen was unclear on the question of how to encourage ethnic separatism without weakening the original ideal of a single society. One critic warned that cultural pluralism would "result in the Balkanization of these United States." But Kallen made his attack on Anglo-centered assimilation at a time when critics of the melting pot could reasonably assume the solidity of the overarching framework. Because he considered political unity a given, he put his emphasis on the protection of cultural diversity.

The gospel of cultural pluralism was at first largely confined to academics, intellectuals, and artists. The postwar years saw much popular disenchantment with Europe, a Red Scare directed largely against aliens, the rise of the anti-Catholic Ku Klux Klan, and a campaign, realized in the Immigration Act of 1924, to freeze the ethnic composition of the American people. The new law established quotas on the basis of the national origins of the population in 1890, thereby drastically reducing the flow from southern and eastern Europe.

The xenophobic nationalism of the 1920s was followed in the 1930s by crises that, on some levels divisive, nevertheless strengthened the feeling that all Americans were in the same boat and might as well pull together. The Great Depression and the Second World War showed the desperate necessity of national cohesion within the frame of shared national ideals. "The principle on which this country was founded and by which it has always been governed," Franklin D. Roosevelt said in 1943, "is that Americanism is a matter of the mind and heart; Americanism is not, and never was, a matter of race and ancestry. A good American is one who is loyal to this country and to our creed of liberty and democracy."

Gunnar Myrdal in 1944 showed no hesitation in declaring the American Creed the common possession of all Americans, even as his great book *An American Dilemma* provided a magistral analysis of America's most conspicuous failure to live up to the Creed: the treatment by white Americans of black America.

Noble ideals had been pronounced as if for all Americans, yet in practice they applied only to white people. Most interpretations of the national identity from Crèvecoeur on were for whites only. Even Horace Kallen, the champion of cultural pluralism, made no provision in his "democracy of nationalities" for black or red or brown or yellow Americans.

Tocqueville was an exception in factoring persons of color into the American equation. With his usual prescience, he identified racism as the irremediable flaw in American democracy. This "most grasping nation on the globe" had doomed the red man to extinction; and the presence of a black population was "the most formidable of all the ills that threaten the future of the Union." The more optimistic Emerson and Zangwill had thrown nonwhite nationalities into their smelting or melting pots, but Tocqueville saw racist exclusion as deeply ingrained in the national character.

History supported this judgment. White settlers had systematically pushed the American Indians back, killed their braves, seized their lands, and sequestered their tribes. They had brought Africans to America to work their plantations and Chinese to build their railroads. They had enunciated glittering generalities of freedom and withheld them from people of color. Their Constitution protected slavery, and their laws made distinctions on the basis of race. Though they eventually emancipated the slaves, they conspired in the reduction of the freedmen to third-class citizenship. Their Chinese Exclusion acts culminated in the total prohibition of Asian immigration in the Immigration Act of 1924. It occurred to damned few white Americans in these years that Americans of color were also entitled to the rights and liberties promised by the Constitution.

Yet what Bryce had called "the amazing solvent power" of American institutions and ideas retained its force, even among those most cruelly oppressed and excluded. Myrdal's polls of Afro-America showed the "determination" of blacks "to hold to the American Creed." Ralph Bunche, one of Myrdal's collaborators, observed that every man in the street—black, red, and yellow as well as white—regarded America as the "land of the free" and the "cradle of liberty." The American Creed, Myrdal surmised, meant even more to blacks than to whites, since it was the great means of pleading their unfulfilled rights. Blacks, new immigrants, Jews, and other disadvantaged groups, Myrdal said, "could not possibly have invented a system of political ideals which better corresponded to their interests."

The Second World War gave the Creed new bite. Hitler's racism forced Americans to look hard at their own racial assumptions. How, in fighting against Hitler's doctrine of the Master Race abroad, could Americans maintain a doctrine of white supremacy at home? How, with China a faithful American ally, could Americans continue to forbid Chinese to become American citizens? If the war did not end American racism, at least it drove much racial bigotry underground. The rethinking of racial issues challenged the conscience of the majority and raised the consciousness of minorities.

Emboldened by the Creed, blacks organized for equal opportunities in employment, opposed segregation in the armed forces, and fought in their own units on many fronts. After the war, the civil rights revolution, so long deferred, accelerated black self-reliance. So did the collapse of white colonialism around the world and the appearance of independent black states.

Across America minorities proclaimed their pride and demanded their rights. Women, the one "minority" that in America constituted a numerical majority, sought political and economic equality. Jews gained new solidarity from the holocaust and then from the establishment of a Jewish state in Israel. Changes in the immigration law dramatically increased the number arriving from Hispanic and Asian lands, and, following the general example, they asserted their own prerogatives. American Indians mobilized to reclaim rights and lands long since appropriated by the white man; their spokesmen even rejected the historic designation in which Indians had taken deserved pride and named themselves Native Americans.

The civil rights revolution provoked new expressions of ethnic identity by the now long-resident "new migration" from southern and eastern Europe—Italians, Greeks, Poles, Czechs, Slovaks, Hungarians. The ethnic enthusiasm was reinforced by the "third-generation" effect formulated in Hansen's Law, named after Marcus Lee Hansen, the great pioneer in immigration history: "What the son wishes to forget the grandson wishes to remember."

Another factor powerfully nourished the passion for roots: the waning American optimism about the nation's prospects. For two centuries Americans had been confident that life would be better for their children than it was for them. In their exuberant youth, Americans had disdained the past and, as John Quincy Adams urged, looked forward to their prosperity rather than backward to their ancestors. Amid forebodings of national decline, Americans now began to look forward less and backward more. The rising cult of ethnicity was a symptom of decreasing confidence in the American future.

Ethnic as a word has had a long history. It originally meant "heathen" or "pagan" but soon came to mean anything pertaining to a race or nation. In this sense everyone, even the Lowells and the Cabots, were ethnics. By the time Henry James used the word in *The American Scene,* however, "ethnic" had acquired an association with foreignness. As applied since the 1960s, it definitely means non-Anglo minorities—a reversion to the original sense of being beyond the pale.

The noun *ethnicity* meanwhile made its modern debut in 1940 in W. Lloyd Warner's Yankee City series. From its modest beginning in that sociological study, "ethnicity" moved vigorously to center stage in popular discourse. The bicentennial of American independence, the centennial of the Statue of Liberty, the restoration of Ellis Island—all turned from tributes to the melting pot into extravaganzas of ethnic distinctiveness.

The pressure for the new cult of ethnicity came less from the minorities en masse than from their often self-appointed spokesmen. Most ethnics, white and nonwhite, saw themselves primarily as Americans. "The cravings for 'historical identity,'" Gunnar Myrdal said at the height of the ethnic rage, "is not in any sense a people's movement. Those cravings have been raised by a few well-established intellectuals, professors, writers—mostly, I gather, of a third generation." Few of them, Myrdal thought, made much effort to talk to their own ethnic groups. He feared, Myrdal added with a certain contempt, that this movement was only "upper-class intellectual romanticism."

Still, ideologues, with sufficient publicity and time, could create audiences. Spokesmen with a vested interest in ethnic identification repudiated the ideal of assimilation. The melting pot, it was said, injured people by undermining their self-esteem. It denied them heroes—"role models," in the jargon—from their own ethnic ancestries. Praise now went to "the unmeltable ethnics."

In 1974, after testimony from ethnic spokesmen denouncing the melting pot as a conspiracy to homogenize America, Congress passed the Ethnic Heritage Studies Program Act—a statue that, by applying the ethnic ideology to all Americans, compromised the historic right of Americans to decide their ethnic identities for themselves. The act ignored those millions of Americans—surely a majority—who refused identification with any particular ethnic group.

The ethnic upsurge (it can hardly be called a revival because it was unprecedented) began as a gesture of protest against the Anglocentric culture. It became a cult, and today it threatens to become a counter-revolution against the original theory of America as "one people," a common culture, a single nation.

* * * *

The attack on the common American identity is the culmination of the cult of ethnicity. That attack was mounted in the first instance by European Americans of non-British origin ("unmeltable ethnics") against the British foundations of American culture; then, latterly and massively, by Americans of non-European origin against the European foundations of that culture. As Theodore Roosevelt's foreboding suggests, the European immigration itself palpitated with internal hostilities, everyone at everybody else's throats—hardly the "monocultural" crowd portrayed by ethnocentric separatists. After all, the two great "world" wars of the twentieth century began as fights among European states. Making a single society out of this diversity of antagonistic European peoples is a hard enough job.

The new salience of non-European, nonwhite stocks compounds the challenge. And the non-Europeans, or at least their self-appointed spokesmen, bring with them a resentment, in some cases a hatred, of Europe and the West provoked by generations of Western colonialism, racism, condescension, contempt, and cruel exploitation.

Will not this rising flow of non-European immigrants create a "minority majority" that will make Eurocentrism obsolete by the twenty-first century? This is the fear of some white Americans and the hope (and sometimes the threat) of some nonwhites.

Immigrants were responsible for a third of population growth during the 1980s. More arrived than in any decade since the second of the century. And the composition of the newcomers changed dramatically. In 1910 nearly 90 percent of immigrants came from Europe. In the 1980s more than 80 percent came from Asia and Latin America.

Still, foreign-born residents constitute only about 7 percent of the population today as against nearly 15 percent when the first Roosevelt and Wilson were worrying about hyphenated Americans. Stephan Thernstrom doubts that the minority will ever arrive. The black share in the population has grown rather slowly—9.9 percent in 1920, 10 percent in 1950, 11.1 percent in 1970, 12.1 percent in 1990. Neither Asian-Americans nor Hispanic-Americans go in for especially large families; and family size in any case tends to decline as income and intermarriage increase. "If today's immigrants assimilate to American ways as readily as their predecessors at the turn of the century—as seems to be happening," Thernstrom concludes, "there won't be a minority majority issue anyway."

America has so long seen itself as the asylum for the oppressed and persecuted—and has done itself and the world so much good thereby—that any curtailment of immigration offends something in the American soul. No one wants to be a Know-Nothing. Yet uncontrolled immigration is an impossibility; so the criteria of control are questions the American democracy must confront. We have shifted the basis of admission three times this century—from national origins in 1924 to family reunification in 1965 to needed skills in 1990. The future of immigration policy depends on the capacity of the assimilation process to continue to do what it has done so well in the past: to lead newcomers to an acceptance of the language, the institutions, and the political ideals that hold the nation together.

Is Europe really the root of all evil? The crimes of Europe against lesser breeds without the law (not to mention even worse crimes—Hitlerism and Stalinism—against Europeans) are famous. But these crimes do not alter other facts of history: that Europe was the birthplace of the United States of America, that European ideas and culture formed the republic, that the United States is an extension of European civilization, and that nearly 80 percent of Americans are of European descent.

When Irving Howe, hardly a notorious conservative, dared write, "The Bible, Homer, Plato, Sophocles, Shakespeare are central to our culture," an outraged reader ("having graduated this past year from Amherst") wrote, "Where on Howe's list is the *Quran*, the *Gita*, Confucius, and other central cultural artifacts of the peoples of our nation?" No one can doubt the importance of these works nor the influence they have had on other societies. But on American society? It may be too bad that dead white European males have played so large a role in shaping our culture. But that's the way it is. One cannot erase history.

These humdrum historical facts, and not some dastardly imperialist conspiracy, explain the Eurocentric slant in American schools. Would anyone seriously argue that teachers should conceal the European origins of American civilization? or that schools should cater to the 20 percent and ignore the 80 percent? Of course the 20 percent and their contributions should be integrated into the curriculum too, which is the point of cultural pluralism.

But self-styled "multiculturalists" are very often ethnocentric separatists who see little in the Western heritage beyond Western crimes. The Western tradition, in this view, is inherently racist, sexist, "classist," hegemonic; irredeemably repressive, irredeemably oppressive. The spread of Western culture is due not to any innate quality but simply to the spread of Western power. Thus the popularity of European classical music around the world—and, one supposes, of American jazz and rock too—is evidence not of wide appeal but of "the pattern of imperialism, in which the conquered culture adopts that of the conqueror."

Such animus toward Europe lay behind the well-known crusade against the Western-civilization course at Stanford ("Hey-hey, ho-ho, Western culture's got to go!"). According to the National Endowment for the Humanities, students can graduate from 78 percent of American colleges and universities without taking a course in the history of Western civilization. A number of institutions—among them Dartmouth, Wisconsin, Mt. Holyoke—require courses in third-world or ethnic studies but not in Western civilization. The mood is one of divesting Americans of the sinful European inheritance and seeking redemptive infusions from non-Western cultures.

One of the oddities of the situation is that the assault on the Western tradition is conducted very largely with analytical weapons forged in the

West. What are the names invoked by the coalition of latter-day Marxists, deconstructionists, poststructuralists, radical feminists, Afrocentrists? Marx, Nietzsche, Gramsci, Derrida, Foucault, Lacan, Sartre, de Beauvoir, Habermas, the Frankfurt "critical theory" school—Europeans all. The "unmasking," "demythologizing," "decanonizing," "dehegemonizing" blitz against Western culture depends on methods of critical analysis unique to the West—which surely testifies to the internally redemptive potentialities of the Western tradition.

Even Afrocentrists seem to accept subliminally the very Eurocentric standards they think they are rejecting. "Black intellectuals condemn Western civilization," Professor Pearce Williams says, "yet ardently wish to prove it was founded by their ancestors." And, like Frantz Fanon and Leopold Senghor, whose books figure prominently on their reading lists, Afrocentric ideologues are intellectual children of the West they repudiate. Fanon, the eloquent spokesman of the African wretched of the earth, had French as his native tongue and based his analyses on Freud, Marx, and Sartre. Senghor, the prophet of Negritude, wrote in French, established the Senegalese educational system on the French model and, when he left the presidency of Senegal, retired to France.

Western hegemony, it would seem, can be the source of protest as well as of power. Indeed, the invasion of American schools by the Afrocentric curriculum, not to mention the conquest of university departments of English and comparative literature by deconstructionists, poststructuralists, etc., are developments that by themselves refute the extreme theory of "cultural hegemony." Of course, Gramsci had a point. Ruling values do dominate and permeate any society; but they do not have the rigid and monolithic grip on American democracy that academic leftists claim.

Radical academics denounce the "canon" as an instrument of European oppression enforcing the hegemony of the white race, the male sex, and the capitalist class, designed, in the words of one professor, "to rewrite the past and construct the present from the perspective of the privileged and the powerful." Or in the elegant words of another—and a professor of theological ethics at that: "The canon of great literature was created by high Anglican assholes to underwrite their social class."

The poor old canon is seen not only as conspiratorial but as static. Yet nothing changes more regularly and reliably than the canon: compare, for example, the canon in American poetry as defined by Edmund Clarence Stedman in his *Poets of America* (1885) with the canon of 1935 or of 1985 (whatever happened to Longfellow and Whittier?); or recall the changes that have overtaken the canonical literature of American history in the last half-century (who reads Beard and Parrington now?). And the critics clearly have no principled objection to the idea of the canon. They simply wish to replace an old gang by a new gang. After all, a canon means only that because you can't read everything, you give some books priority over others.

Oddly enough, serious Marxists—Marx and Engels, Lukacs, Trotsky, Gramsci—had the greatest respect for what Lukacs called "the classical heritage of mankind." Well they should have, for most great literature and much good history are deeply subversive in their impact on orthodoxies. Consider the present-day American literary canon: Emerson, Jefferson, Melville, Whitman, Hawthorne, Thoreau, Lincoln, Twain, Dickinson, William and Henry James, Henry Adams, Holmes, Dreiser, Faulkner, O'Neill. Lackeys of the ruling class? Apologists for the privileged and the powerful? Agents of American imperialism? Come on!

It is time to adjourn the chat about hegemony. If hegemony were as real as the cultural radicals pretend, Afrocentrism would never have got anywhere, and the heirs of William Lyon Phelps would still be running the Modern Language Association.

Is the Western tradition a bar to progress and a curse on humanity? Would it really do America and the world good to get rid of the European legacy?

No doubt Europe has done terrible things, not least to itself. But what culture has not? History, said Edward Gibbon, is little more than the register of the crimes, follies, and misfortunes of mankind. The sins of the West are no worse than the sins of Asia or of the Middle East or of Africa.

There remains, however, a crucial difference between the Western tradition and the others. The crimes of the West have produced their own antidotes. They have provoked great movements to end slavery, to raise the status of women, to abolish torture, to combat racism, to defend freedom of inquiry and expression, to advance personal liberty and human rights.

Whatever the particular crimes of Europe, that continent is also the source—the *unique* source—of those liberating ideas of individual liberty, political democracy, the rule of law, human rights, and cultural freedom that constitute our most precious legacy and to which most of the world today aspires. These are *European* ideas, not Asian, nor African, nor Middle Eastern ideas, except by adoption.

The freedoms of inquiry and of artistic creation, for example, are Western values. Consider the differing reactions to the case of Salman Rushdie: what the West saw as an intolerable attack on individual freedom the Middle East saw as a proper punishment for an evildoer who had violated the mores of his group. Individualism itself is looked on with abhorrence and dread by collectivist cultures in which loyalty to the group overrides personal goals—cultures that, social scientists say, comprise about 70 percent of the world's population.

There is surely no reason for Western civilization to have guilt trips laid on it by champions of cultures based on despotism, superstition, tribalism, and fanaticism. In this regard the Afrocentrists are especially absurd. The West needs no lectures on the superior virtue of those "sun people" who sustained slavery until Western imperialism abolished it (and, it is reported, sustain it to this day in Mauritania and the Sudan), who still keep women in subjection and cut off their clitorises, who carry out racial persecutions not only against Indians and other Asians but against fellow Africans from the wrong tribes, who show themselves either incapable of operating a democracy or ideologically hostile to the democratic idea, and who in their tryannies and massacres, their Idi Amins and Boukassas, have stamped with utmost brutality on human rights.

Certainly the European overlords did little enough to prepare Africa for self-government. But democracy would find it hard in any case to put down roots in a tribalist and patrimonial culture that, long before the West invaded Africa, had sacralized the personal authority of chieftains and ordained the submission of the rest. What the West would call corruption is regarded through much of Africa as no more than the prerogative of power. Competitive political parties, an independent judiciary, a free press, the rule of law are alien to African traditions.

It was the French, not the Algerians, who freed Algerian women from the veil (much to the irritation of Frantz Fanon, who regarded deveiling as symbolic rape); as in India it was the British, not the Indians, who ended (or did their best to end) the horrible custom of *suttee*—widows burning themselves alive on their husbands' funeral pyres. And it was the West, not the non-Western cultures, that launched the crusade to abolish slavery—and in doing so encountered mighty resistance, especially in the Islamic world (where Moslems, with fine impartiality, enslaved whites as well as blacks). Those many brave and humane Africans who are struggling these days for decent societies are animated by Western, not by African, ideals. White guilt can be pushed too far.

The Western commitment to human rights has unquestionably been intermittent and imperfect. Yet the ideal remains—and movement toward it has been real, if sporadic. Today it is the *Western* democratic tradition that attracts and empowers people of all continents, creeds, and colors. When the Chinese students cried and died for democracy in Tiananmen Square, they brought with them not representations of Confucius or Buddha but a model of the Statue of Liberty.

The great American asylum, as Crèvecoeur called it, open, as Washington said, to the oppressed and persecuted of all nations, has been from the start an experiment in a multiethnic society. This is a bolder experiment than we sometimes remember. History is littered with the wreck of states that tried to combine diverse ethnic or linguistic or religious groups within a single sovereignty. Today's headlines tell of imminent crisis or impending dissolution in one or another multiethnic polity—the Soviet Union, India, Yugoslavia, Czechoslovakia, Ireland, Belgium, Canada, Lebanon, Cyprus, Israel, Ceylon, Spain, Nigeria, Kenya, Angola, Trinidad, Guyana. . . . The list is almost endless. The luck so far of the American experiment has been due in large part to the vision of the melting pot. "No other nation," Margaret Thatcher has said, "has so successfully combined people of different races and nations within a single culture."

But even in the United States, ethnic ideologues have not been without effect. They have set themselves against the old American ideal of assimilation. They call on the republic to think in terms not of individual but of group identity and to move the polity from individual rights to group rights. They have made a certain progress in transforming the United States into a more segregated society. They have done their best to turn a college generation against Europe and the Western tradition. They have imposed ethnocentric, Afrocentric, and bilingual curricula on public schools, well designed to hold minority children out of American society. They have told young people from minority groups that the Western democratic tradition is not for them. They have encouraged minorities to see themselves as victims and to live by alibis rather than to claim the opportunities opened for them by the potent combination of black protest and white guilt. They have filled the air with recrimination and rancor and have remarkably advanced the fragmentation of American life.

Yet I believe the campaign against the idea of common ideals and a single society will fail. Gunnar Myrdal was surely right: for all the damage it has done, the upsurge of ethnicity is a superficial enthusiasm stirred by romantic ideologues and unscrupulous hucksters whose claim to speak for their minorities is thoughtlessly accepted by the media. I doubt that the ethnic vogue expresses a reversal of direction from assimilation to apartheid among the minorities themselves. Indeed, the more the ideologues press the case for ethnic separatism, the less they appeal to the mass of their own groups. They have thus far done better in intimidating the white majority than in converting their own constituencies.

"No nation in history," writes Lawrence Fuchs, the political scientist and immigration expert in his fine book *The American Kaleidoscope,* "had proved as successful as the United States in managing ethnic diversity. No nation before had ever made diversity itself a source of national identity and unity." The second sentence explains the success described in the first, and the mechanism for translating diversity into unity has been the American Creed, the civic culture—the very assimilating, unifying culture that is today challenged, and not seldom rejected, by the ideologues of ethnicity.

A historian's guess is that the resources of the Creed have not been exhausted. Americanization has not lost its charms. Many sons and daughters of ethnic neighborhoods still want to shed their ethnicity and move to the suburbs as fast as they can—where they will be received with far more tolerance than they would have been 70 years ago. The desire for achievement and success in American society remains a potent force for assimilation. Ethnic subcultures, Stephen Steinberg, author of *The Ethnic Myth*, points out, fade away "because circumstances forced them to make choices that undermined the basis for cultural survival."

Others may enjoy their ethnic neighborhoods but see no conflict between foreign descent and American loyalty. Unlike the multiculturalists, they celebrate only what is distinctive in their own backgrounds but what they hold in common with the rest of the population.

The ethnic identification often tends toward superficiality. The sociologist Richard Alba's study of children and grandchildren of immigrants in the Albany, New York, area shows the most popular "ethnic experience" to be sampling the ancestral cuisine. Still, less than half the respondents picked that, and only one percent ate ethnic food every day. Only one-fifth acknowledged a sense of special relationship to people of their own ethnic background; less than one-sixth taught their children about their ethnic origins; almost none was fluent in the language of the old country. "It is hard to avoid the conclusion," Alba writes, "that ethnic experience is shallow for the great majority of whites."

If ethnic experience is a good deal less shallow for blacks, it is because of their bitter experience in America, not because of their memories of Africa. Nonetheless most blacks prefer "black" to "African-Americans," fight bravely and patriotically for their country, and would move to the suburbs too if income and racism would permit.

As for Hispanic-Americans, first-generation Hispanics born in the United States speak English fluently, according to a Rand Corporation study; more than half of second-generation Hispanics give up Spanish altogether. When *Vista,* an English-language monthly for Hispanics, asked its readers what historical figures they most admired, Washington, Lincoln, and Theodore Roosevelt led the list, with Benito Juárez trailing behind as fourth, and Eleanor Roosevelt and Martin Luther King Jr. tied for fifth. So much for ethnic role models.

Nor, despite the effort of ethnic ideologues, are minority groups all that hermetically sealed off from each other, except in special situations, like colleges, where ideologues are authority figures. The wedding notices in any newspaper testify to the increased equanimity with which people these days marry across ethnic lines, across religious lines, even, though to a smaller degree, across racial lines. Around half of Asian-American marriages are with non-Orientals, and the Census Bureau estimates one million interracial—mostly black-white—marriages in 1990 as against 310,000 in 1970.

The ethnic revolt against the melting pot has reached the point, in rhetoric at least, though not I think in reality, of a denial of the idea of a common culture and a single society. If large numbers of people really accept this, the republic would be in serious trouble. The question poses itself: how to restore the balance between *unum* and *pluribus?*

The old American homogeneity disappeared well over a century ago, never to return. Ever since, we have been preoccupied in one way or another with the problem, as Herbert Croly phrased in 80 years back in *The Promise of American Life,* "of preventing such divisions from dissolving the society into which they enter—of keeping such a highly differentiated society fundamentally sound and whole." This required, Croly believed, an "ultimate bond of union." There was only one way by which solidarity could be restored, "and that is by means of a democratic social ideal. . . ."

The genius of America lies in its capacity to forge a single nation from peoples of remarkably diverse racial, religious, and ethnic origins. It has done so because democratic principles provide both the philosophical bond of union and practical experience a civic participation. The American Creed envisages a nation composed of individuals making their own choices and accountable to themselves, not a nation based on inviolable ethnic communities. The Constitution turns on individual rights, not on group rights. Law, in order to rectify past wrongs, has from time to time (and in my view often properly so) acknowledged the claims of groups; but this is the exception, not the rule.

Our democratic principles contemplate an open society founded on tolerance of differences and on mutual respect. In practice, America has been more open to some than to others. But it is more open to all today than it was yesterday and is likely to be even more open tomorrow than today. The steady movement of American life has been from exclusion to inclusion.

Historically and culturally this republic has an Anglo-Saxon base; but from the start the base has been modified, enriched, and reconstituted by transfusions from other continents and civilizations. The movement from exclusion to inclusion causes a constant revision in the texture of our culture. The ethnic transfusions affect all aspects of American life—our politics, our literature, our music, our painting, our movies, our cuisine, our customs, our dreams.

Black Americans in particular have influenced the ever-changing national culture in many ways. They have lived here for centuries, and, unless one believes in racist mysticism, they belong far more to American culture than to the culture of Africa. Their history is part of the Western democratic tradition, not an alternative to it. Henry Louis Gates Jr. reminds us of James Baldwin's remark about coming to Europe to find out that he was "as American as any Texas G.I." No one does black Americans more disservice than those Afrocentric ideologues who would define them out of the West.

The interplay of diverse traditions produces the America we know. "Paradoxical though it may seem," Diane Ravitch has well said, "the United States has a common culture that is multicultural." That is why unifying political ideals coexist so easily and cheerfully with diversity in social and cultural values. Within the overarching political commitment, people are free to live as they choose, ethnically and otherwise. Differences will remain; some are reinvented; some are used to drive us apart. But as we renew our allegiance to the unifying ideals, we provide the solvent that will prevent differences from escalating into antagonism and hatred.

One powerful reason for the movement from exclusion to inclusion is that the American Creed facilitates the appeal from the actual to the ideal. When we talk of the American democratic faith, we must understand it in its true dimensions. It is not an impervious, final, and complacent orthodoxy, intolerant of deviation and dissent, fulfilled in flag salutes, oaths of allegiance, and hands over the heart. It is an ever-evolving philosophy, fulfilling its ideals through debate, self-criticism, protest, disrespect, and irreverence; a tradition in which all have rights of heterodoxy and opportunities for self-assertion. The Creed has been the means by which Americans have haltingly but persistently narrowed the gap between performance and principle. It is what all Americans should learn, because it is what binds all Americans together.

Let us by all means in this increasingly mixed-up world learn about those other continents and civilizations. But let us master our own history first. Lamentable as some may think it, we inherit an American experience, as America inherits a European experience. To deny the essentially European origins of American culture is to falsify history.

Americans of whatever origin should take pride in the distinctive inheritance to which they have all contributed, as other nations take pride in their distinctive inheritances. Belief in one's own culture does not require disdain for other cultures. But one step at a time: no culture can hope to ingest other cultures all at once, certainly not before it ingests its own. As we begin to master our own culture, then we can explore the world.

Our schools and colleges have a responsibility to teach history for its own sake—as part of the intellectual equipment of civilized persons—and not to degrade history by allowing its contents to be dictated by pressure groups, whether political, economic, religious, or ethnic. The past may sometimes give offense to one or another minority; that is no reason for rewriting history. Giving pressure groups vetoes over textbooks and courses betrays both history and education. Properly taught, history will convey a sense of the variety, continuity, and adaptability of cultures, of the need for understanding other cultures, of the ability of individuals and peoples to overcome obstacles, of the importance of critical analysis and dispassionate judgment in every area of life.

Above all, history can give a sense of national identity. We don't have to believe that our values are absolutely better than the next fellow's or the next country's, but we have no doubt that they are better *for us*, reared as we are—and are worth living by and worth dying for. For our values are not matters of whim and happenstance. History has given them to us. They are anchored in our national experience, in our great national documents, in our national heroes, in our folkways, traditions, and standards. People with a different history will have differing values. But we believe that our own are better for us. They work for us; and, for that reason, we live and die by them.

It has taken time to make the values real for all our citizens, and we still have a good distance to go, but we have made progress. If we now repudiate the quite marvelous inheritance that history bestows on us, we invite the fragmentation of the national community into a quarrelsome spatter of enclaves, ghettos, tribes. The bonds of cohesion in our society are sufficiently fragile, or so it seems to me, that it makes no sense to strain them by encouraging and exalting cultural and linguistic apartheid.

The American identity will never be fixed and final; it will always be in the making. Changes in the population have always brought changes in the national ethos and will continue to do so; but not, one must hope, at the expense of national integration. The question America confronts as a pluralistic society is how to vindicate cherished cultures and traditions without breaking the bonds of cohesion—common ideals, common political institutions, common language, common culture, common fate—that hold the republic together.

Our task is to combine due appreciation of the splendid diversity of the nation with due emphasis on the great unifying Western ideas of individual freedom, political democracy, and human rights. These are the ideas that define the American nationality—and that today empower people of all continents, races, and creeds.

"What then is the American, this new man? . . . Here individuals of all nations are melted into a new race of men." Still a good answer—still the best hope.

QUESTIONS TO CONSIDER

1. What did de Tocqueville and Myrdahl see as the great exception to the American creed? Why? What event stimulated the rethinking of that exception? Why?
2. What was the source of the ethnic movement? What congressional act encouraged it? How?
3. How has European bashing distorted reality in academe?
4. In what ways do the sources and arguments of critics of Eurocentrism undermine themselves?
5. "Is the Western tradition a bar to progress and a curse on humanity?" Why or why not?
6. What evidence does Schlesinger advance for the shallowness of the ethnic craze? Are you convinced?
7. What is your response to Schlesinger's arguments?